Soldiers
and aliens

# Soldiers and aliens

Men in the Australian Army's Employment Companies during World War II

JUNE FACTOR

MELBOURNE UNIVERSITY PRESS

*To the 'aliens' in the Australian Army's Employment Companies,*
*and to all who offered friendship and support, then and ever since,*
*to those seeking a decent life in a free land.*

MELBOURNE UNIVERSITY PRESS
An imprint of Melbourne University Publishing Limited
Level 1, 715 Swanston Street, Carlton, Victoria 3053, Australia
mup-contact@unimelb.edu.au
www.mup.com.au

First published 2022


Chapter 13 was first published in the *Australian Jewish Historical Society Journal*, vol. XX, 2011, Part 3.



Text design and typesetting by Megan Ellis
Cover design by Pfisterer + Freeman
Cover photograph: Members of 6th Employment Company.
Source: Jack Friedman.
Printed in Australia by McPherson's Printing Group

NATIONAL LIBRARY OF AUSTRALIA
A catalogue record for this book is available from the National Library of Australia

9780522878585 (paperback)
9780522878592 (ebook)

# Contents

# Author's note

The word 'alien' has a long history—from Latin via French into English. Its suggestion of a largely negative otherness—difference, foreignness—has been consistent through the centuries.

Names can be a marker of difference, including of nationality, language and class. It was not uncommon for 'foreign' names to be mispronounced, misspelled or significantly altered. Some of the 'aliens' in this book were given or chose an English-sounding version of their name; others were given, or opted for, spelling variations or even entirely new names. I have used the name and spelling provided by the men I interviewed, by family members, or as found in archival and published sources. I apologise for any unintended misnaming or misspelling.

# Acknowledgements

It has taken a long time to bring this book into the world. My apologies and sincere thanks to all who have shown me encouragement, support and patience.

It was my good fortune to meet and interview men who served in a number of the Australian Army's alien Employment Companies, and to receive photos and verbal and written communication from them, and from other 'alien' soldiers. There were also welcome gifts of stories, photos, and other material from family and friends of the men. Together with my father's stories, and a copy of a talk he gave on 6 April 1986, at a celebration of his eightieth birthday, this treasure-trove of material was an essential source for this book. To all these informants, I owe a great debt for their generosity and their commitment to this project. My grateful thanks to Alf Barr, Harry Barr, Paul Baxter, Yosl Bergner, Yossel Birstein, Dennis Bluth, Bern Brent, John Callinicos, Albert, Guido and Allan Ceen, Victor Chapkoun, John Cohen, Fred Cohn, Mary-Ann and Michael Cohn, John Cohn, Charles D'Aprano, Robert Exiner, Adrian Factor, Juliet Flesch, Evelyn Flitman, Jack Friedman, Helmut Graf, Julius Guest, Gerard Herbst, Gary Hughes, Orpheus Kandiliotis, Frank Klepner, Richard and Kurt Langfelder, Stephen Leahy, Fred Lester, Eric Liffman, Karl and Kurt Liffman, Vane Lindesay, Henry Lippmann, Kurt Lippmann, Hannah Loney, Werner Lowenstein, Margot Lustig, Laurence Maher, Peter Meyer, David Nachinsky, Klaus Neumann, Maurice Nirens, Vic O'Connor, Themis Paizis, Harry Peters, Speros Polites, John Pollak, Nicholas Raftopoulos, Stavros Raftopoulos, Elizabeth Ridge, Johnny Ridge, Mollie Ridge, Ivan (Icko) Rostkier, Alfred Ruskin, Gerald Ryle, Robert Salter, Walter Schnock, Paul Seefeld, Wolfgang Sievers, Ann Smith, Theodore Spirakos, Keith Steinhardt, Rose Stone, Gershop Tryster, Ann Tundern-Smith, Jack Waller, Louis Waller, Felix Werder, and Emil, Ron and Nic Witton.

A number of historians, historical organisations and subject specialists shared useful information. Norman Brown from the British Royal Pioneer Corps Association sent a CD of Major ER Rhodes-Wood's *War History of the Royal Pioneer Corps 1939-1946*. Lieutenant Colonel JA Stirling sent details of the history of both the British and the New Zealand Employment Companies. Graham R McKenzie-Smith provided an early draft of his informative *Unit Guide: The Australian Army 1939-1945*. Associate Professor Bruce Pennay offered ongoing support, as well as a copy of his writing on the 4th Employment Company men who loaded and unloaded trains at Albury station. Professor Peter Stanley gave encouragement and advice. George Paxinos offered access to interviews he had made with some alien Employment Company men, and photos of a number of them. Wendy Rankine introduced me to her pioneering University of Melbourne MA thesis 'The Chinese in Australia 1930 - 45: Beyond a History of Racism'. Rosie Block guided me to valuable material held in the Mitchell Library in Sydney. Andrew Firestone shared information about the Yiddish poet Yossel Birstein and publicised my research on the Birstein Project website he created. Vane Lindesay told of the 'alien' friends he made while working on the army publication *Salt*. Dr Charles Coppel provided access to letters written in support of the Dunera internees by his late mother, Mrs EG Coppel, Honorary Secretary of the Victorian Immigration Appeals Committee. Dr Stephen M Leahy sent an early draft of an article about Swatow-born soldiers in the Australian Army. Ernest Chamberlain and Stephen Faram shared information about Timor, and Laurence Maher and Julian Burnside provided information about the legal case of *Polites v The Commonwealth*. James Waghorne shared notes from Minutes of the Australian Council for Civil Liberties. I am also grateful for the attentive listening and wise comments of History Fellows' seminar colleagues at the University of Melbourne, and the friendly exchange of information and ideas with the late, admirable Professor Ken Inglis.

My thanks to the helpful and knowledgeable staff at the National Archives in Canberra, Melbourne, Sydney, Adelaide and Hobart; the research section of the Australian War Memorial; the High Court of

Australia; the National Library of Australia; the National Maritime Museum; the Mitchell Library in Sydney; University of Melbourne Library; the Jewish Museums in Melbourne and Sydney; and the Army Records Office, Victoria Barracks. A special thanks to the forerunner of ASIO—the Commonwealth Security Service—and to the various State Government police security units. Their efforts, while often initiated by suspicion of 'aliens' and providing evidence of mistrust and misunderstanding, resulted in the accumulation of a large and detailed archive of material devoted to the alien soldiers, much of it now open to public scrutiny.

I am indebted to two Australian institutions whose grants helped make my many research journeys possible. My thanks to the Army History Research Grants Scheme for a research grant of $6000, and to Arts Victoria for an award of $3000.

Over the years of research, a sequence of dedicated young people helped with document checking, sorting and filing: my thanks to Anna Bradbury, Bert Collard, Esther Faine-Vallantin, Anna MacDonald, Rebecca Mason and Anna Murdoch.

Friends provided both support and practical assistance. Jenny and Keith McKenry offered a comfortable roof over my head on my visits to archives in Canberra. My neighbour and friend Norman Gardiner typed out every interview on an old typewriter. Wendy Pomroy, a friend from schooldays, spent many months, without complaint, following the information—sent on cassettes from Melbourne to Geelong—to build the organisation of the mass of collected material. Her wisdom and understanding were a special bonus. The cassette machine used was provided by my dear friend the late Margaret Tomkins. She, like Wendy, Elise Callander, Gwenda Davey and Maureen Dyer, never wavered in friendship and encouragement, and an ongoing belief in the value of my work. Rosalind Price, the best of editors, provided early critical heft to both argument and expression.

My good friend, Judy McKinty, enhanced my modest computer skills, brought order to lists and systems, found missing sources, and provided countless hours of invaluable, thoughtful and skilful assistance to the very last full stop. My dear son, Ian Rogers, was patient, practical, wise and constantly supportive. My heartfelt thanks to them both.

My apologies to anyone whose name has been overlooked or misspelled—once notified, the correction will be made in future editions.

June Factor

# Introduction

How long does it take my father to persuade my mother that he should join the Australian Army? In June 1941 the Germans invaded the Soviet Union; in December 1941 the Japanese bombed Pearl Harbor, and Darwin not long afterwards. It's time, my father says, for him to help defend us from a possible Japanese invasion. My parents have been in Australia for less than three years; they are struggling to master English and make a living. My father is barely 5 feet 4 inches in his socks, and weighs a modest 9 stone. But he is a persuasive man.

According to family folklore, my father writes twice to the Minister for the Army, offering his loyal service. When that fails, he persuades two more prominent members of the Melbourne Jewish community to sign a letter to the Minister with him. He is pleased when the reply this time is 'Yes': the government has decided to allow 'friendly aliens' to join the army. Soon, choice will be replaced by compulsion; military or civilian conscription is extended to all but neutral or suspect 'enemy' aliens.

On 16 May 1942—my mother's thirty-third birthday—my father enlists in the Australian Military Forces. His army record book registers him as Szulem Faktor, and, under the heading 'Restrictions Regarding Employment', notes that he has 'poor physique'. Very soon, he will be hauling large sacks of potatoes and helping move bombs and other ammunition at the Victorian–New South Wales railway junctions of Tocumwal and Albury. He becomes a soldier who never fires a gun. He wears the khaki uniform and the slouch hat until 15 September 1945; the next day, his young daughter's birthday, he is in civvies again.

There are so many questions we wish we could ask the dead. I never thought to ask my father what the weather was like that first day, when he went to enlist at the Caulfield Racecourse in Melbourne. I never asked my mother what they promised each other before he walked away from our small, rented North Carlton cottage.

I have only fragmentary memories of my father in uniform—I was very young then. He was a great raconteur, but stories of his time in the army were rare; those early post-war years seem to have been filled with talk about how to bring the handful of family survivors from Europe to Australia. While I never forgot my father the soldier, it was not until quite late in his life that I began to ask questions about those army years. The stories of one anti-fascist Polish Jew have led me to a multitude of tales peopled by Italians, Greeks, Yugoslavs, Germans, Chinese ... And to even more questions. How did these mostly non-naturalised men come to be in the Australian Army? What did the army want them for? What did it mean to be an 'alien' in the Australian Army? What did they do when not soldiering in their khaki uniforms, slouch hats and solid boots—the formal dress of all Australian soldiers? How did the locals view this polyglot collection of Diggers? How did the men with heavy foreign accents and unpronounceable names regard the locals? And, in the end, why does it all matter now?

'Modern warfare is a potent generator of memories', wrote the historian Catherine Merridale.[1] Perhaps it would be more accurate to say that contemporary historians have found ways to access and disseminate war memories on a scale previously unimaginable. Oral history has played a significant role in this process.

But not all memories are equal. As in other spheres of life, groups on the periphery have little voice or visibility. This book is an attempt to restore to public memory a part of our history largely forgotten: the experiences of men like my father, many recent immigrants and refugees, who willingly or reluctantly joined the Australian Army and found themselves in the military's Employment Companies (also called Labour Companies).

At the core of this book are the experiences of the participants: the 'aliens' whose military task was the hard physical labour needed to maintain the war effort and support the fighting forces. They were a heterogeneous lot: scholars and peasants, musicians and factory workers, communists and royalists, Jews and Catholics, animists and atheists. Diverse in nationality, and in their capacity to undertake demanding physical work, fastidious or rough-and-ready, they lived in tents and huts in crowded proximity.

A strong bond of solidarity developed from the men's broadly common circumstances, the work they performed, and their widespread commitment to contribute to the defeat of the Axis powers. Each Company was a community of about three hundred to five hundred men, with subgroups as small as a tent full of friends or as large as a national, religious or language cohort. As well as work, there was sport, gambling, dances, concerts, political debate and hunger strikes—when, according to the painter Yosl Bergner, in the 6th Employment Company 'we had home-cooking in our tents and ate more than ever'.[2] A camaraderie among 'the boys' (as many of the Europeans called themselves) generally ensured fundamental stability when political or personal enmity erupted.

In writing this book, I have had the good fortune to sit at kitchen and dining-room tables in many homes, talking to the old about their youth, to the children about their fathers. Some of the men wrote memoirs, and some families have kept letters, photos and other documents from those long-ago days and generously shared them with me. As well, there is a wealth of material scattered throughout the Australian War Memorial, the National Archives and various other record depositories. These rich sources, together with the writing of historians, have provided layers of knowledge and understanding, and added the perspectives of politicians, military officialdom, the media, supporters and opponents to the central voices of the approximately four thousand Employment Company men who created a multicultural force in the Australian Army—long before the word 'multicultural' had entered the nation's lexicon.

# 1

# Coming to Australia: home is no longer home

Until well into the 1940s, almost everyone who came to Australia travelled by boat. It took about five to six weeks to come from Europe, a leisurely voyage via the Suez Canal, stopping at various ports in the Middle East and Asia along the way. Ships also travelled via the Cape of Good Hope, or through North America and across the Pacific.

For some of the people in this book, the journey was like a holiday—a calm interlude between the fears and anxieties they were escaping and a hopeful but uncertain future in Australia. Kurt Lippmann, an eighteen-year-old from Hamburg, who later served in the 4th Employment Company, remembered his family's voyage on the Blue Funnel liner *Ulysses*—a ship appropriately titled for passengers travelling into the unknown. He called it 'the highlight of our lives, chiefly because it was a complete relief from the past, and the worries of the new life were still in the future.'[1] Most knew very little about Australia. 'Full of black-fellows and kangaroos, that is about the sum total of what we knew of the country,' wrote Robert Exiner, remembering, more than fifty years later, his reluctance to leave Berlin until interrogated by the Gestapo in 1938. 'That finally forced me to see the light.'[2] He too became a soldier, with a varied career in the 6th Employment Company.

Most of the approximately four thousand men who served in the 'alien' Employment Companies arrived in the 1920s or 1930s.[3] The majority came from Europe; a smaller number from Asia.[4] Some were young single men; others older, with families of their own. Diverse in nationality, religion, class, culture and language, they shared the need to find a country that would take them.

Australia was not everyone's first choice of haven. Keith Steinhardt's eldest sister went from their home in Bad Nauheim, Germany, to Frankfurt in 1938, to see if she could arrange for the family to go to South America. Nobody from that large continent was available to interview her on the day, but the Australian office was open.[5] Sheer chance. Others preferred the United States, but its severely restrictive quota system made some turn to Australia. One Hungarian applied for entry permits to Rhodesia, Canada and New Zealand as well as Australia; when, in 1939, only the Australian permit had arrived, he was desperate and took it.[6] For many, as one of the men pointed out, 'it was not a question of which country to choose, rather which country would choose to take you.'[7]

Some saw Australia as a fresh opportunity: the promise of a new life. That was particularly true for those escaping privation. Many were leaving families, and sometimes whole districts, that were wretchedly impoverished. Through word of mouth, they heard this was a country where hard work would allow peasants and working men alike to live in modest comfort. Orpheus Kandiliotis' father was one who acted on this hope. Orpheus was born in Ithaca, Greece, in 1920. His father fought in Greek wars for years and got 'sick and tired of it'; leaving his wife and five children, he bought a bag of salted bread ('which wouldn't rot') and sailed with a friend to Australia. Orpheus, the last of the children to be brought over, arrived in 1939, aged seventeen.[8] For Joe (Giuseppe) Zammarchi, born in 1901 in Parma, Italy, penury and oppression were a double spur. He arrived in Australia in 1927, escaping both Mussolini's fascist regime and poverty. 'It was hard to live, wages were very low. I thought Australia was a better place to live than Italy.'[9] Jankiel Waligora (anglicised to Jack Waller), a Jew from Poland, travelled to Australia with his small family in 1938. According to his son, Louis Waller, his father emigrated because life in Poland was hard: poverty, not politics, or fear of another war, was the major motivation.[10] All three men—the Greek, the Italian and the Polish Jew—became comrades in arms in the 6th Employment Company.

Cruel regimes stimulate emigration. For the majority of those who came from the European Axis countries (initially, Germany and Italy), and from countries occupied or threatened with occupation, it was a peaceful and humane sanctuary they sought: 'a chance to work and live in freedom'.[11] In the Berlin of 1938, Wolfgang Sievers knew it was impossible for him to study his chosen profession of archaeology: his family was Lutheran but there was one Jewish grandparent. His father had been an art historian in charge of the cultural department of the German foreign office until dismissed by the Nazis in 1933. He urged both his sons to leave Germany soon after the Nazis came to power. When Wolfgang, initially reluctant, finally asked his father where he should go, he replied, 'Well, two things. As far away from Europe as possible. And go to a British country.' Wolfgang asked: 'Why to a British country?' 'Because it is better to be suppressed by the British than by anyone else,' said his father. More than fifty years later, Sievers remarked, 'And I think he was right. He was very sensible.'[12]

That practical advice, plus the help of a South Australian nurse studying childcare in Germany who arranged for sponsors, brought Sievers to Australia in September 1939, and, three years later, into the 4th Employment Company.[13]

Some came involuntarily. The British used the grand ship the *Queen Mary* to bring to Australia 266 Europeans (mainly German and Austrian Jews), many of whom had sought temporary refuge in the Straits Settlements of Penang, Singapore, Malacca and Labuan. Fear that all those born and bred in an enemy land could pose a danger to security was the reason for transporting them.[14] And, in an action echoing a practice long familiar during the early settlement of Australia, refugees were sent as prisoners from Britain, deported during the panic after the British defeat at Dunkirk in June 1940. They were mostly

German and Austrian men and boys, chiefly Jews, who had escaped to Britain before the war. They were detained there as 'enemy aliens', a bitter irony made plain in the first stanza of a song composed at a detention centre near Liverpool:

> We have been Hitler's enemies for years before the war,
> We knew his plan for bombing and invading Britain's shore;
> We warned you of his treachery when you believed in peace,
> And now we are His Majesty's most loyal internees.[15]

With protests mounting at home, the British Government persuaded a reluctant Australian Government to take approximately two and a half thousand of these detainees and imprison them here.[16] (Churchill later referred to this episode as 'a deplorable mistake'.[17]) The men endured a grim voyage under armed guard on a ship called the *Dunera*, followed for many by internment in rural New South Wales and Victoria; and, finally, late in 1941, gradual release: some to return to Britain to join the British Army's Pioneer Corps, some to live in the community, and others to become soldiers in the Australian Army.[18] 'The strangest boatload ever to reach this country', according to the sociologist Sol Encel,[19] was to provide more than five hundred volunteers for the 8th Employment Company.[20] These men were surprised to discover their destination was Australia. 'Few of us knew anything about the country,' one of them later recalled. 'I think that, generally speaking, we knew of it as the place "bottom right" on the map, or, more disrespectfully, as the arse of the world.'[21]

Whether emigrants leaving their homeland while they could, or refugees expelled or escaping, all those fleeing fascism and war saw Australia as a temporary safe haven, a quiet place in which to live until the disasters at home were ended. In the beginning, few thought of Australia as their new home.

## Enough scum here already?

Emil Witton (Witkowski), born in Berlin in 1919, seemed destined for a comfortable life. His father was a doctor, his mother the daughter of one of the founders of the German publishing house Rudolf Mosse Verlag and famous daily newspaper the *Berliner Tageblatt*. A happy family life, a first-class education—but when Witton finished school in 1937, further study was impossible: he was a Jew. That also meant he was stateless: the Nuremberg Laws of 1935 declared that 'A Jew cannot be a citizen of the Reich. He has no right to vote in political affairs and he cannot hold public office.'[22] A year later, the German State Secretary went further: 'The fundamental principle of all measures is to foster the emigration of the Jews.'[23]

By the time Witton arrived in Australia in April 1939 he had experienced some of the Nazis' 'measures', including Kristallnacht, the regime's organised attacks on thousands of Jewish shops and synagogues on 9–11 November 1938, and the temporary imprisonment of his father in Buchenwald concentration camp. More than half the Jewish population of Germany had already fled the country.[24] In a letter he wrote many years later, Witton remembered:

> It had been clear for a long time that emigration was going to be an absolute necessity, but when it actually came, it turned out to be a traumatic experience. Not so much the daily difficulties and troublesome dealings with hostile officials, than that everything I had taken for granted during my youth, was now negated for ever. I grew up being a German. My family had lived in Germany for many generations. My father had been an officer in the First World War (Oberstabsarzt, EK1 and EK - Major in the Medical Corps, with the medals of the Eiserne Kreuz [Iron Cross] first and second class) and was not anymore allowed to practice, and all that culminated eventually in the deprivation of my nationality.[25]

Taking advice to depart Germany, Witton and his girlfriend, both just nineteen years old, hastily married, and the young couple and Witton's parents applied to emigrate to Australia. It was, he explained, an imperative decision to leave. As to where to seek refuge, he and his family were fortunate: Emil's brother Paul was already in Australia and could sponsor them. The young immigrant cum refugee arrived in Australia just months before the beginning of World War II, and in 1942 became a soldier in the 3rd Australian Employment Company.[26] But before he was transformed from an 'enemy alien' into an Australian soldier, much had to change in government policy and community attitudes.

In 1940 Prime Minister Robert Menzies received a letter from a woman in Western Australia:

> I have heard on the wireless the news that Australia would be willing to receive internees from England. I beg to protest; we have enough of the scum here already, too many in fact. I am not a vindictive woman, these aliens are God's creatures just the same as we are. All the same I sincerely trust that a U-boat gets every one of them.[27]

The 'scum' she rejected so emphatically were the German and Austrian refugees, predominantly Jewish, soon to travel to Australia as prisoners on the *Dunera*. That they were European, white and, with few exceptions, anti-fascist made no difference: for this woman, and many others, non-British foreigners were aliens in more than just the legal sense.

There is an oft-quoted line from LP Hartley's memorable novel *The Go-Between*: 'The past is a foreign country: they do things differently there.'[28] Australian society in the 1930s and early 1940s was markedly less heterogeneous than it is now. The population was 7 million when World War II began in September 1939. For at least a decade before the war the country suffered what is still called the Great Depression, with a peak of 29 per cent of the working population unemployed in 1932.[29] Its people were predominantly of Anglo-Celtic origin; few had travelled overseas, and, when they did, mostly visited 'Home'—the British Isles or Ireland. Information about the world was available chiefly from local newspapers and radio stations. This was a relatively isolated community, not highly educated, generally unaccustomed to foreigners, and uneasy with unfamiliar languages and traditions. The official term 'alien', which applied to those who were not British subjects, carried emotional as well as legal weight.

In the same period, fascism in Italy, and its even more pernicious variant, Nazism in Germany, moved from brutalising and murdering its internal 'enemies'—parties and people on the Left, unionists, religious opponents, Jews, gypsies and homosexuals—to invading neighbouring countries. In Asia, Japan's assault on China, begun in 1937, was followed by the bombing of the US naval base at Pearl Harbor in December 1941 and a subsequent powerful military attack on a series of South-East Asian countries.

Terror and war in Europe and Asia produced a cascading sea of refugees seeking asylum. Between 1933 and 1939 alone, more than ninety thousand German and Austrian Jews fled,[30] some first to neighbouring countries, and then, if they could, to safety beyond the reach of the encroaching fascist regimes.

For the Australian Government, the inheritor and advocate of a policy of preferencing British immigrants, international pressure to accept non-British 'aliens' created significant political and ideological difficulties. Something of the government's attitude can be gauged from a discussion that took place just a few months before the war began. On 17 February 1939 Brian Fitzpatrick, an historian and the Secretary of the Australian Council for Civil Liberties (ACCL), led a deputation to meet the Minister for the Interior, John McEwen, and the head of his department, Joseph Aloysius Carrodus. The deputation had been arranged by the Victorian International Refugee Emergency Council, a body closely associated with the ACCL and chaired by Professor Woodruff from Melbourne University. Fitzpatrick's report to the ACCL included the following:

> The deputation had been informed that there were already 40,000 applications [for landing permits]; these could not all be dealt with, even with increased staff ... At present refugee immigration was being considered first – applications from concentration camps were considered urgent. It had been necessary to depart to some extent from the policy of not discriminating on grounds of race and religion, in order to prevent the growth of anti-Semitism in Australia. Thus Australia House [in London] would be empowered to grant permits to suitable non-Jewish applicants under 45 with £200 capital, to Jewish & 'Aryan Christian'[31] applicants with £1000 capital. Sub-quotas had been established within the quota, but the Minister would not divulge them ... [T]he suggestion ... that only persons with capital would be admitted, was wrong; some poor persons would be admitted, with a strong preference for young non-Jews ... Only Austrians, Germans & Czechoslovakians subject to political discrimination, and Italian Jews covered by a recent decree, would be classed as refugees ... [The Minister] said he could not give first preference in all cases to persons in concentration camps, as there were more than 15,000 of such applications, but offered to give preference to them all things being equal. He acknowledged the value of refugees to Australia, and stated that he had referred to the Prime Minister the question of protesting to the German Govt about their persecution.[32]

The Australian Government expressed regret for having to depart from 'the policy of not discriminating on grounds of race and religion' while proudly upholding its White Australia policy, and limiting Jewish entry with the specious argument that it would encourage anti-Semitism. Not surprisingly, Fitzpatrick and his ACCL colleagues were not impressed.[33] They were dismayed at the entry restrictions for Jews, the most vulnerable of all the applicants for refuge, as well as the consideration of a preference for moneyed applicants. Perhaps they recalled a statement by Robert Menzies (then Deputy Leader of the governing United Australia Party) on his return from a visit to

Germany in 1938: 'Hitler is not an administrator as Mussolini is. He is a dreamer, a man of ideas, many of them good ones.'[34]

Despite the government's determination to limit the groups who could be called refugees, international circumstances were making such distinctions implausible. More and more Europeans were fleeing the threat of persecution and extermination, and the British Government was applying polite pressure for Australia to accept a larger number of asylum seekers than it wanted.[35] Consequently, the differentiation between immigrants and refugees is much less in evidence at this time than in the post-war period. Government documents from as early as 1938 refer to 'Jewish refugee migrants';[36] and the term 'refugee alien', one of the categories of aliens, becomes the label for many who had in fact paid for a landing permit and did not require financial assistance on arrival.

Far more significant for the government at the time was the attempt to regulate and, where possible, curb the arrival of so many people of non-British stock. The policy was spelled out by the Australian delegate to the international conference on Jewish refugees held in Évian-les-Bains, France, in July 1938:

> … it will be appreciated that in a young country manpower from the source from which most of its citizens have sprung is preferred, while undue privileges cannot be given to one particular class of non-British subjects without injustices to others. It will no doubt be appreciated also that, as we have no real racial problems, we are not desirous of importing one by encouraging any scheme of large-scale foreign migration.[37]

Five months later, in December 1938, the same Minister ended a speech in parliament about the Évian Conference and Australia's refugee commitments with the words:

> The British people should be told that there is room in Australia for them and their families. We must encourage them to come

> here so that we shall maintain the predominance of Britons in our population and have the right kind of manpower to ensure our safety and progress.[38]

The glib reference to 'no real racial problems' not only ignored the Aboriginal community but also non-white residents and refugees such as the Chinese. With a White Australia policy largely implemented by the Immigration Restriction Act's dictation test, first passed in 1901,[39] the arrival of refugees from places such as China and the East Indies caused the government considerable anxiety. But refugees from Japanese invasion could not easily be turned away, and many of these men became Australian soldiers. When Prime Minister John Curtin, in his famous broadcast to the United States in March 1942, declared of Australians, 'We are all the one race, the English-speaking race',[40] he was conveniently ignoring all the aliens—non-British by definition—whom his government was in the process of recruiting into military service.

At the time of the Évian Conference, Australia had a quota per year for Jewish immigrants: 1500 refugees were guaranteed entry; another 3600 might be accepted but entry was not guaranteed.[41] As a result of international pressure at Évian, the government agreed to increase its quota of refugees (of any faith) to 15 000 over three years. This was only 'a slight increase on previous admissions', the aptly named government representative at the conference, Lieutenant Colonel Thomas W White MP, assured the parliament: 'Australia having pursued a policy as liberal as that of any other country.'[42] These refugees were required to be healthy, of good character, have an Australian sponsor or provide £200 landing money.[43] 'Preference would be given in the selection of refugees to artisans and industrialists who could give some help to Australia.'[44] White then went on to urge the Opposition to support 'the admission to Australia of people of our own [British] race … our own kith and kin.' Unfortunately, there was an 'excess of departures over arrivals of persons of British stock.'[45] It is clear the government considered the refugees a very poor substitute for their own 'kith and kin'.

Nine months later, Germany invaded Poland, and France, Britain and most British Empire countries, including Australia, declared war on Germany. That ended all but a trickle of refugees from Europe; only about six and a half thousand of the 15 000 Jews Australia had promised to take actually arrived.[46]

It is not difficult to build a strong case to show how governments of this staunchly Anglo-Celtic outpost of the British Empire resisted the efforts of thousands of people desperate to find refuge here. Despite this, there were 53 037 aliens registered in the country in 1940. While some were longstanding residents who had never been naturalised, a considerable number were official or unofficial asylum seekers.[47] For them, in Sievers' words, 'there was no way back'.[48]

# 2

# Life before the army

Even in the best circumstances, emigration is a major enterprise. When it is the result of trauma and fear, and sometimes involuntary, often organised hastily, with limited choices and even more limited knowledge of the destination, then settlement is unlikely to be easy. Torn from the familiar, separated from loved ones, infantilised by a foreign tongue and foreign ways, not everyone who arrived in Australia in the 1920s and 1930s was initially enthusiastic about this new land.

> I saw Australia and hated it immediately. At first I was homesick and wanted to go back to Poland. Father sent me to buy eggs in a store, so that I'd learn English. I came in and said I wanted 'six exs' and they said they had only one ax.[1]

That was the response of 17-year-old Yosl Bergner, brought to Melbourne in 1937 by his father, the writer and Polish Jewish community leader Melech Ravitch. Having seen with his own eyes the fate of Jews in Germany under the Nazis, Ravitch urged Polish Jews to leave: 'You *must* get out of here!'.[2] True to his conviction, he brought first his daughter and then his son to Australia; and later, his wife.

Ravitch, an inveterate traveller, shortly left for Mexico, never to return.

Bergner and his sister went to board near the cemetery in working-class Carlton, where the landlady gave them bread pudding for supper: 'poor folks' food'.[3] He took on a series of unskilled, poorly paid jobs. Often hungry, he was always drawing and painting. 'What saved me was the knowledge that I wanted to paint. Nothing could stop me; I never stopped painting.'[4] And gradually his view of Australia changed. Although his travels into the countryside with a fellow artist to paint proved unproductive—'I hated the Australian landscape, hated the eucalyptus trees'[5]—the poverty he saw in the city was reassuringly familiar: 'The minute I came to Melbourne I felt very comfortable … From the Warsaw street I moved straight into the Melbourne street.'[6]

My father, Saul Factor, remembered his 'first shock in Australia' when, in 1938, he went to Queen Victoria Market:

> I saw people picking out rotten tomatoes from the dustbins. I thought to myself: I ran away from a country, a very poor country, and came not to a country but a continent, large and rich, with a population of only six and a half million people. Seeing that made a terrible impression on me. That such a country couldn't afford even to feed her own people … Later on, when I learned the history of Australia, when I realised that the Depression existed here in this rich country, I thought to myself: you can run and run and you always find the same thing.[7]

Poverty was a problem common to locals and newcomers alike. Language, however, was a particular difficulty for immigrants, and went well beyond Bergner's mispronunciation of 'eggs', or locals' constant mispronunciation of their non-Anglo names. Speaking a foreign language in public, especially German, could arouse suspicion and outright abuse. Richard Langfelder's son Kurt recalls his parents' story of a truncated tram trip in Melbourne, when they were ordered off because they spoke to each other in German.[8] Bob Exiner only spoke German with his mother: 'Even amongst our friends we spoke English, it was advisable anywhere in public to speak English because people used to object if you spoke German.'[9] 'In those days,' wrote George Strauss, a refugee from Vienna, 'a foreign accent attracted immediate attention':

> A foreigner asking for a tram ticket loudly enough to be heard caused heads to turn. People avoided speaking a language other than English in public, as if not being Australian was something to be ashamed of, and explained their German accents by saying they were Dutch. The refugees resented this, but their previous experiences had taught them that it was best to avoid stares, hostile comments and awkward situations by lowering their voices.[10]

Opposition to the use of foreign languages in public could also come from well-established immigrants and their organisations. Before the influx of European Jews in the 1930s, the majority of Jews in Australia were either locally born or came from Britain. They deliberately differentiated themselves as little as possible from their Anglo-Celtic neighbours, seeking, in the words of one historian, 'group invisibility and non-distinctiveness'.[11] The marked difference in the newcomers' appearance and speech was recognised by both the new arrivals and the Anglo Jews. Stephen Lovas, a Hungarian immigrant, describes the way the Middle Europeans stood out from Australians: 'As an immigrant of the 1939 period, I remember that we would recognise each other from a distance. The style of men's suits, ladies' costumes, the length of our overcoats, the kind of briefcase we carried and the English we talked gave away our origins.'[12]

As for the government, there was ample correspondence on the subject of 'Use of Enemy Languages in Public Places'.[13] Much of the correspondence reflected the conflicting suspicion of such use with the danger 'that the prohibition of the use in public of tongues of allied nations or of neutral nations may be undesirable for reasons of diplomacy.' However, there was support for prohibiting 'the use of the spoken languages of all nations with which we are at war.'[14] No such prohibition eventuated, but there were restrictions on enemy language publications.[15]

Both foreign language and appearance caused many of the Anglo Jews considerable unease. Their discomfort was defended in an editorial in *The Westralian Judean*, which asserted that 'it is a simple but irrefutable fact that no society in its earliest stages of development can receive with ease an alien in vast numbers. Almost invariably the young sinews would regurgitate the unaccustomed dose.'[16]

More prosaically and urgently, the President of the Australian Jewish Welfare Society, Mr Saul Symonds, advised 'a large gathering of [Jewish] migrants' in Sydney in April 1939 to be on their best behaviour. The report of his remarks included a warning:

> Mr Symonds spoke on the objectionable impressions created by congregating in groups, and speaking in a foreign language on trams ... The Jewish community has incurred serious responsibilities – and it was expected that the new comers would so act that there would not be distinguishable any difference between local members of the community and the new arrivals.[17]

He was followed by another leader of the Australian Jewish Welfare Society, who offered his listeners a simple road to happiness in the new land: 'In Australia there is but one language – English – so make up your mind to speak English and to think in it. That is the way to become Australian and be happy.'[18]

Problems with language, including adjusting to the constant Anglicising of people's names, are common among immigrants. It is one of the reasons they may suffer a sense of dislocation and sometimes alienation. For the pre-war immigrants, there was also the difficulty of finding work and a decent place to live. Wolfgang Sievers, one of the few with a reasonable grasp of English, and helpful connections, rented his first flat in Melbourne's salubrious South Yarra.[19] The majority, lacking either the new language or connections, and with very little money, lived in cheap boarding houses or shared a rented room with others recently arrived. Some, more fortunate, were welcomed by relatives already here, but these families also generally lived in poorer neighbourhoods. Like Bergner and his sister, many arrivals found their first dwelling in working-class suburbs in the inner city—in the Bergners' case Melbourne's Carlton, then 'the densest enclave of Melbourne's Jewry'[20] and also the 'heartland of the Italian community in Victoria.'[21]

Difficulty finding satisfying work in their original trades or professions is an experience familiar to many immigrants to this day. Richard Langfelder was an engineer in Vienna, but his qualifications weren't recognised here, so for a time he worked as a fitter and turner.[22] Jack Waller (Jankiel Waligora) had been a carpenter in Poland, and worked in that trade briefly on his arrival in Melbourne in 1938. He earned a little over £2 a week, not enough to live on, so he chose to learn to be a cutter and sewer in his brother-in-law's handbag factory.[23] Albert Marius Ceen (Achille Menotti Coen), with a degree in business (Dottore in Scienze Commerciale), had been a prosperous commodities trader in Rome. Strongly opposed to Mussolini's fascist regime, he brought his wife and two small boys to Melbourne in March 1939, and at first managed to get work in a similar role. But once Italy declared war on the Allies in June 1940, he was informed by the managing director of his firm that he could no longer do this job: 'an enemy alien could not be seen to represent the company.'[24] Yet he was still required to come to the office every day, with nothing to do but read the newspaper. Ceen was saved from depression by winning a scholarship for a correspondence course for cartoonists; until he was able to join the 6th Employment Company, his 'desk was covered by cartoon sketches'.[25]

Not all employers were honest. Robert Exiner, with a modest training in textiles, worked night shift in a weaving factory, making elastic ribbons. He was paid about £4 a week, the basic wage then, with a few shillings extra because he worked at night. But there was a catch:

> On Fridays, after I got paid, I had to go and see [the boss] and hand him back £1! This practice of undercutting the basic wage was then quite a common practice amongst employers, both Jewish and non-Jewish, who gave jobs to refugees. As the money had to be handed back in cash no breaking of the law could be proved. Low language skills and lack of technical know-how by these employees was used as an excuse for the bosses.[26]

Necessity is also the mother of resourcefulness. Joe (Guiseppe) Zammarchi arrives from Italy as a twenty-six year old in 1927, having previously worked at labouring jobs in Europe. He is unemployed for a few weeks, then gets a job in the building trade in Melbourne. The job peters out and he heads off to rural Victoria, timber cutting and carting wood, then fruit picking; back to Melbourne, working for a blanket factory; to the country for harvesting; then, with another man, buys a second-hand truck and wins a contract to cart wood. Later he's in the Northern Territory prospecting for gold. When he appears before the Aliens Tribunal in 1941, challenging the government's decision to detain him as an enemy alien, his lawyers have no difficulty acquiring glowing references from his previous employers and fellow workers.[27]

Speros Polites, who, in 1937, came to Australia from Greece as a twenty-two year old, stayed for six months with an aunt in Melbourne, where he was well looked after. But when he determined to get a job and live independently, it was hard. The Depression, he remembers, meant that 'Australians didn't have enough jobs to keep themselves and their families—how could I, with no language, no trade, a foreigner, ask for a job? It was impossible.'[28] He finally, through contacts in the Greek community, was given work in a Swanston Street milk bar, earning £1 10s a week and paying twelve shillings a week rent for a room in Brunswick Street, Fitzroy.

A determined and resourceful man, Polites sought a new job at a coffee lounge that required him to speak English. When interviewed for the job, he said, 'I want to work with Australians to learn the language.'[29] By the time he was conscripted into the 6th Employment Company, in September 1942, he had worked at the Hotel Australia, and later bought his own milk bar and coffee shop. He was helped by advice from someone he trusted—an older Greek man who had been a schoolmate of his father and came from the same village to Australia in 1905.

Such examples of support from more established members of an immigrant's home community feature in many of the stories of the men who served in the Employment Companies. Robert Exiner, finding difficulties with both work and accommodation in Sydney, travelled down to Melbourne, and remembered with special gratitude and affection the generosity to a number of new arrivals of a large, well-established Jewish family there, the Mushins:

> All the Mushin crowd was terribly nice and helpful to us. They opened their homes to us, fed us copiously with very welcome meals, introduced us to interesting people, such as the writer Judah Waten, and gave us good advice and information on the Australian scene ... They were open to all cultural and political influences, and this was reflected in the high spirited and interesting conversations at social evenings.[30]

Like Exiner, Bart Srhoy (Bartul Srhoj), from Dalmatia, found a welcoming Yugoslav community when, aged seventeen, he arrived in Fremantle in 1938. But he learned quickly that he was expected to work very hard to earn his keep:

> Initially I worked long hours in the market gardens, for twenty-five shillings a week. I carted horse manure and wheat from farmers in various country towns. I worked in quarries and shovelled coal ... I was exploited, used and cheated by many. But I was too young and too naïve to confront people, especially those who were experiencing the same tough life I was. At the time, it was almost impossible, especially for migrants, to break through the economic and social barriers.[31]

For those called enemy aliens, it was government regulations that made their lives the most difficult. At the outbreak of war, the 1939 Aliens Registration Act required a register of all aliens in each state, and the National Security (Aliens Control) Regulations, which followed, obliged the details in these registers to be held by the police and the security service.[32] These regulations also placed severe restrictions on those non-British subjects who were classified as 'enemy aliens': 'a person, enjoying His Majesty's protection, [who] possesses the Nationality of a State at war with His Majesty'.[33]

'Enemy aliens' was a classification that, until the government in February 1942 created the new category of 'refugee aliens', included anti-fascists and Jews from Germany, Austria and Italy.[34] These men and women, many of them refugees from fascism, had restricted rights to travel beyond their suburb or district, were required to report to the local police once a week, and couldn't change their names or seek naturalisation. There was a special Aliens Control (Prohibited Possessions) Order, which carefully listed banned items. The order prohibited 'all aliens of enemy origin' from possessing or using 'signalling apparatus' (such as a torch) and maps and charts 'without permission'. Enemy aliens were also forbidden to possess, 'without authority, wireless apparatus, petrol or other inflammable liquid, motor vehicles and boats, aircraft or cameras or other photographic apparatus.'[35] Bold young men like Robert Exiner were undeterred—he concluded that 'these regulations were silly and went on my bike wherever I wanted to.'[36] But for most people, the classification was an insult, and the restrictions a hardship and a humiliation.

For some seven thousand of those designated enemy aliens, government policy was even more severe.[37] Yet, internment in detention camps did not reach the level of the incarceration of people of German extraction during World War I. The Menzies government's temperate policy on internment was spelled out in September 1939:

> The general policy which it is intended to adopt is to intern the minimum number of persons consistent with the requirements of

> national security. Whilst the national interest must be paramount, sympathetic treatment will be accorded to enemy aliens who, having left their own country on political, racial or religious grounds, or having been in this country for many years, are known to have lost sympathy with the country of their origin.[38]

However, this nuanced policy lasted only briefly. After the swift conquest by Germany of a series of European countries, the fall of Dunkirk in May 1940 and Italy's official military alliance with Germany in June 1940, Britain was under threat, and the Australian Government followed it in imprisoning enemy aliens in internment camps. At its peak, in June 1942, six months after the Japanese attack on Pearl Harbor, and with the Labor Party in government, there were more than 12 000 people interned, without trial, in detention camps around Australia.[39] Some were born-and-bred Anglo-Celtic Australians suspected of pro-fascist sympathies, but the vast majority were not 'natural born or naturalized British subjects'.[40] They included 4022 Japanese (almost all detained until the war's end); 3836 Italians (some for many generations Australian-born); and 2661 categorised as German, even though German Jews had been made stateless by the Nazi regime.[41] With the exception of the Japanese, and some Germans, such as the Christian Templers, almost all the detainees were men.[42]

Among the internees was Julius Guest (Weingeist), a young Viennese Jew who became a soldier in the 8th Employment Company in April 1942. After Germany annexed Austria in March 1938, he decided it was time to leave: 'I immediately thought—if I don't get out of Austria, I won't have many more birthdays.'[43] He managed to get the necessary documents to leave the country and take refuge in England, where, at first without any English, he worked on a farm, and later as a milkman in London. In Britain, he was initially classified as a friendly alien—a refugee from Nazism. But after the British defeat at Dunkirk and the German threat of invasion, Guest was picked up by the police and interned with thousands of other German- and Austrian-born men—now declared enemy aliens.

Guest was one of the more than two thousand men and boys, some Nazi and Italian prisoners of war, but the majority refugees from Nazism, who travelled to Australia on the notorious ship the *Dunera*: 'the first convict ship since penal days'[44]—arriving in Sydney on 6 September 1940.[45] For some of the young men, the voyage provided an education. Felix Werder, another 8th Employment Company soldier and later a leading Australian composer, remembers the lectures on a variety of subjects provided by fellow internees: 'We had so many German professors, there were enough to start several universities!'[46] But the opportunity to learn from professors did not nullify the humiliation and ill-treatment experienced by the majority on the voyage.[47] For most, including Werner and his sick father, it was a miserable time. 'We hadn't shaved for two months', Guest recalled. 'We were a raggedy lot, louse-infested, really on the nose.'[48] Kurt Lewinski, another German-born refugee who later joined the 8th Employment Company, wrote that day in his shipboard diary:

> Fifty-eight days, almost two months, on the Dunera! Fifty-eight days on the way to Australia, and we volunteered for a voyage of a fortnight at the most to Canada! ...[49] Two months ... without a toothbrush, without shaving gear, without a change of underwear, almost without soap, bad and insufficient rations, almost uninterrupted diarrhoea! Fifty-eight days exposed to the attempted bullying of the Nazis [on board], and also to the 'kindness' and the bayonets of the guards ... The chapter Dunera is closed for us at long last![50]

In contrast with their *Dunera* experience, the men found the Australian soldiers who guarded them on the trains to the Hay internment camp in southern New South Wales generally both relaxed and friendly. That may explain the widespread repetition of a story that has become apocryphal—told by many of the men as if it had happened to each of them—of the guard who asks a detainee to hold his rifle while he rolls a smoke, has a pee, gets a cuppa … In one man's account, the story is embedded in a larger narrative of welcome change:

> After disembarking, we got into this train and an old sergeant walked round with a whole pile of sandwich loaves. He chopped them into huge slices with his bayonet and opened tins of bully beef. Real meat two inches thick, and there was tinned butter too! ... He said, 'Have a sandwich, boys.' So we chewed away on these bloody great Dagwood sandwiches. They were three inches thick, the best food I've ever tasted. And these soldiers were completely different. We could move through the whole train. One soldier said, 'I'm going for a piss. Hold the rifle!' and he gave one of our chaps his rifle and bayonet! I took a liking to Australians. Talk about the lucky country, and it was only a beginning![51]
>
> Another man wrote, many years later, of the guard in his carriage who said, 'Just hold my rifle for a sec while I roll myself a smoke': He later sat down with us in our carriage for a chat, making clear that he considered us human beings entitled to a fair go. I shall always remember that fair dinkum Aussie. It was a heart-warming introduction to Australia.[52]

Of all the aliens who were later to become soldiers in the Employment Companies, the 'Dunera boys' are the only significant group to have had books written about them, to have been the subject of a television series and an exhibition in the National Library of Australia.[53] They alone have some recognition in public memory.

What is not so widely known is that their experience of internment—in Hay, and in Tatura, in rural Victoria, and Orange in New South Wales—was, with some variations, also the experience of many other equally innocent enemy aliens. These included about two hundred and seventy refugees from German fascism who had taken refuge in the British-controlled Straits Settlements—Penang, Singapore, Malacca and Labuan—and then been transferred to Australia on the grand

*Queen Mary*, converted into a troop ship.[54] A number of this group also became Employment Company soldiers.

Detention in internment camps was an unexpected and unwelcome experience for the new arrivals. Scattered across several states, and sometimes holding both internees and prisoners of war, the camps varied in size, and in standards of care. In some, such as Hay and Tatura, the guards—mostly World War I veterans—were generally kindly disposed to their civilian prisoners. There was ample food. Religious Jews at these camps were able to maintain kosher kitchens.[55] Some Jewish and Christian organisations, as well as civil liberties groups, offered material and political support.[56] There was a range of scholarly and cultural activities, including concerts and lectures. The men produced their own newsletter, enlivened with cartoons drawn by the gifted artists among them. According to Erwin Fabian, who later joined the 8th Employment Company, and in civilian life became a leading artist and sculptor:

> The Australian military presence, right from arrival [on the Dunera] was minimal and tolerant … At Hay, the academics continued teaching … I think a lot of people started their academic careers at Hay … There was a lot of activity in camp: students read and discussed, others organized and practised music, any artistic or intellectual pursuit was acceptable … A library had been established, and there were some art books.[57]

Julius Guest was one of the young men who benefited from the 'first-class university' established by the internees at the Hay and Tatura camps.[58] He saw it as an 'accidental' benefit of internment:

> We had some mathematicians there … and I was taught by three or four of them … One gave me lessons every day. By the time I was released, I was already a third-year mathematician … it only took me about a year. And that was very good indeed. I had my future mapped out as becoming a mathematician, which did happen.[59]

But even a detention centre with friendly guards is a prison, and it would be an error to focus only on the positive experiences of some internees. A petition to the Governor-General, Lord Gowrie, signed by 126 adults on behalf of the refugees from the Straits Settlements and Malay States interned at Tatura, conveys the disbelief and shock felt by many internees. In the four-page petition, dated 2 March 1941, they say:

> Your Excellency will understand that it is very hard for us to believe that there should be no possibility of finding a more satisfactory solution to our problem, if even only for the duration of the war, the more so as our fate must be considered undeserved and our present internment unjust ... All our hopes were shattered when we were delivered into this Internment Camp, where until now we are kept interned together with Italian, Nazi and other anti-British internees.[60]

In a number of detention centres, including Orange in New South Wales, Loveday in South Australia, and Tatura in Victoria, supporters of fascism were indeed housed in close proximity to Jews and other anti-fascists. In Loveday, where many Italians were interned, an Italian anti-fascist was murdered.[61] A former Australian member of the pro-fascist Australia First Movement who spent time in the Tatura internment camp later commented sardonically 'It is ironical to contemplate that the only institution dominated and run by Nazis in the Second World War in Australia was an internment camp.'[62] An exaggeration, but there were numerous appeals from detainees to be separated from the fascists: 'my life is absolutely hell in Tatura for me, being an anti-Nazi,' wrote one desperate German to the government's Aliens Tribunal.[63] Military Security was worried enough to report Nazi activities at Tatura, including 'lectures on National Socialism' and 'ardent Nazis' endeavouring 'to inculcate the principles of Nazi ideology on new arrivals'.[64] The report neglected to mention the Nazis at Tatura celebrating Hitler's birthday and Kristallnacht (Crystal Night)—the night in November 1938 when the German regime organised violent attacks on Jewish shops and synagogues throughout the country, and sent thousands of Jews to prison and concentration camps.[65]

Most of the men were deeply frustrated at being imprisoned by the enemy of their enemy: they had sought shelter here from German and Austrian Nazis and Italian fascists, and were being treated as if they were allied to the hated regimes they had fled. Some gained their freedom by appealing to their state's Aliens Tribunal.

The Aliens Tribunal was a semi-judicial body established under the National Security (Aliens Control) Regulations in November 1940, to hear pleas from enemy aliens against restrictions, or for release from detention.[66] The members of the tribunals, many of them lawyers, were not bound by the rules of evidence, and their recommendations could be rejected by the Minister for the Army, but the tribunals provided an avenue for enemy aliens to detail their grievances and, in some cases, to gain release from internment. While the 'Observations for the Guidance of Aliens Tribunals' made it clear that 'In cases of doubt the benefit should be given to national interests rather than to the individuals',[67] there is evidence that a number of tribunal members gave serious and sympathetic consideration to the appeals before them. One Victorian Tribunal report in March 1941 politely but firmly rejected the attempt by a representative of the Minister to suggest that the Tribunal's assessment of risk couldn't compare with that of the Defence department:

> [T]he task of reaching their own conclusions is imposed on the Aliens Tribunal by law, and a Tribunal can but form its own opinion on the material submitted to it. The proceedings before the Tribunal moreover may have afforded the first opportunity of fully investigating the matters which led to an objector's detention, or may have supplied fresh evidence which throws new light on his record.[68]

In 1940 Joe (Guiseppe) Zammarchi tried for months to gain release from internment, but was strongly opposed by the Intelligence section of the military in the Northern Territory, where he had been working.

Their reasons: 'Zammarchy [sic] was a member of the Victorian Council Against War and the Argus unit of the Communist Party. He was still actively interested in Communism at the time of his arrest.'[69] His possession of a number of books distributed by the Left Book Club in Britain was regarded as evidence of his communist attachment.

Zammarchi was finally able to present his circumstances and arguments before the Aliens Tribunal in Victoria in May 1941. His barrister, JV Barry (instructed by the legal firm Slater and Gordon), pointed out that he had been interned with Italian fascists at Hay, where 'he had been threatened with the baton and the razor'.[70] Zammarchi denied being a Communist,[71] declared his hatred of fascism—'I will never go to Italy as long as there is the Fascist Regime there'—and when asked why he had joined the Left Book Club, replied: 'For cheap books to read.'[72] He said he read *Hitler and Europe*, *Hitler and Russia*, and *Mein Kampf*.[73] Such evidence elicited a firm comment from the tribunal's chairman, Mr C Book KC: 'It is not the Minister's practice to intern men because of their social views.'[74]

Witness after witness testified before the tribunal to Zammarchi's admirable character and loyalty to this country: 'I have always regarded him as a fine type of citizen obeying the laws of the land that was giving him protection,' said one employer.[75] A man who worked with Zammarchi declared: 'He has been with me for two years on the Tennant Goldfield and one could not wish for a more honest and considerate mate and partner.'[76] The Hay internment camp commandant reported that his behaviour 'has been excellent – he conducts a class of ten or fifteen internees in English, twice daily'.[77]

In June 1941—more than a year after his arrest—in a unanimous decision, the three members of the tribunal recommended Zammarchi's release from internment:

> The Tribunal was greatly impressed by the directness and straight-forwardness of the objector as a witness. He has been ever since his arrival in Australia a very active anti-Fascist. No doubt his social views are of a radical kind. But the Tribunal is satisfied that he is

> not a Communist and that he has no subversive tendencies ... The Tribunal is satisfied that the continued detention of the objector is neither necessary nor advisable for the public safety, the defence of the Commonwealth or the efficient prosecution of the war, and that his release would not be likely to occasion unrest in any Australian community.[78]

No further objections came from the military, and Zammarchi was released, joining the 6th Employment Company on 6 April 1942.

By that time, government policy towards the undifferentiated 'enemy aliens' category had already changed. There had long been critical articles and letters in the press, as well as considerable lobbying of ministers, to reform a policy that treated opponents of the Axis powers and refugees from their depredations as if they were allies of the enemy.[79] The British Government sent an emissary to persuade the Australian Government to release the very enemy aliens the British had sent here as prisoners.[80] But the main reason for the change in policy was practical. The war was going badly, and the new Labor government had urgent need of more men in agriculture, industry and the military.

Barely a month after the Labor Cabinet was sworn in on 7 October 1941, the Minister for the Army, FM Forde, was authorised to release from detention refugees from Nazi oppression who had been sent from Britain and the Strait Settlements.[81] By the following January, Forde was recommending that 'excluding technicians and other specialists who can be of use in a civilian capacity ... it seems that [the] services ... of these persons of active military age ... should be used under the Defence Act rather than that they should proceed abroad (a return to England is a course open to the majority) or be released to undertake, to the possible chagrin of the public, some non-essential civil occupation.'[82] (The government was always worried about public reaction to the subject of aliens.)

And so, in large part, it came to pass. In February 1942 the government amended its legislation to permit the enlistment of 'refugees from enemy countries when no objection from a security aspect was seen',[83] and declared most of the 'enemy' aliens on the *Dunera* and from the Straits Settlements to be worthy 'refugee' aliens, no longer subject to detention or to civilian restrictions. Before they were released, some of the men were sent to pick fruit in places like Shepparton, Victoria, where labour was in short supply. Helmut Newton (Neustaedter), with his unblinking photographer's eye, describes the scene on arrival in the town:

> On one side of the factory yard stood two hundred Jews of different ages – anything from eighteen to twenty to decrepit old Jews of fifty or more, professors, teachers, doctors, writers, and musicians, all this intellectual flotsam and jetsam from Berlin that had washed up on the factory yard in Shepparton – and opposite these two hundred guys, about fifty Australian fruit-growers from the Shepparton area looking for a workforce to do the harvesting in their fruit orchards.[84]

The fruit picking only lasted about three months, and Newton declared that 'the natives didn't take kindly to us, as the girls were intrigued by us. Foreigners of our kind had never been seen before.'[85] Whether this was true or boastful, such tensions did not prevent the Shepparton paper publishing a number of articles and letters indicating that a friendly relationship had developed between the foreigners and the locals. That was certainly the view of a refugee who wrote a farewell article for the paper in April 1942. According to the enthusiastic 'young journalist':

> We have seen that, in nearly all cases, the Australian farmer harbors a kind heart, an understanding for arising difficulties and, above all, an appreciation of our specific position. This gives him the trait of a pretty broadminded man.[86]

Considering the writer's later assertion that Shepparton 'can stand up to any modern city in the new world and outstrip the corresponding areas in Europe',[87] it is possible that flattery was one purpose of the article, and perhaps even the reason for its publication.

The men from the *Dunera* and the Straits Settlements had the option of returning to Britain to join an army Pioneer Corps there, or to become soldiers in one of the newly formed Australian Army Labour Corps (soon retitled Employment or Labour Companies). According to some accounts, it was an opportunity that came with a threat: 'If you don't volunteer for the army, you know what we're gonna do with you, we're gonna put you back into the camp,' is Newton's recollection of the offer made to the men.[88] For Felix Werder, there was an ugly bait. His father was ill and needed hospitalisation. Then an officer arrived:

> He had a long chat with me and said, 'Look, we can't do anything for your father because he's a prisoner … But what we can do, if you join the Australian Army, then he becomes a dependant. Then we can put him into hospital.' So, that's how it finished. You think I volunteered for the army? You must be joking![89]

In the end, about four hundred and fifty men sailed back to England, and approximately six hundred and forty remained in Australia, the majority joining the 8th Employment Company.[90] One of these men composed a ditty including the following verses:

> We know the world from Norway down to Greece
> We left our homes and sailed the Seven Seas;
> We answered the call, when they asked for volunteers
> For the Home Defence as Pioneers
> In Austra-li-a-a-a …
>
> Ev'rybody thinks we're a funny looking crowd,
> Being in the Army makes us feeling mighty proud,
> We adore the Skipper and salute the Rising Sun,
> Until Victory is won.
> For Peace and Victory,
> FOR VICTORY![91]

•

Beneath the clamour of daily life, those seeking refuge had in common a deep-seated anxiety about family members left behind. Parents, siblings, wives and children: how could they be helped, how could they be saved?

Refugees desperate to bring a family member to Australia first had to find a person or an organisation to sponsor them. Not only that, sponsors themselves had to have a job, and were required to guarantee maintenance of the new immigrant for five years.[92] For refugees with little influence and few contacts, this was daunting.

A number of organisations, Jewish and non-Jewish, took on the responsibility of sponsoring and supporting refugees, as did numerous individuals.[93] The historian Michele Langfield tells the story of a young man, Fred, who came from Vienna and then tried to bring over the rest of his family. He was helped by a Mr AB Davis, who himself had immigrated in the 1890s and, though a stranger, offered to sponsor Fred's family:

> Fred said, 'How, you don't know us?' And [Davis] said, 'I've guaranteed for twenty-seven Jewish families from Austria whom I didn't know and they all got their permit.'[94]

Robert Salter, 'a refugee from the Nazis',[95] arrived in Melbourne in September 1938 from Vienna via Batavia, capital of the Dutch East Indies (now Indonesia). He was advised to make an appointment with Dr W Maloney, the Labor Party MP for Carlton. Maloney listened to his story and said immediately, 'I will try and help you.' Salter learned that Maloney's mother had been 'nursed back to health' by a Jewish family, 'perfect strangers to her', years earlier in California. 'She had taught her son, in gratitude, always to be kind to Jewish people.' This Catholic parliamentarian and member of the Australasian Knights of Labor[96] arranged permits for Salter's fiancée and, later, for his parents. Dr Maloney and his secretary attended Salter's wedding at the St Kilda Synagogue on 6 May 1939. There, said Salter, 'he gave me my residency permit, as well as permits for my parents, as a wedding present from the Australian Government.'[97]

A year before he died, my father wrote down some memories of his early days in Australia. From the day he arrived, in July 1938, he wrote, 'my mind was already occupied with the thought, what is happening now in Poland? Will I be able to manage in time, [before war breaks out], to bring my wife and child to Australia?'[98] Within a fortnight, he'd discovered that a Mr Brown was the Immigration Department person to see in Victoria. My father wrote that, after a number of fruitless visits:

> I took the photo of my wife holding our child in her hands and looked up in the dictionary the word 'love' … I went up to him and [showed him the photo] and the only thing I said was 'a permit, I love'. I couldn't say 'I would like to have a permit'… because I couldn't speak any English. [99]

Mr Brown's secretary took my father's particulars—name and address, names of wife and infant child—and, after four weeks, he received the permits he needed. Love may have softened hearts. But, my father noted wryly, it was lucky he couldn't understand Mr Brown's questions, one of which included the word 'job'. He didn't yet have one.

# 3

# Joining up

On 16 May 1942—my mother's thirty-third birthday—my father found his way from North Carlton to the Caulfield Racecourse to enlist in the Australian Army. He was an anti-fascist who had been trying to join up for some time before he was finally accepted.

Later, my mother would tell me about one of the arguments my father used in an effort to persuade her that he should enlist. He said there was a need for every able-bodied man to fight against a possible Japanese invasion; if he joined the army he would be helping to protect her and their small child. My father, who had persuaded her in 1938 that they should emigrate from Poland to Australia because he took seriously Hitler's warmongering and anti-Semitism, now added imperial Japan to the list of fascist enemies. Much later, he wrote:

> I had run away to the end of the world, to the unknown land, just to avoid what I could envisage so vividly ... Later I decided to volunteer for the Australian army to defend this country, to fight the same fascism that I was so afraid of, that I had run away from. And to fight Japanese militarism.[1]

My father was thirty-six years-old, 5 feet 4 inches, a slightly-built textile worker who wore glasses—not a convincing bulwark against the invading hordes. His passion was politics, not fighting. Like many other volunteers, he must have seemed unpromising material for a soldier. But, by the time he enlisted, the government had begun a massive mobilisation of men between the ages of eighteen and sixty: there was an urgent need for more manpower, both in the military and civilian spheres.

## Gearing up for war

Despite the cruelty, bellicosity and overt aggression of the fascist regime in Italy and the Nazi fascists in Germany, conservative Australian governments followed the British policy of excuse and appeasement. In 1938 Robert Menzies, then Attorney-General and Minister for Industry in the Lyons government, made an official visit to Germany. On his return, he challenged the opinions of those who did not appreciate Nazi Germany's good qualities. The *Sydney Morning Herald* in November 1938 reported him as expressing the view that 'those who thought France was always right and Germany always wrong were the sort who made international trouble.' He recognised that 'the dictator in Germany had been guilty of unspeakably bad things, but there were also points in the dictatorship that Australia could learn from.' He was particularly impressed by Germany's industrial efficiency. A month later, speaking to a church gathering in Melbourne, he called for people to appreciate the German perspective. 'I think', he said, 'there is a good deal to be said for German re-arming.'[2]

Five months later, Menzies became prime minister, and, in another five months, was declaring war on Germany. Then began a scramble to provide the military resources needed for battle.

Initially, intermittent attempts by the Menzies government to 'turn this country into a great war production unit'[3] were resisted by both the Australian Labor Party and the trade union movement.[4] One historian summarises the first two years of the war as a period when 'it is difficult to discern any coherent approach, on the political level, to the problems of labour in a war economy, which can be dignified with the name of manpower policy.'[5]

But a dramatic shift in government policy became necessary when Japan entered the war in December 1941, with attacks on Pearl Harbor, Hong Kong and the Malay Peninsula, followed by the imminent arrival of American forces and General MacArthur.[6] Once again in Australia's short European history, the needs of the military dominated government strategy, as they had done more than two hundred years earlier, when, for some thirty years after British settlement, the convict colony of New South Wales was controlled by naval and military officers.

Within months of the establishment of a minority Labor government in October 1941, a series of amendments to regulations ensured that the overall direction of capital and manpower was in the hands of government-appointed authorities. This was done to secure the resources needed to fight the war. Prime Minister John Curtin gave a stern warning of what was to come in a speech in December 1941:

> The Government must make the decisions … and when those decisions are made, there must be no argument about the wisdom of them … I now say to the people of Australia that I cannot wait upon debate. There will be governmental decisions where they are called for … [7]

By February 1942 Curtin was able to announce:

> The full Cabinet today directed the War Cabinet to Gazette the necessary regulations for the complete mobilization and complete ordering of all resources – human and material – in this Commonwealth for the defence of the Commonwealth. That means clearly and specifically that every human being in this country is now, whether he or she likes it, at the service of the Government to work in the defence of Australia … [And] every material thing in this country … when so required, can be diverted to the purposes of war … [8]

A number of trade unions and civil libertarians initially opposed such extraordinarily comprehensive government control (including 'conscripted labour'), but most came to accept—grudgingly or otherwise—the primacy of national defence policy. That it was a policy promulgated by the Labor Party, led by a man whose 'basic political thinking' was liberalism,[9] may have suggested to even the most ardent opponents the gravity of the situation.

In the same February speech, Curtin referred to Australians as 'sons and daughters of Britishers' who had come from England, Scotland, Wales and Ireland. Then, in an unusual extension, he declared that Australians also contained 'the best qualities of other races'.[10] It is unlikely he was hinting at the admirable qualities of Aboriginal Australians. More probably, it was an allusion to the non-British immigrants and refugees whose labour power he was about to enlist along with that of the descendants of 'Britishers'.[11] Certainly, 'every human being in this country' was soon to include a significant number of male non-British subjects.[12] When Curtin broadcast to the American people a month later, determined to convince this crucial ally of Australia's commitment to the war effort, he emphasised the totality of his government's control of the able-bodied population:

> There are three means of service – in the fighting forces, in the labor forces and in the essential industries. For the first time in the history of this country, a complete call-up has been made ... only the infirm remain outside the compass of our war plans. [13]

In fact, the situation was nowhere near as tidy as Curtin suggested. Government regulations created a Manpower Directorate in January 1942 to control industry and labour.[14] In February the Allied Works Council (AWC) was established. Headed by 'Red Ted' Theodore, a man with a long and sometimes controversial history in the labour movement, government and business, the AWC directed and controlled projects required to support all military effort in Australia.[15] These two federal bodies needed to cooperate with each other, and to work with numerous Commonwealth and state agencies—which was no simple enterprise, given the delicate relations between the two.

The defence services, meanwhile, were facing their most serious challenge: recruitment. The 'phoney war' that lasted until Hitler's invasion of Norway, Denmark and Holland in April and May 1940 was long over, but enlistment into the armed services continued to be slow. During the first two years of the war, fewer than 189 000 volunteers (only about 2.7 per cent of the population) enlisted in the Australian Imperial Force (AIF), the army's critical fighting force. By contrast, in the first two years of World War I the volunteers numbered almost 308 000, 6 per cent from a considerably smaller population.[16]

Japan's sudden entry into the war in December 1941 spurred a surge in enlistment, but it was not enough. The motivation behind the government's increasing focus on various categories of aliens was both the dearth of volunteers, and the urgent need for labour for war-related industry and infrastructure.

Necessity, the mother of change, forced a decision on a matter that had been the subject of consideration in military and government circles from the earliest days of the war: was it legal to enlist aliens? On 5 September 1939 the Commander of the 3rd Military District of the Australian Military Forces (AMF) sent the Secretary of the Military Board advice provided by Captain EG Coppel, who was a practising barrister and part-time lecturer in Law at the University of Melbourne, as well as a consultant to the army's legal division. Before the war broke out, Coppel had undertaken the task of evaluating 'the possibility of enlisting aliens as members of the Commonwealth military forces'.[17] After canvassing the legal position in Britain and Australia, and noting the probability that the large number of men made stateless by the Nazi regime and now in Australia 'will be desirous of rendering assistance to the country which has conferred on them at least the right to live', he concluded that 'there is no legal obstacle to the enlistment of aliens in the Commonwealth military forces'.[18]

The Judge Advocate-General challenged Coppel's legal assessment,[19] and the subject remained in dispute. Largely unknown to the public, a steady stream of correspondence on the enlistment of 'unnaturalised aliens' criss-crossed the Military Board, the departments of External Affairs, Defence and the Army, the Defence Committee (representing the army, navy and air force), the Department of Defence Co-Ordination, the Attorney-General's Department and, finally, the Prime Minister's Department.

When the war began, in September 1939, navy regulations required recruits to be 'of pure European descent and sons of natural born or naturalised British subjects.'[20] This was in accord with the country's longstanding tradition that favoured 'white' Europeans in general and British subjects in particular. The Air Force regulations did not specify nationality, but the 'approved conditions of entry' prescribed conditions almost identical to those of the navy.[21] The army's rules limited volunteers to those 'substantially of European origin or descent.'[22] All three forces required recruits to swear allegiance to the King.

The British response was different. Within weeks of the outbreak of war, its government issued an Order in Council under that country's Emergency Powers Act, providing that 'aliens may hold a commission or may be enlisted or entered in any of His Majesty's Forces as if he were a British subject.'[23] The British Government then proceeded to remove the requirement (seen as particularly offensive to American citizens, and therefore politically unwise) that aliens should swear allegiance to 'Our Sovereign Lord the King'.[24] New Zealand and Canada followed suit not long after.

By August 1940, when the British High Commissioner gave a polite nudge to Australia, expressing the 'hope that the Commonwealth Government will be prepared to take similar action',[25] air force regulations had been altered to allow the enlistment of aliens other than enemy aliens in the Royal Australian Air Force (RAAF). Senior RAAF officers had been urging this for some time, but the government, perhaps wary of public opinion, underplayed the change. The Melbourne *Herald* reported on 25 June:

> Because pre-war Royal Australian Air Force regulations would prohibit the service from getting men who were really, if not legally, 100 percent Australian, the regulations have been altered. Aliens will now be permitted, in special circumstances, to join the forces ... The Minister for Air (Mr Fairbairn) ... pointed out that the amended powers would only be used in exceptional cases, because the waiting list of Australians was sufficient reserve for all ordinary requirements.[26]

It is doubtful the RAAF shared the Minister's faith in an adequate 'waiting list of Australians'. As for aliens eager to join the AIF—and many were—sometimes the absurdity of their situation was sufficient to arouse even the ire of a government minister.

In August 1940, the Minister for External Affairs, 'Black Jack' McEwen, wrote a courteous letter to his colleague, the Minister for the Army, Brigadier the Honourable GA Street. McEwen directed the Minister's attention to the circumstances of Andrew Zanelli, who, he said, 'has been well and favourably known to me for many years.' Zanelli was only three months old when his family came to Australia from Italy, but he was technically still an enemy alien. While a younger brother was already in the AIF, Andrew Zanelli had been rejected. McEwen was prepared 'to personally testify to the loyalty of this man.'[27]

In due course, McEwen received a reply: 'the proposed provisions for the enlistment of aliens do not contemplate the enlistment of aliens of enemy origin. Until and unless Mr Zanelli receives a certificate of naturalisation he cannot be considered as eligible for enlistment in the A.I.F.'.[28]

McEwen's next letter was far less civil:

> Speaking in the Australian language, I am fed up to the back teeth with the treatment which this case has received by the Department of the Army. I might state that Zanelli is a farmer and neighbour of mine, whom I have known for probably 20 years ... Many months ago, I sponsored an application by Zanelli to the Department of

> the Interior for naturalization. To the best of my knowledge, that Department still holds his £5 deposit.[29]

McEwen went on to assert that he'd raised the matter in the War Cabinet and received assurances from various military heads that all would be well. This was indeed the result. In less than a week, Spender's private secretary sent a note to the Secretary of the Military Board:

> With reference to the communication from Mr McEwen, Minister for Air, of 28th of February regarding Andrew Zanelli, the Minister has informed Mr McEwen that he has given approval for the enlistment of this man. Will you please arrange for immediate action to be taken to carry out the Minister's direction?[30]

That was not a question—it was an order, carried out immediately. But for Zanelli, there was an insurmountable hurdle. Southern Command informed the Military Board that he had 'failed to pass the medical examination, he was given a Medical Unfitness Certificate and return rail warrant to his home.'[31] He was, nonetheless, granted naturalisation.

Few aliens had the support of a government minister pursuing their case. It took almost a year, after much to-ing and fro-ing of proposals and objections—the latter particularly from the army, to removing the oath of allegiance—for the National Security Regulations to be further amended. On 2 April 1941 the regulations were revised to enable 'aliens, not being enemy aliens', to enlist in the Royal Australian Navy and the AIF. The result was the opening of the services to a range of fresh talent, as the *Argus* reported three days later:

> A former baron of Imperial Germany was among the first 'friendly aliens' to be enlisted in the A.I.F. yesterday ... The former baron came to Australia before the Nazis took office in Germany. Other men enlisted yesterday were born in Russia, Latvia, Greece, Poland, Holland, Turkey, Iraq, and Jugoslavia.[32]

This change required a solution to the problem of the oath of allegiance. In January 1940 the War Book Officer had written to the Secretary of the Department of Defence, pointing out all that was needed to allow aliens to enlist were 'brief regulations to be passed' in connection with the National Security Act, 'and a schedule to such regulations [that] could contain a special oath of enlistment for aliens in which the words "Our Sovereign Lord the King" in the Defence Act oath could be substituted by "His Majesty King George VI".'[33] More than two years later, the government accepted an even simpler solution: 'When an alien has signed the declaration at the foot of the form of attestation, has been passed medically fit and is accepted, he is duly enlisted.'[34] In practice, an alien was 'at liberty to take [the] oath or not as he pleases'.[35]

Not until after the Labor government came to power in October 1941 were non-enemy aliens permitted to join not just the AIF but also the Citizen Military Forces (CMF, commonly referred to as the Militia).[36] In November a Cabinet decision led to the release from internment of 'a substantial number of refugees from Nazi oppression who, because of a state of emergency and strategic requirements respectively were transferred from England and the Straits Settlement to Australia.'[37] Though free from detention, these and other enemy aliens 'of the refugee type against whom no suspicion exists'[38]—notably, Jews born in Germany or Austria, and anti-fascists from Italy and other 'enemy' countries—had to wait until February 1942 before they could enlist as refugee aliens.[39]

Finally, the categories of aliens eligible to volunteer or be conscripted for military service encompassed almost all alien groups. Male aliens between the ages of eighteen and sixty were required to register for national service. All but non-refugee aliens could volunteer for service in the AIF or CMF; in practice, almost all found themselves in a section of the CMF the army variously called Labour or Employment Units. If aliens did not register promptly—within fourteen days of 3 February 1942—they could be compulsorily enlisted in civilian labour under the authority of the Minister for Labour and National Services.[40] Allied aliens who did not volunteer could be sent to CMF units.[41]

Nationals of neutral countries, such as Sweden and Switzerland, could volunteer but not be compelled to serve. Some efforts by the authorities to conscript them for service in the Civil Constructional Corps foundered when both the Swedish and Swiss Consul-Generals protested at what they viewed as a 'definite breach of international law';[42] the government finally chose to avoid conflict by saying that neutral aliens could work in 'essential industries' of a civilian kind instead.[43] Enemy aliens—persons whose 'sovereign or state' was at war with Australia and its allies and who were not reclassified as refugee aliens—could be detained, or conscripted for civilian labour, but could not serve in any military or military-related capacity.[44]

In the wider community, there were those who not only feared aliens as a potential fifth column but also resented what they saw as foreigners profiting from civilian occupations while Australian men were required to serve in the military. Newspapers around the country published many letters of complaint. One was written by a 'Soldier's Mother' in September 1940:

> While Australian soldiers are going abroad to endure all the dangers and horrors of modern warfare, aliens in Australia continue to live their pre-war existence. During the weekend, many aliens toured this district [Shepparton] with the object of purchasing land. Australian territory is passing into foreign hands, while our men make all the sacrifices, which will be in vain if they are to come back and discover that aliens have usurped their places. Refugee doctors are agitating to be permitted to practise here, while our own medical men are prepared to sacrifice their practices for the army. Aliens are prepared to fight for the last man of British stock.[45]

There was a prompt letter of rebuttal in the paper the very next day:

> It is deeply distressing to see that 'Soldier's Mother' joins the people who are spreading calumnies against defenceless aliens. She must know that many of them would gladly fight Hitler, but are

> by Australian law forbidden to do so; she must know that refugee doctors gladly would work for the army, but are not allowed to either. She surely knows that aliens from enemy countries are forbidden to purchase land. I am very grateful for being here, but I protest strongly against incorrect and unjust statements of this kind. The British Empire is fighting for justice.[46]

The compulsory inclusion of aliens in war-related work helped alleviate such rumours and a more general sense of grievance—what a War Cabinet memorandum referred to as 'the widespread opinion that there should be equality of sacrifice between Aliens and Australian citizens.'[47] That was exactly what many aliens themselves had been calling for; in the words of a feisty Austrian refugee, 'best use should be made of the services of all hands and brains available.'[48]

While alien enlistment in the military could, on occasion, depend on the whim of the recruiting officer, John Curtin's ambitious 'complete mobilization' was a little closer to fulfilment.

## Joining the army

Long before the government acknowledged the necessity of including aliens in the services, many of the men who would ultimately find themselves in the army's Employment Companies were trying to join up. Most were initially unaware of the regulations that excluded them because they were not British subjects; all who attempted to enlist wanted to fight against regimes they had reason to hate both personally and politically.

Helmut Graf, a young Jewish carpenter from Drossen, Germany, declared the police in Hobart were 'gentlemen', and spoke warmly of an Army Intelligence Major there. But when he tried to join the air force a few months after the war broke out, because he 'wanted to fight Nazis', it was 'no go'.[49] A later attempt to join the army was stymied by an officer who was a partner in the building company he worked for. Finally, he left for Melbourne in February 1943:

> Tried the Air Force again. No ... So I just walked into Royal Park and joined up, hoping to get into a fighting unit or at least [the] Engineers. But I was sent to Tocumwal [the 6th Employment Company] with an escort.[50]

Wolfgang Sievers, from a cultivated Berlin family, tried energetically to join up, and was initially rejected for being 'a German bastard':

> When the war broke out I went to the Town Hall, on the 1st of September, and the military asked me where I came from. 'German, you said? Get out, you bastard!' But a couple of months later, I was accepted in the air force, the RAAF, to be a teacher at Point Cook. But as soon as that became known in Canberra, they protested, and I was called up to army headquarters. And I said, 'Why can't I do it?' He said, 'Well, because an enemy alien cannot be an officer.' I said, 'I don't care a damn whether I'm an officer or not,' but he said, 'No, this job carries the rank of an officer.' Bureaucracy forever.[51]

When bureaucracy finally submitted to reason, he joined the 4th Employment Company.

On the other side of the continent, Bart Srhoy, from a small village in Dalmatia, listened on shortwave radio, along with Yugoslav family and friends in Perth, to the grim war news:

> The German army was advancing on all fronts leaving behind a trail of death and destruction ... Everybody was talking about the war and the need to fight the enemy and to beat the German Nazi and Italian fascist forces. I was toying with the idea of joining up.[52]

He wanted to join the navy, but he was not a British subject. Then he tried the air force; same result. The army seemed to him a very poor option: 'It sent the message to me that the navy and the air force were the elite services and the army was second-rate.'[53] But in June 1942 he willingly accepted army service, though his initial impressions of the

11th Labour Company (later called the 12th Employment Company) were not complimentary.

Emil Witton, a Berliner and self-described 'refugee from Hitler' who joined the 3rd Employment Company in Sydney in 1942, spoke for men of many European nationalities when he said:

> My attitude to the war was absolutely clear. That was my war, the war against Hitler, and that was the reason for joining the army. The Japanese problem, for me, was of less importance. But Hitler, his ideas and Nazi Germany had to be defeated. I tried to enlist several times between 1939 and 1942, but as I was an 'enemy alien' I was refused every time. I joined right at the beginning of 1942 as soon as we were allowed.[54]

Witton points to at least one significant difference between the motivation of local Australian men and of European-born aliens to volunteer for military service. This difference also applied to many of those who were conscripted. The war in the Pacific, and the real fear of Japanese invasion, was a spur for locals to enlist. Men who had escaped fascism, either as immigrants or refugees, were preoccupied with what was happening in Europe; it affected their family and friends, and for many it was also a political issue—the defeat of fascism and the restoration of democracy. For these men, political concerns were to play a significant role in their army lives.

Once 'all male aliens of and above the age of 18 years, who are not exempt,' were required to register, the army distributed notices to post offices around the country.[55] Letters commanding the men to appear at recruiting centres followed. John (Constantin) Callinicos,[56] who was fourteen when he came to Australia from the Greek island of Ithaca in 1936, was working at a fruit shop in Toorak Road, South Yarra, when both he and his employer were ordered to attend a call-up centre at a weatherboard hall nearby. His boss was exempted—at least for a time—because he had a business; Callinicos was marched with others up Punt

Road and then taken by train to Caulfield Racecourse. That is where he and hundreds of others began their army lives.[57]

All recruits needed to pass a medical examination to ensure they were fit. While the AIF consisted largely of men between the ages of twenty and forty, not less than 5 feet 5 inches, and with emphasis on the highest fitness classification, A1,[58] standards for the Employment Companies were understandably lower: these men were not going to be front-line fighters.

Most of the recruits were young, but there were also older men (though few over forty-five);[59] and many, young or older, whose previous occupations did not demand great physical stamina: tailors, watchmakers, musicians, mathematicians, factory workers, fruiters, coffee shop proprietors, artists, clerks and students.[60] As the commanding officer of one Employment Company noted, 'Members, with the exception of Officers, are not usually persons medically fit for service with field formations.'[61] In fact, officers and men alike mostly comprised 'B class personnel',[62] with many ranging from B1 to C3. 'Disabilities' listed in army records included 'feet unfit for long marching', 'astigmatism', and 'skin problems'.[63]

The men lining up to be examined knew little or nothing of the military's medical standards. Erwin Fabian, already an aspiring artist before he was shipped to Australia on the *Dunera*, recalled his medical examination at the Tatura internment camp, before release:

> ... there was a medical officer who listened to your chest. I remember I had cut off a piece of my thumb on a bread-cutting machine, and had a dressing round it. The soldier who sat there – they were elderly soldiers who had been in the First War – said, 'Are you fit?' He looked at the dressing and said, 'Uh, you'll pull the trigger!' [64]

In March 1942 Keith Steinhardt enlisted at Caulfield Racecourse. He remembers wryly:

> They gave you a bottle to go to the toilet ... Some of [the men] couldn't do anything, so someone said, 'Give us a bit of yours.' It didn't matter ... Wearing glasses didn't count. Flat feet didn't count either. I think you would have to be half dead before they sent you home. [65]

Racecourses and showgrounds were popular military enlistment centres. In Sydney, Emil Witton, Gerhard Steuerwald and Emery Barcs, all members of the 3rd Employment Company, were processed at Ascot Racecourse. Steuerwald wrote with dry humour (in a 1942 article the army refused to let him publish) that 'it was pitiful to see our N.C.O.'s making their first efforts to produce sounds which were intended to resemble our names ...'[66]

Bart Srhoy and some of his Yugoslav friends 'gathered in the Newcastle Hotel, Fremantle, for a few drinks' before reporting at the Royal Showgrounds at Claremont in Perth in June 1942. Their drinking, yarning and singing made them late:

> We reported at the camp in mid-afternoon and were given a friendly lecture for being late, and told it must not happen again. We are now members of the Australian Military Forces and we must abide by its rules, we were advised. We went though the induction procedures, including the swearing of allegiance, taking photographs for the paybook and army records, measuring height and weight, a medical examination and other formalities. They then issued us with the necessary army gear ...[67]

Srhoy and his friends were keen to take an active role in the fight against fascism, but found the Labour Company 'a sorrowful looking unit': they 'carried no guns, bayonets or anything that resembled a soldier, other than shabby-looking uniforms that didn't fit.'[68] These young men were not alone in their disappointment, and Srhoy, like a number of others in various Employment Companies, sought to join more active units.

In Melbourne, some men were sent to Caulfield Racecourse, others to Flemington Racecourse. It was at Caulfield that Bob (Robert) Exiner became 'the proud wearer of a most unfitting khaki uniform' and, like several other recruits, managed to sleep at home, rather than on the palliases the army provided as beds on the stands.[69] Frank Klepner was not so fortunate: he was one of those who 'slept on the stands, on the gangways leading up to the seating area, on the seats.'[70] More comfortable were the stables, which had been cleaned out to accommodate the men.

For Helmut Newton, Flemington seemed 'very low key':

> I reported to Flemington Racecourse with all my friends, and in true Australian fashion everything was very relaxed. The induction into the army was very low-key. We had to be on the racecourse, which was treated like a parade ground, every morning, so our names could be called, and then we were told that we had the day off, that we didn't have to come back until the evening. The Australians didn't quite know what to do with us. They knew they wanted to use us, that they needed a labor force, but they hadn't worked out exactly how they should go about it. [71]

Newton was wrong. The government had well-developed plans for the growing number of non-British subjects now part of the Australian Military Forces.

# 4

# We're in the army now

## Principle and pragmatism

In the same month—February 1942—that friendly and refugee aliens began registering for service in the Employment Companies, the Captain of the Intelligence Section (Ib) of Eastern Command wrote a strongly disapproving memo. According to Captain GHV Newman, it was rarely possible 'for an alien to produce proof that he was forced to emigrate from enemy territory on account of actual or threatened religious, racial or political persecution.'[1] And he was convinced the Nazis would go to any lengths to plant spies in Australia:

> It is only reasonable to expect that enemy Intelligence Service arranged to send several agents here in the guise of refugees, and knowing the efficiency of their Intelligence they would, no doubt, even go to the extent of placing some of them in concentration camps to give them the full and appropriate background before sending them out to carry out their work.[2]

Having declared his suspicion even of those 'enemy' aliens who had escaped concentration camps, Captain Newman turned his attention to the uniform all aliens would wear in the new army companies. 'No indication is given as to how these aliens are to be dressed,' he grumbled, insisting that this was a security concern:

> It is felt that if they are dressed in the uniform of the Australian Forces or in any uniform resembling that of the Australian Forces a most decided objection will be taken by Australian troops and the public with prospects of serious trouble developing quickly.[3]

Not an auspicious beginning to army life for the aliens, one might think. And it was not just the extreme view of one Intelligence Captain. A month later, the Director of the Commonwealth Security Service wrote to the Director of Military Intelligence on the same subject:

> As there will be potential enemy agents amongst those called up, the recommendation is repeated that no person affected by the National Security (Aliens Services) Regulations should be allowed to wear the same pattern (or colour) of uniform as the Australian Forces ... If orthodox Australian uniforms were used by any of these persons ... it would of course ... lead to considerable public and, no doubt, Service resentment. [4]

Military and Commonwealth Security spoke as one. But on this issue at least, they were unsuccessful, as were those, like leaders of the Returned Sailors', Soldiers' and Airmen's Imperial League of Australia (RSSAILA; in 1965 renamed the Returned Services League (RSL)), who regarded the aliens as potential fifth columnists—any one of whom might 'wreak damage under cover of his A.M.F. uniform'.[5] Letter writers to the Prime Minister, such as SJ Barry from Leichhardt, New South Wales, agreed. His passionate three-page missive included a heartfelt rebuke:

> You have clothed enemy nationals in the uniform of the Australian soldier which my son and other relations wear and respect. For me and others it is the work of clever enemy agents enjoying the confidence of the Federal Government ...[6]

With the government's intention to conscript certain categories of aliens enacted,[7] and the urgent military need for these recruits, the army leadership responded to the controversy over uniforms with a mixture of principle and pragmatism. The Deputy Chief of the General Staff pointed out that the aliens being enlisted 'are persons of whose loyalty Military Intelligence is satisfied or about whom nothing adverse is known', therefore 'it is not considered necessary from the security point of view that the Labour Units should be clothed in entirely distinctive uniforms'—though a new colour patch would be provided.[8] The Master-General of Ordnance (the army corps responsible for supplying uniforms) added that, from his department's point of view, 'it is undesirable to have a special type of uniform in view of the difficulty of obtaining production of additional new types and the necessity of holding large stocks of them.'[9] Fine, said the Deputy Chief of the General Staff, but be careful about the colour used in the patch: 'It is suggested no yellow should be included in any colour patch adopted ... since a yellow badge was forced in certain European countries on Jews as a mark of dishonour, and many of the overseas ex-internees are Jews.'[10]

In the end, it was determined that the alien Employment Companies would wear the same uniform as all other soldiers in the Citizens Military Forces (CMF) and have the same colour patch as all other Employment Companies: a 1-inch white square cornered over a 1½-inch red square.[11] They also received the same pay. Initially five shillings a day, it rose over time to 6s 6d, and increased for those men who rose in rank.[12] Yet the contretemps over uniform, a minor matter in the larger story of the enlistment of aliens into the Employment Companies, illustrates how, for a time, their recruitment continued to be a subject of controversy. As late as December 1943, the Captain of the 20th Australian Employment Company, stationed in Milne Bay in Papua New Guinea, wrote to headquarters that his men 'resent' the fact they 'wear the same colour patch as Alien Emp. Coys.'[13] A similar sentiment was expressed in the War Diary of the 33rd Australian Works Company in June 1944: to wear the same patch as those from alien Employment Companies, the writer insisted, 'has always been a point of dissatisfaction with personnel of this Unit.'[14]

Well after the Companies were bedded down, Private Kurt Honigsberg, an Austrian who had volunteered and was serving in an Employment Company, visited the Melbourne offices of the Commonwealth Investigation Branch, inquiring why his application for naturalisation had been refused without explanation:

> In the course of the conversation I pointed out to the interviewing clerk that my application should be given favourable consideration, since I was a soldier in the Australian Army, wearing the King's uniform. The clerk answered as follows, 'You are not in the Army, you are not a soldier, you are in the Labour call up.' I asked him if I was not even given credit for having volunteered, to which I did not get an answer.[15]

## The Employment Companies

A clear, brief outline of the official structure and functions of the Employment Companies (Coys, as they were often called) was written for the Military History Section of the army by an officer of the 22 Australian Works Company, CF O'Neill, at the end of 1944. His report is marked 'Secret'.

O'Neill noted that there were thirty-nine Companies, requiring 'personnel of robust physique and the ability to handle difficult jobs of the most varied nature.'[16] In fact, thirty-eight Employment Companies were established (there is no evidence of the existence of number 13), and, over the period of the war, some of the Companies were amalgamated.[17] O'Neill's own company, like almost all the others, consisted of four platoons. (The overall number of soldiers in each Company was initially intended to be approximately four hundred and fifty, but some were smaller and others larger, with up to six platoons.[18])

A platoon could be detached for a particular purpose, such as 'to assist in the transhipment of stores; to work at [railway] break of gauge points; maintain dock facilities and to co-operate with ... similar [military] services ... In conjunction with these duties the [22nd] Company covered the basic military training in small arms weapons and successfully completed a course of anti-gas instruction.'[19] And, in a warning against seeing these men as useful adjuncts to other sections of the military, the Quartermaster General of the Army reminded his colleagues:

> Labour Companies are raised for the purpose of supplying military labour for works projects and labour tasks and the personnel of such Coys will NOT be employed as cooks and batmen nor to provide camp fatigues other than within their own units.[20]

Although the Companies were 'not required to perform duties of a combatant nature',[21] basic military training in small arms weapons was provided to the non-alien Companies, some of which were based in combat zones such as New Guinea. Alien Companies received no such training: these men were not armed.[22] For many, this was a distinction that rankled. Henry Lippmann, from the 8th Employment Company, remarked that 'you didn't receive any military training although many of us would have liked to.'[23] The reason for this discrimination, and the passion it could arouse, is caught in a passage from a short story written many years after the war by Charles D'Aprano from the 6th Employment Company. The men have been discussing 'proper training in the use of firearms', to which a young officer replies:

> 'Come on, you chappies know that the military brass will not allow you to handle fire-arms.' ...
>
> A short, heavily-built Italian pushed his way to the front until he was facing the young officer. Then, with a ham-like hand thrust

> forward he said, 'I want to fight the fascists with a gun. I want to destroy them. And all I do is unload and load trains.'
>
> 'But Private San Marco, you're an Italian. I mean, put yourself in their place. They think that you could not be trusted with a gun in your hands, that's all.'[24]

Alien Company officers, however, were provided with weapons because of a fear that the 'alien personnel … of several nationalities' in each company might give rise to 'racial feeling'.[25] Pistols being in short supply, twenty-eight rifles per alien Company were distributed.[26] I have found no evidence that these rifles were ever used.

As mentioned in an earlier chapter, not all members of Employment Companies were 'personnel of robust physique'. An army brigadier was one of a number of senior military officers who pointed to 'the high percentage of unsuitable personnel at present in Employment Coys together with the similar percentage still being allotted who are physically unfit for such duty, viz. manual labour.'[27]

The Regulations permitted the enlistment of men 'of the age of eighteen years and upwards but under sixty years',[28] so it was not surprising that many were not in prime physical condition. This explains the establishment of a special 'standard of medical fitness'[29] for those eligible for Employment Companies. Men were accepted even with a hernia 'if controlled by a truss', varicose veins, flat feet, bunions and hammer-toes.[30] While young men like Werner Lowenstein were 'A1—young and fit',[31] there were many others, like Albert Ceen (Achille Coen), who were not. He was thirty-nine years old when he joined the 6th Employment Company. A prosperous Italian businessman from Rome, who brought his wife and two small boys to Australia in 1939 to escape persecution by the Mussolini regime, Ceen volunteered for the army but struggled to lift the heavy bags of cement and stores that were the responsibility of the Company in its early months in Melbourne. Two months after his enlistment, he wrote to his wife:

> Haven't written for over a week – lack of time and place and tired – need sleep. No difference between weekdays and weekends – we work day and night … Biggest change in my life – perhaps will do me good. [32]

It seems that many men did indeed grow fitter during their army years, Ceen included, but, fortunately for him, his Commanding Officer decided after a few months that he would be more useful in a clerical capacity. In August he wrote happily:

> I have an office of my own (!): one tent with a table and a bench. But I'll improve that and in my spare time I'll dig out my old carpenter's skill and will make some furniture to keep records and files. [33]

The Employment Companies were modelled on the British Pioneer Corps, but the military in Australia chose to use different titles. The British had established a Labour Corps during World War I; the World War II version was renamed the Royal Pioneer Corps 'because of class association with Labour'.[34] The term 'labour' did not appear to trouble the Australians—there was, after all, a Labor prime minister from October 1941.

Almost all these Companies were established early in 1942. Initially referred to as Labour Corps, the majority were known as Australian Labour Companies, but in October 1942 they were renamed Australian Employment Companies—'to make it sound a little bit nicer' was the acerbic assessment of Wolfgang Sievers.[35] From May 1944, when soldiers were gradually being discharged and Companies amalgamated, many of the non-alien Companies were formed into specially created Works Companies.[36]

## Alien Employment Companies

Before amalgamation or disbandment, there were eleven alien Employment Companies: the 2nd and 3rd enlisted in New South

Wales; the 4th, 6th and 8th in Victoria; the 10th in South Australia; the 7th, 11th, 12th and 23rd in Western Australia; and the 36th in Queensland.[37]

The Companies with a majority of non-British subjects generally had the word 'alien' included in brackets after the Company title: 4th Australian Employment Company (Alien), and so on. The three exceptions to this practice were the 7th Employment Company, made up of overseas Chinese; the 23rd, with a considerable proportion of Koepangese (from what was then called Dutch Timor); and the 36th, with Javanese (Indonesians). For reasons unstated but most probably related to the overarching White Australia policy, each of these Companies had its nationality added to the Company title. Although enlisted in the Australian Army, these Asian foreigners were apparently regarded as even more alien than the Europeans and required very specific labelling.

Many in the alien Employment Companies never knew that their Company was just one of a large number established by the army during World War II. And few in the general community were familiar with this branch of the military. Ivan (Icko) Rostkier, from Poland, who had somehow managed to join the AIF in 1941 but was transferred to the 6th Employment Company in 1942 because he wasn't naturalised, said he knew nothing about Employment Companies.[38] The same is true for Nicholas Raftopoulos, who came from Greece in 1934 as a fourteen-year-old to join his father and grandfather, and was conscripted in May 1942. Wishing 'to help make Australia a safer place', he expected to be in 'the fighting forces'. Instead, he was also sent to the 6th Employment Company. 'Before joining', he wrote, 'I knew nothing about the Company or reasons for its formation.'[39] Robert Salter left Vienna in September 1938 to escape the Nazis. When he volunteered for the army, in 1941, he had a wife and child, and a business in Melbourne. He volunteered, he said, because 'I felt it was my war even more than most Australians' war … and I didn't want to be sitting here in business whilst other boys are out there in the army … I did not know what [the army] was going to do with us when I joined, where they would send us.'[40] Apart from a few people who knew of the Employment Companies from friends who were already enlisted, this was a common response from members of alien Employment Companies.

For a number of the men, enlistment in a Company that offered no prospect of fighting the enemy was a humiliation and an outrage. John Cohen's response is typical. He came from Cologne, Germany, in January 1938 as an eighteen-year-old, and spent some time in the 11th Employment Company, first in Western Australia and later in Queensland.

> I was fitted out with the normal army uniform. We went to Northam for some elementary marching up and down, no real military training of any kind ... It was very much, as far as I was concerned, a painful experience ... in the sense that I wasn't deemed good enough to join the fighting services of Australia. Because when I arrived in Australia ... I'd made up my mind ... that I want to be an Australian: it's going to be my land, my country, my home, and therefore why should I not be accepted in the fighting services? Why should I be pushed off into a pioneer corps, a labour corps ... the lowest spectrum of the Australian army? [41]

Cohen wrote 'one application after another' to be transferred to a 'combatant unit', without success. He suspected that his applications 'all finished up in the waste-paper basket', because the Commanding Officer needed to keep a certain number of soldiers in order to maintain a desirable quantity of officers. In the end, by what he calls 'most fortuitous circumstances', Cohen succeeded in being transferred—though not to a combat unit. In Perth, he was recognised by the father of one of the students he'd taught German at Wesley College before being in the army: this man was a subeditor at the *West Australian* newspaper. That resulted in a letter to a WA Senator, and not long after, to the fury of Cohen's Commanding Officer, he was transferred to General Blamey's headquarters on the Atherton Tablelands.[42]

While Cohen's desire to be a member of the AIF was probably not how the majority felt, the commitment to contribute to the defeat of the Axis powers united men across age, class and nationality. As Frank Klepner explained, 'You felt you were part of the whole nation doing its bit; you were doing your bit in the army towards the achievement of the win of the Allies.'[43]

There they were: volunteers and conscripts, a remarkable congregation of 'aliens' in the strongest arm of the state—the military—of a dominantly Anglo-Celtic nation. By November 1943 the army recorded forty-one nationalities serving in the Labour Corps, totalling 3360 men, including '520 ex-British Internees'—men from the *Dunera*.[44] The list is neither complete nor always accurate: there was more than one Macedonian in the 6th Employment Company,[45] and many more than one Javanese (Indonesian) in the 36th and 170 Chinese in the 7th. None the less, the number of nationalities is some evidence of the broad range of ethnicities in Australia at the time, however small some of the communities. (In 1940 there were 53 037 aliens registered here;[46] in 1942 the Military Board lists fifty-nine 'alien nationalities known to be resident in Australia'.[47]) According to the military, by November 1943 the largest number of aliens serving in the Employment Companies came from Greece (797), Germany (724), Yugoslavia (366), Austria (353), Poland (276) and Italy (273).[48] Jews are not listed separately, but most of the men from Germany, Austria and Poland were Jewish.

Intermittently, the army tried to control the placement of certain categories of aliens. In March 1942 instructions regarding the registration of volunteer refugee aliens, sent by Major Christophers from Eastern Command in New South Wales, included a warning: 'It is imperative that when the Labour Company is formed that no large number of the same nationality will be in the same platoon.'[49] As the Company with the largest number of volunteer refugee aliens—the 8th—consisted almost entirely of fugitives from fascism in Germany and Austria, it seems the Major's warning went unheeded. As late as January 1944, orders were being given to prevent allied nationals and neutral aliens from being posted to an Employment Company consisting of refugee aliens.[50] How then to explain the composition of Companies such as the 2nd, 3rd, 4th and 6th, with their polyglot mixture including Greeks (allied aliens) and the occasional Swiss and Swede (neutral aliens) alongside mostly Jewish Germans and Austrians (refugee aliens)?[51] In Charlie D'Aprano's description of the 6th, he lists eighteen nationalities:

> There were Swedes and Norwegians and Russians and Swiss and Poles and Hungarians, Italians, Greeks, Cypriots ... There was even one American, whom I suspected of being an FBI agent.[52]

According to military regulations, Norwegians were not to be allocated 'to any units of the C.M.F., including Labour Units.'[53] Even in the army, head office does not always control realities on the ground.

## A challenge to the system

It is a curious accident of history that a legal challenge to conscription during the war—a challenge that reached the highest court in Australia—was brought by two 'allied alien' members of an Employment Company.

Speros Polites was twenty-two years old when he came from Greece to Australia in 1937 in search of a better life. Initially, he lived with an aunt in Melbourne, found work in a Greek bar and café, and then in a popular Australian coffee lounge—he was determined to learn English. By the time he was required to join the army, he had his own milk bar.[54]

It was Orpheus Kandiliotis' father—'sick and tired of fighting' in the Greek wars—who came to Australia in the 1920s, and gradually brought out his three sons and, later, his wife. Kandiliotis was twenty-three years old when he was conscripted, and had not long acquired a milk bar in Swanston Street, Melbourne, in partnership with an older Greek man. He was the younger of the two partners: 'One of us had to go, and of course I was the younger one.'[55]

Some time after joining the 6th Employment Company, the two men, with some support from other members of the Company and the wider Greek community, decided to test the legality of the government's conscription of foreign nationals. The court case, in December 1944, aroused both public and legal interest. Newspapers such as the *Launceston Examiner* provided an approximate and incomplete summary of the case:

> CALL-UP OF GREEK MELBOURNE
>
> On behalf of Speros Polites, 29, of Camp Pell, Melbourne, a writ has been taken out in the High Court against the Commonwealth and the Minister for the Army (Mr Forde). Polites claims that he has been called up wrongfully for service in the Citizens' Military Forces. He states that he is a national of the kingdom of Greece. [56]

The plaintiffs' lawyers argued that public international law, with which English law was presumed not to conflict, could not conscript aliens for military service against the state's enemies. The government argued on a number of grounds, including that there was no 'accepted practice' on this subject in international law, and these allied aliens weren't actually required to fight.[57]

The six judges brought down their judgment on 10 April 1945. Theirs was a unanimous finding in favour of the government: it had the authority as a sovereign state to make such laws, 'even if that law should violate a rule of international law'.[58] But there were qualifications. Chief Justice Latham wrote:

> The practice or rule of civilized nations [regarding the conscription of aliens] is … rather vague and undefined … The Commonwealth Parliament can legislate on these matters in breach of international law, taking the risk of international complications … It is not for a court to express an opinion upon the political propriety of this action. It is for the Government of the Commonwealth to consider

> its political significance, taking into account the obvious risk of the Commonwealth having no ground of objection if Australians who happen to be in foreign countries are conscripted for military service there.[59]

The ruling in this case remains a pillar of Australian law.

# 5

# Officers and NCOs

Officers and the men they command: the folklore of military service encompasses two dominant contradictory narratives. At their simplest, there is the tale of the gallant officer leading men who respect and admire him; and then there is the other tale, of the officer who is mocked, despised and even defied by his men.

Both stories emerge from oral and written records of the alien Employment Companies, but while the traditional officer–soldier relationship is often marked by class distinctions (officers being well-bred and well educated compared with ordinary soldiers) the situation in the alien Companies was more complex. Most officers spoke only English, while the men under their command spoke an array of languages but sometimes little English. There was also clear evidence that many lowly Privates were far more sophisticated and better educated than those who gave them orders. This caused discomfort on both sides. To these complications were added suspicion on the part of some officers as to the reliability of 'reffos' or 'chinks', and the disgruntlement of some aliens at their mundane roles or even at being enlisted at all. The situation was ripe for tribulation, vexation, friction, and comedy—deliberate or unintended.

Many of the officers were older World War I veterans—men whom the army considered no longer suitable for front-line service because of age or disability. A number of the Commanding Officers and Non-Commissioned Officers were born in the 1880s and 1890s. Their civilian occupations prior to the war could be called reasonably modest: Captain Richardson of the 6th Employment Company was a bank officer;[1] Sergeant Totterdal of the 6th had been a builder,[2] and his colleague Sergeant Doyle was reputed to have been an official of the Waterside Workers' Federation.[3] According to Cary Roth, whose rhyming ballads of army life entertained the 4th Employment Company:

> There is also Captain Harrison
> The C.O. of the garrison
> Who before this blooming war
> Ran the local hardware store.[4]

Captain Walker of the 4th Employment Company was described by Wolfgang Sievers as having been 'a second-hand furniture dealer from Ballarat', [5] which may have been true. But this is the same Captain he remembered welcoming his men with the words 'I notice a lot of you chaps are Germans and Austrians; I just want to tell you the only Germans and Austrians I like are dead ones', so Sievers may have exaggerated slightly.[6] However, he is not alone in recalling that the initials the Captain proudly attached to his name—VD (which stands for Volunteer Officers' Decoration, a World War I military award)[7]—were quickly deflated to Venereal Disease. And Albert Ceen, in the 6th, recalled an ugly experience, described years later by one of his sons:

> One day the Sergeant Major asked that all soldiers who had ever served in a foreign army to step forward. [My father], who nineteen years earlier had attended officers' training in the Italian Army, stepped forward. He and his mates were ordered to report to the kitchen and peel potatoes and wash dishes.[8]

Such officers came from an older generation of Australians whose attitude to non-English-speaking foreigners was likely to be cautious, if not suspicious. These recollections tend to support the observation of the historian Paul Fussell that the war was a time when 'Anglo-conservative(s)' reaffirmed traditions and marginalised outsiders.[9] Felix Werder, in the 8th, was not the only 'alien' soldier who, despite his uniform, was abused in public: 'Why don't you go back to where you came from?'[10]

But this is not a simple story. John Cohen had applied for the AIF, and was not happy to find himself in the 11th Employment Company—'it's not a fighting service!' He didn't think the officers were 'the crème de la crème of the officer corps', but none the less remembered, with some gratitude, that he had been 'treated with a little concern' (perhaps because he had been a teacher at Wesley College in Perth), and was rescued from tree felling and made a medical orderly.[11] In the 4th Company, Sievers observed that an Orthodox Jew in the 4th Employment Company '*was allowed to live in his own hut and make his own food. He didn't march with us, didn't work on the railways … he had a little hut, all on his own … I must say, I did have respect [for the captain] for that.*[12]

The 4th was also a Company that put on theatrical and musical shows that today might be called multicultural, and celebrated its first anniversary in March 1943 with 'a special dinner with free wine provided by the Regimental Fund.'[13] The dinner was attended by representative officers from other sections of the army, who all supported 'Captain Walker's words of thanks and satisfaction to the members of the Unit for the splendid work they have carried out during the past year. By doing so [the men] had fully played the very important part they are allotted in the common task to win this war.'[14]

A feature of the celebration—at the Albury camp where the 4th was based—was a remarkable 26-page illustrated ballad of camp life in rhyming couplets, called 'A Day in Camp', created and illustrated by two members of the Company, Cary Roth and Tim Walton.[15] This comic epic opened with words of warning about censorship:

Like one's intestines by the growth of a cancer
Opinions are threatened by the knife of the censor.
So I have to be careful and weigh my words
Not to criticize – even if it hurts ... [16]

Despite the warning, the ballad offers plenty of sly pokes at military authority and methods, including a quatrain describing the men's response to the Captain's lengthy address to soldiers on parade:

So to bring his many words down to a few,
There is little that's pleasant and nothing that's new.
They jump to attention, chilled to the heart,
And captain and officers slowly depart. [17]

Captain Walker may well have been a product of Anglo-conservatism, yet spoke quite warmly of the Greek soldiers in his Company on the occasion of a Greek national holiday celebration in Albury:

> I am impressed with the dignified and worthy way in which the Greek soldiers under my command are wearing the Australian uniform. While younger men served in Greece in the trying days, we older officers are to direct the older Greeks in Australia. They are giving their best and the majority are doing a worthy job.[18]

Captain Walker overlooked the youth of many of his Greek recruits, but he certainly had some understanding of the progress of the war: in the camp canteen, a picture of Joseph Stalin hung next to the picture of King George VI.[19]

At a more pragmatic level, officers sometimes chose to overlook certain activities. Gambling, though against standing orders, was rife in the alien Companies, as elsewhere in the army.[20] John Cohen from the 11th Employment Company, initially based in Western Australia, remembered numerous card games, including a Greek version of poker. 'There was a fair bit of gambling going on', he says. 'I think the officers turned a blind eye to that.'[21] A soldier from the 6th, reflecting on similar experiences, views the officers' benign neglect as a sensible way of keeping peace in the camp.[22] And for some soldiers, it was a distraction from war-induced anxieties and sorrows. In his eloquent essay on life in the 4th Employment Company, written in 1963, Gerard Herbst recalls the daily BBC news broadcast, with its catalogue of sailors drowned, pilots burned:

> Unfathomable numbers of those murdered arrived with every World Service … An Australian, downcast and embittered about the 'theatre of war' was pulled gently by the sleeve. A Greek it was, who whispered to him: 'Come on fellow, you must learn to be philosophical', and moments after succeeded in enticing him away to a gambling two-up school in progress somewhere.[23]

Bern Brent, a Dunera boy in the 8th, remembered when he overstayed the 24-hour leave granted to the men on the Victory in the Pacific Day celebrations. He was stationed in the New South Wales border town of Tocumwal and wanted to get to Sydney to see his girlfriend. Once there, he realised he wouldn't be able to get back in time—the train took more than twelve hours. 'So I thought,' he says, 'if I can't get back in time I might as well overstay a day or two.'[24] Which he did. While he was away, one of his mates had responded on his behalf when his name was called on morning parade, but the Lieutenant and Sergeant knew he was absent. Ignoring the rules, they didn't report him to headquarters. When he appeared before the Lieutenant and told him the story, the officer said, 'It's not VP Day every day: a fortnight confined to barracks.' Brent was grateful:

> That didn't get into the records, you see. And a fortnight confined to barracks was a joke, because there wasn't anywhere to go anyway. I thought it was rather nice—the Lieutenant could have raised a fuss, but he didn't.[25]

The relationship between the officers and their soldiers ranged from respect and affability to outright rebellion. Andy Factor (Abraham Faktor), an eighteen-year-old in the 6th Employment Company, remembers the men getting on 'reasonably well' with the officers. There was a Lieutenant who was 'a very meek man, a very sedate man, very easy to get on with', and an impressive Sergeant Major:

> There was Sergeant Major Grogan—now, he could really yell 'Attention!' in the morning. He was a real military man; if he strode up and down the parade ground, you respected him … He was the epitome of a military sergeant.[26]

Speros Polites, in the same Company, recalled with pride the six Greek members of his working gang: 'We used to [work] a hundred percent—we wouldn't let our officer be disappointed.'[27] And Orpheus Kandiliotis, also in the 6th, spoke of a Corporal who was very good to the men— 'he would bring round dry towels in the morning.'[28]

Emil Witton, in the 3rd Employment Company in Sydney, wrote with admiration of a Sergeant Major:

> This officer deserves a special mention. He was a cockney, which was clear after the first command he made. He could be as rough as any other army officer, but also extremely understanding. Every morning he called out all the names on parade to send people to working parties. Our names, mostly foreign, from very difficult long Slav and German names to involved Greek and Italian ones, were certainly not easy to pronounce for an English tongue. He asked every new soldier with a difficult name to teach him the proper pronunciation. When he called the name out on the next parade it was perfect.[29]

The same Sergeant Major, learning that Witton had been sent to a timber camp 250 kilometres from Sydney around the time one of his children was due to be born, called him in when he was sent back to Sydney and said, 'You had a bit of a rough trot. I have a job for you as guard in a Comforts Fund Store.[30] You are married, so I expect you will behave yourself.'[31]

Interviews and memoirs offer examples of friendship, and even solidarity, among officers and men. Gerard Herbst, from the 4th Employment Company, tells the story of a fellow soldier, a young man from Prague he calls Jüngerle—'young fellow' in German. On leave in Melbourne, Jüngerle, together with 'the "bonza" chap of an Australian Officer as he was called by everyone in the unit', were enjoying a tram ride:[32]

> An elderly lady sitting opposite stared at both for some time, obviously realising that the Jüngerle was a foreigner, but what about the Lieutenant? So she plucked up courage and asked him: 'Excuse me, and what country do you come from?' The Officer obliged with his Scottish accent, 'Oh Madame I'm a bloody Hun!' Screaming with terror, the lady as if bitten by a tarantula pulled the cord and alighted at the next stop. Both Officer and Jüngerle smiled in silent comprehension for one another. [33]

Captain Richardson, Commanding Officer of the 6th Employment Company, was regarded by some of his men as lacking in sympathy for foreigners, but he responded firmly to racist attacks on his soldiers. He sent a sharp official letter, headed 'Offensive Behaviour', to the units of the AIF, AMF and RAAF that were also stationed, along with the 6th, near Tocumwal:

> It is repeatedly brought to my notice by members of this Coy. on leave in the town of TOCUMWAL that they are being subjected to offensive remarks made by members of other units (A.I.F., A.M.F., & R.A.A.F). Such remarks as "woggs, dagos, jews, ectr." [sic]
>
> It will be appreciated that members of this Coy. are doing a job of national importance and are deserving of better treatment by fellow men in the same uniform.
>
> Such behaviour reflects bad discipline within units to which offenders belong and is most aggravating to maintaining a high standard which is my aim within this Coy.

Perhaps recognising the aspersion he was casting on the disciplinary capacities of fellow officers, he added a handwritten note to the typed letter:

> Instruct units at Tocumwal this must cease & inform R.A.A.F. also in a nice way.[34]

Captain Richardson's admonition was quickly supported by the Major responsible for all military units in the region.[35]

Sometimes there was friendship and solidarity; often there was unintentional comedy, a by-product of cultural and language differences. Witton's Sergeant Major's effort to correctly pronounce the men's names was exceptional, for the accounts by soldiers in the alien Employment Companies are peppered with tales of mispronunciations. As Gerhard Steuerwald of the 3rd Employment Company remarked, it was pitiful to see the Anglo NCOs 'making their first efforts to produce sounds which were intended to resemble our names.'[36]

Frank Klepner tells the story of a Sergeant drilling the new recruits to the 6th Employment Company at Caulfield Park and wanting to test their alertness:

> The sergeant said to us, 'If I tell you to do left turns, right turns, halt, don't do it unless I say "Simon Says"'. One fellow nudged another and said (in Yiddish), 'Simon? Who is Simon? What is he talking about?'[37]

Klepner notes wryly, 'This exercise was not very successful, and they didn't persevere much with that part of our training.'[38]

In the same Company, a Lieutenant whose knowledge of musicians must have been minimal determined that one of the men should play a bugle to rouse sleepers every morning. Andy Factor was a talented violinist, who in his free time formed a quartet consisting of two fellow Employment Company members, both from Vienna—Fred Bohm second violin and Robert Schreiber viola—and a cellist, Ron Oakley, a local railway worker at Tocumwal. One day, the Lieutenant said to him, 'You are a muso, I've got a bugle here, I want you to wake up the camp in the morning, reveille.' According to Factor:

> I said, 'I can't play the bugle, I've never played the bugle.' He said, 'Here's the music, you're a muso. You've got to be able to do it.' So I looked at this thing, this rusted thing ... He said, 'I'll give you the day off, you can practise', which I did. I tried to. I couldn't get a sound out of it. And so, at the end of the day, he came to me. He said, 'Are you going to play tomorrow morning?' I said, 'I can't blow it.' He said, 'Blow it now,' and I really made a tremendous effort to get the sound out of this thing, and I collapsed, and they had to take me away to hospital. [39]

It turned out that the bugle, an ancient World War I instrument, was blocked. When Factor was released from hospital, the Lieutenant said, 'I still want you to play that thing.' Fortunately, Factor got hold of a record of the requisite bugle music, and from then on he only had to play the record every morning.[40] Meanwhile, the Commanding Officer ordered him to stop carrying crates. For a month he became the office runner, which left time for him to practise—the Captain wanted him to play 'Ave Maria' on his violin to the officers during mealtimes.[41]

In a letter to the *Sydney Morning Herald* in 1992, Frank Wheener (Frantisck Wiener), who had served in the 2nd Employment Company in Sydney, described an occasion when the men became 'a column of rumbling discontent' because they were forced to march from Mascot to Botany Bay. It was hot and dusty, and the Sergeant decided they would do better if they sang. The younger men knew a few popular songs in English, but they soon petered out:

> Our sergeant urged more singing, but the youngsters refused; he urged the middle-aged and elderly to sing into the breach until one rather timidly told him that the only marching songs they knew were Austrian or German ones.

> Our sergeant rose to the occasion: 'Sing them!'
>
> And thus it came to pass that in the darkest days of World War II, as Hitler's hordes swept towards Moscow and Leningrad, a bunch of fellows in Australian uniforms were cheered by women and children in Botany Road singing such songs as Ich hat' einen Kameraden, Prinz Eugen der Edle Ritter, and 100,000 Mann die zogen ins Manoever … (Translated: I had a comrade, or perhaps more appropriately, I had a mate; Prince Eugene the noble knight; and 100,000 men headed for manoeuvres.)[42]

There was the comedy of misunderstandings, misjudgements and making do; and then there were officers whose attitudes, from unease to contempt, left a mark remembered decades later. Wolfgang Sievers recalled the Warrant Officer in the 4th who was a heavy smoker, always coughing. 'He never feared to tell us', said Sievers, '"Got that from the Germans [in World War I], you know."'[43] In the 6th, a Warrant Officer told Robert Salter that the only decent people in the world were 'the bloody Australians'. He didn't even like the Poms.'[44] Members of this Company haven't forgotten the officer who addressed them as 'you people'.[45] In one of the short stories he wrote years after the war, Charlie D'Aprano has a Sergeant use those words as the men wait to be moved from the Caulfield Racecourse:

> The conversation was cut short by a sudden yell from somewhere behind them. They turned to see a little man with three stripes on his arm, barking at them to be quiet. 'You people'll have to learn to do as you're told or I'll make your life a misery.' From the back came mumbles of protest. 'So, we are just "you people"' …[46]

In an interview, D'Aprano spoke grimly, remembering an incident that epitomised an officer's lack of understanding of what men in the Company were having to endure:

> Michael Kaminsky, a Polish [Jewish] boy, had received news from the Red Cross that all his family had been killed, all of them—his

> cousins, his uncles … And this bastard [a Warrant Officer] comes along, on parade, and we were the usual noisy bunch early in the morning … and he yelled, 'You people don't understand, do you, that there is a war on!' I looked at Michael and I thought, oh cripes … There is Michael, grieving, and we are all grieving with him because he was our mate, our comrade, our friend. I thought, oh Jesus, some people never understand, never … It still brings tears to my eyes, I'm so angry about it.[47]

Even in the 8th Employment Company, led by the remarkable part-Maori Captain Broughton, whose care and attachment to his men became a byword for decency, not all officers followed his example. Felix Werder, a young Jew from Berlin, remembered being abused 'for being a bloody intellectual, telling me even though I was in uniform, "Why don't you go back to where you come from!"' Like the majority of the 8th, he was a 'Dunera boy' who had joined the army.[48] He saw the problem as a cultural gap: he didn't drink beer, he wanted coffee, not tea, he preferred to play soccer rather than Australian Rules football. Small things in themselves, but they came to represent something more serious: 'It's a feeling you had, a feeling of being constantly a second-rate citizen … treated with disdain.'[49]

There were officers the men admired, respected, even liked. But the history of every alien Company, even the 8th, features stories of animosity and dissent. Fred Lester, a young German Jew in the 4th, provides one explanation for the hostility that erupted on occasion. He wrote:

> The main drawback in army life was the carry-over of many outgrown ideas and inflexible attitudes from the top which [caused a] flare up from time to time. Such things as marching to and from working areas in Summer heat or Winter downpours twice a day, when other army units were transported in trucks, became a bout between troops and administration.[50]

The men's resentment at what they regarded as unjust and discriminatory rules led to direct action: a hunger strike. Hunger strikes occurred in a number of the alien Companies. Stopping work, the more conventional means of labour protest, would have resulted in severe punishment, even court martial, in the army. As well, those men who felt a deep need to contribute to the defeat of fascism would not countenance a stoppage that might affect the war effort. In the 6th Employment Company at Tocumwal, one strike was partly the result of long-held grievances over food. Charlie D'Aprano remembered:

> We used to get horrible meals. I mean really horrible meals. We had meat with maggots crawling over slices of lamb. Maggots. Beautiful beef: maggots. Butter—never saw butter.[51]

But the turning point from dissatisfaction to hunger strike was the rumour that an officer—'the same person who called us "you people",' said Charlie—was 'selling butter, all the good meat, all the good cuts, to the cafés in Tocumwal, Shepparton, Cobram. So we went on strike. We just refused to eat. We would go on mess parade, with our dishes, but walk past the cooks.' After three days, a few 'trouble-makers' were transferred to the 4th Employment Company for a time, but they were not charged. And, said Charlie triumphantly, 'the food improved no end. You know, we got good food.'[52]

Resentment of 'outgrown ideas and inflexible attitudes' gave rise to a conflict between the men in the 6th and their first Commanding Officer, Captain Fogarty. In a memoir written in the 1990s, Robert Exiner remembered the 6th's first camp 'in a bend of the river Murray' near Tocumwal in mid-1942:

> There were only three water-taps for the use of several hundred men. There were long queues in the morning and the ablutions were rather superficial. However, our company commander … explained to us that if facilities were good enough for him they should certainly be sufficient for us. This did not go down well with the troops and

> he was booed. We were rather a disrespectful lot and had inhaled enough Australian air to be rebellious and undisciplined towards our superiors whom we did not consider to be our betters … The army had not selected its elite human material to lead this non-combatant horde of 'bloody foreigners' … Our officers were only saluted when we could not avoid it.[53]

This proved to be a very bad place for a camp—it was soon flooded and had to move to higher ground. And it appears that the aggravation Exiner noted in his 6th Employment Company comrades was sufficient to reach the ears of the Major-General who headed the Victoria Line of Communication Area (the military control centre in Victoria). The Adjutant-General wrote a preliminary report about the Company, recommending 'urgent investigation'. One of his concerns was the claim that 'there is little sympathy between the officers and the Alien personnel' and that 'the officers of the unit have various grievances, one of them not dining with the other three.'[54]

The army sent an officer to Tocumwal on 22 November 1942, 'to make a thorough investigation'. He stayed with the Company for a week, and remarkably, found 'no lack of sympathy between the officers and the alien personnel.'[55] The summary of the situation, signed by the Major-General, noted gloomily that 'this Unit has received more attention from Inspecting Officers from [Victorian army headquarters] … than any other Unit in this … area.'[56] His report praised the new camp, the catering facilities, and the 'periodical visits' of 'religious and consular representatives of various nationalities, and a Y.M.C.A representative … for the purpose of distributing comforts.' Any trouble in the ranks was blamed on 'Balkan nationalities whose inter-racial hatreds are indigenous'. More generally, according to the Major-General, any problems with the Company were the consequence of its diversity of nationalities, and the fact that many of the men 'were previously engaged in sedentary occupations, and were of an age that militated against adaptability to entirely new surroundings, and the manual labour required of the Unit'.[57]

In practice, nothing much changed as the result of what seems to have been a superficial inspection.[58] Years later, the painter Yosl Bergner, a Private in the 6th, gave his own summary of relationships in the Company: 'There were about 20 nationalities there, and we all lived happily together, Yugoslavs and Italians and Jews and Greeks and so on. We were all united of course against the Australian officers.'[59] And, according to Frank Klepner, thanks to food parcels from home, 'we never ate better than during that hunger strike.'[60]

In one alien Company, the behaviour of some NCOs led to a formal military inquiry. The 2nd Employment Company was based in Sydney, with working parties sent to rural centres in New South Wales. Its multicultural and multilingual recruits included men from Germany and Austria. Here, as in all other alien Companies, men spoke to fellow nationals in their own language, but the Company's Routine Orders censured only those who spoke in German: 'The speaking of German is prohibited. Disciplinary action will be taken against offenders ...[61] It is reported that personnel will speak in German over the Bureau phone. If this practice is continued with, the phone will be cut off.'[62]

It is precisely the German speakers who feature as the innocent victims in the inquiry.

The military Court of Inquiry, consisting of three army Majors, assembled at the Victoria Barracks in Paddington on 16 September 1942. Its purpose was to inquire into 'the circumstances surrounding the dismissal of five NCOs of 2nd Labour Coy ... and is based on a report given to Mr Mulcahy M.H.R. by ex-Sgt. J. W. Jackson, V.C.'[63]

The core of the complaint by Sergeant Jackson and his fellow NCOs was what they declared to be improper 'pampering' and preferential treatment of the alien soldiers in the Company.[64] The NCOs were all facing dismissal for a range of offences, including drunkenness, violence and insubordination. Perhaps it was his World War I Victoria Cross that emboldened Sergeant Jackson to attempt to put his case to the most senior officer of Eastern Command, General Fewtrell. The approach failed, and he was warned 'not to seek political assistance on the matter.'[65] Undeterred, he did just that, meeting a government

Member of the House of Representatives, Daniel Mulcahy, on Sunday, 13 September. The very next day, Mulcahy met with the Minister for the Army, Frank Forde, and handed him a three-page document based on information from Jackson.[66] Forde immediately instituted a military Court of Inquiry; it began its hearings two days later.

Such speed. Mulcahy must have been persuasive, or at least influential. It may have been because of his role as a Labor Party dissident—a member of the Premier of New South Wales Jack Lang's break-away Non-Communist Labour Party until its disbandment in 1941. When he chose to address the Military Court towards the end of its inquiry, he declared himself well justified in bringing the matter to the attention of the Minister; cheerfully acknowledged that when soldiers couldn't get the results they wanted through military means 'they find possibly that they will get there through a member of Parliament'; and made it clear that 'before the Minister received the Report', he would 'have a chat' with him about what he believed should happen to the NCOs. In Mulcahy's view, 'if they do not want to leave the Army, they should be used somewhere other than in this Labour Coy.'[67]

The Court received documents and called numerous witnesses, including the five NCOs, the Captain, and other senior officers of the 2nd Employment Company. The Commanding Officer of the 3rd Employment Company also gave evidence, as his Company was based at the same site—Ascot Racecourse—as the 2nd. In large part, the questioning focused on accusations raised by the NCOs against alien soldiers. Were they trustworthy? Did they work hard enough? Did they get preference in leave and other benefits? Evidence from all witnesses other than the five NCOs was yes to the first two questions and no to the third. In its final report, the Court declared that 'the majority of complaints made to Mr Mulcahy were grossly exaggerated and in many cases no evidence could be produced by the NCOs or others in support of them.'[68]

What is notable for a contemporary reader is the manner in which the evidence against the five NCOs—a litany of violence, drunkenness, 'abusive and filthy language' and other 'military misdemeanours'[69]—is flavoured with their own statements against the aliens under their command. Regardless of what their officers said, they could not work with aliens. When asked by the Court, 'Why do you object to the Germans?' Sergeant Jackson replied, 'I have a lot of reasons – we fought them in the last war and I know their sympathies are not with us.'[70] According to Sergeant O'Brien:

> There are Germans out there belonging to the 2nd Lab. Coy – they are refugees and they say they have no time for Hitler – they have been hunted out of Germany and they would not stand for Hitler. I think there would be a lot of propaganda in those cases … I think that those men on the whole – I will include the lot – that they are detrimental to the conclusion of the war. They are not friendly aliens – they are enemy aliens.[71] I call them Huns …[72] I definitely say that a German, whether a Jew or a Gentile, he is still an enemy.[73]

Corporal Smith went further: 'I would not ask a Jew for anything … I don't like them at all. I have no time for any Jew … I just want to have nothing to do with them.'[74]

In the end, the three Majors who conducted the military Court of Inquiry decided that, despite the overwhelming evidence against them, the NCOs had not been entirely fairly treated, and recommended they be transferred, 'if vacancies exist', to a non-alien Company.[75] Drunkenness and general insubordination, not racism and anti-Semitism, were criticised. And members of the Court appear to have shared some of the NCOs' prejudices, as they also recommended that 'in the public interest Alien Labour Companies should be provided with a distinctive uniform and/or badge to distinguish them from Australian Fighting Services.'[76] The Court did acknowledge that government policy made the enlistment of aliens legitimate, and therefore 'it was not competent for the N.C.Os to object … and that in objecting to and reporting against such enlistments the N.C.Os concerned showed lack of discipline', but qualified this criticism by noting that 'in view of ... their experiences in the war in 1914-1918 this is understandable.'[77]

A few weeks after receiving the Court of Inquiry report, Major General Fewtrell forwards the document to the Minister for the Army with a friendly covering letter. 'My Dear Minister,' he writes, 'The Court dealt exhaustively with the matter and disclosed that many of the allegations were without foundation and were mainly caused by jaundiced opinions of the NCOs concerned.' After more of the same, he lists the actions he has taken 'in respect of the discharges contemplated, and which were held in abeyance pending the Report of the Court':

Sergeant JW Jackson: his request for discharge granted; '... it is not proposed to re-employ him'.

Sergeant L O'Brien: discharged because of his 'heavy drinking', 'abusive and filthy language', and because 'on one occasion [he] threatened a member of 2 Labour Coy with an axe'.

Corporal R Gamble: discharged as 'unsuitable', a 'heavy drinker' with 'a long record of convictions for military misdemeanours'.

Corporal S. West: because of cardiac condition, given discharge for medical reasons.

Corporal Smith: demoted to Private and sent back to Garrison Battalion from which he came.

Corporal McLennon: to be transferred back to Garrison Battalion from which he came, 'but as now is absent without leave, when he has been apprehended I intend his discharge to be proceeded with'.[78]

The Major General has made his own decisions, only some of which coincide with those of the Military Court. And he adds a sharp rebuke for the behaviour of Mr Mulcahy, MHR:

> In the presence of these NCOs, Mr Mulcahy stated that if he was a man like Sergeant Jackson he would refuse to be dictated to by an alien NCO, he would not give him his pay book, and would not ask for a pass into Camp, and that he would not live in the camp. Such statements coming from an Officer of the Commonwealth, and a member of the party now controlling the Government of the

> country is to be deplored as it was an incitement to the men to resist authority, and his statement made to the NCOs and to the Court that he was astonished to know that aliens could wear the uniform of an Australian Soldier and have a Rising Sun badge on his coat, appears to be a reflection on the policy of Cabinet. I stress these matters in view of the statement made by Mr Mulcahy that the matter would be heard of in another quarter. [79]

Having ensured that the Minister is forewarned and forearmed, the letter ends with a friendly gesture: 'As you will appreciate many of the allegations were of a flimsy nature with which I will not weary you.'[80] When, in the following year, Mulcahy attempts to raise the matter again with the Minister, he is sent a polite letter setting out the decisions Major General Fewtrell has made months earlier.[81]

## Alien NCOs

> Men desirious [sic] of being considered for promotion to rank of Corporal will submit their names to the platoon Commander immediately.
>
> (Notice in Routine Orders of 4th Employment Company, 14 April 1942) [82]

One of the Court of Inquiry's recommendations, also not endorsed by the military leadership, concerned the promotion of alien soldiers. According to the Inquiry, 'alien Non Commissioned Officers should be confined to the rank of L/Corporal.'[83] The military simply did not have enough 'British subjects' to allocate as Non-Commissioned Officers to the alien Companies, so they determined that 'from the inception of the Companies, 50% of the Corporals were to be obtained by promoting Aliens'.[84]

In every alien Company, men seen as capable and reliable became Lance-Corporals and Corporals, and occasionally Sergeants, especially if they had reasonable English. In September 1942 the 2nd Employment Company had only one alien—a Greek—among its thirteen Sergeants, but ten of its fourteen Corporals were aliens: three Germans, two Greeks, a Hungarian, a Rumanian, an Austrian, a Pole and a Palestinian.[85] In the 6th Company, in D'Aprano's words, 'the more likely elements from the ranks received their first stripes … a Swede, a Norwegian, German and Austrian Jews, Yugoslavs, Greeks and Italians'.[86] According to a military report of June 1945, '60% of all NCOs in Employment Companies are Aliens', but while the report notes that 'no authority can be found which prevents the promotion of Aliens to the rank of Sergeant', there were at that time only twelve alien Sergeants in Victoria, and only one in New South Wales.[87]

One of the alien Sergeants was Albert Ceen, of the 6th Company, who described in a letter to his wife how he'd learned of his promotion:

> Yesterday morning, on parade, I saluted the Captain and he told me I was not properly dressed. I thought he meant I was not supposed to wear an American shirt, but he told me that the reason was that I had one stripe missing on my right arm. I answered back that I would immediately go to the tailor to fix it up and after ten minutes I was a sergeant. It was not a bad surprise at all although I was waiting for it. [88]

To have officers who understood the language and culture of significant cohorts of their troops was an obvious benefit to a Company's operation. And there were also advantages for those who were promoted, including a pay rise: from six shillings a day to ten shillings.

But not everyone was interested in rising through the ranks. Some thought it might cause a rupture with mates; others were not attracted to military hierarchy. Henry Lippmann, in the 8th Company, said, 'I wasn't very ambitious in the army and I never had a stripe. I never wanted … to push myself forward there.'[89] Both Orpheus Kandiliotis and Speros Polites, from the same Company as Ceen, were offered promotion but declined. As Greek allied aliens, they regarded their conscription as improper; Polites thought it would enmesh him too closely in the military.[90]

Comments from men in the Companies suggest that status was as important as salary to some aspiring NCOs. Steuerwald from the 4th Employment Company humorously describes the response:

> During the early days in the history of our company a stripe was something to be regarded with supreme respect and admiration. Almost everyone of us believed himself worthy of at least two of them, while our newly-appointed [alien] lance-corporals strutted around the camp as if they were field-marshals … [91]

There were men, according to one of the 6th Company soldiers, who were prepared to 'be very nice to officers, they paid them compliments, they put themselves out to volunteer, perhaps, for certain tasks nobody else wanted to do, in order to get a stripe.'[92] Felix Werder, whose acerbic comments on his experiences in the 8th are a salutary reminder that memory does not always grow more benevolent with time, is uncompromisingly critical of the men who were promoted:

> They were more officious than the Australians. The Australians were inclined to be stupid, but they were lackadaisically stupid: she'll be right mate … they [didn't] really care. But our own guys … should have been in a German Prussian army … [93]

A more benevolent view comes from Eric (Erich) Eckstein, also a Dunera boy and a member of the 8th:

> The Australian military authorities were confronted with a ticklish task in their selection of NCOs from among us. They tended to choose older men and also those who stood out for any particular reason. While the authorities' choice was, on the whole, quite sound, our own NCOs were by no means always popular. As a result all sorts of cheeky rumours circulated about their competence for the job. One, it was said, had been appointed because he possessed a typewriter, another because he was a musician and played the saxophone. Others

again were conspicuous because of their appearance and bearing, causing the authorities to suppose that they were likely to assert themselves. Generally speaking, we got on reasonably well with our NCOs, both Australian and our own.[94]

An example of the fortuitous nature of some promotions comes from the experience of Alfred Ruskin, who left Germany in 1938 to escape persecution and was a member of the 6th Employment Company for a year. Ruskin had spent four years as a medical student in Berlin, and his training proved useful very soon after he joined the Company in 1942. The men were sent to the Melbourne wharves to 'unload cement ships that had been diverted from Java to avoid the Japs'.[95] According to the story at the time, the waterside workers' union refused to do the work without being paid danger money. It was certainly dirty work:

> Many of the sacks were already broken, quite a lot broke because of the handling by inexperienced people, and cement dust was everywhere. There was no medical station at the wharf. So I slipped out, telling the guards I was sent to get some medication from a chemist. I did indeed go to a nearby chemist and bought some eyedroppers, small eye troughs, bandages, splints, eyedrops, iodine, mercurochrome, etc, etc. [96]

Having added a Gladstone bag to hold his purchases, and a Red Cross armband, he returned to the wharf. 'I found work immediately wherever I went,' he wrote. 'I washed eyes closed with cement dust, I looked after minor abrasions, all sorts of other damage that the chaps had suffered – I had arrived as a medical orderly.'[97] The Commanding Officer, Major Richardson, demanded to know what he was doing:

> I pretended to lose my temper and told him off (a Private to a Major) for not having a medical officer on the staff. He took it quite well, asked me where I had the knowledge from and then appointed me as his first foreign Corporal and his medical orderly on the spot.

> I became a Sergeant a short time later and was put in charge of the Medical Hut.[98]

In the end, as Jack (Jonas) Friedman from the 6th said philosophically, 'Some of the officers were very nice, some of them were not so nice.'[99]

# 6

# Hard yakka

The official history of the Employment Companies is scattered through the army's Routine Orders, and the War Diaries that each Company was required to keep.[1] According to regulations, the Diary was 'the principal war record'. Guidelines for compiling this important record were detailed at some length in a document overseen by Dr CEW Bean, the official Australian historian for World War I, and Gavin Long, who had the same role in World War II.[2] In practice, few Employment Company scribes attached the same importance to the task as its initiators. Most wrote entries with the clipped economy of a telegram, often ignoring advice against 'the omission of pronouns, possessive adjectives and prepositions'.[3] Date, place, and a few words about daily activities represent the common practice. Yet, despite the rigid format, each diary is as distinctive as the thumbprint of the officer who wrote it.

The 4th Employment Company's War Diary is a model of economically presented information:

> 16/7/42 2 Off [Officers] 11 NCO's [Non-Commissioned Officers] 173 O/Rs [Other Ranks] transfer Ammunition at Wodonga &

> Albury. Large US Convoy passed through Showgrounds Camp, was bedded down, provided with evening meal & breakfast.[4]

Occasionally, economy of presentation creates odd juxtapositions. The 5th Labour Group diarist's entry for 15 August 1945 records: 'Acceptance of Surrender terms by Japan announced. Very heavy rain.'[5] Some record keepers focused almost entirely on the weather; others, the comings and goings of officers and men. The 10th Employment Company, which had many aliens but was not always officially designated as an Alien Employment Company, was stationed at Springton in South Australia, chopping down trees for firewood. Its straight-faced War Diary account of digging a bore, initially without success—'no sign of water'—and then finding water that was not suitable for drinking, reads like a comic farce.[6] Elsewhere, the officer who documented the activities of the 1st Australian Works Company in Townsville often resorted to clumping a number of days together with the comments 'Nothing of interest to record', 'Nothing of value to record', and 'No events of historical value.'[7]

For some officers, maintaining an historical record of a Company's activities was not, one suspects, a high priority.

The scribe for the 6th Employment Company listed the work the men were doing in Melbourne in the early months: loading stores, drying hessian, digging slit trenches at Yarra Bank, Racecourse Flat, Fishermans Bend and Wesley College, stacking timber, loading petrol drums, unloading onions, and working at Victoria Dock.[8] John Callinicos, from Ithaca in Greece, was not the only young man who was 'a skinny fellow when he went into the army and came out very strong'.[9]

There is no mention of the fact that soldiers of the 6th sometimes replaced striking wharf labourers[10] because the wharfies refused to handle broken cement bags without extra pay.[11] Albert Ceen recalled 'three days unloading cement, causing great discomfort to eyes, nose and throat due to dust.'[12] According to Helmut Newton:

> We were sent down to Port Melbourne for two weeks to unload these big bags of cement. The [American] ships were never-ending. I remember for two weeks I was white, because the cement used to set under the shower and you couldn't wash it off.[13]

Paul (Helmut) Seefeld, from the 8th Employment Company, remembers a similar experience —'when the work was finished we were covered in cement'—but with a happier ending: 'Before going back to camp we went to the baths, to the City Baths, and could wash with hot water.'[14] Perhaps that indulgence exemplifies the devoted concern that Captain Broughton, the 8th Commanding Officer, demonstrated towards his men, as does the willingness of officers in that Company to find lighter work for men like the slightly-built Julius Guest:

> There was a lot of physical work; some of it I could do and I did ... Sometimes they asked you to lift cement bags for about 8 hours a day, and I couldn't do that. I just said, I'm sorry, I can't do that sort of thing, I'm just not strong enough ... They found me another job that was lighter.[15]

The first working party from the 4th Company—sixty men commanded by one Lieutenant—were sent to dig slit trenches in Caulfield, only three days after their enrolment. No time was wasted.[16]

There were men, elated at finally being accepted into the army, who initially made light of the mundane and the difficult. Albert Ceen, previously an Italian businessman, now in the 6th Employment Company, wrote reassuringly to his wife from Caulfield Racecourse:

> 5.30 reveille – work at the [railhead] unloading bales of jute weighing 300kg. Hard hard hard work, but I made it and so did everybody (it was Sunday, naturally). We came and returned in a convoy of fast trucks – the Sunday crowds were amazed. We looked brutish (from the hard work) but we were satisfied. We had lunch on the

> platform – bread, butter, cheese, jam and tea. Excellent. There was also stew – very tasty but too spicy and I did without ... I am very happy with my new life. I have some good comrades already ... I'm very happy with the decision [to enlist] I made and I hope it's for the best once more ...[17]

Occasionally, there were perks. Men from the 8th Company were stationed at Camp Pell, in Parkville, close to an American base. Seefeld was part of a working party sent to the American canteen, where they were set to peeling large quantities of potatoes. The tedious job had its benefits: 'We could buy American products—cigarettes, chewing gum and nylon stockings'[18]—articles difficult to obtain in the tightly rationed Australian market.

According to directions in the War Diaries, the men, when at work, were meant to wear their 'working trousers, working jacket and working hat'[19]—the last item often absent, much to the irritation of the more rigid officers. As with so many other military regulations, the direction about clothing was adapted to suit the circumstances. Bern Brent, in the 8th, recalls the men wearing summer shorts and short-sleeved shirts, and removing the shirts at work when it was very hot. He tells of one man in the Company who always wore a long-sleeved shirt. It was rumoured that he had been made welcome in a pub by a couple of wharfies who got him thoroughly drunk and then took him to a tattoo parlour. The resulting risqué tattoos—one on each arm—were supposedly the reason for his preference for long sleeves.[20]

In the early months, many of the Companies were based in large public spaces in capital cities. Bart Srhoy's 11th Employment Company camped at the Claremont Showgrounds in Perth. The men slept on palliasses 'straight onto the mother earth'.[21] One of his companions, finding this arrangement not to his liking, went home to sleep.[22] While frowned on in Perth, this seems to have been generally accepted by the officers of the Companies stationed in Melbourne. The men in the 6th were expected to sleep on palliasses on the stands of Caulfield Racecourse, but many, like Robert Exiner and Jack Waller, slept at home.[23] As long as they were back in camp for morning parade and rollcall, nothing was said.

Across the country, parties of Employment Company soldiers were directed to factories for packing and transporting goods; others dug trenches, repaired roads, and drove trucks loaded with military equipment. In Sydney, some of the men in the 2nd/3rd were sent to regional areas to assist the locals in a variety of ways. Emil Witton was part of a small group that spent a few weeks in Goulburn, cleaning a psychiatric hospital. At Spring Hill, twenty of the soldiers were sent to load timber on to railway trucks. A more clearly military task was undertaken by John Pollak, one of fourteen soldiers selected to staff a camouflage unit. Under the supervision of 'a nice lieutenant', the men travelled in two trucks along the east coast Pacific Highway, camouflaging buildings as required. Later, Pollak served in a camp at Bogan Heights, 'dismantling cannon and rifle shells, getting rid of explosives and sending the metal parts back to the factories so that new shells could be manufactured.'[24] Back in Mascot, where the Company was based, the men worked on the wharves and on the railways. Witton later wrote that 'at times, if necessary, we worked hard. For instance when we unloaded the NSW wool clip from railway trucks on to lorries. This we did in three 8-hour shifts for several weeks. We learned quickly how to move the heavy bales with iron hooks. On the other hand, if it was pick and shovel work, you grabbed a shovel, if possible. You cannot lean on a pick.'[25]

The men in the 11th/12th Company, initially based in Western Australia, were similarly put to work on a variety of non-military tasks, including cutting timber around Dwellingup, in the south-west. John Cohen, who spent a year in the Company, remarked that no one explained what the timber was to be used for. Later, the Company travelled by troop train across the Nullarbor. Cohen recalled the Aboriginal people who would come to the train when it stopped to take on water, hoping for cigarettes or other small items. Some of the soldiers wanted to take photos of them, and Cohen retained a memory of one Aboriginal man who refused to be photographed and said: 'Me no monkey'. He understood exactly what the man felt. Once in Brisbane, the soldiers of the 11th /12th spent time on the wharves, 'lumping oil drums and what have you to supply [the] troops'.[26] Their 'gangs' worked alongside those of the waterside workers without conflict, despite knowing that the wharfies received a decent wage while the soldiers were paid six shillings a day. There was, after all, in Cohen's words, 'a national emergency.'[27]

The 4th, 6th and 8th Employment Companies spent much of their army service near the border of Victoria and New South Wales because of a quirk in the railway system. A lasting disadvantage of the early British settlement of Australia was the differing railway gauges constructed by separate states. As long ago as 1895, the American writer Mark Twain commented wryly after his visit:

> The oddest thing, the strangest thing, the unaccountable marvel that Australia can show. At the frontier between NSW and Victoria our multitude of passengers were routed out of their snug beds by lantern light in the morning in the biting cold to change cars. Think of the paralysis of intellect that gave that idea birth, imagine the boulder it emerged from, on some petrified legislator's shoulders.[28]

What was a nuisance and an inconvenience in peacetime became, in wartime, a serious impediment to the speedy movement of soldiers, armaments and supplies. With little shipping available, rail transport between Victoria, New South Wales and Queensland was critical.[29] Victoria and New South Wales were the states with the largest populations and centres of industry, with a number of government departments, particularly Defence and the War Cabinet, based in Melbourne.[30] When the American General Douglas MacArthur, appointed Supreme Commander for the South West Pacific with control over all Allied personnel, shifted his headquarters from Melbourne to Brisbane in the middle of 1942, Queensland became the major centre for US troops readying for battle in the South Pacific, and on leave. By September 1943 about ninety-six thousand of the 119 000 American military personnel in Australia were based in that state.[31] Ammunition, goods and services were mostly heading north.

Loading and unloading trains at Tocumwal and Albury, two centres where the mismatched Victorian and New South Wales railway gauges lay side by side, 'bearing their renowned insignia of origin, Sheffield and Krupp',[32] became a major task for the men in the 4th, 6th and 8th Employment Companies. It was not until many years after the war that the expectation of the American troops in Australia interviewed by an army journalist—that '[Australia] must have a single railway gauge system as soon as possible'—became a reality.[33]

The first group of men to be sent to Tocumwal came from the 4th Employment Company. Each man was issued with a groundsheet, water bottle, haversack and mess tin.[34] They had already received their paybooks and their often ill-fitting uniforms: 'size 10 hats for size 6 ½ heads'.[35] Erwin Fabian recalled that they were warned 'not to leave their tents without wearing boots, because of the tiger snakes.'[36] The Company's War Diary notes, in a tone of disapproval, the 'very primitive nature' of the facilities on their arrival at the camp: 'There were no Cook houses, latrines or washing arrangements, water was not laid on [*sic*] onto the Camp-site.'[37] The men's first task was 'to concentrate entirely on establishing the Camp to the best permitted by the circumstances.'[38]

In his ironically titled short story 'The Heroes of Tocumwal', Charlie D'Aprano describes the arrival of the 6th at their Tocumwal camp:

> We left Melbourne one cold, damp morning ... and arrived at the little station of Tocumwal late in the afternoon, in brilliant sunshine, and went straight to a military camp near the river [the Murray] ... Huge gums grew between the tents. Past the latrines, erected under two ancient Murray gums, the broad waters of the Murray flowed ... We had been there two weeks when it began to rain heavily. On the morning of the second day ... the camp was flooded. The river had risen during the night ... The huge marquees that were our mess huts were all under water, the kitchen was being lapped by the rising flood and the latrines were under two feet of water ... A few days

> after this episode we were moved to a new camp site near the Finlay Road, away from flooded billabongs. No treacherous river was going to catch the heroes of Tocumwal unawares![39]

In the new camp, 'on a flat rather dry and dusty area',[40] the men slept in 6-men tents–good Australian tents, with a fly over each that protected against heat and cold.[41] Certainly better than the American variety, according to Frank Klepner, because they could be opened at the sides to catch a passing breeze.[42] Some men remember sleeping on palliasses filled with straw or leaves from corn; others recall folding canvas stretchers. Andy Factor's mother, worried about her 18-year-old son, persuaded an older fellow recruit to make him a bed, which he did—out of chicken wire.[43] A pillow could be made from a rolled-up overcoat or boots covered with a blanket. Each man was given four blankets—one to lie on, the others for warmth. In the winter, many slept with their clothes and boots on.[44]

Albert Ceen, almost always a determined optimist when writing to his family, sent a letter to his wife in May 1942:

> Beautiful Darling,
> Tomorrow morning at dawn we leave for Tocumwal. It is a good camp and I hope we will be well there … Don't tell anyone where they are sending us, it's forbidden, but I write you in a closed envelope [civilian mail] so that you may know that I am close and in a safe place. We are all very happy because life will be better and the work more varied and less heavy.
> P. S. I pay 2 1/2d when I send mail outside military channels.[45]

Ceen broke the rules to reassure his wife, but his expectation that Tocumwal would offer better living and working conditions than those at Caulfield Racecourse were only partially fulfilled. In one letter, he described (and sketched) a shower the men improvised when they first arrived at their Tocumwal camp: 'a jerrycan with a tap at the bottom, from which a tin was suspended. They pierced the bottom of the tin with many holes ... The lot was suspended from the branch of a tree.'[46] His view of the laundry facilities was more positive: 'I am wearing clean clothes because we have organized an excellent service with a laundry in town. They work well and are not very expensive.'[47]

The army recognised that 'personnel of 6 Emp. Coy ... have had to use temporary structures for cookhouse, mess hut, ablution benches, and latrines', and promised huts that, when completed, would have 'a beneficial effect on the morale' of the men.[48] According to one of the locals, it didn't take long for the men to compare their living conditions with those of the American soldiers and airmen housed in a large area on the other side of the town. When Ceen's son Guido visited Tocumwal in 1996, he was surprised to see some still-existing structures on the Americans' site: 'a huge bomber base: enormous hangars, quonset hut living quarters with all conveniences.' His guide from the local historical society acknowledged the disparity and remarked, 'Ah yes, when they met in town they used to fight like buggery!' [49] A dramatic possibility, not verified by evidence from the men themselves.

While some of the soldiers were detailed to work around the camp—in jobs such as cooks, hygiene, health and clerical workers—the majority were used as labourers: loading and unloading military personnel, ammunition and stores on the trains. As Ceen soon discovered, almost everyone worked hard and there was little rest. When his wife complained that he didn't write often enough, he responded:

> Please remember that we are on our feet from 5.30am and work until 5.30pm, after which we have to wash and eat. Considering that we have to go to bed by 9.30pm to get a decent night's sleep, there is only limited time for other necessities. [50]

Gerard Herbst, from the 4th, wrote a short memoir of his army experience. It includes a poetic evocation of working on the trains:

> Time: one hour after midnight. Platoon One on the march for the border station. In disciplined formation the men reached the railway

> transit platform … Out of the darkness rolled the shunted carriages from the South. A starless sky. Silently they rolled in, like monsters to a clandestine meeting, hidden under the cover of tarpaulins. 'Ready fellows!' was heard in a half loud voice. The sound of ropes being pulled off, the sliding of tarpaulins, preceded the exposure of 'fighters of steel' returning from the desert war. Bren-gun carriers – sand coloured, sinister. Heavy ropes untied fell like satisfied reptiles onto the platform, and so freed, the war machines from the desert began to make the crossing on plates of steel.[51]

Tying down these monsters and other large equipment with ropes was called 'lashing', and required considerable strength and cooperation. Yosl Bergner of the 6th coined the phrase 'the local aristocracy' about the men who did it most quickly and efficiently.[52] Jack Friedman was a member of one of the 6th's lashing gangs, and remembers his role with some pride: 'You can either join the boy scouts or you can become a member of the lashing gang … We were quite proud that we were the lashing gang':

> Lashing meant tying up with ropes: tanks, big armoured vehicles, trucks, jeeps, cars, anything that had wheels … Those vehicles had to be tied up in such a way that when they were shunting from one place to another … they didn't smash or get damaged … You really had to make sure it was done correctly … In those days we had to do it with ropes and saplings. We used to cut saplings from gum trees … in order to turn it, twist it [to tighten the ropes]. Then we had to tie up that sapling somewhere so that it didn't unwind. That was our job. [53]

Charlie D'Aprano, another strong young man in the 6th, was also in a lashing gang. He remembered the advantage of youth and strength:

> You were given your allotted duties, and when you finished your three trucks, your 75 tons, you went back to camp. The younger ones, the

> stronger ones, finished much earlier than the older ones, of course. We were very selfish. There were five of us to a gang. We wanted to finish as quickly as possible, get back to camp and do our own thing. So, we had a group of five young men—bang, bang, bang, and away you go.[54]

Other accounts stress cooperation rather than selfishness. My father, slight of build, wearing glasses and at thirty-six already regarded as an 'older man', vividly recalled the strong young Italian, Joe Zammarchi, gently pushing him aside as he struggled to lift a large sack of potatoes: Joe did the lifting with ease.[55] Certainly there was a high level of camaraderie among friends, and this extended to their work. Speros Polites spoke proudly of his 'Polites gang'—the six Greek men who shared a tent and worked together: 'we used to be a hundred per cent. We wouldn't let our officer be disappointed.'[56] But this group also worked cooperatively with others, especially some of the Jewish men: 'Jack [Friedman]—he was helping us and we helped him. Jews were always with us.'[57]

'There was nothing the military used that we didn't transport,' said Fred Cohn of the 4th.[58] This included a whole hospital. The US 4th General Hospital—equipment and staff—had been shipped from America in 1942 and housed in the newly built Royal Melbourne Hospital; in 1944 it was packed up and sent by train to Brisbane, and from there to Finschhafen in New Guinea.[59] In Albury, the work was undertaken by seventy men under the command of an officer and five NCOs. The hospital was loaded into forty-two trucks, and, according to the Company's War Diary, the men were 'complimented by the US Officer i/c [in charge] for their quick and efficient job.'[60]

The loading and unloading also included tanks, driven down a ramp from one train and up a ramp onto another, where they were chained for stability; and heavy ammunition—250-pound and 500-pound bombs—a regular item in the 4th Employment Company's War Diary.[61] A journalist later wrote, 'Men who were not allowed to carry arms spent their days loading bombs on trucks.'[62] Fred Lester, one of the youngest in the Company, described bombs being stacked, pointed side down, on the wooden floors of the railway carriages, and reflected on the potential danger of such an arrangement if there had been a railway accident. 'But they were in a great hurry,' he said.[63]

Inevitably, there were accidents. The most common injuries, according to the historian Bruce Pennay, were crushed fingers or toes.[64] Paul Baxter, in the 6th Employment Company at Tocumwal, jumped from the platform on to the rails and broke his ankle.[65] Louis Waller says that his father, in the same Company, stopped wearing his wedding ring: the mates in his tent made him take it off because one of the soldiers, when working on top of a truck, jumped down, caught his ring on a protruding bolt—and lost his finger.[66] Wolfgang Sievers, in the 4th Company, tried to unload some 500-pound aerial bombs alone. One dislodged from its rack and hit him in the back. Two days later, he collapsed from the injury. 'I was unfortunate in being very stupid' was his comment many years later.[67] There were also some deaths, including that of Private Y Unkovich of the 11th/12th Employment Company. The report of a military Court of Inquiry includes a description of the event that led to the fatal injury:

> During the morning of the 29 March '43 a party of woodcutters of whom Pte Unkovich was one were working in a Mr Johnson's property opposite No. 2 Farm, Harvey [Western Australia]. Pte Unkovich was using a hammer and wedges in splitting a log when he appeared to have been struck suddenly and staggered back … Blood was noticed coming from the left groin …[68]

The court determined that his death resulted from 'a massive haemorrhage which was uncontrolled for at least ten minutes', and that 'the fatal injury sustained was directly attributable to the conditions of service'.[69] Private Unkovich, who came from Dalmatia, Yugoslavia, died a few days before his thirty-third birthday.[70]

Some of the men were sent to work at ammunition depots. Keith (Kurt) Steinhardt went with other soldiers from the 4th Company to the Hume depot, near Albury, to clean shells, including mustard gas shells. They were cleaned with wire brushes, and then repainted. No one appears to have explained why mustard gas shells were being cared for, nor were the men provided with any protective clothing.[71] Soldiers from the 6th worked at an ammunition dump between Tocumwal and Deniliquin. According to Charlie D'Aprano, 'it stretched for miles and miles.'[72] When, in old age, he remembered the dump, he noted the absurdity: 'This is the ridiculous part of it: we weren't allowed to carry guns … and yet we looked after the largest ammunition dump in the Southern Hemisphere. All it needed was a cigarette butt dropped down one of the chimneys and you'd blow the whole camp, the whole ammunition dump up'.[73]

Occasionally, it was the quick responses of soldiers that avoided disaster. Private Fred (Werner) Cohn from the 4th described an incident that occurred while unloading boxes of small arms ammunition from a Victorian train at Albury. Each box weighed about 10 pounds, and they were thrown by the men on the train onto an improvised roller conveyer, from which they were stacked and packed on the platform by Cohn. He said:

> I was very quick and fast and strong in those days, and I really packed them very quickly and tightly. Suddenly there was an explosion—the last box I had packed opened up like a bomb going up in the air … The boxes around me started to burn, and the small ammunition started to fly everywhere …[74]

He and Sergeant Johnny Buckland, the only other man on the platform at the time, dragged a tarpaulin over the boxes and smothered the fire. No one was hurt, other than some minor injuries to men who had jumped from the train, but it could have been catastrophic: nearby was a truck filled with TNT. 'If that fire would have taken hold,' said Cohn, 'the whole of Albury would have gone up into the air.'[75] There was an official inquiry at which he and Buckland gave evidence ('no hardship because we spent three days in Melbourne'). The inquiry led to the construction of another railway platform some miles from Albury, in order to protect the town.[76]

Loading and unloading stores—what the officer responsible for the 4th Employment Company's War Diary called 'mixed Goods'[77]—was another task, and one that aroused some resentment among the soldiers. While the importance of handling boxes of food and other non-weaponry essentials was generally acknowledged as a necessary contribution to the war effort, the arrival of goods intended for large private companies, or for the wealthy, could provoke indignation, and, occasionally, a form of collective disobedience. At its mildest, there are comments such as that from Jack Friedman: 'We were unloading or loading articles that went to shops; and we were thinking in terms of somebody doing good business whilst we are doing this for them, at six shillings and sixpence a day.'[78] Nicholas Raftopoulos, also a member of the 6th, remarked: 'I expected army life to be regimental, but in fact we were used to unload railway wagons for civilian use. Goods from Myers and other department stores were unloaded from the Victorian side to the NSW side.'[79] When asked by interviewer George Paxinos about his attitude to what he called 'civilian work', Raftopoulos replied: "We didn't like the idea. We were in the army. Why would we work for bloody civilians?'[80]

Albert Ceen described an occasion when the men devised their own kind of direct action. The cargo was Sydney rock oysters sent from New South Wales to Melbourne. Guido Ceen summarises his father's story:

> The idea that soldiers had to work to satisfy Melbourne's civilians' desire to eat oysters which were superior to those obtainable in Victoria annoyed the men exceedingly. Consequently they slipped several sacks over the side, and that night in camp they all ate oysters served by a Greek soldier who opened them for sixpence a dozen, lemon included.[81]

Pilfering also occurred for other reasons. Bob Exiner explained it as a consequence of a kind of anonymity the military uniform provided: 'When you wear a uniform, in a certain way you lose your individuality and you become a sort of collective that would do things you would never dream of doing in civilian life.'[82] Richard Langfelder's son Kurt points out a practical cause—providing for one's family. 'If they were unloading bananas, they'd always manage to drop a case of bananas, and then they'd take them home—it provided food for the families.'[83] More generally, pilfering from supplies happened throughout the military; it was certainly not a peculiarity of the alien Employment Companies. Army Routine Orders include regular warnings against 'the offences of stealing and fraudulent misapplication of stores and supplies', and reject terms such as 'pilfering' and 'scrounging' because they 'tend to obscure [the] gravity' of the offences.[84] And moral imperatives still prevailed. Emil Witton of the 2nd/3rd Company described an occasion when he and two other soldiers from the Company were sent to guard 'a store full of rare goods':

> It would have been easy to open a fruit tin or even take some tobacco. We three talked about it, and we all felt the same way about it. We never touched anything in that store.[85]

On occasion, working conditions led to outright rebellion. Emil Witton wrote that he and his fellow soldiers 'had adjusted well to the Australian mentality of striking':

> If NCOs or officers from other units, while telling us what to do, used words like 'you people' in an offensive way, or if the word 'foreigners' should be mentioned, we complained immediately, even went as far as stopping work. But we always got away with it and our officers straightened things out very quickly, nearly always taking our side, stating that we were Australian soldiers and were to be treated as such.[86]

At one time, the 4th Employment Company based in Albury was required to work three shifts a day unloading ammunition: from 8 a.m. to 12 p.m. and 1 p.m. to 6 p.m., and then from 8 p.m. to midnight. 'Those times were very desperate', John Callinicos remembers, 'we were over-tired, and we didn't know what to do. So we decided to have a hunger strike.'[87] According to Callinicos, the strike succeeded: 'they took us off these 3 shifts and left us with 2 shifts, morning and afternoon.'[88] The men in this Company were also successful when they stopped work because of a procedure they regarded as unjust: they were required to march a mile from the camp to the railway station and back again four times a day, regardless of the weather. According to Fred Lester, 'we just walked out on a hunger strike, just walked straight through [the mess hut] and refused to eat.'[89] Within a couple of days, the men were provided with trucks to make the journey.

In the 6th there were several hunger strikes over working conditions as well as food. The only consequence of any significance was a message of appreciation to the Employment Companies from the Commander-in-Chief, General Blamey.

The story behind this message typifies much of the military policy development regarding these Companies: events force reluctant attention to a problem, there are conflicting views, and sometimes, modest action follows. In this case, a brigadier—a senior military officer—writes to the Commander-in-Chief, offering his advice. He believes the Employment Companies are, in the main, doing excellent work, but there is a complaint that in the military hierarchy they are 'nobody's baby' and hence 'there probably is a tendency to treat them somewhat cavalierly'. He makes three suggestions for improvement: 'the work of the men and officers would benefit if the Commander-in-Chief thought fit to (a) issue some message of appreciation; (b) use press in capital cities for a tribute to their work; (c) appoint some last-war senior officer now holding good rank as Director with instructions to visit, encourage and vitalise.'[90]

The response, via a major general, is rather huffy, rejecting any suggestion that the Employment Companies are 'nobody's baby', and praising the existing Director of Labour, Major RW Hamer, as more than adequate. Only one of the Brigadier's recommendations is to be fulfilled: 'a message of appreciation of the work being performed by Employment Companies [is] to be prepared for despatch ... at an early date.'[91]

In due course, every Employment Company received the following message from General Blamey in November 1943:

> 1. It has been brought to the notice of the C-in-C [Commander-in-Chief] that personnel of Aust Employ Coys, both on the Mainland and in New Guinea, though serving their Country in a most unspectacular role, are carrying out important and often very strenuous work, without which the many arms of the Forces could not properly function.
> 2. Their duties are such that a continuous maintenance of a high standard of 'esprit de corps' is necessary to offset the sometimes monotonous nature of the tasks allotted to them, and this is borne out by the willingness and conscientiousness with which these tasks are performed.
> 3. The C-in-C, therefore, desires that his appreciation of the services being rendered be conveyed to all ranks.
>
> (Signed) J.H. Cannon
> Major General
> Quartermaster-General
> 29 Nov 43[92]

At this time, the army recorded the existence of thirty-six Employment Companies, consisting of approximately fourteen thousand men and two hundred officers.[93] According to Major General Cannon, writing just two months later, the 'promulgation to all ranks' of the C-in C's statement 'is known to have done much to make members of these Companies realise that their service to their country does not go unnoticed, but is appreciated.'[94] There is, however, no evidence I could find to substantiate the Major General's opinion. The men continued to work: some sustained by a commitment to defeat the enemy, others because they had no other option.

By 1944, as the army began demobilising, it renamed all the non-alien Employment Companies as Works Companies. This change came after much lobbying by some in the military who continued to desire a clear distinction between the alien Companies and those regarded as truly Australian.[95] The War Diary of the 33rd Employment Company reflects this attitude in an entry dated 28 April 1944. The Company was then based in Port Moresby:

> Advice was received today that pursant [sic] to LHQ SM3926 dated 18 April 44 this Unit has been redesignated the 33 Australian Works Company. This has removed, to some extent, the stigma of being in the same category as Alien Employment Coys and when our new color patch is issued everyone will be much more satisfied.[96]

In fact, there was to be no new colour patch, and very soon a number of the Works Companies included naturalised men from alien Employment Companies.[97] The army was reducing and consolidating its labour force. The government was also soon encouraging those in the alien Companies to become naturalised—amending naturalisation regulations 'to enable an alien who is serving or has served with a good record in an Employment Company being granted a certificate of Naturalization free of charge.'[98] This change not only enabled naturalised aliens to join Works Companies but also made them eligible to join the AIF.

A few men took this opportunity.[99] Robert Exiner transferred from the 6th Employment Company to the AIF Medical Corps after his naturalisation late in 1944. At Puckapunyal, he was trained in the prophylactic treatment of venereal diseases—'an enemy more deadly than the Japanese', according to his beloved Commanding Officer, Major Colqhoune.[100] He was promoted to Corporal and sent to man the prophylactic depot at Flinders Street station —twenty-four hours on, twenty-four hours off. This urbane Viennese was so good at his job that the army was reluctant to release him at the end of the war.[101]

Fred Lester from the 4th Employment Company received his naturalisation papers in mid-1945 and immediately applied for a transfer to the AIF. Within a month, he was accepted and posted to a training camp in Nowra, New South Wales, but his time in the unit was short: a month later the war ended and he was transferred to Bonegilla Army Hospital to serve out the rest of his time until his discharge in July 1946. While in the training camp he had managed to fire just five shots—at tin cans.[102] Paul Baxter, who grew up as a boy in Germany reading about heroic soldiers in World War I, yearned to be a hero in the Australian Army. The prospect of naturalisation allowed him to leave the unheroic life in the 6th Employment Company and be sent to the Atherton Tablelands near Cairns, and then, he hoped, to Borneo. But the war finished and instead, thanks to a series of military errors, he ended up as the batman to the commander of the Australian military police in Morotai, then part of the Dutch East Indies.[103]

More commonly, transferring from an alien Employment Company meant serving in a Works Company. By January 1945 the Deputy Assistant Director of Labour in Queensland was sending out terse notices to the officers commanding soldiers who had been reassigned to these Companies. 'It is noticed that Works Coy personnel are being employed in Salvage stores cutting buttons off old clothing,' he wrote. 'This is considered uneconomical and also is not the type of work that comes within the scope of these personnel.'[104] A month later, his sights are on the men:

> It is desired that when coys have available personnel, that such personnel are NOT permitted to lay about the camp without being economically employed. These occasions are excellent opportunities to train personnel so that the soldierly bearing of all personnel in the Labour Service will be of a high standard.[105]

These urgings went on for some months; their repetition suggests a lack of success. The war was drawing to a close.

# 7

# The enjoyment companies

Humour, that scourge of pomposity and foundation for solidarity, is a commonplace of military life, especially among those who receive orders but rarely give them. It has sometimes been declared 'a prominent and typical characteristic of the Australian soldier', and even 'an integral part of the Australian character.'[1] While humour is more likely a ubiquitous human characteristic with local variations, it certainly pervades the stories of men in the alien Employment Companies.

One historian has written that 'war provided a thousand settings – in bad food, ill-fitting clothes, contradictory commands, pompous behaviour – for the expression of a rebellious, verbally inventive Australianism.'[2] The 'aliens' were yet to be regarded as Australians, but their verbal playfulness was just as inventive. Officers were prominent targets for such wit—as Exiner in the 6th observed, the men 'had inhaled enough Australian air to not consider our superiors to be our betters'.[3] The army's headquarters in Melbourne was known as 'zebra row' because it was inhabited by men with stripes,[4] and the well-meaning officer in the 8th who told one of his young soldiers that he'd better polish up his English received the straight-faced response: 'Don't you think that my English is Polish enough?'[5]

Officers were not the only targets. There were derogatory names for other branches of the military. The men in the air force were 'blue orchards': 'they had it soft, with lovely blue uniforms, proper beds in huts instead of tents, and no deep trench latrines … out in the open'.[6] And there were certainly 'aliens' who shared with other Australian soldiers a mixture of admiration, envy and contempt for the thousands of American soldiers—'Yanks'—brought here: 'over-paid, over-sexed, and over here!'.[7] It's unlikely the Australian soldiers had access to the small booklet titled *Instructions for American Servicemen in Australia 1942*, which included many comments on Australian character and behaviour, such as 'a lively sense of independence', 'rugged individualism', and talent as 'a rapid, sharp and unsparing kidder.'[8]

Unfamiliar or badly cooked food received short shrift: the Jewish men in the 6th, who were accustomed to rye bread, named the standard-issue white bread 'nylon'.[9] There were comical nicknames for nationalities: in the same Company, the Jews called their Greek friends Gimelech, a diminutive of Gimel, the third letter of the Hebrew alphabet, while the Greeks called their Jewish mates Americanos or Canadesos. The Italians called the Greeks 'fish and chips', the Greeks called the Italians 'maccoronathas' and 'spaghetados'.[10] Sometimes, different subgroups within an ethnicity had their own nicknames. Yosl Bergner, a Polish Jew, mocked the German and Austrian Jews who 'wanted to assimilate' and 'changed their names to super-English-sounding names', by referring to them as 'Yekke pots', a sardonic and vulgar Yiddish prod at their supposed Germanic obsession with order and punctuality. Frank Klepner, an Austrian who became Bergner's close friend, and later his biographer, turned the tables when he discovered that Bergner had been born in Vienna, and was thus himself a 'Yekke pot'.[11] In the 8th Company, the Germans and Austrians who had been living in the Middle East, mainly in Iran, were called 'Persians'; and a handful of men of German nationality who had served with the French Foreign Legion were known as 'Foreign Legionnaires'.[12] The Chinese in the 7th poked fun at Australian-born Chinese by naming them 'ABCs'.[13] And while a brigadier noted that the Employment Companies were sometimes referred to in the military as 'nobody's baby',[14] it was friendly irony that led Yosl Bergner to name his own Company, the 6th, 'The Enjoyment Company'.[15]

The men in these Companies worked hard—sometimes, night and day. They also managed an array of 'extracurricular' activities. Sundays were commonly declared rest days,[16] and during the working week, groups of men were allocated some time off. Keith (Kurt) Steinhardt, from the 4th, gives a description of a typical pattern of work and rest:

> We worked whenever work was there. Everything was work. Very often we went out in the morning and did an ammunition train, and we were told the food train was coming ... We were finished, perhaps one or two o'clock in the afternoon and we went out in the evening again, did the food train, which took us about four or five hours, then we came home. We had the next day off, the whole day off.[17]

The grand ballad of life in the 4th Employment Company, 'A Day in Camp', created by Cary (Hermann) Roth, and written and illustrated by Tim Walton, includes a couple of stanzas celebrating the pleasures of free time:

> Now an hour or so is devoted to rest
> And every man is trying his best
> To devote this hour of lazy leisure
> To a little nap or a little pleasure.
> Some are discussing Hitler or Goring;
> Some are reading and some are snoring,
> Some play two-up and some play chess,
> Some do nothing and others still less,
> They indulge in pleasures great and small
> And a jolly good time is had by all.
>
> The lucky boys of the rest-platoon
> Parade in the early afternoon.

The Captain inspects them from tip to toe
And compliments them – a jolly good show!
He is obviously happy and very pleased
That tunics are buttoned and trousers creased.
In the office there is a bit of a jam
When the boys get their passes and quickly scram
And soon they are streaming out of the gate
Down to the town where the girlfriends wait.[18]

Almost without exception, the stories told by men in the Employment Companies include fond memories of socialising both in camp and in the wider community, whether in a country town like Tocumwal or the 'big smoke' of the capital cities. Robert Salter said he spent most of his free time in camp 'reading, socialising and playing cards', although sometimes, after a long day of heavy physical work, reading was beyond him.[19] The 4th Company's camp at the Albury/Wodonga Showgrounds had a reading room with a library. It was funded by the Young Men's Christian Association and built by the Company men.[20]

Even in this well-endowed Company, men depended on family and friends, as well as the generosity of welfare organisations, for reading material. Fred Lester, who was just sixteen when brought to Australia with nineteen other youngsters by the Jewish Welfare Society only months before the outbreak of war, recalled 'a lot of lending and borrowing' of books', especially from friends in Melbourne.[21] The same was true for Bob Exiner of the 6th;[22] while Bern Brent, a Dunera Boy in the 8th, apart from receiving occasional books from his mother in England, searched for and found treasures in the Melbourne Public Library.[23] Felix Werder, another Dunera Boy in the 8th, remembered, with a mixture of disdain and gratitude, the load of German classics donated by the Jewish Welfare Society to the internees at Tatura, but clearly preferred the best of these books to some that were provided by the army: 'Jane Austen and company. Stuff that I still detest to this day!'[24]

Reading was widespread, but not universal. In its own way, it was a marker of social difference in military communities encompassing the tertiary educated and the barely literate. Yossel Birstein and Yosl Bergner, both just seventeen, came out to Australia from Poland on the same boat in 1937, and they served in the 6th Employment Company together. Birstein became a writer, and his short story 'Weger', first published in 1974, is strongly autobiographical, with its opening section a darkly humorous account of life in the 6th, though the Company is not named. Birstein describes his central character, Weger, a Jew, sitting on his cot in the evenings, 'reading by the light of a lamp and several candles on a box nearby'. His tent mate, a Macedonian, Papadimitrio,

> would sit opposite on his own cot, elbows on knees, face in hands, and eyes fixed on Weger. The reading of books was a thing unknown to him, and no one he knew read them … After watching Weger for a long time, Papadimitrio got himself a small black-bound prayer book with a cross embossed on its covers. Whenever Weger sat down to read in the evening he, too, would place some lighted candles on a box beside his own cot and begin chanting in his native tongue prayers whose words and tune kept recurring endlessly. [25]

If books signified class and educational differences between the men, gambling united many across these often inherited disparities. According to the army, 'Gambling in a camp or other Military premises … is forbidden … Breaches of this regulation will be severely dealt with.'[26] The Routine Orders of the 2nd Employment Company in Sydney insisted that 'card playing during spells on working parties will only be allowed on the strict understanding that no gambling is indulged in; any infringement of this instruction will invoke disciplinary action against the NCO in charge of the party and [the] personnel concerned.'[27] All these warnings and threats, common in the documentation of every Employment Company, seem to have been universally ignored, though oft repeated.[28] Indeed, it is from some of these futile repetitions that one learns about the kinds of gambling that took place.

Though by no means as popular as card games, Two-up is often officially castigated: 'Gambling is forbidden, and the game of "Two-up" in the tent lines will cease forthwith. Disciplinary action will be taken against offenders.'[29] John Cohen recalled Two-up as being favoured mainly by the English speakers in the 11th in Western Australia,[30] but it seems to have appealed to many men in other alien Companies. Felix Werder referred to it irreverently as 'the Australian way of life.'[31]

Card games were ubiquitous, so that at least one Captain excluded those playing for small stakes from the general order forbidding gambling.[32] Emil Witton from the 3rd Company remembered the group of German-speaking youngsters he spent most of his time with in camp at Mascot in Sydney, 'playing chess or cards: poker, bridge, skat, bezique.'[33] Albert Ceen from the 6th wrote to his wife that in Tocumwal he played bridge 'by candlelight on a board supported by two camp beds. I am winning enough to keep me in cigarettes.'[34] Jack Friedman, from the same Company, recalled a number of the card games: 'Those who had a brain or two played solo; some of them played bridge, but that was only the intelligentsia and they were far and few between. In the main, they were playing poker.'[35] While there are some accounts of soldiers gambling away all their ready money, Friedman points out that 'all' was hardly great riches to lose:

> You are getting £4.10 a fortnight. You had to buy your own soap, you had to go and buy your shaving gear. Perhaps you bought a small bucket of ice-cream out of that money. So, what did you have left? You might have had two pounds left. [So, when gambling,] that two pounds might have lasted you five minutes, or else you might have made a fortune. That's all the money there was—there was no money.[36]

Other than for sleeping, the men's tents were largely used for conversation, reading and writing. The recreation hall, hut or tent was the centre of much social activity:

With billiards, draughts, and chess, and cards
Now a night of pleasure starts.
There is laughter, there is brawl
In the Recreation Hall
Where resides our independent
Recreation-Hut attendant.
Behind a counter of hickory
He sells some coffee with chicory …

At the wet-canteen a merry crowd
Laughs and drinks and hangs about,
Orders beer and orders shandy …
Some of the boys are having a wager,
Some talk a lot of the sergeant-major,
And some just silently stand and drink
Until their world looks rosy and pink … [37]

The 4th's recreation hut, the site of these verses by Roth and Walton, had been 'placed at the disposal' of the Company 'through the kindness of the Catholic United Services Auxiliary'.[38] (Auxiliaries almost always consisted of women, and it is women from different religious and welfare auxiliaries who provided many practical material comforts to the soldiers.) The hut also housed a wireless set 'with amplifying equipment', a gift from the Melbourne Greek community and installed by experts from a signals unit.[39] The recreation hut for the 2nd Company included reading and study rooms.[40] The 8th Company, while stationed at Camp Pell in Parkville, Melbourne, had a recreation hut open from 2 p.m. to 10 p.m. It boasted a billiard table, writing facilities and a refreshment canteen.[41] Its opening, on 9 March 1943, was a grand affair, attended by His Excellency the Governor of Victoria and other important guests. In his Routine Orders, Captain Edward Broughton thanked the 8th Company's orchestra 'who rendered such an excellent program at the opening'.[42] That orchestra would have included a number of the Dunera Boys whose musical education, like that of Felix

Werder's, was augmented on the *Dunera* and while in internment at the 'Collegium Taturense'.[43]

The 6th Company, stationed at Tocumwal, had a less salubrious event for its more modest facilities. Albert Ceen described the occasion in one of his many letters (in Italian and English) to his wife in Melbourne:

> Last night it was the inauguration night of the recreation hut. It is a big tent – and at the end of it a very [big?] stage has been erected, with two [Tilley?] lamps to provide the lighting. We had plenty of music: piano accordions, chitarra [guitars], mandolini, ecc [etc]. [44]

The piano in this hut is remembered in Yossel Birstein's short story about Weger, who plays Bach and Mozart until the day the Captain declares he should give up the classics and play dance music: 'Girls from the township would be invited to dances.' Weger refuses, much to the Captain's annoyance. 'He never touched the piano … again.'[45]

There were talented musicians in a number of these Companies, as well as men familiar with a range of musical traditions, from folk songs to operatic arias. Singing was popular and required no instruments. Bart Srhoy, a member of the 11th Company stationed at Davilak in Western Australia, where conditions were poor and food inadequate, writes that singing was 'our popular pastime': 'I remember, with some nostalgia, how I loved singing Paul Robeson's 'Old Man River' while dishing up our evening meal to queued soldiers out in the open. Everybody would join in.'[46] In the canteen of the 4th Company, a choir organised by the Hungarian Erwin Rado[47] 'sang Russian songs in Russian, all taught by Rado. There was a really rich cultural life', remembered Wolfgang Sievers.[48] And, like much of the politics, it tended to the Left.

A famous singer to serve in the Employment Companies was Eric Liffman (Erich Liffmann). From the Rhineland in Germany, he had a promising career as a young tenor before the war, and after taking refuge in England, began to build a reputation there as well. But the disaster of Dunkirk and the subsequent British Government's panic about aliens found him on the ship *Dunera*, headed for Australia. Like so many of the Jewish Dunera boys, he became a soldier in the 8th Employment Company. His musical talent saw him play the lead role of Prince Charming in that Company's popular theatrical musical *Sergeant Snow White*—a production so successful that it raised a lot of money for charity and, according to one of the men in the 8th, 'members of the cast were continually recognised in the streets when on leave.'[49]

Very soon, often in spick-and-span army uniform, Liffman was singing in concert halls in and around Melbourne and on commercial radio. He sang for Australian and American troops; he sang in town halls and met, as he later wrote, 'many prominent and famous people.'[50] He remained a Private in the 8th Employment Company and shared with most of his fellow soldiers a warm affection for its Captain, Edward Broughton. The Captain recognised his talent and his commitment to the war effort. In May 1943 he sent Liffman a letter, written in Maori and translated into English. He wrote:

> These words of affection are founded on thoughts emanating from the depths of my soul that some day you will ascend to the peak of the mountain of song and there dwell forever. May the creator bless you and guide you always. [51]

Liffman was not the only significant musical talent in the Employment Companies. Another was the conductor of the 2nd Employment Company choir—an internationally famous Jewish musician from Germany, Curt (Kurt) Prerauer.[52] The very fact of the choir's existence was challenged during a Military Court of Inquiry by five NCOs dismissed from the Company because of their drunkenness and their 'jaundiced opinion' of Jewish aliens. The NCOs claimed that the choir was allowed to practise at times when its members should have been in training or working, but the Court declared this allegation to be without foundation.[53] It is said that officers behaved quite differently in the 8th Company, where the Captain, ever considerate of his men, excused musicians from hard labour in order to protect their hands.[54]

The 6th Company's repertoire included chamber music, played by a quartet. Three of the players, two from Austria and one from Germany, were members of the Company; the cellist was a Tocumwal railway worker.[55] They took their music seriously, and Yosl Bergner, who declared that 'all the Germans were intellectuals'[56] and who insisted on counting Austrians as German, happily recalled in his memoir an occasion when the quartet 'gave a concert of classical music and the wind blew their sheet music away and they couldn't go on. The Greeks stepped in and improvised, without a score.'[57]

Musical and theatrical performances were also part of the military's deliberate policy of outreach to the local community, as well as a way of raising money for patriotic causes. Only a few months after its establishment, the 4th Company provided the orchestra for a Red Cross Ball at Tocumwal's Masonic Hall,[58] and later put on a 'Variety Show' in their recreation hut at Albury , which Captain Walker described proudly in the Company's Routine Orders:

> A Variety Show was held in the Recreation Hut including musical items and sketches. The hall was crowded with men of the unit and visitors from Albury. The show that was put on by members of this unit proved to be a great success.[59]

The musicians from the 6th Company performed concerts at the large air force base near Tocumwal.[60] The Company also had a choir of about twenty-five men, conducted by my father, whose repertoire included 'Soviet Land' and a song about the Russian air force. 'I think we would have been the only Company choir in the Australian army who would have marched through Tocumwal singing these songs,' reflected Bob Exiner with some pleasure, many years later.[61]

Staging plays was a major commitment for a number of men. Like the musicians, those with artistic talents found an outlet in cultural activities legitimised by the military. Albert Ceen, well educated and a gifted artist, represents this enterprising cohort. While in Tocumwal with the 6th Company, he threw himself into the production of a play. His enthusiasm is conveyed in a letter to his wife Flavia:

> The latest of my activities in camp is that I am rehearsing on the stage the part of Trotter in 'Journey's End', a show which will be put on shortly by our Company, first of all in our recreation Hut and if it is successful afterwards in the Tocumwal Theatre.
>
> It is a dramatic show of great renown: the scene is an English dug-out in the last War. Only Officers and Soldiers are on the stage, no women, thanks God, so that we have not to transform a poor labourer into a glamour girl, neither have we to recruit authentic glamour girls among the few if any Tocumwal beauties.
>
> Although I have not been on the stage since I was eighteen, our regisseur expressed his satisfaction at the way I am playing my new role. As you see your husband, although getting old, discovers every day new avenues … [62]

Ceen, at thirty-nine among the older members of the Company, was careful in his letters to subtly reassure his wife that he was not interested in other women. But his enthusiasm for the play is genuine, and soon he is also painting the scenery, and making posters to advertise performances in Tocumwal and in Finley, a nearby town. Many of the rehearsals take place in the Company's medical hut, where the Sergeant in charge, one of the actors in the play, ensures that the performers are marked as 'unfit' for work during rehearsal time.[63]

Ceen's letters are full of details about the play, accompanied by complaints about being overworked (he was promoted from Corporal to Sergeant and responsible for the Company's accounts), as well as the heat—it is January: 'a climate that compares very favourably with Hell.'[64] But he is gratified when the play's performance in Shepparton receives a positive review in the local paper, including 'a special reference to “perfection of the scenery”’.[65] It seems that audiences were not disturbed by British World War I officers who ‘spoke in reffo accents’.[66]

Ceen’s pride in the 6th Company’s performance is tempered by his knowledge that the 8th produced ‘Sergeant Snow White, a Happy-go-Lucky musical revue of bad old and good new times’ at Melbourne University’s Union Theatre for three nights to considerable popular success, raising £880 for patriotic funds.[67] He points out, not unfairly, that the 8th Company’s show included professional artists.[68] Cyril Pearl, author of one of the first books about the Dunera Boys, agrees that ‘it was an ambitious production in three acts and 22 scenes with a cast of more than 50’:[69]

> The show deployed an abundance of talent. The choreographer and solo dancer, Corporal Peter Schmitz, was a former member of the Russian Ballet in London … A magnificent tenor, Private Eric Liffman was well known to radio audiences in England and Holland … One of the six accordionists had played by command for the Duke of Windsor. [70]

While some Employment Company soldiers devoted spare time to cultural activities, others played sport. At Tocumwal, Wednesday afternoons were allocated for the 6th Company to play sport. Orpheus Kandiliotis says they had two options: play sport or undertake work around the camp.[71]

For those with a passion for exercise, such as Fred Lester, sport was combined with a personal fitness schedule. While platoons of the 4th Company were stationed at Albury, Lester spent the time between morning call at 6 a.m. and breakfast at 7 a.m. jogging around the camp ground. ‘There was a very nice bike track there, and I used to look after my fitness by doing about a couple of miles there … and occasionally a bit more.’[72] He also spent his free days in Sydney playing junior soccer for a Jewish sports team, Hakoah, and football with members of the left-wing Eureka Youth League.[73]

For most of the Europeans in the Employment Companies, football meant soccer. Ceen tried to learn to kick the oval ball used in Australian Rules football, but without much success. Writing to his young son Guy, he commends the boy for starting to play the Australian game at school, and admits his own incompetence: 'it is rather hard for me to learn now the drop-kick which is the basis of the game; it is very different from soccer.' He goes on to praise the soccer team 'our boys here have formed: [they] gave a very nice exhibition last Sunday. With a bit of training, I am sure they could favourably compare with some of the Melbourne soccer clubs.'[74]

Like the 6th, a number of the Companies had soccer teams. Captain Walker included an account in his War Diary of a match involving the 4th Company's soccer team in May 1942, writing with satisfaction:

> The afternoon provided a sporting event of great interest amongst the men, when a team representing No.4 Labour Coy played a soccer match against the R.A.A.F., concluding the game with a victory, scoring 4 to 1 against the R.A.A.F. As Showgrounds Camp was open for visitors, the news of this encounter attracted quite a number of spectators, who enjoyed the congenial game. [75]

Soccer even features in Company Routine Orders. On 27 June 1945 the officer of the 3rd Company writes in the margin at the bottom of the page: 'Army Soccer Football Team defeated English Golden Hind 4-2.'[76] And dotted through the Routine Orders of many of the alien Companies are references to sport, especially when it involves success for men in the Company. Typical is the pleasure expressed by the 4th Company officer as he notes that 'members of this Unit have been very successful in local Army Sports Event (Soccer, Bike-Racing, Foot-Running, etc.) gaining first place in almost every event to [*sic*] took part in.'[77] This Company even had a Unit Sports Officer.[78]

Sports, like cultural activities, were viewed by the military as both morale-boosting and a bridge to local communities. Sunday, generally a rest day, was a favourite time for team events. The 10th Company, cutting timber in the bush around the small community of Springton in South Australia, played a cricket match against the locals; the War Diary doesn't record who won the game.[79]

Less organised physical recreation included fishing and swimming in the Murray River. Swimming was popular enough to warrant an official warning—a sensible precaution when many of the men had little or no experience of Australian rivers, or indeed of any kind of swimming:

> All ranks are warned against the dangerous nature of Murray River, particularly as regards currents, deep holes and snags.[80]

One man from the 4th did drown, and the men in the Company were then prohibited from swimming unless 'under the supervision of a competent person or persons appointed by the C.C. for this purpose.'[81] It is unlikely this order was obeyed for long. Certainly, the pleasure of cool water on hot days lured men from all the Companies stationed near the river, including Ceen, who wrote enthusiastically during a hot December in 1942 of 'wearing a pair of underpants in the river ... It was simply lovely!'[82] A few months later, in the February heat, he is just as keen on the water, and the surrounding bush:

> Yesterday, Sunday, I took two hours off and went for a swim in the river. It was simply gorgeous. I went on a bike with a few mates. They undressed and went into the water and I took all their gear on the bike and went to wait for them about one and a half mile down the river. There was a beautiful beach, not a soul, and while waiting for my mates I had a couple of light dips and got dried in the sun.
>
> It was probably the best swim I had in Australia: the scenery in that spot is really picturesque and the colours worthy of Cezanne's brush. [83]

Ceen also uses his leisure time to explore well beyond the camp at Tocumwal. He makes friends with a local sheep farmer, and spends an exhilarating free day on the 7500-acre farm:

> I had the thrill of my life when, in the afternoon, Mr. Lawrence and a friend of his, Mr. Beale, took us driving in two motor cars through the paddock running after kangaroos and emus. The poor brutes were sometimes cornered by fences and it was very nice to see them running for their lives at thirty miles per hour and then jumping over the fences. Specially interesting to see how the emus can run fast …
>
> The weather was very nice, we had two good meals and talked a lot at night near the fireplaces so that I really enjoyed my day off.[84]

Some men kept dogs (Orpheus Kandiliotis called them 'army dogs')[85] and went hunting for rabbits;[86] some grew tomatoes and greens to supplement the army rations.[87] And almost everyone seized opportunities to mix with civilians, whether in the small towns such as Tocumwal or the big capital cities.

They took advantage of local facilities such as the cinema—the 4th Company was given late passes twice a week to see films in Albury.[88] That rural town also boasted a Rest Room, which issued 'a cordial invitation' to members of the 4th Company 'to attend … on Sunday evening and to bring any musical instruments with them, also to participate in the singing, etc.'[89] Greek cafés—in Albury and other rural towns—were a magnet for men yearning for something tastier and more varied than bland camp food; Bob Exiner was not the only one to declare army food 'unspeakable'[90] and remember with affection 'the social highlight of life—steak and eggs at the Greek's'.[91] (It was not lost on the men that the officers ate separately and were served better food.)[92] When Orpheus Kandiliotis recalled a brief spell at the army hospital at Royal Park, he commented: 'better food and nice nurses.'[93] He also mentioned the hotel in Tocumwal—there was only one—where some of the men went to drink. Sometimes, there were enough of them to crowd out the locals.[94]

The towns and cities also provided a more beguiling recreation: dances. For the younger men especially—and many were young—it was an opportunity to meet young women. ('We talked about food and girls,' remarked John Cohen from the 11th Company.[95]) Servicemen often had free entry to dances, such as one featuring the Merry Maker Girls in Albion Street, East Brunswick, in November 1943.[96] Town halls held dances for servicemen, sometimes with quotas of men from different Companies.[97] In Tocumwal, there were 50-50 dances, with an even split of the modern and the old, every week,[98] but some young men chose to go to a dance at Shepparton, or Cobram, or Finley.[99] Finley was 12 miles away; it meant hopping on and off a commercial train and a lot of walking. In his autobiographical novel, *Tears, Laughter and the Revolution,* Charlie D'Aprano writes of 'the dances at Cobram, Shepparton, Finlay [*sic*]; the young nurses from the Mooroopna hospital; the Land Army girls …'[100] As Jack Friedman remarked, 'You'd be amazed how you find a way to have a personal life.'[101]

As always, the 8th Employment Company created special opportunities for its men—including dancing lessons. Cyril Pearl describes 'a monocled dancing master of the old school' giving 'expert instruction while grizzled guards looked on in wonder' as the men danced with each other.[102] And these men had the benefit of the writer Alan Marshall's counsel on how to talk to Australian girls: don't use up your conversational gambits in the first meeting seems to have been the essence of the advice.[103]

Henry Lippmann, one of the Dunera boys in the 8th Employment Company, gives a vivid description of the dancing and socialising in Sydney and Melbourne:

> There were hundreds of dances. That was the marvellous thing, the good thing, about this time … At night we were on leave and … you would go into the YMCA —there were many places in town, there were activities for the soldiers … there were thousands of soldiers at dances. Fantastic jazz bands … Glenn Miller music and Artie Shaw and all these arrangements, that was the beauty of this time … Then the jitterbug … they were fantastic, they were acrobats, the Americans particularly … And we would just sit there, and dance, and mingle—girls, smart girls, that's how it was. We would take girls out and stroll around the park and come back [to camp] in the morning tired and

> sleepy … We had a fantastic time … There were also dances from different communal organisations. There were Catholic dances, Jewish dances, all sorts of political organisations …[104]

Many of the men spoke English with a strong foreign accent, and that aroused, at best, simple curiosity. Lippmann's approach when a girl asked, 'Where do you come from? Where are you from originally?' was to reply, 'I can't talk about it, it's a military secret.'[105] One of his fellow soldiers pretended to be Dutch, only to be introduced by his girl to another 'Dutch man' so that the two could speak Dutch together. Fortunately, the second soldier was also a German pretending to be Dutch. 'So they speak in German and the girls think they speak Dutch, because they don't know the difference,' chuckled Lippmann.'[106] Gerhard Steuerwald, from Hanover, Germany, wrote of the efforts of some of his fellow 3rd Employment Company soldiers to disguise their origins:

> For fear that the word 'Germany' may create a bad impression most of our men born in that country pretend, when asked, to be of any nationality that appeals to their fancy. Whenever we got to a dance girls we meet are puzzled. In most cases our dancing partners are under the impression that we are American soldiers. Their curiosity is very great. 'Why do you wear an Australian uniform?' they will ask … One of us privates … likes the idea of being taken for an American. The fact that he wears an Australian uniform does not worry him. 'I lost my American uniform in a game of poker. As I have to return to camp in uniform, I borrowed this one,' he will explain …[107]

In a letter sent from three of the Jewish ex-'enemy' aliens in the 6th Company to a friend in the 4th, they write that 'Tocumwal is still a place of "quiet romance" (very quiet), of "social activities" (oh yeah!) and varied diversions (very varied!).'[108] A description that covered every country town where soldiers congregated.

Some of the men took advantage of the opportunities the army provided for the enhancement of their cultural and intellectual passions. Among their number were musicians, painters, poets, and a variety of scholars. What one writer has called 'the greatest cultural migration since the fall of Constantinople in 1453'[109]—the exile from Germany after 1933 (and, later, from German-occupied countries) of Jews and anti-fascists—resulted in a level of cultural and educational sophistication in a number of the alien Employment Companies not found elsewhere in the Australian military at the time. Wolfgang Sievers, himself part of that forced diaspora, and a brilliant photographer, remembered the good company he had in the 4th: 'We had very interesting friends and concerts and poets. Intellectually, it was a very interesting collection of people.' Among his army friends were two Hungarians, Andrew (Andor) Fabinyi, later to become one of Australia's leading publishers and booksellers, and Erwin Rado, a photographer and pianist, who co-founded the Melbourne Film Festival in the 1950s.[110]

Yosl Bergner, the poor boy from Warsaw with a rich cultural heritage, shares a tent with other émigrés. 'We worked very hard ... but our tent was very cultured, we read, we discussed ...'[111] He paints in his tent at night by the light of a kerosene lamp: 'hundreds of mosquitos and crickets got stuck on the wet paintings'.[112] He paints the Aboriginal Australians he remembered from his time in working-class Fitzroy; the men around him in the 6th Employment Company; and, before there was much information about the destruction of Warsaw, he paints his old home in flames and ruins. His imagination proved sadly prescient.

Another artist, Klaus Friedeberger, was a refugee from Germany to Britain in 1937, and later, one of the 'enemy aliens' sent to Australia on the *Dunera*. At the internment camp in Hay, he develops his skills, learns art history and colour theory from experts (other detainees), and begins a lifelong friendship with a number of young painters and sculptors. But it is not until he is a soldier in the 8th Employment Company that he exhibits work publicly, with the Contemporary Art Society, and, while in the army, establishes connections with the

Australian artists William Dobell, Arthur Boyd and Sidney Nolan. It is in Tocumwal, loading and unloading trains, that he produces his first oil paintings.[113]

In the 6th Company, Albert Ceen, the successful Italian businessman with several degrees and a talent for art, paints a large portrait of the Captain surrounded by his men, in the mode of a king's court. This humorous work is popular with everyone, and brings Ceen considerable satisfaction.[114] He is later commissioned by the Commanding Officer to paint an oil portrait of himself in full uniform.[115] In his letters to his wife, he mentions that he and others are organising a series of conferences and talks at the camp in Tocumwal, to which he will contribute 'a talk about the technique of silk screen printing.'[116] Charles D'Aprano, one of the Italians in the Company whose previous education had been limited, remarked when interviewed not long before his death, 'We didn't feel culturally deprived—there was always something going on in the camp.' He attributed much of his learning, both cultural and political, to his time in the army.[117]

Learning from the talent around them—scholars as well as artists—provided ongoing informal education. And despite the heavy work, and the periods of isolation from major educational and cultural institutions when stationed outside capital cities, a number of the men spent their free time persevering with their studies. The Army Education Service (AES) offered a range of cultural and educational programs. Established at the urging of men such as CEW Bean, the famous World War I correspondent and historian, the AES was officially established in October 1943, although education classes of various kinds were available much earlier.[118] The AES's programs included English lessons, lectures on current affairs, and a range of courses, many of which could be taken by correspondence. The Routine Orders for the 8th Employment Company on 20 March 1943 include paragraphs urging the men to consider taking up courses, followed by a full page listing 'Subjects Available for Study by Correspondence' and 'Subjects Available for Study by Personal Tuition.' The emphasis in both lists was on 'skilled trades', which were declared to be in short supply.[119]

Among the men interviewed, a number took advantage of the AES's programs. Those stationed at Albury were offered classes in Arithmetic and English at the local high school.[120] The well-educated Robert Exiner took four AES courses, including bookkeeping and managerial tactics.'[121] Bern Brent, a Dunera Boy, was helped (probably by Margaret Holmes, Secretary of the Australian Student Christian Movement) to begin his matriculation subjects while interned, and finished them with the assistance of an AES correspondence course by the end of 1944.[122] And Holmes, ever concerned for the welfare of the ex-internees in the 8th Employment Company, went as far as writing to various clergymen, requesting both their fellowship and the provision of a quiet space for the men to study in their free time. In a letter she noted that many of these men were Jews, but she was sure 'they would appreciate any gesture of courtesy and hospitality from the Christian community and townspeople generally.' In case the point needed emphasis, she added, 'In our work for this group we have drawn no distinction between Jews and Christians ...'[123]

John Cohen, who served in the 11th Employment Company until he was transferred, first to General Blamey's headquarters, where he was made a Sergeant ('you had to be at least a sergeant at Blamey's headquarters'), and then to the AES, found himself giving lectures to army units 'about the war, about the Atlantic Charter, about Indonesia'. He spoke with approval of the opportunities the AES provided for soldiers to further their education.[124] One talented artist in the 8th Company, Erwin Fabian, was transferred to the AES on the recommendation of an officer who had seen one of his drawings reproduced in the AES magazine, *Salt*. He spent the last year of his army service in congenial company in Melbourne, producing covers and illustrations for the AES's fortnightly *Current Affairs Bulletin*.[125]

While the opportunity to gain skills and knowledge likely to be useful in civilian life was one goal of the AES, it is the broader education—the films and lectures and library books—which may well have had the most profound and enduring influence on men in the army, including those in the alien Employment Companies.[126] The range of speakers is impressive, including leading socialists such as Percy Laidler, whose illustrated lectures to the army were encouraged by Prime Minister Curtin.[127] The 8th Company's Routine Orders for 14 October 1942, under the heading 'Education', urged the men to attend an illustrated talk by Laidler on the subject of 'Red Army and Russian People':

> The Commander wishes as many members of this unit as possible to attend this programme, which will prove to be of high topical interest to all.[128]

Russia was also the topic of a lecture to the 4th Company in March 1943 by Ian Milner, a left-wing political scientist from Melbourne University. According to the Company's Routine Orders, 'a large audience gave him unlimited support and tremendous applause'.[129]

While the Soviet Union was an extremely important ally during the war, the positive views of the country and its military coincided with the political leanings of many in the AES. In 1974 the historian Ian Turner wrote fondly of his lively and enlarging time in the AES among 'personnel overwhelmingly on the left ... the times were radical; the Russians were popular, and the dreams of post-war reconstruction were grand.'[130] His was a fairly typical AES routine: he lectured to the soldiers about the war and current affairs, showed documentary films, encouraged fledgling writers and artists, and introduced jazz records to men for whom they were a puzzle or a revelation.[131]

The AES also published *Salt*, a lively little magazine that provided information about the war (including much historical and cultural background of the countries involved in it), as well as a range of educational and literary material. It was entertaining as well as informative. Soldiers contributed to *Salt*, and in the case of a handful of men from the 8th Employment Company, labouring work on the magazine led to their becoming contributors. The artist Vane Lindesay, who worked on *Salt*, became close friends with two of these men: Bruno Simon and Erwin 'Teddy' Fabian. Together with Freddy (Fritz) Schonbach and

Klaus Friedeberger, the men worked packing the fortnightly issue of *Salt* in the building of its printers, Truth and Sportsman Ltd, only a few yards from the *Salt* office in Melbourne. Their proximity to the friendly and cultured soldiers who produced the magazine led to the discovery of their talents as artists and their subsequent publication in its pages.[132]

In the midst of a bitter war, the Australian Army had the foresight and commitment to establish the AES. For many soldiers, including those in the Employment Companies, its educational services—both professional and cultural—provided immediate engagement and the long-term prospect of a fulfilling civilian life.

# 8

# 'Most satisfactory service': the Chinese Employment Company

If the story of the majority of European 'aliens' in the Australian Army's Employment Companies during World War II has been generally neglected,[1] there is even less historical recognition of the Asian 'aliens' who similarly wore the regulation khaki and provided essential labour for the war effort. Of the eleven Companies defined as composed of aliens (with the exception of commissioned officers), three consisted largely of non-European men: Chinese in the 7th, Koepangese (Timorese) in the 23rd, and Indonesians (often called Javanese) in the 36th. The largest of these was the 7th Employment Company, made up of Chinese whose presence in Australia was generally a by-product of the war.

The exigencies of war reshaped many Australian expectations, and occasionally challenged long-established regulations. The White Australia policy, that determined bulwark against the 'deadly, coloured alien biped',[2] faltered. What to do about Chinese seamen whose ships were stranded in Australian ports following the outbreak of the Pacific conflict? How could the policy legislated by the very first Commonwealth Parliament in 1901 deal with non-white refugees from the Japanese invasion of Singapore, Malaya, Indonesia, New Guinea and Timor?

According to the Director-General of Security, 'up to the 31st of March 1945 there were 7,638 Registered Alien Chinese living within the Commonwealth.'[3] Arthur Calwell, speaking in parliament as the Minister for Immigration in 1949, focused on refugees; he said there were 5473 non-European refugees in Australia during World War II, of whom about three thousand were Chinese.[4] Escaping the Japanese military expansion, the majority of non-European refugees arrived after the outbreak of the Pacific War in 1941, and were permitted entry on special humanitarian grounds that circumvented the White Australia restrictions.[5] The historian Barry York calculates that 2033 of these Chinese received Certificates of Exemption from the Dictation Test—the notorious language test he describes as 'an all-encompassing mechanism for exclusion by subterfuge'.[6] Others were permitted entry as evacuees on humanitarian grounds.[7] It is from this varied assembly, particularly the stranded seamen, that the 7th Employment Company was formed.

Not all these men ended up in an Employment Company. Some continued as seamen, working on Australian ships; some were employed by various manpower instrumentalities across the country; a number were enlisted in other areas of the military; and a few found a way to conduct small private enterprises, such as Chinese restaurants.

Those who remained seamen were generally assured of Australian rates of pay and working conditions, thanks to the vigorous efforts of the Australian Seamen's Union and the body it helped form, the Chinese Seamen's Union. Arthur Gar-Lock Chang, who became the Assistant Secretary of the Chinese Union, remembered EV Elliott—the Communist Party Secretary of the Australian Seamen's Union and a powerful figure industrially—declaring: 'We're all brothers, why shouldn't all seamen get the same wages and conditions?'[8] Such egalitarian attitudes influenced the men who joined the Chinese Seamen's Union, and the politically progressive Chinese Youth League of Australia.[9] When many were conscripted for military and manpower service, they carried with them a preparedness to resist perceived injustice.[10]

In most official documents, the full title of the 7th Australian Employment Company was bracketed with the word 'Chinese'.[11] Similarly, the 23rd Australian Employment Company was bracketed with 'Koepangese', and the 36th with 'Javanese'. The Chinese, Timorese and Indonesians were categorised as allied aliens, and the term 'alien' was defined as a non-British subject, with no reference to colour.[12] Yet government and military documents almost never list the Asian Employment Companies as 'alien'—neither in the title of the Company nor in discussion of the alien Companies. This suggests that whatever the legal definition of alien, in practice, Asians were regarded as more foreign than any Europeans.

The main reason for the founding of the 7th Employment Company was the same as for all the alien Employment Companies: a desperate shortage of manpower to conduct the war. In 1940 the government was firmly opposed to the notion of aliens joining the military, because 'the admission of aliens or of British subjects of non-European origin or descent to the Australia Defence Forces is undesirable in principle.'[13]

In fact, this 'principle' had already been breached for the RAAF—because of its shortage of personnel.[14] By 1942, with the war dragging on with no end in sight, and the army 5000 under strength,[15] that exception was widened well beyond the RAAF.[16] This was probably known to Dr Hsu Mo, the Minister for China in this country, when he wrote to the Minister for the Army in February 1942, urging the government to form an AIF unit consisting of Chinese seamen who were now refugees here.[17] Instead, the authorities were already planning to draft Chinese crews not required for shipping into 'labour units of our Military Forces'.[18]

The establishment of the Employment Companies freed fitter and/or more 'suitable' men to fight the war. Wendy Rankine, who wrote a detailed account of the Chinese in Australia during World War II, suggests that another reason for creating the 7th Employment Company was to control these non-European aliens, to keep them under relatively easy surveillance.[19] In a country with a long-established White Australia policy, these men, while categorised as allied aliens, posed troubling and sometimes unexpected difficulties to both government and the military. A forest of trees was needed to sustain the correspondence among officialdom that their presence engendered.

The Security Service kept a watchful and often worried eye on aliens in general and the Chinese aliens in particular. Rankine provides a comprehensive summary of Security's approach to the Chinese:

> Early in 1944, the Director-General of the Commonwealth Security Service established a separate 'Chinese Section'... [D]espite the chronic manpower shortage, security personnel were employed to investigate, collect, grade and control information covering every aspect pertaining to the Chinese. They were to watch all Chinese refugees, Chinese seamen, Chinese diplomats, Chinese survivors from ships lost at sea, Chinese called up for National Service and the Allied Services (both at work and when on leave), Chinese deserters, Chinese restaurateurs and their clients, Chinese drug and gambling organizations, Chinese cultural, patriotic, social or other societies and Chinese banks and trading houses. [20]

All this effort appears not to have uncovered any spies among the Chinese aliens. As one Security document noted about some of the 7th Employment Company men arriving to work for the US Army in Townsville: 'In all cases the treatment given these men [by the Japanese] was such that they all expressed hatred of the Japanese and would present no security risk.'[21] And Security's own records acknowledge the system's inability always to keep a check on these men.[22] None the less, the letters the men received from Japanese-occupied China—all subject to censorship—provided useful intelligence information.[23]

The 7th Employment Company was formally established in Western Australia—the landing place of most of the seamen—on 17 March 1942. The first intake consisted of 411 Chinese.[24] Its initial cohort of officers were all Anglo-Celts, mainly World War I veterans or men from the Western Australia Militia. As in the other Employment Companies, alien officers up to and occasionally including the rank of

Sergeant were soon appointed.[25] Similarly, the Chinese were proper soldiers in army uniform, paid the rate for Privates of 6/- a day, and subject to all army rules and regulations.[26] Proper soldiers—but without guns.

For some time, the men in the 7th were kept busy with projects not directly military but none the less essential. Based at the Claremont Showground in Perth, working parties of men usually from the same Chinese districts or cities were sent to various places in the state: loading and unloading goods on the wharves,[27] helping erect telephone lines at Yanrey,[28] constructing camouflage at Springhills,[29] and bringing in the potato crop at Harvey, which had been an Italian internment camp.[30] Wendy Rankine interviewed a woman—herself Italian—who remembered the Chinese 'for their continual rhythmic singing and diligent work – they dug twice as many potatoes per day as the Italians.'[31]

This woman wasn't the only admirer of the Chinese effort. The Minister for Commerce and Agriculture, WJ Scully, prepared a paper for Cabinet on 9 January 1943. It begins:

> The rural labour position in Western Australia is more severe than in any other State ... in July 1942 only 40% of the pre-war permanent hired labour force remained ... The potato harvest in November/December 1942 could not have been handled without emergency measures. A labour corps of Chinese and Enemy Aliens was organised and their use gave an indication of what could be achieved by a mobile labour force.[32]

Although Chinese labour was clearly valuable, not everyone welcomed these diligent workers. The Kalgoorlie District Council took offence when a party of Chinese from the 7th Company was sent to work there for a short time. In an angry telegram to the army, the Council declared: 'This is the first time in history Chinese allowed on goldfields work. Strong protest against introduction.'[33] Ship owners grumbled because they were deprived of labour, and there were some contretemps with naval authorities who didn't want the Chinese on the Fremantle wharf.[34]

Hertz Berkowicz (Harry Burke) and Szulem Faktor (Saul Factor) on board the *Moreton Bay*, July 1938. Source: June Factor

*Left:* 'Hitler' Preliminary sketch by Albert Ceen, 6th Employment Company. Source: Guido Ceen
*Right:* Andy (Adrian) Factor's ID tags and colour patch. Source: Andy Factor, 6th Employment Company

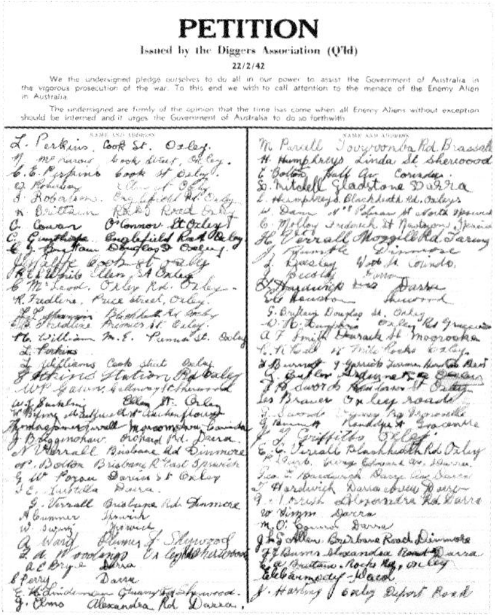

PETITION

Issued by the Diggers Association (Q'ld)

22/2/42

We the undersigned pledge ourselves to do all in our power to assist the Government of Australia in the vigorous prosecution of the war. To this end we wish to call attention to the menace of the Enemy Alien in Australia.

The undersigned are firmly of the opinion that the time has come when all Enemy Aliens without exception should be interned and it urges the Government of Australia to do so forthwith.

NAME AND ADDRESS

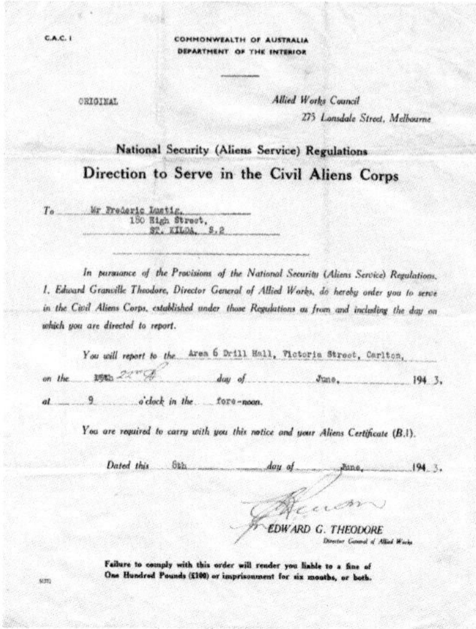

C.A.C. 1

COMMONWEALTH OF AUSTRALIA
DEPARTMENT OF THE INTERIOR

ORIGINAL

Allied Works Council
275 Lonsdale Street, Melbourne

National Security (Aliens Service) Regulations

Direction to Serve in the Civil Aliens Corps

To Mr Frederic Lustig,
150 High Street,
ST. KILDA. S.2

*In pursuance of the Provisions of the National Security (Aliens Service) Regulations, I, Edward Granville Theodore, Director General of Allied Works, do hereby order you to serve in the Civil Aliens Corps, established under those Regulations as from and including the day on which you are directed to report.*

*You will report to the* Area 6 Drill Hall, Victoria Street, Carlton,

*on the* 22nd *day of* June, 1943.

*at* 9 *o'clock in the* fore-noon.

*You are required to carry with you this notice and your Aliens Certificate (B.1).*

*Dated this* 8th *day of* June, 1943.

EDWARD G. THEODORE
Director General of Allied Works

**Failure to comply with this order will render you liable to a fine of One Hundred Pounds (£100) or imprisonment for six months, or both.**

*Left:* Diggers' Association of Queensland petition demanding the immediate internment of all enemy aliens, 1942. Source: NAA: A373, 1272
*Right:* Direction to Frederic Lustig to serve in the Civil Aliens Corps. Source: Margot Lustig

*Left:* Henry (Heinz) Lustig, 4th Employment Company. Source: Margot Lustig
*Right:* Frederic (Fritz) Lustig, 6th Employment Company. Source: Margot Lustig

Nick Raftopoulos, 6th Employment Company, Tocumwal, 1942. Source: Nick Raftopoulos

Emil Witton, 3rd Employment Company, with his wife Hannah in Pitt Street, Sydney. Source: Ron Witton

Charlie D'Aprano, 6th Employment Company, and his wife Zelda on their wedding day. Source: Seona D'Aprano

Members of 3rd Employment Company at Mascot. From left: Front row standing, Jacky Hirsch, on the right of the Captain with cap and light tunic, Paul Witkowski (Witton) and his brother Emil, 3rd and 2nd last in front standing row. Source: Ron Witton

Members of 6th Employment Company, Ivan Rostkier (far left), Sol Brustman (third from left). Source: Ivan Rostkier

*Left:* Saul Factor and Israel Bluthal, 6th Employment Company. Source: Charles D'Aprano
*Right:* Mates in 6th Employment Company: Mick Pennisi, Ivan Rostkier and an American. Source: Ivan Rostkier

Members of 3rd Employment Company, including Harry Bruhl, his brother William Bruhl, the Commanding Officer and John Pollak. Source: John Pollak

Three members of 3rd Employment Company: unknown, Harry Bruhl and John Pollak. Source: John Pollak

Mates in 6th Employment Company in camp. Source: Ivan Rostkier

*Left:* Theo Spirakos and Nick Raftopoulos, 6th Employment Company, Tocumwal, 1942. Source: Nick Raftopoulos
*Right:* Andy Factor's ink sketch, 'Army Camp'. Source: Andy Factor

John Ridge (right), cleaning his boots, 6th Employment Company. Source: Elizabeth and Mollie Ridge

Yossel Birstein and Yosl Bergner, 6th Employment Company, 1942–3.
Source: *Yosl Bergner, Art as a meeting of Cultures* by Frank Klepner

Members of 6th Employment Company with snake. From left: George Collins, Nicholas Raftopoulos, Con Vlasopoulos and Gery Valianos.Tocumwal, 1942.
Source: Nick Raftopoulos

Members of 6th Employment Company loading hessian sacks, Tocumwal, 1943. Saul Factor second from left, Israel Bluthal far right. Source: Charles D'Aprano

Members of 6th Employment Company unloading railway trucks. Photo by Wolfgang Sievers, 4th Employment Company. Source: Wolfgang Sievers

Members of 6th Employment Company sitting on a pile of hessian sacks, Tocumwal, 1943. Israel Bluthal bottom left, Saul Factor bottom right. Source: Charles D'Aprano

Members of 6th Employment Company, Saul Factor second from right.
Source: Charles D'Aprano

Members of 6th Employment Company emptying artillery shells, Mangalore, 1943. *Top:* John Koumanis. *Middle:* Bill Tseapkoun. *Front, from left:* Theodorakis (Theo), 'Lofty' (over 6 feet) and Orpheus Kandiliotis. Source: Orpheus Kandiliotis

Members of 6th Employment Company emptying artillery shells, Mangalore, 1943. The men used to drink from the water tank until one day someone looked inside and found skeletons of snakes and rats. Italian prisoners made little gardens around some of the huts. Source: Orpheus Kandiliotis

Max Jedwab and Charles D'Aprano, 6th Employment Company, Tocumwal, 1943. Source: Charles D'Aprano

Members of 3rd Employment Company working party, Mascot, 1943/44. *From left:* Paul Witkowski (Emil's brother), Jacky Hirsch, Emil Witkowski (Witton) and Claude Newcombe. Source: Ron Witton

Andy Factor's ink sketch, 'Lashing Gang!!' Source: Andy Factor

Andy Factor's ink sketch, 'Comforts'. Source: Andy Factor

Members of 6th Employment Company playing two-up: Ivan Rostkier, second from left. Source: Ivan Rostkier

Members of 6th Employment Company hunting rabbits with dogs, Mangalore. From left: John Koumanis, Bill Tseapkoun and Nick Raftopoulos. Source: Orpheus Kandiliotis

Illustration from *A Day in Camp*, by Cary Roth and Tim Walton. (Illustrated ballad created for the 4th Employment Company on the occasion of its first anniversary, 9 March 1943.) Source: Wolfgang Sievers

'Camp Pell International Hotel', watercolour painting by Albert Ceen, 6th Employment Company. Source: Guido Ceen

Eric Liffman, 8th Employment Company, with Lady Angliss, planning a series of charity concerts. Source: Karl and Kurt Liffman

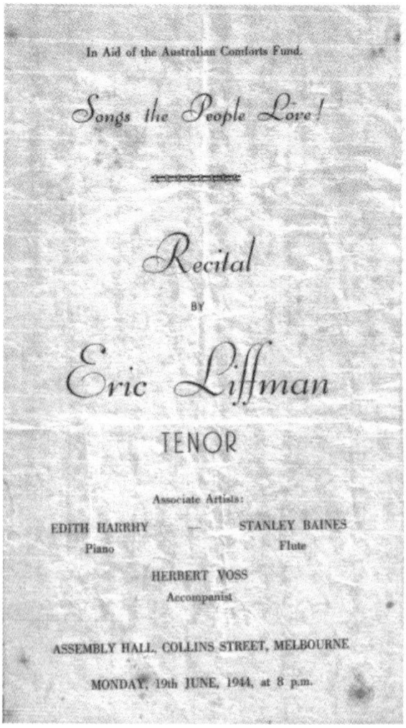

In Aid of the Australian Comforts Fund.

*Songs the People Love!*

*Recital*

BY

*Eric Liffman*

TENOR

Associate Artists:

EDITH HARRHY — STANLEY BAINES
Piano Flute

HERBERT VOSS
Accompanist

ASSEMBLY HALL, COLLINS STREET, MELBOURNE

MONDAY, 19th JUNE, 1944, at 8 p.m.

*Left:* Eric Liffman, 8th Employment Company, looking at a poster advertising a performance in aid of the Australian Comforts Fund. Source: Karl and Kurt Liffman
*Right:* Leaflet for a recital by Eric Liffman, 8th Employment Company, in aid of the Australian Comforts Fund, 19 June, 1944. Source: Karl and Kurt Liffman

It seems the army was largely unmoved by these complaints, but the Labor government was sensitive to any suggestion that members of the alien Employment Companies were displacing civilian labour. Only a month after the establishment of the alien Companies, the Director of Recruiting and Mobilization wrote to reassure the Department of the Army that government policy was being adhered to:

> Members of the labour coy have not displaced civilian labour which had formerly been employed at award rates, and are not being used on work for which skilled tradesmen would be employed … Instructions have been issued to all [Headquarters]… in conformity with the Minister's direction, that in no case is a labour coy to be used in such a way as to displace civilian labour. [35]

The men in the 7th Company worked hard, and their diligence and initiative were not restricted to working hours. They grew their own vegetables, did their own cooking, and built a Taoist temple in the camp.[36] They attended English classes provided by the army, local volunteers and the Western Australian Education Department.[37] They got to know the local Chinese community—most visibly, the restaurants and the prostitutes.[38] And their political awareness, which is a marked feature of their story, made them generous supporters of good causes: they bought poppies on Remembrance Day; and in the Allies Day Fund Queen Quest in 1942, they voted for their favourite, Miss China, who won; each vote cost 1/-.[39]

The Minister for Commerce and Agriculture was right: the 7th was certainly mobile. In November 1942, 238 men and three officers left by train from Claremont station, heading to Mount Isa. The Company War Diary records that 'Everything went satisfactory. Colonel Biles, Major Quartermaine, Major Pullin [and] the Consul for China … were on the Station to see the departure.'[40]

Soon, other sections of the Company were on the move. The *Canberra Times* in September 1943 devoted a column and a half to an evocative description of 'a complete Chinese crew – bosun, mess boy and all' who were a unit of the 7th Company sent to the Northern Territory. They were no longer sailors:

> The captain has become a sergeant, the bosun wears a corporal's stripes, and the mess boy, deckhands and the rest are privates. The war has taken them from the sea and formed them into a platoon of an army employment company which embraces some hundreds of their fellow-countrymen, all of them refugees. [41]

The article points to the men's commonality with other Australian soldiers: 'They wear the army uniform of shorts, shirts and slouch hat – this latter as to the manner born – and their camp is run like any other.' But the writer discerns a difference: 'no other camp can quite rival it in cleanliness or neatness ... This is as true of each individual tent or hut as it is of the camp as a whole.' Moreover, there are carved and decorated pieces of furniture, and a 'pagoda-like recreation hut' in which the men play table-tennis and listen to Chungking radio. Their work, while not dissimilar to that undertaken by other alien Employment Companies around the country—loading and unloading supplies—included splitting hawsers and mending fences.[42]

Fifty men from the 7th Employment Company were sent to help the non-alien 28th Employment Company in the Northern Territory; the latter, that Company's War Diary asserted firmly, were 'essentially soldiers, and manual workers afterwards'.[43] But there was gratitude for the 'manual workers': the Captain of the 28th recorded his appreciation of the Chinese contingent, as well as the work of Aboriginal Australians: both 'helped to lighten the burden from this Coy ... The Chinese have taken over the work of handling stores.'[44]

While a shifting core of 7th Employment Company men continued to be based in Western Australia, and the Company was not formally disbanded until February 1944,[45] the majority were sent to Queensland—to Townsville, Cairns and Brisbane. The last 7th Employment Company soldier to be sent interstate left Western Australia on 30 June 1943.[46] For most of these men, though few knew it at the time, the US Army was beckoning. Of the 1552 Chinese who were at some time employed by the US Army's Small Ships Branch of its Services and Supply division in Queensland, 600 or more began their working lives in Australia as members of the 7th Australian Employment Company (Chinese).[47]

In April 1942, the American, General Douglas MacArthur, was appointed Supreme Commander for the South West Pacific, 'with authority over all Allied personnel'; the head of the Australian forces, General Sir Thomas Blamey, had 'charge of all land forces in the area'.[48] After a few months in Melbourne, where Australian military command was based, MacArthur moved his headquarters up to Queensland—much closer to the battlefields. Suffering a shortage of men for a variety of essential skilled and unskilled work, he first proposed importing 'from China or India between two or three thousand Chinese labourers, drivers and clerks for work in New Guinea and Queensland.'[49] The Australian War Cabinet, with the government's White Australia policy clearly in mind, gave the proposal somewhat grudging and restrictive agreement in September 1943: 'Asiatic labour imported … may be employed on the mainland of Australia, but not south of the 20th parallel, nor permanently anywhere on the mainland.'[50]

It turned out that Chinese labour was not going to be easy to acquire from these sources, so MacArthur made a second proposal. The Services, his representative, Colonel Kramer, pointed out, were 'in urgent need of a very large number of small ships, ranging from 25 ft. to 50 tons.' The parts were already being prefabricated in the US, 'shipped to Australia and assembled at shipyards to be established in Brisbane on the reaches of the Brisbane river.' What was needed was appropriate labour, and the man who would control the project had overseen similar projects 'in Singapore and elsewhere, [and] had always employed Chinese labour and found them superior for the type of work required, as they were peculiarly adapted to monotonous and repetitive work. It was therefore desired to employ Chinese labour solely on the undertaking.'[51] MacArthur wanted about five hundred men, though in the end triple that number worked for the US Army.[52]

The government agreed, and soon Chinese from the 7th Employment Company, from the Native Labour Company (Chinese) who had been working in the wolfram mines in the Northern Territory, and from manpower projects such as the Warragamba pipeline development outside Sydney, were being transported to Brisbane as well as to Townsville, another US base.[53] Those who had been in the Australian Military Forces were discharged, and immediately signed on to work for the US Army, 'to be employed as carpenters, fitters, welders, etc'.[54] Louis Wong, a wireless operator on a ship whose crew was stranded in Fremantle in December 1941, became a Corporal in the 7th Company. In the 1980s he recalled that period of his life:

> We were in the Australian army for about eighteen months and then more useful work was found for us. The US army, stationed at Brisbane, needed us to work for them to build small ships for the counter-offensive against the Japanese in the Pacific Islands. So we were transferred to Brisbane ... There we were discharged from the Australian army and we worked for the US army as civilians and got the award rate ... As a wireless operator, I knew the fundamentals of electricity and I was employed as an electrician, repairing welding equipment.[55]

To their considerable satisfaction, the men found that their pay—now at least £6 2s 6d a week—was much better than in the Australian Army (six shillings a day) or when they laboured on manpower projects. Their working conditions were also much improved.

Dennis Burchill, a young Brisbane boy at the time, remembers the Chinese working on the small ships at Bulimba shipyard:

> The workforce comprised about 800 Chinese labourers who were housed in barracks built along Baldwin Street and terraced down the hill. The barges that they were building were about sixty feet long by about 25 feet wide. They had a chisel bow at each end. The barges had one refrigeration cold room at each end with a self-contained

> plant room in the middle. One cold room was for frozen goods while the other was for perishables. The barges were designed to be taken as deck cargo to New Guinea and then towed by tugs to where they were needed. As soon as an island was secured by the yanks around the corner would come the barge loaded with coca-cola and ice cream. As the barges were steel, the Chinese were taught to weld and they worked three eight hour shifts. At six o'clock every morning, (which was the change of shift) the whole district would be awakened by loud Chinese music blasting over the speakers.
>
> The entrance to the Chinese camp was at the end of Hood Street. Just outside the front gate the yanks put in a recreation hut which was about forty foot long and about two feet off the ground. The Chinese filled it up with all types of gambling tables and games. The building had a hardwood floor with large gaps between each plank. We [the children] would set ourselves up at about 7pm under the hut and wait for the coins to start dropping through the floor boards. Once a coin dropped through the cracks the Chinese wrote it off. It helped to supplement the pocket money.[56]

Outside of working hours, the US Army allowed the men considerable freedom. Quickly, word of the good pay and conditions spread to their comrades in other places. The Security Service, already concerned about the influence of the Chinese Workers' Club and the Chinese Seamen's Union,[57] and with a list of Chinese who were 'not amenable to control,'[58] 'ring-leaders', 'trouble-makers', 'malcontents'[59] and 'undesirables',[60] now had another problem. According to a telegraphed report:

> [Chinese] members of same unit now at [Mount] Isa are receiving letters from their discharged friends urging come and join [us]... Unit exceedingly restless and on the verge of refusing duty. Oriental mind cannot follow logic of such diverse conditions of pay between two masters. They request to be allowed to join their friends at US rates of pay, which is natural and to be expected. One section actually refused to obey order [to] proceed to Dunmara for duty. So

> far dissension has not spread to detachments at Larrimah but will assuredly happen ... Position difficult as undesirable [to] place whole unit under arrest. Chinese have very strong sense of justice and think we are exploiting them. [61]

Similar expressions of discontent came from the men in the Chinese Labour Corps in the Northern Territory. Fung Hoi, who with 600 other Chinese was rescued from Nauru by a French ship, landed in Brisbane, and later worked as a cook for the Chinese wolfram miners in Hatches Creek. He remembered the men as unhappy about the low pay and poor living conditions, as well as the contemptuous treatment by some of their bosses. 'Our fellows were angry... They felt insulted.'[62] Despite their distance from major population centres, they were also politically alert. An official observed that the men blamed negative reports about them on the government, 'which they believe is planning to prejudice Australian opinion against the Chinese as an answer to any campaign against the White Australia Policy.'[63]

For all these reasons, Fung Hoi and his fellow Chinese miners were keen to work for the US Army. Like the 7th Company men, they found both their pay and conditions much improved at the US Army camps at Townsville and Brisbane. 'I'd never had such good wages in my life,' said Fung Hoi. 'We lived in army huts just like US soldiers, and wore US uniform ... the conditions were very good ... Our job was to build boats for the US army.'[64]

For the Australian Government, the transfer of the Chinese from the Australian Army to the US Army did not end its responsibilities for these men. Arrangements were made with the US Army's Intelligence Section to keep the Australian Security Service 'informed concerning hiring and firing of Chinese in their employ'[65]—although it appears, from Security files, that cooperation was at best haphazard.[66] And when trouble arose in their new employ, as over some notorious tinned fish, it was the Australian authorities who oversaw negotiations.

In a detailed report from the District Security Officer to his superiors, titled 'Unrest Among Chinese Employed By U.S. Army' and stamped 'Confidential', we learn that 'trouble has been simmering for some time at the Chinese Camp at Armstrong Paddock [Townsville].'[67] A key issue was food: inadequate rice rations, and tinned fish packed in Hong Kong—the latter appropriately described as a 'bone of contention with Armstrong Paddock Chinese.'[68] On 14 July 1944 a high-level visit to the camp was arranged; it included an Australian Security officer and Professor KL Chau, Director of the Chinese Ministry for Information in Australia. Professor Chau gave grudging assent to the rice ration, but both he and the Security Officer were unimpressed by the tinned fish:

> A sample tin was opened. It had a rather nauseating odour and the contents looked dry and shrunken. The taste was unpleasant, and it was hard to conceive that it would be acceptable to any palate. The Chinese had consistently refused to eat it after the first meal.[69]

Unfortunately, the fish had been 'pronounced edible' by US Army authorities. It was therefore necessary for Professor Chau and the Security Officer to meet with US Army Lieutenant Colonel Halstead the next day. After 'an exchange of compliments', Halstead pointed out that the fish, together with other foodstuff, had been bought from the Australian Government 'as suitable food for the Chinese'. Some of the other foods were weevil-infested or otherwise rotten, and had to be destroyed. 'The fish had been certified as edible but of doubtful palatability by the appropriate U.S. officer', who was then called in. More tins were produced and opened. It was solemnly agreed one 'line' of fish was palatable. The US Lieutenant Colonel insisted that 'the U.S. Army could not destroy or write off the fish as long as its own officers could not condemn the consignment.'[70] Stalemate.

In his report, the Security Officer shows that he understands the larger implications of this comical saga. 'There seems to be some danger that this little problem may develop into an awkward situation involving some considerable repercussions,' he writes. 'This situation is likely to develop into serious trouble if the agitators in the camp can work upon the men. They are liable to represent this dispute over food with the other disputes over transport and holidays as national slights due to white people treating Chinese as a lower and servile race.'[71]

A Security operative noted solemnly, 'there is a disturbing element fermenting trouble.'[72] Fermenting or fomenting? Perhaps the unintentional slip was occasioned by disturbing reports of the Chinese enjoying Australian beer, as well as spending time in 'gambling dens'[73] and opium smoking.[74] Drinking sometimes led to brawls. One such event, at a hotel in Bulimba run by a Mrs McFadden, Security reports as involving 'a number of Europeans and about 1,000 Chinese from the Camp. One Australian soldier was stabbed and several Chinese injured.'[75] A local resident offers a somewhat different perspective:

> The Chinese workers caused quite a lot of friction with the local workers. The yanks paid them well and they always had plenty of money. As beer in those days was rationed and was only served in sessions, the Chinese who had worked all night would have a sleep and then stroll down to the Balmoral Pub when the session started. When the meatworkers and the stockmen arrived after work they found that the Chinese had downed most of the beer on tap. This led to several nasty brawls with the stockmen chasing them down Oxford Street on their horses and hitting them with palings that they had ripped off fences.[76]

To add to government and military aggravation, newspapers such as *Truth* and the *Sunday Mail* inflamed popular prejudice against the Chinese working for the US Army. There were stories asserting that these non-white aliens were taking over businesses in Brisbane, and threatening this law-abiding city with oriental crime.[77] *Smith's Weekly*, notoriously racist, targeted the Chinese camp at Bulimba, declaring the men were over-paid and under-worked, with privileges unavailable to other residents of Brisbane.[78] Security reported that 'one of the newspapers is preparing material in an attempt to prove that there is to be a co-ordinated attack on the "White Australia Policy" by Chinese now resident in Australia.'[79]

Such troubles occupied the time of Australian officials, but the Americans were largely satisfied with their Chinese labour force. They probably never saw a statement sent to Security from an unhappy local shipbuilder, a Mr A Wright. After three pages of complaints about the lazy Chinese and the excessively lenient Americans, he concluded: 'I set about observing them closely and found that only about 10% were any good. The majority we found, much to our regret, to be lazy, insolent, disobedient, untruthful and thieves.'[80]

This negative assessment of the Chinese did not accord with the opinion of either the Australian or the American military. Among the former, there is evidence of regret at the loss of the Chinese to the US Army. An Australian military officer, reflecting on the movement of Chinese from the 7th Employment Company to the US Army in May 1943, regarded the shift as 'unfortunate, as Chinese are excellent workers and have given most satisfactory service in Labour units.'[81] Security even suggested that 'some American officers' had encouraged Chinese dissatisfaction, presumably in order to lure them to United States employ.[82] The fact that an ex-Secretary of the Chinese Seamen's Union was Superintendent of the Chinese section of the United States Small Ships workforce at Bulimba was another sore point for Security.[83]

For the American Army, the approximately 1550 Chinese aliens[84] employed by the Small Ships Branch at Bulimba in Brisbane, and Armstrong's Paddock in Townsville, provided the essential labour to build the small boats that carried supplies to American and Australian forces fighting in the Pacific. Designed so that they could manoeuvre through the coral reefs, and largely manned by Australians (wearing American uniform and serving under the American flag), they were, according to one commentator, 'the lifeline of the Allied armies' advance in New Guinea':[85]

> A lifeline of the allied troops at the front, the Small Ships carried up guns and ammunition, bully beef and biscuits, fuel, army tanks and tents. They took up fresh troops, and returned with tired, sick, wounded soldiers, and those killed in action.[86]

While the European war ended in May 1945, Japan did not surrender until August. By the end of October, all the Chinese aliens who had worked for the US Army were discharged, and once again were the responsibility of the Australian Government. To the annoyance of the government, many of these men continued to demand justice. The Queensland branch of the Demobilised Sailors, Soldiers and Airmen's Association of Australia wrote to the Minister for the Army on 23 October on behalf of approximately two hundred 7th Employment Company men who believed they were owed pay in lieu of leave. The Association declared 'the boys concerned are all of a high intellectual character', and concluded that in view of 'the wonderful help the Chinese have given to our lads overseas during their trials as prisoners-of-war, we feel that your Department should leave no stone unturned to see that these boys get what is justly theirs.'[87]

Not only did the army reject the validity of the Chinese soldiers' complaint, but very soon the Australian Government was shipping out refugee Chinese in large numbers. As a brief letter in June 1945 from the Director-General of Security to the Secretary of the Department of Interior made clear, the Chinese being discharged from US Army service and living in various parts of the country 'remain … under the Aliens Security Regulations … prohibited immigrants.'[88]

More generally, the White Australia policy was being implemented by the Labor government with considerable diligence, led by the Minister for Immigration, Arthur Calwell. While the government had made clear as early as March 1944 that the application of 'white internees' to settle in Australia would be considered 'on their merits',[89] no such opportunity was offered to the Chinese. In December 1945, two ships took 1600 Chinese back to Hong Kong; others went later.[90] Captain J McNeir, from the US Army, was reported as saying that many of the Chinese had 'wives and families in China, Singapore, and the Pacific Islands. They were now earning no money and were eager to return home.'[91] Rankine suggests that most went willingly, for reasons such as readily available work in overseas ports,[92] and she estimates no more than about one hundred and twenty remained in Australia—working, married to Australian women, or too ill to travel.[93] But a number of Chinese and Indonesians challenged Calwell's determination to deport them.[94] Some did so actively, testing the deportation law in courts and garnering considerable public support. Others quietly disappeared into the community.

To enhance the government's legal authority to deport aliens, Calwell introduced the Aliens Deportation Act in 1946, and the War-Time Refugees Removal Act in 1949. At that point, the major focus of the government was the deportation of non-whites. But Calwell's insistence 'that people who had the status of non-British aliens should be liable for deportation on the basis of poor character or conduct no matter how long they had been settled in Australia' had an enduring effect on Australia's immigration policy.[95]

# 9

# Refugees and rebels: Indonesians and Timorese in Employment Companies

## Indonesians

*Refugees and Rebels: Indonesian Exiles in Wartime Australia* is the title of one of the few extensive published studies of the more than five thousand Indonesians who spent some of the war years in Australia.[1] The book's author, Jan Lingard, comments that it was 'the exigencies of war' that enabled 'natives' from a number of Asian countries to come to this country despite the government's passionate commitment to the White Australia policy.[2] And there is added irony that among these refugee 'natives' were a group who rebelled against European domination in their own country and ultimately helped influence Australia's foreign policy.[3]

Almost all these Indonesians—men, and some women and children—were brought to Australia by their colonial masters, the Netherlands East Indies (NEI) Government seeking refuge from the Japanese invasion of Indonesia in March 1942. The Australian journalist Rupert Lockwood, himself a radical and an active participant in the political struggles of the period, wrote that the Dutch brought with them, 'in merchant ships, warships and aircraft, thousands of

Indonesian servicemen, clerks, medical orderlies and merchant seamen. With the Indonesians were imported the frictions of a stratified colonial society.'[4] Brisbane became the official base for the NEI Government, thereby making Australia the site of a colonial government-in-exile.

The story of the more than five hundred Indonesians[5] who were enlisted in the 36th Employment Company in January 1943 is peppered with complaints and misunderstandings, as a result of two governments—Australian and Dutch— struggling to administer these men in tandem. There was also the irritant—from the NEI Government's point of view—of growing Indonesian nationalism among the men.

Among the refugees who arrived with the Dutch was a special group of over six hundred political prisoners—mostly Indonesians 'guilty' of pro-independence activities. They included Mohamad Bondan, who was shortly to become a leading figure in the Australian campaign for Indonesian independence. He had been arrested by the Dutch in 1933 and imprisoned until 1943, when he was brought to Australia and interned at Cowra for eight months.[6]

Freed from imprisonment in what was then NEI-controlled west New Guinea,[7] these were the men who most worried the Dutch authorities—and with good reason: many had not lost their convictions, nor their capacity to organise, and they came to play a significant role in the local campaigns for an independent Indonesia.[8]

Initially, a large number of Indonesians were interned in the Cowra prisoner-of-war camp in New South Wales and the detention centre at Loveday in South Australia.[9] Alongside the political prisoners were many Indonesian seamen who, within a month of arriving in Australia, and supported by the Australian Seamen's Union, were on strike, 'demanding Australian standards of pay.'[10] Their imprisonment, requested by the Dutch Consul, was legitimised under a special provision of the Australian National Security (Aliens Control) Regulations, which gave the government the power to arrest and detain alien seamen who deserted or were 'absent without leave' from their ships.[11]

Protests from the Australian Seamen's Union and civil libertarians encouraged the release of the seamen, and the Dutch authorities were forced to improve their conditions and salaries.[12] Still, many of the men, like their Chinese counterparts, refused to go back to sea—it was too dangerous.

The Australian Government had felt obliged to accede to the NEI demands for imprisonment, but the Australian military was not convinced that internment was the best solution. The response of the Adjutant-General was typically pragmatic:

> I am of [the] opinion that these Javanese [Indonesians were often called 'Javanese' in Australia] seamen should not be allowed to remain in internment camps as it depletes the reserve of accommodation, and also on account of the difficulty of employing greater numbers than are already accommodated without materially increasing guards and escorts.[13]

Instead, suggested the senior officer, they could be employed 'as Labour units' and 'paid at their ordinary rates of pay'—that is, their previous rates as merchant seamen—if the NEI Government agreed.[14] This proposal was accepted by the Dutch authorities in Australia, possibly encouraged by the occasional prods from the Australian Council for Civil Liberties (ACCL). In his annual report in 1943, the secretary of the ACCL, Brian Fitzpatrick, referred to cases the organisation had taken up in 1942 and 1943 that included seamen — Dutch subjects— 'who had been treated unjustly by various authorities'.[15] A letter from Fitzpatrick inquiring about the release of Indonesians from Cowra annoyed Dr van der Plas, a leading figure in the NEI Government, although he acknowledged the letter was 'couched in courteous terms'.[16] Fitzpatrick was able to inform the members of the ACCL that most of the cases of injustice to these men 'were pushed to satisfactory conclusion.'[17] However, it is likely the military's advice to the Australian Government was a more potent reason for the freeing of the Indonesians than Fitzpatrick's eloquent advocacy.

The same National Security (Aliens Control) Regulations that were used to imprison the Indonesians gave the government the authority to put them to work. As the Lieutenant-Colonel who was Director of Prisoners of War pointed out:

> Paragraph (3) of Regulation 14 a. of the National Security (Aliens Control) Regulations provides that any alien detained in pursuance of such Regulation may be employed on such labour and in such place as the Minister from time to time determines. [18]

At first, it was suggested that the Indonesians be employed by the Allied Works Council, a civilian authority. This proposal received the qualified approval of the Director of Military Intelligence. Security had no objection to the use of the Javanese to undertake work such as 'constructing strategic roads in Queensland', he wrote, but they must only be employed 'in an area from which they can be quickly evacuated in the event of an invasion'. It was not the Indonesians he sought to protect from the invaders, but the Australian forces on whom they might become 'an encumbrance'.[19]

Instead, it was into the newly formed 36th Employment Company that the Indonesians were inducted in January 1943. As 'militarised civil labour', they were based at Wallangarra, Helidon, Blackbutt and Toowoomba in Queensland.[20] While the Captain, Lieutenants and Sergeants were all Australian Army personnel, one officer was provided by the Royal Netherlands East Indies Army. It was this Dutch 'liaison' officer who was responsible for 'the administration and maintenance of discipline' of the Indonesians.[21] It was he and his staff, including six interpreters temporarily holding the rank of Sergeant, who were to give the orders and ensure they were obeyed. Punishment, according to the Company regulations, was theirs to enforce:

> The powers of punishment prescribed for a Korps-Commandant under the regulations at present in force for Royal Netherlands Indies Army Forces has been delegated to the liaison officer and the interpreters. [22]

Was there another Company in the Australian Army in which such authority was delegated to representatives of a foreign country? This was a situation quite different from that of the other alien Employment Companies. There, non-citizens could be promoted to Corporal—and, on rare occasions, to Sergeant—but were never a separate source of command, and officers certainly could not impose punishments according to the military rules of another nation. Little wonder that the 36th Employment Company was, from its beginnings, a site of confusion and conflict.

Like other Employment Company men, the Indonesians were issued with clothing—in their case, generally much too large.[23] The work they undertook was essentially similar to that of alien Employment Companies elsewhere. In Toowoomba, a major centre for both Australian and American forces, the men were kept busy loading and unloading supplies. For the 353 men sent to the small town of Wallangarra, on the Queensland–New South Wales border, it was loading and unloading trains—yet another place where old colonial rivalries had resulted in two differently gauged railway lines meeting at the border. According to one account, 'during WW2 thousands of Allied troops passed through Wallangarra Railway Station on their way north or south. Due to wartime secrecy arrangements, railway staff were only given about 2 hours' notice of the arrival of a troop train. This gave the dedicated railway staff enough time to cook and serve on arrival, hearty meals of sausages, mashed potato and gravy.'[24] (This is a reminder that the difficulties facing 'alien' soldiers included the strange new foods they were expected to cook and eat. For these Muslim soldiers, there appears to have been no provision of *halal* food.) The men handled stores and ammunition, though, like all the alien Companies, they themselves were not armed.[25]

Weaponry featured in the work at Blackbutt, where the men reconditioned spent shells, and at Helidon, near Toowoomba, where the military had established an area for the storage of armaments, and the demolition and burial of unwanted explosives of various kinds.[26] They were also engaged in the many other tasks required to maintain the base. Mohamad Bondan worked at Helidon. His Australian wife, Molly Bondan—also known as Aussie Molly[27]—later wrote of him and his army mates 'shifting cases, loading and unloading trucks, keeping tallies … and the like.'[28] According to Lingard, the men at Blackbutt wore 'Australian army uniforms dyed prisoner-of-war maroon for work', but looked smart in sarongs and white jackets when socialising in the town.[29]

Within a couple of months of the formation of the 36th Employment Company, the Captain was writing to the Major-General in charge of the Queensland region, pointing out some problems. One was clothing. The men were meant to be issued with two pairs of dungarees per person, but the supply provided by Ordnance Services was inadequate. That wasn't the only inadequacy:

> In view of the extreme cold weather at Centres where the Javanese are stationed … it is suggested that a special issue of a Service Uniform be provided for the Indonesian personnel of the Company …

To persuade the Major-General that this wasn't merely—or even mainly—for the comfort of the men, the Captain outlined the disciplinary value of his proposal:

> This will, in addition of providing the men with clothes to go on leave, also be the means of identification, so that some method of control can be exercised by the Military Authorities over the Indonesians when away from their Camp. At present, because of the state of wear of their working dress, the boys are allowed to wear their civilian clothes and it is very difficult for the Military Police to determine whether these men are civilian or Militarised Civil Labour. Cases have come to my notice where many of the Javanese have been found visiting townships many miles from their Encampment.[30]

Having made clear his disapproval of the Indonesians feeling free to move beyond the centres in which they were based, the Captain proceeded to ask for recreation huts at the four camps, as well as canteens. The latter were important, he explained, because the Indonesians 'are not expected to partake of Canteen Comforts in company with Australian personnel.' He did not allow 'the natives' to fraternise with Australian personnel, he insisted, because 'it would be inadvisable for disciplinary reasons.'[31]

All too soon, this Captain and his superior officers would discover that 'the natives' were more than capable of making trouble without the assistance of traditionally rumbustious Australians, in or out of uniform.

There were some minor episodes of attempted sabotage at Blackbutt,[32] and a much more serious attempted assassination at Wallangarra. According to the military record of the event:

> Soon after midnight on 5 July 43, a hand grenade was thrown and exploded in the 36 Employment Coy, Camp Area Wallangarra. This grenade exploded within a foot of the entrance to an American Type Tent, occupied by … Pte. Hookeywin W.A. a member of the 3 A.A.O.D. [Australian Army Ordnance Department] who is attached to the Coy. The grenade riddled the tent and narrowly missed the occupant … This is the culmination of numerous explosions which have taken place during the last few weeks and was no doubt an attempt to kill Pte. Hookeywin.[33]

(Private Hookeywin, an Australian, not only survived the grenade attack but ended the war as a Corporal.)

Despite an official inquiry, no one appears to have been convicted of the grenade offences. The Camp Staff Officer reporting the event commented that in his opinion, 'the Javanese had no more reason to attempt to kill this soldier than any other, but … his tent was the closest and easiest to get at.'[34] If his assessment was correct, the relationship between the Indonesians and the Australians attached to the Company was sometimes less than comradely.

Such a dramatic event might temporarily have overshadowed a much more widespread grievance among the Indonesians in the 36th Employment Company: pay. A convoluted story, it began when a Dutch officer promised the men, while they were still prisoners at Cowra, that they would receive the same wage in the 36th Employment Company as that of other Australian soldiers (including 'alien' soldiers in other Employment Companies): 6s 6d a day.[35] This amount was initially confirmed by Australian officers of the Company.[36]

The Australian Government had other ideas. At first, they planned to pay the Indonesians only 1s 5d a day, but after protests, they decided on three shillings. This was recommended by the army, together with £2 4s a month 'towards the purchase of small commodities in their canteen.'[37] How was the daily wage calculated? According to the military, 'though it is not the absolute lowest initial salary (minus all bonuses) paid on the K. P. M.[38] [Dutch] ships, it corresponds roughly to the salary (minus war bonus) paid to ordinary servants on board, the class to which these labourers belong.'[39] Indonesian seamen had been 'translated' into 'ordinary servants', and thus could be paid less. Yet, army officers responsible for the men's work were reported as being 'very satisfied by the work done by the labourers'.[40]

When even the small extra amount of pay was not received, nor the back pay that had been promised, the protests intensified. On behalf of the men in the 36th, Boestami, described as 'leader of the Indonesians of this Coy',[41] wrote to both the Dutch and the Australian governments. After setting out the history of the payment imbroglio, he makes a claim for equal pay (with a few odd spellings, possibly the result of the poor spelling of a translator):

> Seeing we are no longer Internees and are not enemy-prisoners and are doing the same exentual (sic) duties as the Australian-army has been doing, we consider we are quite intitled to the same pay 6/6 shilling per day, which was promised to us by the Dutch-Officer when we left the Internment-Camp Cowra to come to this work.[42]

The argument over pay dragged on for months. It may well have been a contributing factor to the acts of sabotage and violence. More than a year after the polite letter from Boestami on behalf of his fellow

'Indonesian workers' in the 36th Employment Company, Dr van der Plas, signing himself Netherlands Indies Chief Commissioner, wrote directly to the Minister for the Army, the Right Honourable FM Forde. After pointing out that earlier he had recommended the men be paid seven shillings a day because of the 'really hard work' required of them, he declared that the matter had become urgent:

> ... while thus far I have been able to prevent action by the people concerned who have direct relations, not only with the communist party, but also with several labour unions, I fear that, unless their reasonable objections against what by all labour standards in Australia is serious underpay, are eliminated, we are in for unpleasant publicity which would do harm and for which from our side we could not be held responsible. [43]

Van der Plas' letter seems to have been an attempt to shame—or frighten—the Australian Government into agreeing to pay the men the rate then standard for soldiers undertaking heavy work.[44] It failed. So did his telegram eighteen days later, in which he tells the Minister that one Indonesian who refused to work for three shillings has been 'locked up in a cell', and that he fears 'further trouble if unfavourable decision maintained.'[45] The army remained obdurate, using the argument that the Indonesians' 'standard of efficiency and the type of work performed' didn't justify the pay rise, and noting that 'rations and clothing are issued free by the Commonwealth'.[46] At this point, the NEI Government gives up, and van der Plas writes again to the Minister for the Army, telling him that 'to prevent serious trouble', it will pay the men doing the hard work the extra four shillings.[47]

Not surprisingly, this did not restore harmony in the 36th. As the Quartermaster-General pointed out, 'some personnel in this Company will be in receipt of 3/- per day and others 7/- per day. Obviously dissension will arise and as a result thereof it is anticipated that further difficulties will be involved in the near future.'[48] Indeed, the men's complaints about underpayment, and later about the non-payment of moneys owing, were still being heard as late as May 1944, when some were gradually released from the 36th into a number of the army's Works Companies, and others back under Netherlands East Indies command.[49] The loss of these men was regretted by the army because of its 'serious affect [on] the labour programme' (no mention here of the Indonesians' supposed lack of efficiency), but was reluctantly accepted in order to maintain 'the friendly cooperation of our allies.'[50] The 36th Employment Company (by then renamed as a Works Company) was disbanded on 31 May 1945.[51]

While inadequate and unjust levels of pay was a running sore for the duration of this Company, for some of the men there was an even more important issue: the future independence of Indonesia. According to Mrs Laura Gapp, of the Civil Rights League, the men she initially met 'behind barbed wire' at the Liverpool prison camp were constantly talking about the end of Dutch rule in their home country: 'We shall return to Indonesia – but the Dutch? Never.'[52]

Mohamad Bondan, who had been imprisoned by the NEI Government before the war for his opposition to Dutch colonial rule, is credited with being one of the first to publicise the news of Soekarno's declaration of Indonesian independence on 17 August 1945, just two days after the announcement of the Japanese surrender.[53] The news spread quickly among the Indonesians, and Indonesian Independence Committees were formed in cities across the country, with Brisbane—holding the largest number of Indonesians—the site of the Central Committee for Independence. (This was the same city in which the Dutch had earlier established their government-in-exile.) The leaders of this independence movement came largely from men who had served in the 36th Employment Company.

These men became part of a larger story, their campaign to support the fledgling independent state linked with that of radical and anti-colonial groups in the Australian community. The Communist Party of Australia's newspaper, *Tribune*, edited by Rupert Lockwood, was the first to publicly support the cause of Indonesian independence;[54] and the Australia–Indonesia Society, established late in 1944 in Sydney 'to educate Australians about Asia and Asians about Australia',[55] played an increasingly active role. One of its leaders, Molly Warner, together with Mohamad Bondan (whom she later married), helped set up the Centre for Indonesian Intelligence in Brisbane in September 1945. The Centre received broadcasts from Indonesia and distributed press releases. It had close contacts with the more radical unions.[56]

Indonesians refused to man the NEI ships that the Dutch were planning to return to Indonesia, to restore their colonial regime with soldiers and weapons. The Australian Waterside Workers' Federation then placed a ban on the ships. This ban of the Black Armada, as Lockwood called it, was, in Molly Bondan's view, critical. In an interview given many years later, she declared:

> Had there been no strike against Dutch ships in Australia the whole history of the republic would have been a different one … It would have been a much more complicated struggle if not for the strike.[57]

Ultimately, the strike received the support of the Australian Labor government. In parliament, the Prime Minister, Ben Chifley, made the government's—and the labour movement's—position clear:

> The hold-up of ships bound for Javanese ports is a matter between the Dutch authorities and their own subjects. Indonesians refuse to work those ships. If the Dutch authorities cannot make their own subjects do the job, I can easily imagine that the subjects of another country are not likely to take action which might be regarded as 'scabbing'.[58]

Later, the government's position against the re-establishment of Dutch rule in Indonesia hardened. Chifley declared in Parliament that 'the old order in Indonesia will not go on.'[59] This policy was reflected in the actions of a ship's captain whose response to Dutch demands gained some publicity at the time. When the *Manoora*, an Australian ship bringing Indonesians back to their country, was confronted by armed Dutch soldiers demanding those Indonesians who had once been the

NEI Government's prisoners be handed over, the ship's captain, Allan Paterson Cousin, refused. He said:

> I brought these Indonesians from Australia and I have been trusted by our Australian Government to hand them over to the Indonesian Republic and no one else.[60]

One of the Australian seamen on the ship recalled the outcome:

> All the former political prisoners of the Dutch and any others who might be in danger of reprisals were escorted by Gurkhas [from the British Army] at Captain Cousin's request, to Republican territory, about 60 miles from Batavia. Women and children were escorted ashore later.[61]

In 1947 the Immigration Minister, Arthur Calwell, boasted (not entirely accurately) that 'every Indonesian left these shores voluntarily':[62]

> I did not have to issue a single deportation order against one of them. And when they landed in Indonesia, they were handed over to their own people. They were not delivered into the hands of any persons who might exact revenge upon them because of their political opinions.[63]

The Indonesians were part of the Australian Army for only two-and-a-half years.[64] Yet, from a political perspective, they could be regarded as the most influential of all the 'alien' groups who served in the military during World War II. Their presence in this country, and their vigorous public refusal to return to a Dutch-ruled Indonesia, helped change Australian government policy. For the first time in Australia's history, its government supported the legitimacy of an indigenous population in Asia to create its own government against the claims of a European power.

## Timorese (Koepangese)

Of all the aliens in the Employment Companies, the Timorese—often called Koepangese[65]—have received the least attention. Their period as members of an Employment Company is also the shortest. From modest archival sources, as well as the research of a number of scholars,[66] it is possible to garner some details of the contribution of the 'natives' and 'half-castes' (as one official report referred to them)[67] to the military—in their case, initially in the 23rd Employment Company.

When, in February 1942, the Japanese invaded Timor, an island in the Malay Archipelago between Australia and Indonesia, two European powers controlled the country. East Timor was a Portuguese colony, West Timor belonged to the Dutch. The Portuguese Government had opted for neutrality, but despite this, the Japanese military overran both parts of Timor. Australian soldiers who had entered the country before the invasion, with the support of the Dutch, maintained a guerrilla campaign in East Timor for some months, with the essential aid of local Timorese.[68] This support was not mentioned in the statement from the Governor-General, Lord Gowrie, when he thanked the army for 'the bold and enterprising detachments in TIMOR', which 'harassed the enemy and delayed their development of that island for many months.'[69]

Some of the Timorese men, together with others who had served the colonial regimes, were included in the evacuation of Portuguese and Dutch to the safety of Australia.[70] One scholar estimates that more than six hundred Portuguese and Timorese escaped to Australia from Portuguese Timor alone.[71] When the army, in May 1942, determined an urgent need for fourteen additional Labour Companies 'for work of national importance in the handling of cargoes at ship's side or in transit to and from the various Australian ports', the Koepangese were allocated to the 23rd Employment Company, based in Western Australia.[72]

While the name 'Koepangese' was attached to this Company in official documents, its composition included men from other parts of the Malay Archipelago.[73] One example is Amat Bin Abu, whose name is listed on the Honour Roll of the Australian War Memorial in Canberra because he died of an illness while in the Company. His birthplace is given as Boyan, an area in Malaysia. Another is Samsudin bin Katib, who gave his birthplace as Sumatra. Before the war, he had been a pearl diver in Broome.[74]

The War Diary of the 23rd Employment Company is incomplete, and brief—ending in February 1943 and commenting mostly on the movement of officers. There is one reference to five men sent for 'lugger work', another five men to be trained as cooks, and one man transferred to enlist with the Dutch Navy Authority. In February 1943 four officers and fifty-three men were moved to the 12th Employment Company.[75] Four months later, these Koepangese were transferred to the 3rd Australian Water Transport Company (Small Craft).[76] It was most probably from this Company that a number of the Koepangese were recruited into 'Z' Special Unit, which attempted a guerrilla war against the Japanese in Timor.[77] One of the many Special Operations to Timor was code-named 'Lagarto'; on 1 July 1943 a small boat with 'Portuguese, Timorese and one Australian signaller' landed in Timor. The men were captured by the Japanese on 29 September.[78] The account of this Operation describes the cruel treatment of the Australians, but no mention is made of the fate of the Portuguese or Timorese.

A search of the World War II Nominal Roll[79] using the names of Timorese and Malay members of Z Force indicates that a number were initially in the 23rd Employment Company, and many others, though not similarly labelled, enrolled in the same place and around the same time as these men.[80] One of these men was Samsudin bin Katib.

The official record marks February 1943 as the date on which the 23rd Company was disbanded. And yet, the record of a number of the men serving in the 23rd lists them as discharged as late as March 1945.[81] After the war, 580 Timorese were repatriated to Portuguese Timor.[82] Most of the rest were sent back in November 1945 aboard the SS *Angola*.[83] There is still much to learn about the men who served in this Company.

# 10

# Antagonists, allies and advocates

Times of danger encourage paranoia. The war, which for a time appeared to lead to the threat of Japanese invasion, heightened the public expression of suspicion, fear and sometimes loathing of foreigners, especially those who came from an enemy country. In March 1942 the leader of the Country Party, Arthur Fadden, demanded that the government 'intern all [male] aliens in Australia, excluding nationals of our Allies and friendly nations'; that female enemy aliens should be investigated and their activities restricted; and an inquiry be established into the granting of naturalisation certificates for the past five years.[1]

With Australians dying in battle abroad and digging air-raid shelters at home, it might be expected that not only politicians but the media and community leaders would settle for the supposed wisdom of 'better safe than sorry', and accept that aliens would best be constrained for the greater public good. It is a measure of the complex relationship between principle, prejudice and pragmatism in this period that the story does not follow quite such a simple trajectory.

There was certainly no shortage of public urgings and warnings about the danger of foreigners in our midst. In May 1940 the Melbourne *Age* printed a letter from a man from South Yarra:

> I went to the front in 1914 to fight for the protection of the British Empire and freedom of Australia and my children, not to have this country taken possession of by foreigners. I appeal to returned men and their wives, and all Australian women who have families to think of, to wake up and help check foreign invasion out. Teach your children every day, Australia for Australians.[2]

If this man's viewpoint was common among World War I ex-servicemen, it helps explain the generally anti-foreign position of the ex-servicemen's organisation, the Returned Sailors', Soldiers' and Airmen's Imperial League (RSSAILA)—described by the historian Geoffrey Bolton as 'the most powerful pressure group in Australia' then and for many decades.[3] Some RSSAILA state branches called for the internment of all aliens, including those who were naturalised—they could be spies, according to Mr John Black, a member of the RSSAILA's New South Wales State Council. He insisted that it was better to have ninety-nine innocent refugees in safekeeping than to allow a single guilty one to be free.[4] This position was supported by E Hardy Johnston in a letter to the *Sydney Morning Herald*, the day after Black's statement was reported in the paper:

> Love of country is the first thing instilled into man from birth, therefore we should be doubly careful even of the naturalized alien. Country of birth will always come first. Internment should not be regarded as a penalty but as a sacrifice towards victory undergone willingly by those refugees who are loyal.[5]

In 1942 the RSSAILA was still passing resolutions demanding that the government abolish internees' right of appeal, warning darkly of 'the danger of subversive activities [by aliens] in canneries and pulping factories', and calling on branches 'to co-operate in stirring up public opinion towards general acceptance of the proposals'.[6] The Mosman RSSAILA sub-branch—displaying the RSSAILA's motto, 'The Price of Liberty is Eternal Vigilance'—wrote to the Attorney-General, the

Right Honourable WM Hughes, in September 1941, demanding that 'all enemy aliens be de-franchised, as was done in the Great War of 1914-18'.[7] In February 1942 the chairman of the RAAF recruiting drive, Sir Donald Cameron, declared that no enemy aliens were to be admitted to the RAAF. Naturalization, he explained, 'does not enable an alien to overcome the barriers raised by his enemy origin'.[8]

Some ex-servicemen, and families of servicemen, were unhappy with the presence of aliens in any part of the military. In a letter sent to the Prime Minister, John Curtin, in April 1942, Mr SJ Barry from Leichhardt asserted that he had 'interviewed all sections of the community' on the subject. He then launched a verbal assault on the PM for:

> having clothed enemy nationals in the uniform of the Australian soldier which my son and other relations wear and respect. For me and others it is the work of clever enemy agents enjoying the confidence of the Federal Government ... Infiltration is a successful strategy of the enemy as you are well aware and here under your protection as Prime Minister in the Alien Labor Corp is an army organized and dressed in our military uniform ... [This is] treachery to our country.[9]

In response to such attitudes, one of the 8th Employment Company men, signing himself G.H.N., wrote to *The Age*:

> As a member of the Alien Labor Battalion I would like to express the indignation we feel at the suggestion that we should not be allowed to wear the same badge on our uniform as Australian soldiers do.
>
> We are just as much enemies of Nazi Germany as the Australians are, even more so. The greater part of us volunteered for service; in our company, for instance, every single man is a volunteer. In England, where a similar unit, the Pioneer Corps, was formed at the outbreak of war, there has never been a question of the Pioneers not being allowed to wear the English Army badge, although they are mainly Germans.

> I invite those gentlemen who feel so deeply concerned about us to come down to the docks with us at 5 o'clock every morning and work 12 hours seven days a week as we do. Perhaps they may change their opinion then.[10]

G.H.N. was George Hans Nadel, Viennese born, who after the war became a social and political historian writing about Australian colonial culture.[11] His letter in defence of aliens in the military (which somewhat exaggerated the 8th Employment Company's working conditions) was by no means an isolated example. Newspapers were the major news media of the time, and the metropolitan dailies, the weeklies and the smaller regional and local newspapers devoted space to matters concerning the circumstances of aliens. The letters columns in particular hummed with arguments on the subject, and there was also regular editorial comment.

*Truth*'s proprietor, Ezra Norton, had written a year before the war that 'We do not want Jewish refugees! ... As a racial group they are a menace to our nationhood and standards'.[12] The Melbourne *Argus* published two adjacent articles in May 1939 that neatly focused on prejudice against foreigners, especially Jews. The first article, under the heading 'Industrial Danger', presented the views of Sir Frank Clarke, President of the Victorian Legislative Council, who informed the annual meeting of the Malvern branch of the Australian Women's National League that 'the eastern European Jew was deficient in some of the qualities that made citizens of the British Empire'—these people lacked 'good physique and good education' and were not 'decent citizens'. The second article, titled 'Rich Refugees', reported that an officer on the ship *Nestor* had learned 'from a most reliable source' that the sixty-eight Jewish refugees on board had a 'total wealth of £173,000'.[13]

For some, Jews were not welcome, whether poor or rich. The police department in Carlton, a Melbourne working-class suburb with a considerable 'foreign' population, reported a series of attacks on Jews in the streets and in shops in June and July of 1943. The culprits—'street corner larrikin types' according to a senior detective[14]—mostly received good behaviour bonds. But after a report that 'the word "Jew" was cut into the glass of the Display Windows of three Jewish shop-keepers in Chapel St, Prahran', a note in July from the office of the Chief Inspector of Police to the department's Special Branch recommended that such incidents be investigated 'with a view to ascertaining if any persons in Melbourne are attempting to emulate certain overseas methods of propaganda.'[15] Chapel Street, Prahran, also required investigation by the Commonwealth Security Service in October of that year, when a Mr Riddell, a shopkeeper of second-hand goods, displayed anti-alien signs in his window. They included a picture of a body hanging from a tree with the text: 'This is what the German refugees will do to you and your children if they get a chance. Don't talk to Foreigners.'[16] Mr Riddell, according to the Security officer, was 'allowing his patriotism, if patriotism it is, to outweigh his sense of judgment in these matters.' He was asked to remove the 'offensive' material from his shop window.[17]

But Jews were by no means the only foreigners subject to newspaper—and local community—calumny. In 1942 *Smith's Weekly* was still publishing articles with headings such as 'Over-generous payments to refugees.'[18] Sydney's *Bondi Daily* devised a dramatic editorial in July 1940, addressed to the Prime Minister, Robert Menzies; it included the following capitalised exhortations:

> Do not, Mr. Menzies, unless you want to smash yourself and turn Australia again you – DO NOT, we say, PLACE ANY ENEMY ALIEN (naturalized or otherwise) IN ANY KEY POST, or any other post, IN ANY OF OUR WAR ENDEAVOURS … CLEANSE AUSTRALIA AT ONCE of all taint of foreign eney [sic] blood. You have already greatly annoyed countless thousands of good Australians, Mr. Menzies, by your inattention to this matter …[19]

This kind of editorial outburst certainly had some popular support. Even before Italy officially declared war on the UK and France in June 1940, there were attacks on Italian businesses. In May 1940 twenty women demonstrated in front of a Bondi fruit shop owned by a naturalised Italian. The *Sydney Morning Herald* reported that despite the owner putting up a notice that the money he received from sales of fruit would be donated to the Anzac Buffet in Hyde Park and to St Vincent's Hospital, 'this failed to satisfy the women. Their demonstration was so hostile and their remarks to persons entering the shop were so bitter that an ugly scene was threatened for several minutes. The proprietor tried to reason with the women but eventually was forced to close the shop.'[20] Once Italy was part of the Axis powers, public antipathy increased. In a case before the Aliens Tribunal, a lawyer described a threatening situation at Tennant Creek in the Northern Territory in June 1940, where 'a Vigilante Committee was in process of formation with the intention of running the Italians out of town'.[21] As late as October 1942, the New South Wales branch of the Security Service was warning the Aliens Classification and Advisory Committee against trusting naturalised Italians:

> So far as Italians are concerned, it has often been shown that naturalisation means little or nothing to them as far as loyalty to the Empire is concerned and when it is remembered that those of prior nationality of other enemy countries were born and bred in the enemy country, there is a strong presumption that their sympathies would lie in the ultimate with the country of their birth.[22]

With such widespread attitudes, it is not surprising that the 1942 report of those interned without trial listed Italians as the majority of internees.[23]

In a number of rural communities, self-interest played a part in the hostility to aliens. The Queensland Longreach and Ilfracombe Districts Patriotic Fund wrote to Prime Minister Menzies in 1940, urging the government of the 'NEED and the FAIRNESS of confiscating the property of unnaturalised Italians and Germans who are not pro-british' [*sic*], especially in North Queensland, and insisting that the confiscation of internees not be overturned after the war.[24] In the same year, in Western Australia, the Brunswick War Patriotic Committee from Brunswick Junction, a small farming community in the south-west of the state, passed a seven-point resolution at a meeting attended by 120 people. Points 1 and 2 preface the point that really matters:

> 1. That all people who have migrated to Australia from enemy countries within the last fifteen years be interned whether naturalised or not.
>
> 2. That their labour be utilised to further the country's was [sic] effort in the production of essential commodities.
>
> 3. In view of the serious shortage of agricultural labour due in part to enlistment in the A.I.F. the services of some of these enemy aliens be made available to farmers requiring them.[25]

There was prejudice and self-interest aplenty. None the less, significant sections of the media offered a less fearful and intolerant approach. The usually conservative Sydney *Daily Telegraph* published an article in July 1938 that welcomed the Évian international conference on political refugees as 'a sign there is still an international conscience', and suggested that Australia welcome some of the people 'fleeing before blind religious or racial or political persecution … [to] dismiss the right of homeless refugees to live is to turn back the clock of civilisation.'[26] The New South Wales-based *Sydney Morning Herald* seems to have been more inclined than the Victorian *Age* or *Argus* to editorialise quite early in favour of '[sorting] out the disloyal few [enemy aliens and refugees] and [letting] the majority help the war effort in a military or civilian capacity'.[27] In October 1943 the paper criticised the government for taking far too long—four years—to distinguish between refugees and genuine enemy aliens.[28] All three major dailies increasingly presented to their large readership factual information about government policy towards aliens, and some modestly supportive material that depicted most aliens as victims of fascism, and therefore eager and willing to help defeat the common enemy. This more sympathetic approach occasionally predated but largely echoed the shifts in government policy.

A similar trajectory occurred in a number of regional newspapers, where a friendlier attitude was sometimes the result of growing familiarity with aliens. The historian Bruce Pennay traces this shift in perspective in the pages of one such paper, the *Border Morning Mail*, based in Albury, where the 4th Employment Company—consisting of many Austrians, Germans and Greeks—was stationed during the war. He notes that before World War II, the paper 'boasted that Australia should be 99% British'; by 1946, when the Returned and Services League (RSL) 'passed a resolution that would make it difficult for foreigners to establish a business', the *Mail* editorialised in opposition: 'The paper supported what it termed "strangers in our midst". It called for tolerance.'[29]

Against the ignorant, the fearful, the prejudiced and the self-interested, there emerged a host of organisations, large and small, that focused on the defence and the wellbeing of aliens unjustly demonised or ill-treated. These included leaders and groups representing particular immigrant communities. Probably the best organised was the Jewish community. Long sensitivity to anti-Semitism, and growing awareness of the horrors threatening Jews in Europe, convinced at least some sections of that community—even those generally preferring a quiet and unobtrusive public presence—to organise in the interests of the newcomers. Jewish advocates and lobbyists included the Australian Jewish Welfare Society, the Association of Jewish Refugees, a number of Jewish synagogues and rabbis, the Polish Jewish Welfare Committee and the Jewish Council to Combat Fascism and Anti-Semitism (JCCFAS). While the majority directed their advocacy to the government and, to a lesser degree, the press, the JCCFAS was particularly active in public education, linking the national and international commitment to fighting European fascism with the dangers of anti-Semitism at home. Established in 1942 in response to a local surge in anti-Semitism, which it recognised as a key feature of contemporary fascism, the JCCFAS published a pamphlet titled *1,000,000 Jews in the Armies of Freedom*, underlining the contribution of Jews to allied armies all over the world: 'All Jewish sympathies are on one side: the side of the Democracies'. In bold print, the pamphlet declared:

> Anti-Semitism is a tool of Fascism –
> If you meet anyone preaching it,
> Tell him he is playing Hitler's game! [30]

While regarded with suspicion by both the conservative leadership of the Jewish community and the Commonwealth Security Service (CSS)—each suspecting communist influence—the Melbourne-based JCCFAS became an influential activist organisation. It 'enjoyed broad communal support' during the war years, according to one of its historians.[31] The report of one CSS officer in 1943 stated that the JCCFAS posed no security risk,[32] and sometimes forwarded useful information to Security headquarters.[33] Despite this positive assessment, the fact that its committee included a number of leftists, as well as its regular collaboration with the Australian Council for Civil Liberties (ACCL), ensured that it remained of interest to the CSS.

Beyond the advocacy from immigrant communities, a notable variety of individuals and organisations gave modest or major support to aliens. They include the Australian Council of Trade Unions, the P.E.N. Club, the President of the League of Nations Union, the President of the National Council of Women, the New Education Fellowship, professors and other academics, the General Secretary of the New South Wales ALP, the Premier of South Australia, and members of the ALP Federal Government.[34] Personnel occasionally overlapped and/ or cooperated. In effect, these groups, along with individual advocates for aliens, formed an unofficial and sometimes unintentional kind of resistance movement.

Writers, artists and intellectuals were prominent in a number of these groups. Left-wing organisations such as the Australian Civil Rights Defence League, while predominantly interested in challenging government policies that restricted political activity and free speech, also championed the rights of 'all anti-fascist aliens'.[35] The Defence League established a sub-committee for this particular purpose. Its members included the well-known writers Frank Dalby Davison, Bartlett Adamson and Miles Franklin,[36] while its fortnightly meetings hosted, according to a Security report, 'delegates from the Italian, Greek, Russian, Yugoslav, Chinese, Free French and Scandinavian groups.'[37] As late as April 1945, the League was still actively campaigning; led by its secretary, Mrs Laura Gapp, a small group visited the Liverpool internment camp in New South Wales to interview an Indonesian, Daniel Kamoe. A Security report notes that he was subsequently released.[38] Showing direct concern of this kind for individuals often proved successful.

Like many devoted to supporting and defending aliens, this group made use of the press, especially the letters pages, to influence public opinion and thereby government policy. In May 1943 the *Sydney Morning Herald* published one of their letters, headed 'Aliens in Australia':

> Sir, - Publicity was recently given to the formation of a special labour corps for aliens, and to the question of occupation and position of aliens in this country, the general attitude apparently being quite hostile to them. This attitude we think quite wrong. The test of any person of foreign extraction should be his or her willingness to observe the laws and customs of this country to assist the Allied cause in the fight against the common enemy. This test should be applied independent of birth or nationality ... [39]

From a rather different political perspective, but with a common objective, came an energetic phalanx of Christian individuals and churches. The Society of Friends (Quakers) visited so-called enemy aliens in detention, and their reports were sent to the Governor-General, who forwarded them to the British Government. Their advocacy helped to persuade the British War Office to establish a court of inquiry into the *Dunera* debacle.[40] The Moderator of the Presbyterian

Church in Sydney, RA Smith, was part of a deputation to the Minister of the Interior in July 1940, arguing against the persecution of aliens, and he wrote to the *Sydney Morning Herald* on the subject.[41] The Melbourne Catholic archbishop, Daniel Mannix, called for 'Christian tolerance' towards Italians, and is credited with helping to keep the number of Italians interned in Victoria lower than elsewhere.[42] His influence also secured the release of two schoolboys, the Wolkenstein brothers, who arrived on the *Dunera*, and their enrolment at Xavier College. The writer Alan Gill referred to this event in his obituary for one of the brothers in 2003:

> Since they were Catholic and still of school age their situation aroused the attention of Father Walter Koenig, a Jesuit priest who was a fellow internee. He wrote to the Archbishop of Melbourne, Daniel Mannix, who arranged their early release.[43]

In fact, Archbishop Mannix did not limit his support to Catholic refugees. He responded quickly and positively to an appeal regarding the plight of all the men on the *Dunera* after receiving a letter from Marjorie Coppel, the Honorary Secretary of the Victorian Refugee Immigration Appeals Committee. A handwritten reply from the archbishop makes clear his sympathy: 'I am much impressed by your statement regarding those interned aliens. I have given the facts to the editor of the "Advocate" in the hope that the coming issue will have something to say about this distressing muddle'.[44] The next issue of the Catholic *Advocate* included a prominent article headed 'German Internees in Australia: A Plea for Justice'.[45]

One of the most active and most beloved public Christians supporting aliens was Margaret Holmes, who spent the war years working in the interests of internees. A leader of both the Australian and the World Student Christian Movement, she was described in a privately printed biography as 'a characteristic blend of technical help and human warmth … [together with] innate shrewdness and prudence'.[46] She, too, had influential connections and knew how to use them, but her daily efforts were what we would now call grassroots: providing the men in the internment camps with clothing, books, writing materials, access to education—often in the teeth of military disapproval and even exclusion.[47] And beyond the endless practical assistance, which extended to finding the men accommodation and work when they were released, there was her unguarded friendship. She was especially close to the men who had been transported to Australia on the *Dunera* from Britain, and they felt she was family. Klaus Loewald, one of the Dunera Boys who served in the 8th Employment Company, later wrote fondly:

> All of us owe an inexhaustible debt of gratitude and remembrance to Miss Margaret Holmes of Melbourne. While we had been interned, she was untiring in her efforts, on behalf of the World Student Christian Movement, to provide books, printed music, and instruments as well as to make it possible for us to sit for the London Matric. With unfailing kindness, devotion, and generosity she was a spiritual guide to us when we were in the army. Well into her nineties, she maintained a loving correspondence with many of us in various parts of the world, and all of us who knew her and enjoyed the intellectual and moral benefits which her quiet and consistent attention bestowed on us were united in our admiration and affection for her.[48]

Of all the prominent Christian church leaders, the most persistent high-level advocate for aliens was Charles Venn Pilcher, the Anglican Bishop Coadjutor of Sydney. This urbane English gentleman was a past master of the art of persuasion, and his elevated social position and connections gave him exceptional status and access to those in positions of authority.[49]

Pilcher was a persistent writer of letters to the press, and a polite but unyielding lobbyist of government ministers on behalf of unjustly stigmatised and ill-treated aliens.[50] A typical example of the way in which he set out to influence the community is a letter published in the *Sydney Morning Herald* in May 1940:

> Sir, - I hope that the offer of the seventy refugees to the Commonwealth Government to serve in any capacity, reported in the 'Herald' of May 20, will be accepted.
>
> Australia needs every man who is willing to serve. Britain and France are using thousands of Hitler's victims, including Jewish refugees, to fight the Nazi regime. Why should Australia not use these men who are eager to overthrow the tyranny at whose hands they have so grievously suffered?
>
> Technical obstacles could easily be removed, and a tribunal, presided over by a judge, could be appointed to investigate the antecedents of any case where loyalty was questioned. At this hour of crisis, full use should be made of every genuine offer of service.
>
> I am, etc ...
> Charles Venn Pilcher
> Chairman of the Inter Church Committee for Non-Aryan Christian Refugees
> St Andrew's Cathedral[51]

At a time when public anxiety about the war and the loyalty of aliens was intense, Pilcher cleverly acknowledged 'this hour of crisis', and pointed out how useful refugees could be in the war effort. He built on the recent report that seventy refugees had written to the Australian Government offering to serve 'in any capacity'; co-opted the British and French inclusion of 'thousands of Hitler's victims, including Jewish refugees, to fight the Nazi regime', to strengthen his argument; and offered a simple remedy for 'any case where loyalty was questioned'. And at the end, there is the impressive title, the information about a special organisation with a long and respectable name, which he heads—'Chairman of the Inter Church Committee for Non-Aryan Christian Refugees'—and a true establishment address.

In his public correspondence, Pilcher consistently chose to emphasise the positive. Implicit in almost every letter is the conviction—which, of course, he wished the readers to share—that the vast majority of aliens were decent and loyal men and women, and that the Australian people were also decent and fair-minded. Pilcher most probably organised the fourteen important-name signatories, and wrote the letter published in the *Sydney Morning Herald* in August 1940 under the heading 'Treatment of Refugees. An Appeal for Justice.'[52] It begins:

> Church leaders and other representative citizens in New South Wales have issued an appeal for a fuller understanding of the plight of the genuine refugee from Nazi or Fascist persecution.

The appeal is addressed to 'all citizens of good will', and supports an earlier appeal in Britain issued by 'Dr Temple, the Archbishop of York; Lord Lytton, the Master of Balliol College, Oxford; and other prominent Englishmen.' (One can recognise Pilcher's methodology.) The letter goes on to explain why refugees should not be regarded as 'fifth columnists', why they are eager to contribute to the defeat of Hitler, and how valuable that assistance would be. The harshest term the letter uses to criticise 'ill-informed propaganda directed against refugees' is 'We regret'. The letter ends, as always, positively, using the homely metaphors of hospitality and solidarity:

> We feel that we can appeal with confidence to all fair-minded Australians to meet these people who have sought the hospitality of our shores with understanding and in the spirit of comradeship in the common cause.

When writing to members of parliament, Pilcher demonstrated the same courteous certainty that the recipient was a man (it was always a man) of good sense and goodwill. It appears that he knew a number of Cabinet members well enough to go beyond the usual formalities. Many of his letters to them open with the salutation 'My dear Mr ....', and end 'With every good wish' before the more formal 'I remain Sincerely Yours, Venn Pilcher'.[53]

The Minister for the Army, the Hon Frank Forde, received a number of letters from Pilcher in 1942 and 1943, all concerning unjust restrictions on refugee aliens in both civilian life and in military service. (The government, after much lobbying from many sources, had created the category of 'refugee alien' to cover those who were stateless, such as German Jews, and those 'forced to emigrate on account of actual or threatened religious, racial or political persecution' and who are 'opposed to the regime which forced [them] to emigrate.')[54]

Some of Pilcher's letters were headed 'Personal and Urgent', with copies sent to both the minister's office and his home.[55] Forde began his responses equally warmly—'My dear Bishop Pilcher'—and responded promptly, and very often positively, to Pilcher's requests. A letter from Pilcher dated 29 January 1942 received a friendly acknowledgement on 5 February, and a full response on 2 March, including the welcome words 'You will be pleased to learn that …'.[56] The correspondence was begun again by Pilcher on 17 March—this time, concerning the restrictions on the wives of aliens in the army.[57]

Not all in authority regarded Pilcher benignly. He is most probably the bishop referenced in a November 1940 letter to King George VI from the Governor-General, who expresses unease about the treatment of aliens in Australia and outrage at the interrogation of the prelate:

> Spy mania is a fashionable disease at the present time and one of our most esteemed bishops who pressed for a more thorough investigation into some obviously hard cases [of internees] has been interrogated by the police and warned as to his future activities.[58]

Police warnings made no difference. Pilcher—'the tireless churchman'[59]—must surely be counted among the most persistent, and also among the most effective, high-level public advocates for World War II internees, refugees and enemy aliens in Australia.

Pilcher's equal as an inveterate advocate for aliens, but operating from the secular base of the ACCL, was its secretary, Brian Fitzpatrick. Fitzpatrick was an eloquent exponent of the traditions of justice, fairness and free speech, which he saw as central pillars of a democratic and civilised society. While different in background and ideology, he shared Pilcher's remarkable capacity for work. Fitzpatrick wrote a number of important books on Australian history, as well as devoting decades to public advocacy of his beliefs, and the construction of useful alliances to further their interests. In his time with the ACCL, he helped build a nationwide community of activists for human rights and civil liberties.

Well before the outbreak of war in September 1939, Fitzpatrick was organising deputations to federal ministers on behalf of refugees; in most cases, Jewish refugees. The Minutes of a meeting of the Executive Committee of the ACCL on 6 March 1939, outlined in Chapter 1, reflect the detailed information obtained through personal contact with ministers and heads of department who welcomed Fitzpatrick and his colleagues into their offices.

At the same time, the ACCL was actively coordinating community organisations to speak with one voice to government in support of refugees. Alerted and alarmed by the government's attempts to deny refuge to a group of twenty-seven Jewish men, women and children from Germany, Austria and Czechoslovakia, who arrived as 'tourists' on the Dutch ship *Nieuw Holland* in October 1938,[60] the ACCL began to organise a conference; it finally took place in December 1939. Writing almost two decades later, Fitzpatrick described the conference with considerable satisfaction and a modicum of humour:

> An Immigration and Status of Aliens Committee of the Council for Civil Liberties called a conference of 53 organizations in Melbourne in December 1939 and set up a Refugee Immigration Appeals Committee to help 'to ensure that just and equitable treatment' was accorded to refugees from Nazi persecution. The spirit of the time is indicated by the representation at the conference of the Anglican, Presbyterian, Methodist and Baptist Churches and six other religious bodies; nine trade unions; thirteen Jewish societies; Italian, Chinese and Croat and many various Australian societies; and by the variety of speakers, including the former U.A.P. Minister T.W. White M.P.

> lately Commonwealth representative at the Evian Governmental Commission on Refugees, 1938, and J.D. Blake, an official of the Communist Party.[61]

The ACCL became the home of a number of activists concerned about the treatment of refugees. Fitzpatrick, as its major ideas man, tactician, organiser and spokesman, increased its efforts on behalf of aliens. As he wrote after the war, in the ACCL's annual report in 1945: 'Another of the semi-permanent preoccupations of your Council has been the rights of anti-fascist refugees from Europe, living in our community.'[62]

Fitzpatrick did not work alone. In 1938 three young academics from the University of Melbourne—Austin Edwards, RM (Max) Crawford and EHS (Eric) Burhop—joined the ACCL's executive: likely evidence of the organisation's growing support within the university.[63] Another graduate of Melbourne University and one of the most committed activists was Marjorie Coppel, Secretary of the ACCL's Victorian Refugee Immigration Appeals Committee. She wrote assiduously to organisations and individuals, setting out the facts concerning aliens' internment and other forms of discrimination, and appealing for the government to change its prejudicial policies against aliens. An example is the four-page letter she wrote in May 1941, concerning 'the continued internment in Australian prison-camps of 2,000 deportees from England [in the vessel *Dunera*], nearly all of whom are accepted by the British Government as anti-nazis.'[64] The letter was sent to 'every member of the Federal Parliament, as well as to State politicians, churchmen, trades Unionists and other citizens.'[65] Responses were many and, with few exceptions, polite. The Leader of the Opposition, John Curtin, promises to '[represent] your comments regarding the whole position' to the Minister for the Army and then write back to her.[66] Earle Page, the Minister for Commerce, declares himself 'personally interested in one man interned at Hay, who seems to be just such a case as those you cited', and is 'glad to bring this matter to the attention of Mr Spender, who is the Minister concerned.'[67]

The writer and broadcaster Walter Murdoch is 'moved deeply' by her letter, and promises to do anything he can 'in the way of awakening the public conscience to this iniquity.' [68] And the President of the United Associations of Women, Jessie Street, regretting that Coppel's appeal is outside the scope of her organisation, finishes her letter with a sweeping affirmation:

> ... we as an organisation are deeply sympathetic with the treatment of these unfortunate refugees, and we believe that a great injustice has been perpetrated.[69]

One measure of the effectiveness of Marjorie Coppel's letter is its reproduction in full in a report to Military Intelligence from Major RS Browne, an inspector from the Commonwealth Investigation Branch (the security service) in Melbourne. Major Browne somewhat grudgingly acknowledges that the ACCL has 'a definite sphere of usefulness' in a democratic society, and notes that the internment of the Dunera enemy aliens, 'whose release may have been authorised but whose freedom has not yet been', is 'of some local importance'.[70] Considering the preference of the branch for the continued internment of enemy aliens, this is an unusually balanced assessment.

The ACCL lobbied to get Jewish and other anti-fascist 'enemy aliens' out of internment, and was influential in many of them being reclassified as refugee aliens. Where persuasion of ministers did not succeed, the ACCL assisted individuals to make personal representations to government, and organised legal assistance in court proceedings. Thus, in 1943, when 'deputations ... to the Minister for the Army (Mr Forde) and the Acting Attorney-General (Mr Beasley) did not have the desired effect' of repealing certain inequitable regulations amending the National Security (Aliens Control) legislation, Fitzpatrick could report to members, with some satisfaction, that these alternative tactics largely succeeded.[71]

Like Pilcher, Fitzpatrick was a wonderful networker, but his connections were not in the upper social strata. Instead, he had close associations with writers and artists, with liberal-thinking academics and lawyers, and with the trade union movement and the Labor Party. There is little doubt that the personal friendships, and sometimes long ACCL involvement of men such as Maurice Blackburn, Frank Brennan, Eddie Ward, John Dedman and Bert Evatt—almost all Ministers in the Labor governments from October 1941—enabled Fitzpatrick to gain access to decision makers, and at least a sympathetic ear.[72] Labor Prime Minister John Curtin was not closely associated with the ACCL, but his rejection of the Opposition's calls for the internment of all aliens probably owes something to its influence on Labor thinking.[73] 'The Government,' declared Curtin, 'does not believe in taking people *en bloc* and throwing them into internment camps ... [This was] entirely at variance with all that we are fighting for.'[74]

While much of the ACCL's lobbying took place out of the public eye, Fitzpatrick regularly used his considerable skills as a writer and speaker to put the case for those refugees and immigrants forced from their homes in Europe by fascism. For a time, he wrote a regular column for *Smith's Weekly*,[75] and presented talks on radio about current affairs, usually with a historical perspective.[76] He also produced a number of pamphlets, which were widely distributed through the ACCL, friendly organisations and trade unions. The two printed in 1944 are typical of his approach.

The first, titled *Refugees – Hitler's Loss Our Gain*, was funded and published by the Jewish Council to Combat Fascism and Anti-Semitism (JCCFAS).[77] Written in Fitzpatrick's easy-to-read style—as if engaged in a friendly, but important, conversation—and with illustrations by the left-wing artist Noel Counihan, the pamphlet explains why there were so many refugees in Australia, and their considerable contribution to the war effort.[78] The second pamphlet, published by the ACCL with the assistance of the JCCFAS, has a more dramatic title: *It Can Happen Here!*. In a racy account of the prejudices directed at a Jewish man in Carlton who happened to be both naturalised and in the AIF, Fitzpatrick replicates—or invents—conversations that illustrate the ignorance and boorishness of the anti-Semites. And he cleverly uses the embarrassment the events caused the RSL,[79] whose members were involved, to publicise that organisation's worthy, if belated, efforts to declare their opposition to anti-Semitism and to injustice to anti-fascist aliens. The pamphlet ends rhetorically: 'What influence is trying to destroy the R.S.L. as a democratic force?' And then, beneath a Noel Counihan drawing of a family retreating under the whips of Nazis, are the words: 'We don't want this sort of thing in Australia!'[80]

With Fitzpatrick's radio talks, there was less drama and more argument.

In an elegant, conversational and persuasive broadcast on Melbourne commercial station 3XY on Sunday, 18 July 1943, Fitzpatrick spoke at length on the subject of civil liberties. He didn't hesitate to indicate his political preference for Labor: 'Mr Curtin's Labor Government took office, 21 months ago. There has been far less to complain of, in the period since, than there was in the 21 months before the change of Government.'[81] But nor did he pretend that all was well:

> There is anti-Semitism, stupid prejudice against Jews, among us, there is ill-informed criticism of aliens, of refugees from the Nazis and Fascists. There is bitter campaigning against Communists, whose organization is however, to my knowledge, working wonders in the Labour Movement, and among trade unionists, among generous-spirited young people of the middle classes, for the total war effort we need if we are to keep our country inviolate for a real democracy to grow up in after the war.[82]

This is a talk Pilcher would never have given. Fitzpatrick chose to openly recognise that sections of the community 'let ignorance and prejudice sway them when they think or talk of certain minorities.'[83] He challenged not only racism and anti-Semitism but the antipathy to communists. And linked these prejudices. This is an advocate who confronts his audience; who points to Australian weaknesses, as well as strengths.

It could be argued that such an approach might distance people from your cause, rather than draw them to you. There were certainly members of the ACCL committee who worried about Fitzpatrick's radicalism, especially his openness to the far Left. Some resigned over such issues.[84] He and the ACCL were under constant Security scrutiny.[85] Yet, there is no doubt that Fitzpatrick's untiring efforts at communication and advocacy, the intelligence and skill with which he built his arguments, his gentlemanly demeanour, and the effectiveness of his considerable network of friends, personal and political, made the ACCL a crucial organisation among the groups that supported aliens.

People were grateful to the ACCL. Letters came from such men as Dr Herman Saenger, chairman of the New Australians' Advisory Committee, who wrote to the ACCL in May 1942:

> After a very satisfactory interview with the Minister for the Army yesterday which was kindly and promptly arranged for us by Mr Blackburn, I feel I must tell you how grateful my friends and I are to you. You really set the ball rolling, and it is thanks to your active help and co-operation and to your advice which you have always so readily given us that we were able to put our case to the Minister himself.[86]

Even the conservative, extremely thorough historian of Australia during World War II, Paul Hasluck, recognised the ACCL's and Fitzpatrick's central contribution to the maintenance of human rights and civil liberties. The fact that he was writing during the Cold War did not deter Hasluck from observing:

> Outside Parliament the voluntary role of watchdog was discharged principally by the Australian Council for Civil Liberties, a pre-war organisation with headquarters in Melbourne and a membership in all States, assisted by a legal panel of men eminent in their profession, and also drawing liberally on the Universities and the professions for its office bearers … [The council had] an active and crusading secretary …[87] By and large… democracy was well served [in the early

> war years] by those who kept alive its spirit by their protests against any unnecessary or excessive use of wartime emergency powers.[88]

A stickler for the facts, Hasluck then observed the major limitation on the efforts of those like Fitzpatrick who sought—and seek—to maintain a democratic and just society:

> The most insidious and also probably the most unnecessary infringement of democratic rights and practices was not in those matters that the public knew and for the most part tolerated, but in the information side of communications censorship; and in the activities of Security Service and the Investigation Branch, which were unknown to the public. What was actually done may not have been injurious or unjust but there could be no vigilance against these activities for they were for the most part hidden. If there were injustice it could not be corrected. Such activities require more careful scrutiny than any other for they strike straight at the individual, the inviolability of whom is the foundation stone of democracy. [In the words of Prime Minister Menzies in the first weeks of war]: 'The greatest tragedy that could overcome a country would be for it to fight a successful war in defence of liberty and lose its own liberty in the process.'[89]

# 11

# Religion and politics

## Religion

In pre-war Australia, religious allegiance was one of the defining elements in many people's lives. Since the first British settlement, Protestants held social and political dominance over Catholics, while conducting their own interfaith battles over scripture and parishioners. There were few Catholics in the non-Labor parties until decades after the war.[1] The one Catholic in the Menzies government's 1949 cabinet, John Cramer, was asked during his preselection: 'where does your loyalty lie, to your country or your Pope?'.[2] And, according to one writer, 'Menzies – in many ways the least sectarian of people – had a habit of joking whenever Cramer walked into a room: "Hush, boys. The papist is among us."'[3]

Jews, who were mostly city dwellers like the rest of the population, practised the best-known non-Christian religion. Many Jews were secular, but anti-Semitism made no distinction. During the war, the Jewish Council to Combat Fascism and Antisemitism kept the Commonwealth Security Service informed of anti-Semitic publications.[4] There were quite a number, but the Security Service only listed a handful of what it called 'The Chief Organizations sponsoring anti-Semitism in this country': the Nazi Party of Australia before the war; the Australia First Movement 'and its followers' until 1942; and then 'The United Electors of Australia, and the supporters of the newspaper "The New Times"'.[5]

This modest list doesn't reflect the normalisation of anti-Semitism in a community where its expression is no embarrassment, even to religious organisations. An historian notes that 'only a handful of Protestants spoke up for the Jews after [the attack on Jews in Germany] on Crystal Night.'[6] After the 1938 Crystal Night attacks, a Jesuit publication, the Catholic *Messenger*, justified Hitler and Goering's violence: 'To unify the resurrected nation, the power of the Jews was repressed'. The *Messenger* warned Australians against 'the Jewish commercial and theatrical ring', and called for a stronger campaign to convert Jews.[7]

The historian Paul Bartrop summarises Australia in the 1930s as 'British, monolingual, homogeneous and xenophobic'.[8] Anti-Semitism, though well established long before the arrival of refugees from fascism, was not always distinguishable from an antipathy to all non-Anglo foreigners. This was the view held by one of the Dunera boys, Henry Lippmann, who served in the 8th Employment Company: '... there was this distinction, we were "bloody foreigners" ... Not so much anti-Semitism but anti-foreigners ... In those days Australia was anti any foreigner ...'[9]

As late as January 1941, the Prime Minister's Department was still preparing memoranda that indicate unease about the admittance of foreigners, especially Jews:

> The arrival of a considerable number of foreigners ... would not (it is thought) be welcomed by the Australian public at present, especially as it would appear probable that a large proportion would be Polish Jews. Their absorption would also present difficulties ...[10]

None the less, mistreatment because of religion was one of the criteria demanding sympathetic consideration of an 'enemy' alien, according to government policy announced not long after the war began on 3 September 1939.[11] Just three days earlier, the Victorian International Refugee Emergency Council sent an urgent letter to the Prime Minister. It asked him, 'in the event of war breaking out', to remind the nation 'that the refugees, whilst of German or Austrian nationality, are victims of those very forces which have caused the catastrophe … It would go a long way towards preventing any popular outburst against them as "foreigners" or "Germans".'[12] On 9 September Prime Minister Menzies issued a press statement. Its first two paragraphs could be read as a positive response to the Refugee Council's letter:

> As we have a fair number of aliens living in our midst, I consider it my duty to appeal to the Australian people at this time to avoid treating as enemies those persons who are ready to live peaceably among us and exhibit loyalty toward the Australian Constitution and our political traditions.
>
> Many of the aliens in Australia must now be classed as enemy aliens, but that does not mean that they are sympathetic toward or owe any allegiance to the Nazi Government. Indeed, some of these people have been forced to leave Germany and Austria and as refugees they have sought asylum in Australia. If they are willing to be friendly to us, I see no reason why we should deny them the right of asylum despite the fact that a state of war exists between the country of their birth and the British Empire.[13]

On the same day, a memorandum from the Department of Defence referred to the need for 'sympathetic treatment' of those 'enemy aliens' who had left their country on 'political, racial or religious grounds'.[14] In practice, internment followed for many, until an amendment to the National Security (Aliens Control) Regulations in October 1942. This provided a new classification of 'refugee alien'. The *Sydney Morning*

*Herald* duly reported that 'Refugee aliens … will include European refugees who have been driven from their own countries by Nazi religious or political persecution. They will be treated as aliens and not as enemy aliens.'[15] As well as noting this shift in policy, the paper's editorial criticised the government for taking four years to make this important change.

The military's approach to religious observance appears to have been reasonably straightforward. The army produced hymn books and prayers approved by the Anglican, Methodist and Presbyterian churches, and a Service Prayer Book for the Jewish New Year and Day of Atonement.[16] At the same time, it recognised the right of every soldier to hold a religious faith—or not. The latter could prove a disadvantage on occasion. Good-hearted Captain Broughton was concerned that the Jewish soldiers under his command in the 8th Employment Company should be able to fulfil their religious obligations. According to Henry Lippmann:

> On the first Saturday morning in the army at Caulfield Racecourse our captain asked who wanted to go to synagogue service. Since one would have been detailed for regular work otherwise most of us volunteered for the synagogue.[17]

By September of 1942 the 8th Employment Company Routine Orders include a note that '253 O/RS granted leave for Day of Atonement Services'.[18] Doubtless, there were many secular Jews among the 253. In March 1943 both the religious and secular would have taken advantage of the following:

> Passover. Will those members of the Jewish Faith, who have not a home to go to on Seder night and who desire to obtain Mazzos, please hand in their names to their respective Platoon leaders. Arrangements will be made with the Jewish Welfare Officer, whereby each man will receive 1lb of Mazzoth. [19]

Captain Broughton made sure that Christians were not overlooked. One of the many references in the Company's Routine Orders details church services for both Protestants and Catholics. The latter were offered Holy Mass in the QWO hut, as well as the hearing of confessions there on Saturday afternoons and evenings.[20]

Yosl Bergner, twenty-one years old when he joined the 6th Employment Company, quickly learned that the officers who signed him up also assumed that if you were a Jew, you had a religion. His remembrance of the event he describes is comic and probably happily exaggerated:

> When I enrolled they asked my religion. I said I didn't have a religion. They said: 'Then you must be an agnostic.' I liked the word, so I said yes, I'm an agnostic. Then came the Christian holidays and the Christians were given leave. Then came the Jewish holidays and the Jews got leave. Everyone left, and I was the only one stuck at the camp. So I ran to the staff headquarters and told them that I was a Jew, not an agnostic.[21]

Though rarely mentioned, there were also Muslims in the Employment Companies. One was a friend of Fred Lester in the 6th. He was an Albanian, 'a great bloke', according to Lester, who demonstrated his 'very streetwise' qualities by joining his Jewish (non-religious) friend on an authorised Jewish holiday trip to Melbourne.[22]

Notices of church services feature regularly in the Employment Company War Diaries, and Sunday was generally the day of rest, as befitted a predominantly Christian country.[23] For their regular Sunday church parade, members of the 6th Company were reminded to wear their 'Sunday service dress'.[24] In a memoir written decades after the war, the historian Ian Turner describes choosing Sundays to tidy up the Army Education Service hall, in order to 'escape both church parade and the emu parade (which was the alternative offered to conscientious objectors to religion).'[25] Assigning emu parade (picking up the rubbish, or some other unwelcome task) seems to have been a common response by officers to non-believers.

On Rottnest Island in Western Australia in 1944, Bart Srhoy and his friends in the 11th/12th Employment Company were all from Yugoslavia, and all were Catholics, at least nominally. There were Catholic as well as Protestant and Jewish army chaplains. But one Sunday, all did not go as planned:

> One Sunday morning we were all on parade to attend a church service. Naturally, there were various denominations with the Church of England embracing the biggest number of soldiers. The NCO called out those of the Anglican faith to fall out. My friends and I belonged to the Catholic faith so we stood fast. The men of the Anglican faith were marched off to Church. There were no Catholic or other priests that Sunday so we were detailed to clean the grease traps and other cleaning duties. We soon discovered that a Roman Catholic Chaplain visited the Island on very rare occasions.
>
> The following Sunday when an NCO called for the Anglican men to step forward, we were the first to do so. We were marched off with the others to the church where a service was held which lasted about an hour. After the service we were dismissed and had the rest of the day off whilst other non-Anglicans were slaving around the camp. We decided we were not going to get caught again.[26]

The army initially provided chaplains for six religious denominations: Roman Catholic, Church of England (Anglican), Methodist, Presbyterian, United Churches (other Protestant denominations) and Jewish.[27] Chaplains were regular visitors to all the alien Employment Companies made up of men of European origin, offering support and ensuring that religious duties could be fulfilled. In the case of Jewish soldiers, this sometimes included provision of kosher food. The Captain of the 8th, always devoted to the wellbeing of his men, not only ensured that there was kosher food in the mess hut but established a kosher hut for those who wished to eat apart.[28]

The War Diary of the 4th records a visit from Rabbi Jacob Danglow in December 1942, when the Company was working on the railway platforms in Albury. Rabbi Danglow was the senior Jewish chaplain in the Australian Army, with the equivalent rank of Colonel, and he visited Companies with significant numbers of Jewish soldiers.[29] On this occasion, he was accompanied by a member of the Jewish Welfare Society and another man from 'a Jewish Charity Organisation'. The rabbi conducted a service attended by 150 men. According to the War Diary, 'Rabbi Danglow expressed his gratitude and appreciation to Captain S. Walker for the so very satisfactory and happy conditions under which the men of this Unit serve.'[30] The Diary does not record the men's view of Danglow's glowing assessment of their army experience.[31]

A few months earlier, the 4th Company's War Diary noted a visit from members of the Greek community, and the attendance of 125 soldiers at a Greek Orthodox service at St Matthew's, an Anglican church in Albury.[32] This was an instance of the sometimes powerful unifying effect of the war in an era of sharp distinctions between branches of Christianity. The following year, Greek soldiers in this Company benefited from a day off, thanks to a request from the Consul General for Greece, Mr EC Vrisakis—but that was to celebrate Greek National Day.[33] The 10th Company, in Springton, South Australia, was visited by a padre of the Greek Orthodox Church in August 1943, but such an event is not recorded again in the Company's War Diary.[34]

There were occasions when outsiders' religious prejudice gave rise to a determined response. Charlie D'Aprano recalled a lively incident at a nightclub in St Kilda. A group from the 6th were accosted by some South African soldiers, one of whom kept making anti-Semitic remarks: 'I hate the Nazis but I hate the Jews more. Doing a bloody good job killing the bastards.' Polite attempts by Jack [Jacob] Kornhauser, himself Jewish, to end the abuse—'We're all in the same team, cut it out, it's not nice, we're here for a good time, we're all on leave, I'm not here to fight you'—failed. According to D'Aprano, the South African 'took a swing' at Kornhauser, who responded in kind, with remarkable effect. 'He hit him and hit him and hit him! He hit him downstairs, across the tramlines and back!' Kornhauser's mates—Jews, Catholics, Protestants and atheists—were amazed: they had viewed him as rather meek and mild. Perhaps he had, indeed, once been a boxing champion, a rumour that spread through the Company.[35]

Despite the comic uproar that occurred when Rabbi Danglow was regaling a group of Jewish soldiers in the 6th Company mess hut with the story of the holy days of Hanukkah, and the Greeks sitting nearby took exception to the notion that the Jews defeated the Greeks in a battle, religion seems not to have been a divisive force in the alien Companies. Young Fred Lester from the 6th was adamant: 'There was absolutely no quarrel between [religious groups]—that was a great thing: everybody accepted what the others did, whether they believed in something or not.'[36] And all, including the atheists, benefited from the practical support provided by religious organisations: sporting equipment, books and writing material, a coffee machine from the YMCA,[37] a billiard table from the Jewish Welfare Society,[38] and presents from the Greek Democritus Club at Christmas time.[39] While a common culture and language could provide the comfort of familiarity and often lead to close friendships, religious faith, or none, was neither necessary for warm personal relationships nor the basis of enmity. And, as in the general community, religion could sometimes be seen as a unifying force in the army; what some have called a civil religion, linking state and faiths in the service of a virtuous war, a common cause for the nation.[40]

## Politics

The fall of France to the Germans in May 1940 is often marked as a significant Australian shift in attitudes to the war. Our first major historian of the war, Paul Hasluck, provides a pithy summary: 'The mind of the people had rushed from the dull level of the "phoney war" to the emotional peak of Dunkirk.'[41] As a consequence, the government was 'stirred up',[42] and a new, urgent attention was given to rearming and to '[preparing] the minds of the people'.[43]

War may not be politics by other means, but the political value of emphasising the violence and cruelty of its Fascist, Nazi and Japanese enemies was not lost on the government. Together with an emphasis on patriotism, and support for the gallant British, these were key themes transmitted to the men in uniform as well as to the civilian population.

Radio and newspapers, the two major media of the time, played their part, as did cinema newsreels. Playwright Oriel Gray records in her memoir the way in which the newsreels brought the war very close:

> Most people went to the pictures at least once a week. Continuing the short but already great tradition of the news cameramen, the newsreels brought the Panzer divisions out of the screen and across our Peter's ice-cream bucket … [T]he newsreels were bringing home the realities of war.[44]

The newspapers were forced—both by government pressure and the increasingly war-focused interest of their readers—to utilise some of the pages previously devoted to sport, finance, society events and advertising. The war was no longer just on the front page.[45]

Radio became a site for information, education and political opinion, with learned as well as patriotic speakers, often university academics. A number challenged their listeners to think deeply about the ethics of the war and the Australia that should emerge at its end. Their views did not always coincide with those of a conservative persuasion. The professor of history and political science at the University of Adelaide, Garnet (Jerry) Portus, a regular presenter on the Australian Broadcasting Commission, and a long-time supporter of the League of Nations and the Student Christian Movement, spoke about patriotism as distinct from nationalism:

> This is the magic of true patriotism. It changes narrow nationalistic boasting into a wide international acknowledgement of the beauty and the goodness and the truth in the world.[46]

Another professor, a highly regarded essayist and broadcaster, Walter Murdoch, from the University of Western Australia, expressed his yearning for a better, more humane and more united world. He urged his listeners to read foreign literature:

> One way of getting into contact with another nation's mind and character is by reading that other nation's books. The literature of any people is that people's autobiography ... Our great gain from the reading of foreign authors: not a glimpse of deep-seated racial differences, but a glimpse of a still more deep-seated common humanity ... We learn a lesson of tolerance: it takes all sorts to make a world ... [and] we learn what an immense deal is common to us all.[47]

These progressive and far-sighted views are also a feature of much of the work of the Army Education Service (AES). The establishment of the AES was approved by the War Cabinet in March 1941, and the first issue of its lively, entertaining and informative pocket-sized 'journal', *Salt*, appeared in September of that year, and continued fortnightly publication until April 1946.[48]

The AES was an educational and cultural force, so large and influential that it has been credited with encouraging a renaissance of Australian publishing of books, as well as literary and cultural journals. This was all built on a growing demand for local writing, as well as the decline in access to overseas publishing.[49]

According to an historian of the AES, Darryl Dymock, 'between June 1942 and January 1946 an estimated ten million soldiers ... attended AES lectures, two million heard music recitals, seven million watched documentary films, and more than 66,000 enrolled in correspondence courses.'[50]

The AES's focus was both the immediate needs of the soldiers, and their improvement. The former included some quite basic needs, such as the development of literacy. The *Kalgoorlie Miner* reported in June 1943 that, according to the army, 'Of every 25 men in the Australian army, one cannot read or write or can barely read or write ... Of every 10 men in the Australian army, eight left school at 14 years or earlier.'[51] To encourage literacy, as well as to provide reading material for soldiers, the AES organised a system of box libraries, including books by Australian writers. Another service, skills-focused education, often by correspondence, was intended to provide competence in a variety of occupations. In the words of an article in an early issue of *Salt*, 'Take up the broad studies underlying the kind of specialised training in which you are interested.'[52] There was a lot of spare time for courses, as well as for reading.

In a statement of the AES's aims and objectives, the value of giving a soldier access to education via correspondence courses, lending libraries, lectures and so on, was linked to 'developing in him a faith in the political, economic and social institutions for which he is fighting.'[53] Quite explicitly, this 'faith' was to be contrasted with the Axis powers' militaristic and fascist dictatorships.

John Cohen, initially a member of the 11th Employment Company, was transferred to the AES, and became one of its band of lecturers. (The total AES staff numbered 540.[54]) He went from battalion to battalion in a jeep with a driver, speaking on many topics, ranging from the history of Indonesia to the Atlantic Charter. He shared a tent with the young left-wing intellectual Ian Turner, and got to know one of the editors of *Salt*, Hume Dow.[55] But not all lecturers emphasised serious matters. One among many, Robert Salter, in the 6th Employment Company, enjoyed the humorous and down-to-earth talks by Alan Marshall, who was already a popular writer when he was employed by the AES in 1944.[56]

*Salt* (its title chosen from the saying 'pass the salt'[57]) kept reminding its readers that it was their democratic right, and their responsibility, to think about and plan a future that was to be better than the past. Typical was the approach taken in the editorial of the December 1941 issue. With a heading calculated to attract attention—'Free-beer and Freedom'—the writer moves quickly from beer ('because you have shown that you don't mind paying for it') to politics, constructed as the free and thoughtful development of good ideas:

> You have a chance to have your say, too ... There are thousands of "ideas men" in the Army and Air Force. Many of them have taken pen and paper, and the results have appeared in SALT. These men want to know what's to be done – for you and for the world. "Is the New Order going to be new, or just another order?" That's what they ask.[58]

There is no doubt that the AES and *Salt* engaged in a massive effort to enlarge and deepen the knowledge and diversify the thinking of the men in the army. While the subject matter varied, the emphasis was on democracy, freedom, justice, and lack of prejudice. When it came to local politics, there was care to ensure information without bias, while pointing to the contrast between the politics of democracies and fascist regimes. Before the national election in August 1943, *Salt* published a special issue setting out the policies of the two major parties—Labor and UAP-UCP—as written by their leaders. *Salt's* editorial was headed 'Axis Soldiers Don't Vote'.

References to the AES's politically oriented outreach programs appear regularly in the Employment Companies' War Diaries, sometimes with an added commendation from the officer preparing the Orders:

> Army Education Service – Every Friday Night at 1845 hrs, from Station 5 D.N. there will be a broadcast of Current Affairs Bulletin. All ranks should endeavour to listen in as the broadcasts are very interesting.[59]

The officer responsible for the 4th Company's War Diary on 21 March 1943, noted a lecture held while they were stationed in Albury. The subject was Russia, and the lecturer was 'Mr Millner [*sic*] of the Melbourne University'. According to the officer, 'a large audience gave him unlimited support and tremendous applause.'[60] Ian Milner was a popular and well-informed academic, and a prominent member of the Council for Civil Liberties and the Australia-Soviet Friendship

League.[61] Once the USSR turned against Germany in June 1941, Milner's subject was of widespread interest in Australia.

Decades after the war's end, a member of the AES wrote a letter to a Melbourne newspaper, remembering with pride its impressive depth and reach:

> The service was established in early 1941, with a strength of 43 officers and men, to provide general educational, cultural and vocational services to an army of around a quarter of a million. It was to grow to almost 1000 in late 1945, providing a huge range of activities for almost half a million troops.[62]

But, at the time, not everyone was an admirer of the AES. A Sergeant who attended an Army Education lecture with the topic 'What shall we do with a defeated Japan?' wrote in fury to the *Post and Telegraph Censorship Bulletin*. Apparently, the lecturer had failed to acknowledge that 'the Japs are nothing but barbarians and savages at heart but their intellect is modern ... Not one mention was made of the savagery or Shintoism in which is wrapped all their devilish traits.' *The Bulletin*, published for the eyes of senior government and military officials, included the Sergeant's tirade under the heading 'Communism and pro-Enemy Propaganda Disseminated at Army Educational Lectures.'[63]

From conservative politicians and newspapers there was suspicion of, and even outright opposition to, 'progressive' activities within the army. Little more than a year after the first issue of *Salt*, the magazine was attacked for being a waste of money.[64] One of the first to come to the publication's defence was Australia's official World War I historian, CEW Bean. In a long and passionate letter to the *Sydney Morning Herald*, he declared that *Salt's* production was evidence that 'in some respects at least, our staff has learnt from the failures of 1914-18', insisting that it was 'a godsend' for the times and 'the best magazine that I know'. He wrote, 'Intelligent curiosity and keen desire to increase his knowledge is a special mark of the Australian soldier', adding 'and I have never read a publication better fitted to fill these needs than *Salt*.' He only wished the American forces could benefit from it as well.[65] Later that year, he went further, marking *Salt* as essential to military morale:

> When you hear people criticise it, and you will, remember that we are spending hundreds of millions of pounds on armaments, and that all of it – guns, planes, and tanks – is useless if we fail to keep up the morale of troops. A useful soldiers' magazine like this is not a frill but a basic necessity of the army.[66]

Despite such distinguished support, and the insistence in 1944 of the Acting Prime Minister, FM Forde, that *Salt* had proved beyond doubt that 'the Australian soldier can think and write as well as he can fight',[67] there were conservatives in and out of parliament who were deeply suspicious of what they believed were *Salt*'s left-wing politics. As late as June 1945, the Australian Country Party MP George Rankin suggested in Federal Parliament that *Salt* was guilty of 'bias and unfairness in respect of political matters.'[68]

While this was rejected by the Acting Prime Minister, Ben Chifley, there is little doubt that the left-wing views of a number of the men who worked in the AES and on *Salt* influenced the material that was published, and the character of the lectures—particularly those highlighting the importance of the military collaboration with Russia; challenging racism and anti-Semitism; and encouraging soldiers to consider the possibility of a fairer, less isolated society after the war.

In a short memoir published in 1974, the historian Ian Turner happily acknowledged that there were left-wingers, including communists like himself, who worked for the AES:

> From the editorial offices of 'Salt', in La Trobe Street Melbourne, where there worked, among others, Vane Lindesay, Frank Hardy, Amby Dyson and my future father-in-law, Itzhak Gust, to the lecturers and librarians in the field, the A.E.S. personnel were overwhelmingly on the left ... the times were radical. [69]

Despite conservative distrust (which included the misgiving that *Salt* reflected the Labor government's opinions), even one of *Salt's* most virulent media critics, *Smith's Weekly*, declared—in April 1946, the month the magazine was 'demobbed'—that the publication 'has served a good purpose.'[70] It had provided 'men in uniform with a medium through which they could express themselves, and in which subjects of use to them could be presented.'[71]

Not many members of the 'alien' Employment Companies appear to have been avid readers of *Salt*—for most, English was not their mother tongue. And as the majority were not naturalised, a leading article, such as in the 2 August 1943 issue about the forthcoming federal election, headed 'Axis Soldiers Don't Vote' and detailing all parties' policies, was probably not of direct interest.[72] Yet by then they had already been found a place in the publication. An issue in 1942 included a sympathetic portrayal of the 8th Employment Company. Titled 'They Don't Forget', it focused on 'the men whom Hitler hated': 'First victims of the Nazi madness, the men ... wear the Australian uniform pridefully, voluntarily. This is their war as well as ours.'[73]

And it was four men from this Company who fortuitously developed a close attachment to the publication. Vane Lindesay was posted to the editorial board of *Salt* after surviving the bombings of Darwin. In a memoir, he recalls 'four regularly published contributors: "Dunera boys" working as packers and storemen for *Salt*':

> Bruno Simon the sculptor, Erwin Fabian, a painter and graphic artist of distinction who was then being published in 'Angry Penguins', Frank Schonbach, an enviably talented cartoonist for one so young, and his friend Klaus Friedeberger, another competent artist to contribute joke drawings of army life. [74]

Even those 'alien' soldiers who never read *Salt* benefited from the broader cultural and educational activities of the AES. And, in large part, they also shared the widespread community sympathy for the Soviet Union's determined military and popular resistance to Nazi Germany.

Organisations to express solidarity with, and activate support for, the Russians, such as the Friendship with Russia League, the Australia–Soviet Friendship League and the Society for Cultural Relations with the USSR, had prominent politicians and society figures on their committees and platforms. The Sheepskins for Russia Appeal in Melbourne was registered with the Patriotic Funds Council and operated, according to an April 1943 report from the Deputy Director of Security, 'under the direct control of an officer appointed by the Lord Mayor of Melbourne'.[75] One of its national organisers was Lady Jessie Street, and a vice-president was Robert Menzies, leader of the Opposition in the federal parliament.[76] The appeal received Australia-wide publicity and its progress was regularly featured in newspapers. A typical article, on the second page of the *Advertiser* in July 1943, records the South Australia Russian Medical Aid and Comforts Committee gratefully acknowledging a long list of donations to the Sheepskins for Russia £10,000 Appeal, with special mention of £500 from the Schools' Patriotic Fund. According to the paper, 'a cable was received recently from the Russian Red Cross in Moscow expressing the gratitude of the Russian people for the help which Australia is sending them.'[77]

Public support for such community efforts, and the government's formal expressions of regard for the USSR, including the celebration of Red Army Day on 23 February, appear not to have lessened the fear and suspicion of left-wing, especially communist organisations among many conservative politicians and the various military security bodies.[78] The Communist Party of Australia, outlawed in June 1940 when it supported the USSR's alliance with Nazi Germany, was not officially restored to legality until December 1942. But once the Soviet Union was an ally in World War II, Australian communists became among the staunchest supporters of the war effort. According to an historian of the Party, its leadership directed members to enlist.[79] Of the approximately four thousand communists the Party declared served in the armed forces, there were certainly some hundreds in the Employment Companies.[80]

Immediately after the declaration of war, the government passed a National Security Act, intended to restrict activities that were considered a threat to the war effort. It gave the government ministerial authority to abrogate any Act of Parliament, and later amendments introduced the power to declare any organisation unlawful and to censor publications.[81]

The army added its own regulations. These forbade uniformed soldiers in a military band from playing at 'any meeting, demonstration or procession held for a religious or political purpose' but exempted religious, funereal and religious charity gatherings.[82] More generally, soldiers were not permitted to take part in political processions, canvass on behalf of political candidates at elections, or distribute 'political literature'.[83] For those interested in political activities, the only exemption was the right to attend political meetings in uniform when on leave.

In reality, the rules that attempted to limit political involvement of men in uniform seem to have been not uncommonly avoided or simply disregarded. While there were men in the Employment Companies who took little or no interest in politics, political discussion was commonplace. Jack Friedman, in the 6th Employment Company, emphasised how important politics was to many of his fellow soldiers: 'they always spoke about politics, or discussed it, or argued—they weren't just interested in what's going to win the Melbourne Cup tomorrow, there was more to life than that.'[84] Gerard Herbst, a talented designer in the Bauhaus tradition who arrived in Australia from Germany as a refugee from fascism, served in the 4th from early 1942. In a short memoir, he recalled the 'heated discussion' about 'the siege of Stalingrad and the delay of the Second Front'.[85] An equally popular subject was socialism. Ivan Rostkier, from Poland, listed 'discussion about socialism', along with reading books and listening to music, as the major leisure activities of himself and his army friends in the 6th.[86]

The 6th Employment Company had an active Communist branch. For some of the men, joining the Communist Party connected their emigrant experience of pain and loss with a political movement offering hope and change. The art historian Richard Haese, writing of Yosl Bergner and his Australian artist friends Vic O'Connor and Noel Counihan, notes this connection:

> At a time when the Battle of Stalingrad seemed likely to determine whether European humanism would survive or go under, they felt a link with the 'enlightened' forces of history.[87]

Frank Klepner, a close friend of Bergner from their days in the army, remembered that in the Company, those interested in politics were 'basically mainly strongly to the Left, communists or people who at least felt sympathy [for the communists]. By that time, the Russians had been in the war ... and it was not only acceptable but it was almost accepted to be at least a sympathiser of that cause.'[88]

For young Charles D'Aprano, who had come with his father from Italy in 1937, it was local Italian communists who first interested him in politics:

> I became politically aware when I was 20 when I had been in the Army for about a year. I became influenced by the anti-fascists, the Italian anti-fascists first, and particularly the communists soon after. [B]y the time I was 20, I [had] joined the Communist Party.[89]

D'Aprano regarded the Communist Party as the most noteworthy group in the Company. In old age, he still remembered it as a Party 'which really understood what the war was about.'[90] He estimated forty-six men in the Company were Communist Party members and there were quite a few sympathisers.[91]

Some of his recollections are comic. He recalled a secret meeting of the Party branch while the Company was based in Tocumwal. It was to be held after lights out, in one of the trains the men had been unloading that day. The meeting was underway when the train began to move, requiring a rapid and undignified exit.[92] A more secure arrangement was to meet at the home of one or other of the railway workers who were also members of the branch. Fred Lester, one of the younger members of the Company, recalled 'a lot of talk. It was mainly about assisting with the war effort, but also studying at the same time, and discussing the works of Marx and Engels and all that sort of stuff. It was more educational than anything else.'[93]

According to D'Aprano, the loyalty and commitment of the communists in the Company was recognised by some of the officers. He sold the Victorian Communist Party's newspaper, *The Guardian*, on the parade ground, 'and officers would look the other way'.[94] When there was a rumour that the men might be sent to New Guinea, one of the officers remarked of no. 2 platoon (which held a number of left-wingers): 'every one of you communists will be able to lead the platoon.'[95] Their leadership skills were not put to the test, as the rumour proved unfounded.

By no means were all officers so positive. Very occasionally, political antipathy surfaces in the War Diaries. An example is an entry in 1943 in the 4th's Diary—a disapproving reference to evidence that some of the members were observed at an election meeting for a Communist candidate.[96] A Security report about communists in this Company demonstrates a more balanced view of their activities:

> Communists are very active at the No.4 Aust Emp Coy, Albury. Generally, they only contact people whom they regard as trustworthy, and recently in one afternoon they collected £40 for the Communist Party Election Funds. Weekly Communist papers are sold regularly, and propaganda is being actively disseminated. The soldiers concerned generally are of a very good type, doing the jobs they are requested to do, although they engage in a good deal of controversy with other members of the unit from a class-conscious point of view.[97]

More commonly, suspicion and disapproval were expressed as part of a continuing generalised unease with 'aliens', particularly by the various security services.[98] The October 1942 warning of the Deputy

Director of Security in New South Wales that 'it is regarded as dangerous to presume that an alien would be loyal to the Allied cause merely because he had been compelled to leave his country through racial persecution by the reigning power' specifically listed Jews and Italians as likely suspects.[99] A mountain of correspondence about the suspect 'Jewish Communist Activities' includes reports from a variety of helpful informers, including members of the Jewish community, and on at least one occasion from the Labor MP Arthur Calwell.

In March 1943 Calwell informs the Director-General of Security of a meeting in Melbourne of people from forty Jewish societies, where the discussion focused on raising £70 000 for aid to Russia. According to the letter the Director–General sends to the Deputy Director of Security for Victoria, 'Mr Calwell has suggested that the money may be spent in Communist propaganda in Australia and may never reach Russia, and that steps should be taken to tighten the control of money so collected.'[100] The response from the Deputy Director is comprehensive and reassuring:

> In the past four months, the only appeals in which the Jewish community have been interested have been the Sheepskins for Russia Appeal and Aid for Russia (Medical Supplies) Appeal, both of which are registered with the Patriotic Funds Council and consequently are operating under the direct control of an officer appointed by the Lord Mayor of Melbourne which results in a continuous audit of all funds operating.[101]

Then, perhaps to satisfy both the Director-General and Mr Calwell, the Deputy Director added: 'A check is now being made of all known Jewish Societies and special attention will be given to those in which any Communist Party activity is disclosed.'[102]

The Security branches took a keen interest in what one report refers to as 'activities [that] turn the minds of young soldiers in the wrong direction'.[103] The thousands of American troops who arrived in Australia from early 1942 included black Americans—called

Negroes—who were not welcomed but necessarily tolerated by the Australian Government.[104] An area of concern was the role of the Communist Party challenging what it called 'white chauvinism … the mortal enemy of internationalism' in the Australian Army.[105] This was of sufficient importance to be brought to the attention of the Director of the Commonwealth Investigation Branch in Canberra by the Director-General of the Security Service.

Censorship, including opening soldiers' correspondence, was one method of checking on suspect views or activities. In June 1942, only a few months after the establishment of the Employment Companies, Routine Orders included a warning under the heading LETTERS:

> Acting on instructions from Headquarters, members of this Coy are notified that all letters will be censored and, therefore, must be posted at the Coy Office in the box provided for same unsealed … Any man posting letters outside the Camp Area is liable to place himself under suspicion and the letters are still liable to be intercepted by the Intelligence Authorities.[106]

Unsurprisingly, not everyone obeyed this directive, nor the reminders that dot Routine Orders in the following months, even when they include threats that 'rigid tightening up is to take place, and every case detected will be followed by drastic disciplinary action'.[107] The Communist Party issued a warning to its members: 'In order to minimise the dangers of army censorship, post in civilian post boxes where possible.'[108] Many of the men without any political connections had worked this out for themselves. Albert Ceen was a dutiful and persistent letter writer to his wife and children; only one of his letters was stamped 'passed by censor'.[109] Warnings against posting letters outside the camp seem to have had little more effect than a series of other prohibitions, such as the use of fire buckets to wash clothes, the leaving on of lights in latrines, and leaving taps running.[110]

The Chinese, however, appear to have been very closely watched, their letters opened by Australian military censors even after they are working for the US Army.[111] And, on occasion, there is evidence of such brazen liberties taken by an officer responsible for censoring the letters from members of his Company that it results in worried correspondence from the Captain to higher command:

> It has now been brought under my notice that Lieutenant Roberts has when censoring letters been in the habit of reading out extracts to the orderly Room Staff to such an extent that personnel refer to the 'Session' as the 'Vaudeville Session'. Complaints have also been received that footnotes have been added to letters written by members of the unit, by Lieut Roberts ... Such behaviour for an Officer is tending to seriously undermine the morale of unit personnel, as well as the authority of the O.C.[112]

Military security continued to collect and evaluate a mountain of material about communists and communist sympathisers in the armed forces, as well as those in the AES. This included internal Party correspondence, pamphlets and other documents, and reports of meetings. There was also ongoing suspicion of the activities of 'foreign organisations in Australia', including those that 'are formed ostensibly for the purpose of inculcating loyalty to Australia in their respective nationals'. Surveillance stretched to include Lutheran churches, and cultural organisations such as the Australian–Soviet Friendship League and the Australia–India Association. After listing a range of suspect categories, WB Simpson, the Director-General of Security, emphasised his readiness to maintain 'censorship control of any organisation whose activities are considered to be of internal security interest.'[113]

A mountain of surveillance; yet it seems rarely to have led to action in the military. Typical was the army's response to suspicion about the possible communist leanings of a Lieutenant Wade, who was serving as an education officer in Kenmore Military Hospital. While the Security Service was suspicious, it was noted that 'the fact that Lieut. Wade may be a Communist is not, in itself, sufficient for military authorities to place him under investigation in the ordinary sense and that politically the Army cannot take any action against Communists within the Forces unless they overstep the bounds of Military discipline.'[114] As an historian of the communists in the Australian armed forces during World War II concluded, 'the regulations forbidding political activity were not rigidly enforced against many of those communists ... and this was primarily due to their strong support for the national war effort.'[115]

Similarly, the extensive Security correspondence about 'alien' soldiers seldom influenced the daily lives of the men in the Employment Companies. Their politics—if for many clearly shaped by their experience as foreigners and anti-fascists—were largely in tune with the times.

# 12

# Now the bloody war is over

The war in Europe ended with Germany's surrender on 8 May 1945.[1] VE Day, on 9 May, was a public holiday in Australia, but, in the words of the War Memorial website, 'celebration was tempered with the knowledge that the war in the Pacific was still to be won'.[2] Not so tempered in the Employment Companies composed of Europeans: some Companies declared a special rest day for those men not out on jobs, and it's likely that the 12th Employment Company was not alone in celebrating with special rations of beer and supper.[3]

On 15 August 1945 Emperor Hirohito announced Japan's surrender. On the same day, a 'Message Form' was sent to 'all units under command' by General Sir Thomas Blamey from his base in Borneo. It began with a statement of triumph—'The Japanese have surrendered. Our long and arduous struggle has ended in complete victory'—and went on to praise all those who served in the military: 'No divisions amongst the allies have contributed more to the downfall of our enemies than ours … the troops have been forged into a magnificent army to the pride and glory of Australia … we will go to our homes having done our part in ensuring freedom for all people …'[4]

Many years later, an Australian journalist, reflecting on the war's end, commented that after a war lasting 'five years, 11 months and 11 days, the young nation was proud and dutiful, but it was also tired and anxious.'[5] Some in the community experienced even more complex emotions.

Among the men in the 'alien' Employment Companies, there was jubilation and hope, but also uncertainty, apprehension, and terrible grief. For the Chinese, there was the refusal of the Australian Government to moderate the White Australia policy for even a handful of the men, despite their long and admirable military service. Barely four months after the Japanese surrender, the first two ships left for Hong Kong with 1600 men.[6] For those from war-devastated countries in Europe, the newspapers, as well as letters from 'home', had already carried grim accounts of the Nazi murder of families, destruction of communities and cultures. A Yiddish anthology of writing by Australian Jews, published in Melbourne in 1944, opens and closes with images by the painter and 'alien' soldier Yosl Bergner of the starving Jews of the Warsaw ghetto.[7]

Louis Waller, a Melbourne schoolboy when his father served in the 6th Employment Company, contrasts the two-day celebration for VJ Day, when 'scores of men and women, in and out of uniform, weaved conga lines down Collins Street', with the 'awful confirmation' for Jews 'that most of our near ones in Poland had perished: a singular dreadful tragedy concealed behind phrases such as "the destruction of European Jewry" and today's in-phrase, "The Holocaust"'.[8]

The war had ended, but it took some time before all the men in the Employment Companies were paid wages owed and discharged from the army. Individuals had been released earlier because they were declared medically unfit, particularly those over the age of forty-five.[9] Others were released in order to undertake essential roles in industry and agriculture,[10] or, as in the case of Frank Klepner, to further their studies. When the 6th Employment Company was stationed in Melbourne he had been able to attend lectures in physics at Melbourne University, and his application to the army at war's end for early release in order to study full time led to his discharge in January 1946.[11] Ex-servicemen received free tuition and a small living allowance.

Another dedicated part-time scholar, Julius Guest (Weingeist) from the 8th Employment Company, approached an ALP member of the federal government whom he met in a Melbourne hotel and explained that he wanted to finish his university studies in mathematics. The politician declared this was a good case for an accelerated discharge from the army. Guest was duly discharged on 1 April 1946, having served one week less than four years.[12] A fellow Dunera boy, Eric Liffman, whose much admired tenor voice entertained and comforted multitudes in war-weary Victoria, received his discharge from the same Company on 7 February 1946.[13]

Bob Exiner, whose attempts to enlist were initially rebuffed because he worked in a 'protected' industry, spent less than a year in the 6th Employment Company in 1942 before being transferred to an army medical corp. He wasn't discharged until May 1946. Remembering, he commented: 'I had just as much trouble getting out of the army after peace came as I had to get into the army.'[14] Eric (Erich) Eckstein was transferred back to Melbourne from Albury at the end of 1945 with others from the 8th Employment Company, and sent to work in ordinance stores; he recalled it as 'civilians in uniforms' until discharge in September 1946.[15] Orpheus Kandiliotis, from the 6th Employment Company, spent months in the post-war army in Mangalore, rural Victoria, one of the men allocated the potentially dangerous work of disarming bombs. But even dangerous army life had its compensations. Kandiliotis' account of that time includes a fond recollection of the three 'army' dogs who hunted rabbits with the men. They were beautiful, he said.[16] He was finally released in November 1946, with a suit of clothes and the money he was owed: £120.[17]

While some men—probably most—chafed at any delay in returning to civilian life, in retrospect a few took account of the considerable organisational difficulties. One of the latter was Frank Klepner, who saw sense in the government's actions. When asked how the delay could be justified, he replied: 'You couldn't suddenly stop. There were lots of troops overseas. Some of the work had to continue. A gradual discharge was easier to, A, process and, B, to absorb the people as they were discharged.'[18]

Meanwhile, as ever attendant to the soldiers' needs, the army publication *Salt* provided information on relevant subjects as varied as the clothing coupons for discharged troops and the men's access to free legal services from the Commonwealth Legal Service Bureaus in each state.[19]

In the 27 August 1945 issue, *Salt* presented 'the main points of the AMF Demobilisation Plan', including the three 'priority' categories:

> Normal Priority – order of precedence based solely on length of service, age of enlistment and dependency status. These are the basic factors on which priority is assessed.
>
> Special Priority – the order of precedence given to a man whose demobilisation is to be accelerated regardless of normal priority.
>
> Deferred Priority – the order of precedence for a man whose demobilisation is to be delayed regardless of normal priority or eligibility for a special priority.[20]

*Salt* provided no explanation detailing the basis on which either special or deferred priority was to be assessed. But very few of the men in the 'alien' Employment Companies were reading *Salt* for information about the rules and regulations for army discharge. Some read newspapers; there was a radio in the camps; and more or less reliable information came from their officers, their mates, their families, and from the broader ethnic, religious and political communities. Important information (and rumours) spread by word of mouth.

For the vast majority, civilian life beckoned. By the 22 October 1945 issue, thirteen pages under the heading 'This Way Out' are devoted to '*Salt's* detachable pocket guide to discharge and where you should go for what you need on return to Civvy Street.' The guide outlines the process, which begins with a medical and dental examination, and includes an offer for an 'aptitude test'—meant to be a guide to the soldier's 'civil re-establishment.'[21] The value of this last offer of assistance is uncertain. In an article written many years after the war, Robert Exiner gently mocked the supposed 'specific mechanical gift' the aptitude test determined was his.[22]

There was no choice when it came to the Australian Military Forces Demobilization Procedure Book—the official documentation of 'Authority for Discharge'. This khaki-covered booklet, thirty-two pages and small enough to fit into a coat pocket, was to be guarded 'as closely as your pay book', according to the advice printed on the inside front cover, because it was 'essential to the procedure through which you have to pass before being issued with your Discharge Certificate'.[23] Yet even here, the page headed 'Vocational Guidance Report', to be signed by a psychologist, was sometimes crossed out.

How does 'civvy street' accommodate tens of thousands of ex-servicemen and women?[24] Governments plan for wars' end. As early as 1940, the Menzies government established a committee 'to prepare data and recommendations with reference to the question of preference in government employment to men who serve in the present war.'[25] In 1942 the Labor government created parliamentary committees focused on repatriation legislation, including, with the states, a Rural Reconstruction Commission to consider soldier settlement in rural areas (a project initially developed after World War I),[26] as well as initiating the Department of Post-war Reconstruction.[27] By 1945 a comprehensive Re-establishment and Employment Bill was ready to be debated in the national parliament—part of what Prime Minister Curtin called 'the vital task of post-war reconstruction'.[28]

Writing decades later, Herbert 'Nugget' Coombs, the Director-General of the Department of Post-War Reconstruction and the key public servant responsible for the development of the bill, spelled out its central focus: 'Widening opportunity for all was to be the criterion by which policies were judged.'[29] Thus, the bill specified that 'the demobilisation scheme shall be prepared so as to apply as far as practicable uniformly to members of all sections of the forces.'[30]

Widening opportunity for all was not acceptable to every politician. There was a vigorous parliamentary debate on the Re-establishment and Employment Bill, but Country and Liberal Party members failed in their attempt to exclude 'aliens' from benefiting from access to health services, pensions, and preference in employment and training. The ever-vigilant Australian Council for Civil Liberties, utilising 'strenuous representations against a weight of adverse publicity', helped ensure that 'refugee ex-servicemen were admitted to benefits together with Australians.'[31]

Yet, as late as March 1946, it was considered necessary for the Minister for Post-War Reconstruction, Mr Dedman, to be provided with detailed notes by his department setting out the justifications for allowing refugee aliens from Employment Companies to take up university entry under the provisions of the Re-establishment and Employment Bill. The notes were to be used, if needed, in a parliamentary debate.[32] In such a debate, one of the most vigorous critics of the bill, the Country Party member George Bowden, argued that there was no justification for stateless 'members of the Jewish race' being eligible for reconstruction benefits because 'the tyranny which drove them out [of their own country] no longer exists'.[33] The Liberal Party's Harold Holt, who, twenty years later, would become the Prime Minister of Australia, insisted that he did not 'desire to raise racial or national issues.' None the less, he declared 'I unhesitatingly place our own young men before the stateless aliens.'[34]

It is likely, as the historian Bruce Pennay has suggested, that such a debate 'echoed a wider community uncertainty about the place of European foreigners in the kind of nation that was developing.'[35]

Whatever the pressures, the negative views did not prevail. As early as 1944, an army Major General was informing his superiors that the majority of men of European origin in the 'alien' Employment Companies 'regard Australia as their adopted country; a large percentage have indicated their desire to apply for naturalization as soon as they are eligible.'[36] And the Labor government was already planning its ambitious post-war immigration policy—a policy hinted at in the debate by Charles Morgan, the Labor member for the New South Wales seat of Reid. Responding to Opposition attacks on the bill,

Morgan warned that 'unless we adopt a broader outlook in regard to people who come here from overseas, we shall never make the progress that we desire or develop our country as it should be developed. Our ancestors came from other countries.'[37] He was echoing one of the leaders of his party. In a speech to parliament in 1943, the Minister for Immigration, Arthur Calwell, spoke admiringly of 'the splendid specimens of American manhood walking the streets of Australian cities', who were the product of America's having been 'for more than a generation, a melting port for European nations.'[38] In August 1945 *Salt* published an article by Calwell headed 'Pop. 7,000,000 – Not Enough'. Its final paragraph declared:

> The accomplishment of our immigration policy will require the support of every political party in Parliament and of every public organisation in the community. So much depends on the success of our population policy that failure will spell national disaster.[39]

In an analysis of Australia during World War II, the historian Michael McKernan, at one time Deputy Director of the Australian War Memorial, noted how significantly the war changed the country:

> By war's end Australians emerged as a much more complex and aware people ... [T]he second world war changed Australian attitudes and beliefs far more substantially than had the first world war ... The acceptance of a mass, non-British, immigrant programme symbolised this change.[40]

Only two months after the war, Calwell wrote to his colleague Frank M Forde, Minister for the Army, requesting 'the contribution certain classes and nationalities of aliens had made to our fighting Services'. He wanted this information to support 'the Government's policy on migration and the possibility later of attracting aliens to this country.'[41] As early as March 1944, the federal Cabinet had agreed that the migration authorities could consider refugee applications on their merits 'if they were from white internees'.[42] The second question on the application form for naturalisation asked: 'Is the applicant of European (white) race or descent?'[43]

Those members of the Employment Companies who passed the colour bar and who had been in Australia for at least six years could apply for naturalisation—and did not have to pay the usual £5 fee. Could a quite passionate note to the Prime Minister from the Minister for the Army have helped ensure this modest positive outcome? The note included a summary of the 'alien' men's military role, with the concluding argument that their exemption from the fee 'would predispose them more favourably to this country, in which they choose freely to remain and which, therefore, cannot be uninterested in desiring and encouraging their goodwill.'[44] The Prime Minister acknowledged the 'alien' men had been 'wearing the king's uniform' and had 'served their adopted country diligently'.[45] The Attorney–General's Department was asked 'to draft an amending Regulation accordingly.'[46]

After lengthy debate, the Re-establishment and Employment Bill was passed. As one historian comments: 'The right of returned servicemen to benefit has been, in many ways, considered a sacred right.'[47] On discharge, each soldier received 'civil entitlements', meant to assist him in a society where there was still rationing of food and clothing. The usual 'entitlements' list offered 'Civilian Clothing Card, Civilian Food Book, Special Clothing Book, Special 38 Clothing Sheet', and the odd '6 Hat or Shoes Sheet.'[48] And some, like Robert Exiner, received a war service loan.[49]

Civilians once more, the 'aliens' discarded their army uniforms,[50] embraced family members within arms' reach, and wept for loved ones lost in the pillage of war. Some left Australia—returning to what had once been home, to join surviving family members in old or new lands, or to embark on a different life alone. Of the men transported on the *Dunera*, it is estimated that more than half left at war's end.[51]

There are no exact figures, but the considerable number of 'alien' ex-soldiers who stayed in Australia were able to benefit from Coombs' 'widening opportunity for all'. Among the many who took advantage of what became known as the Commonwealth Reconstruction and Training Scheme were Klaus Friedeberger, from the 8th, who enrolled in the art school at East Sydney Technical College; Steven Strauss, also from the 8th, who enrolled in law at Melbourne University; and Adrian (Andy) Factor, from the 6th, who received a bursary to further his violin studies at the Melbourne Conservatorium.[52] 'Alien' ex-soldiers expanded and enriched both the class character and the culture of Australian tertiary education, and thereby, in the words of one historian, 'access to white-collar jobs and white-collar attitudes.'[53] This class and culture change also occurred as ex-servicemen were preferenced over non-servicemen in appointments to positions in the Commonwealth public service.[54]

Some slipped back into their pre-war occupations. Charles D'Aprano noted that he went into the army as an unskilled worker and came out the same.[55] Orpheus Kandiliotis from the 6th Employment Company was eager to take up his position at his milk bar in Swanston Street, Melbourne.[56] Keith (Kurt) Steinhardt, from the same Company, completed his apprenticeship as a watchmaker.[57] A pre-war pianist resumed his career. On 29 July 1946 the Melbourne *Argus* newspaper published an article about Gualtiero Volterra under the heading 'Solo Pianist Who Worked On Sydney Wharves':

> Mr G. Volterra, Italian-born pianist, who arrived in Melbourne yesterday to be soloist at the last two concerts of Eugene Goossens' Melbourne season, made his first concert appearance at the age of 8 in Florence, and during the war served in the alien labour corps in Sydney.
>
> He volunteered for service in Australia soon after his arrival in Sydney at Christmas, 1939, and was ultimately called up for the labour 1 corps. He worked mainly on the wharves, where his hands became roughened and full of splinters, but he said he had a 'grand time', and enjoyed the company of a group of intellectuals from Central Europe.[58]

Perhaps some of those Central European intellectuals were in the concert audience. Someone like Felix Werder from the 8th, himself a composer of classical music while earning his modest living as a teacher, meeting 'very interesting people' at the Melbourne Chess Club, and even more of them at the Swanston Family Hotel: Judah Waten, Flora Eldershaw, Vic O'Connor, Dalby Davison, Brian Fitzpatrick and Alan Marshall—'a lovely man' with whom he wrote an opera based on Marshall's play 'Kisses for a Quid'.[59] Perhaps also Yosl Bergner from the 6th, gaining new inspiration to shape his work at the National Gallery Art School in Melbourne.

Once held together by military regulation, uniform and commitment, it was personal friendship, or a common culture, religion or politics, that could provide powerful post-army bonds. One group—the Dunera boys—established an enduring organisational structure. Men radicalised by anti-fascist sentiment found comrades in the Communist Party. Among 'alien' ex-servicemen, there was general indignation about the RSL's early insistence (ultimately overturned) that membership depended on a soldier serving 'in the Allied cause during a period of hostilities, either overseas or in an area of war-like activity within his own country.'[60] The discrimination rankled, and led some to join the Australian Legion of Ex-Servicemen and Women, whose charter declared:

> The Legion admits to membership all Ex-Servicemen of this or any war. The test of entry is the fact that you have served in the Armed Forces of Australia and we are not concerned where or how you served.[61]

Jewish ex-servicemen could also join the Australian Federation of Jewish Ex-Service Associations, and, over the years, other ethnic communities established ex-service organisations based on fellowship and welfare.[62]

Anzac Day marches have generally not featured 'alien' Employment Companies.[63] According to one journalist, writing in 1992, his suggestion to a meeting of 'Dunera boys' that they should 'seek permission to march on Anzac Day received only one vote in favour.'[64] And by no means all the 'alien' soldiers chose to maintain army friendships. Henry Lippmann, who served in the 8th Employment Company, provides an eloquent statement of the immediate response to war's end and the freedom of one man seeking 'a complete new life':

> I did not ask for a job … I wanted to get away from all this. I wanted to get away from all my miserable, what I thought was my miserable past. From Nazi German refugees, from the refugees as well as from the Nazis. From the army authorities. From the internment thing. From my mates that drove me nuts. I don't want to see them any more, I want to get away from all that completely and start a complete new life.[65]

For others, army friendships enabled access to some security in civilian life. One instance of many was the experience of Fred Lester, among the youngest of the 'alien' soldiers. Twenty-three years old when discharged in July 1946, he was offered a university place to study engineering, but felt unable to accept the offer: he urgently needed to earn money in order to help his mother come to Australia from Shanghai. After taking a few short-lived part-time jobs, one of his former Employment Company mates gave him the opportunity to learn jewellery manufacturing skills. He accepted with thanks.[66]

Jack Friedman from the 6th suggested that many men were seeking change. 'We were jumping for joy for a few days, and then back to reality … Nobody wanted to go back to their own trade, especially when it required hard work, because we all thought that we worked hard enough—and we did, we worked very very hard.'[67] He himself undertook a course of building and construction at Caulfield Technical School. For Yossel Birstein, also from the 6th, his post-war occupation was a major shift, with long-lasting consequences. 'Changes happened in my life,' he said. 'I stopped being a tailor and became the secretary of the [Jewish] cultural institution J.N.L. Kadimah and became a freelance journalist.'[68] Walter Heine from the 8th became a businessman and shipowner, and Franz Stampfl a leading Australian athletics coach.[69]

My father, who wanted to help change the world, returned without a word of complaint to work with my mother in their small shop in Swan Street, Richmond, selling ladies' blouses and stockings. The little room at the back of the shop, with its window overlooking the Richmond railway line, became a lively site for visitors, political organisation and debate.

We are fortunate to have accounts of some of the considerable, and sometimes remarkable, contributions made by ex-army 'aliens' to Australian life, and the broader world.[70] But it would be a grievous error to neglect or underrate the everyday commitment of those whose 'ordinary' lives enhanced family, work, community and culture. Orpheus Kandiliotis pointed out that 'in an army, not everyone is a front-line member'.[71] The same is true of civilian life.

My father was discharged on 15 September 1945—conveniently, the day before his daughter's birthday. When he joined the army, he was medically assessed as B2; his discharge form states he is B1—much fitter, thanks to the physical work that was part of his daily army life. He was paid the money he was due: £88 9s 6d. And, like so many of the 'aliens', his name had changed: from Faktor to Factor; and all his army mates knew him as Sol, though he spelled that English name as Saul. At home, there was a Polish version: Shulek, and a Yiddish one: Shulem. To be an 'alien' was to juggle the past and the present, often with a different name attached to each chapter.

Months after my father's release, I stepped on to our small front verandah on my way to school, and saw that a large white swastika had been painted on the front of the house. My father scrubbed it off, but its ghostly shape endured. Many decades later, on impulse I drove down the Carlton street to see the house again. On that house, not a trace of the swastika remains.

# 13

# Bergner and Sievers: two 'alien' artists in the Employment Companies

A book of this kind inevitably subsumes personal experience into a broader general narrative. What should not be forgotten in the story of the Employment Companies are the individual stories of men of diverse backgrounds, skills, interests, aptitudes and passions.

At war's end, sooner or later each man was released to civilian life. Some, such as the Chinese, were forced to leave Australia. An unknown number chose to return home—though for many, the old home no longer existed. The majority remained in Australia, to rejoin loved ones or to start afresh; to make a home, a family, and a new life.

No one has calculated the breadth and depth of their contributions to the nation's material and cultural development. This last chapter provides a closer look at the experience of just two Employment Company men whose lives were influenced by their army years and who went on to make notable contributions to their new homeland.

Yosl Bergner was born in Vienna in 1920, but spent most of his pre-Australian life in Poland—first, with his paternal grandparents in Radymno; and then with his parents and sister in Warsaw. When he was a child, his father left a good job in a Vienna bank to return to Poland in order to be an active participant in what was called the Yiddish Revival, a cultural movement focused on the Yiddish language and on mostly progressive politics. The family lived in poverty in Warsaw, but Bergner remembered it as a life full of interests: books, theatre, lively argument, an enormous sense of cultural and political energy. He wrote:

> There was Jewish poverty, there was Polish poverty, but there was hope: socialism, the Bund [a Jewish socialist organisation], communism, Zionism. They all gave people hope. Tremendous cultural activity went on among the poor.[1]

Bergner came to Australia in 1937, when he was seventeen years old, following his sister who arrived a few months before him. Their permits and travelling money were arranged by their father, who recognised the threat Hitler posed to Jews in Europe, and was already in Australia, negotiating with the government to establish a Jewish settlement in the Kimberleys.[2]

On his way to Australia, an extended journey that took almost six months, Yosl Bergner stopped off in Paris, to stay briefly with relatives and to look at art. He had already told his father he was going to be a painter. 'I went to the Louvre,' he later wrote, 'and saw the originals of all the paintings I knew from father's books. I felt a closeness to all the painters, but most of all to Daumier.'[3]

Bergner's initial response to Australia was straightforward: 'I saw Australia and hated it immediately. At first I was homesick and wanted to go back to Poland.'[4] This is a reaction heard from a number of the Employment Company men, and can be found in many a migrant memoir. But Bergner's attitude changed quickly. Australia in the late 1930s was still in the slough of the Depression, something that, paradoxically, for the young painter was both good and bad. On the one hand, he says, 'The minute I came to Melbourne I felt comfortable … From the Warsaw street I moved straight into the Melbourne street.'[5] The poverty here was comfortingly familiar. On the other hand, his well-developed social conscience was outraged. Bergner's early

Australian paintings express empathy for the poor, and an implicit anger at the system that allows such poverty to exist.

Both his background and the circumstances of the time drew him to the political Left. Before he joined the army in 1942, he was already part of a loose group of artists and writers—men like Albert Tucker, Arthur Boyd, George Luke, Jim Wigley, Noel Counihan, Vic O'Connor and Judah Waten —some of whom were communists, most of whom saw themselves, in Tucker's words, as 'politically conscious neo-realists.'[6] (Later, Bergner insisted that he was a social humanist.[7]) Frank Klepner, a fellow soldier and friend of Bergner's who produced a fine book about him, points out that 'It was a time, especially for the younger artists, when to be a "modernist" automatically placed one into the radical, anti-establishment, politically active camp, almost invariably of the committed Left.'[8] While Bergner's period of membership of the Communist Party of Australia was short, his identification with the poor and downtrodden remained a powerful motivator of his art for many years.

Bergner brought the new perceptions and techniques of expressionism and modernism to Australian art. He and Danila Vassilieff—another immigrant— are widely regarded as the first modernist painters in this country. His influence on his fellow artists was considerable. Tucker, whose politics soon diverged from Bergner's, acknowledged his debt:

> Vassilieff and Bergner were 'carriers of another and totally different tradition… [leading to] a widening of my whole conception of what art and artists were about … [They] more or less made a physical reality out of the whole expressionist idea for us.'[9]

Arthur Boyd similarly acknowledged that it was Bergner, the first 'alien' artist he'd met, who led him from naturalism to what the art historian Bernard Smith called 'an expressive realism concerned with human beings and the problems confronting them.'[10]

Bergner also claimed to be the first artist to paint urban Aboriginal people.[11] He seems to have been the first significant white painter to have moved beyond an anthropological or 'noble savage' representation of Indigenous Australians. According to Bernard Smith:

> Bergner was not only the first to introduce a new art here. He was the first to bond his own alienation to that of the Aboriginal people he encountered in Melbourne, the first white artist to feel at home with them as fellow human beings.[12]

Bergner later explained:

> One of the first things that I did see here was an Aborigine playing on a gum leaf near the Town Hall. And I saw this terrible displacement … and identified immediately, and that was my subject.[13] I saw an Aborigine … somehow, to me, he looked like a Jew, with a hat on … So then I painted Aborigines, identifying them with Jews.[14] Till the war broke out. The minute the war broke out I started painting what I imagined was happening in Europe and Poland …[15]

The fate of those left behind—not just family, but all the Jews and, ultimately, all those diminished and destroyed by the Nazis—became Bergner's main subject matter while he was in the army, although he continued to paint Aboriginal Australians who lived on the river bank outside Tocumwal, near the 6th Employment Company camp. He remembers: 'Here I was, a so-called Australian soldier, with a slouch hat, with Greeks, Italians and so on, and [Aboriginal] people not owning their own country … The attitude to the Aborigines was very rough. Unjust.'[16] Fellow left-wing painter Noel Counihan wrote in a letter to Bernard Smith:

> B is as usual our most significant painter in my opinion … He is in a Labour Company away in the bush and is painting magnificent studies of aborigines. For the first time these abused people are being painted by a painter with an understanding of their sufferings and

> exploitation. It has taken a Polish Jew to interpret the aborigine realistically without patronage or sentimentality.[17]

Frank Klepner remembered the circumstances that gave rise to the later paintings of Aboriginal people:

> There was much black and white segregation ... perhaps even worse in some of the country towns. There were a number of Aborigines who lived in their humpies down by the riverside [near Tocumwal] made out of bits of rag and tin ... and they made quite an impression [on us]. A lot of these [people] were represented in Bergner's paintings.[18]

Unlike most Australians at the time, almost every Jew in the Employment Companies, and the majority of men from Europe who were not Jewish, focused on the European war with much greater intensity than on the war in the Pacific. Umbilical cords to family, home and country are not easily severed. For these men, it was the Allies' battle against the fascist armies invading country after country in Europe that gave their participation in the Australian Army a convincing validity. For most, it outweighed their frustration at not being in the fighting forces, and even at the drudgery, physical effort, and isolation from the civilising cities that characterised much of life in the Employment Companies.

It was Bergner who was able, in a work of art, to transmute the experience of alien soldiers in the Australian Army into a requiem of loneliness and loss. There is a painting in the Australian War Memorial, where it is called *Tocumwal – loading the train*; elsewhere, it is titled *End of a Day's Work, Tocumwal.* It was painted sometime between 1942 and 1944, while Bergner was in the 6th Employment Company.[19]

Bergner loved to paint what he saw around him, and, at the simplest level, this painting depicts four Employment Company men tired after a day's work. But that is not the feeling of the painting. It is laden with sorrow, and a sense of lonely hopelessness, emphasised by the men's drooping hands, and the vacant or covered eyes. Only one man looks at another—at the man who hides his face—and it is a look of pity, or regret. His expression is a reminder of the stories told by men in the Employment Companies, of the compassion felt when one of their number heard fateful news of family destroyed. It is a painting of suffering that far exceeds the aches and pains incurred from loading and unloading the trains at Tocumwal. This is indeed the work of a man who declared himself 'a specialist in displacement',[20] and who saw his mission—his work as an artist —'to make Australians aware … of what was going on [in Europe]'.[21] Some of Bergner's paintings of the Warsaw ghetto were created before much detail of that human tragedy was known in Australia.

When Yosl Bergner came to Australia from Warsaw in 1937, he spoke no English; was very young, poor and talented; and ardently Jewish—it was not uncommon for him to introduce himself with the words 'I am a Jewish painter from Poland.'[22] When Wolfgang Sievers arrived in 1938 from Berlin, he spoke good English, was thirty-five years old, a married man, highly educated, a sophisticated European, and Jewish only in the sense that his mother—already dead when Hitler came to power in 1933—was of Jewish descent. He brought with him much luggage, including the camera equipment that had originally provided him with a pleasant hobby, and, in his last years in Europe, a way of earning his living. He had wanted to study archaeology, but the Nazis made that impossible because, though brought up as a Lutheran, his maternal grandfather was a Jewish doctor. He decided his best choice was 'to use my hobby and turn it into a profession'. He recognised that 'you had to have a practical profession to enable you to survive in another country.'[23]

Sievers' father was a highly regarded art historian in Berlin, who, until 1933, was 'in charge of the cultural department of the German foreign office'. He was 'dismissed by the Nazis because he had supported what the Nazis called "depraved art", which was anything that was modern.'[24] His mother had been a writer, and director of an institute for educational films.[25] When speaking of his life, Sievers always expressed gratitude for the rich intellectual and cultural world his parents made accessible:

> Thanks to my parents' intense involvement with the arts, I benefited from living through the most exciting years of the Weimar Republic when Berlin had become the cultural centre of the world .... [T]he very best of Germany's and Europe's culture was so lovingly given to me by both my parents ...[26]

Sievers brought the traditions of high European culture with him, along with his furniture and cameras.

He came to Australia because of his father's urgings:

> 'Father, where should I go?' I said. He said, 'Well, two things. As far away from Europe as possible. And go to a British country.' I said, 'Why to a British country?' He said, 'Because it is better to be suppressed by the British than by anyone else.' And I think he was right. He was very sensible.[27]

Sievers decided on Australia because a German scientist who had been there told him it was 'a marvellous country', [28] and his family's good connections helped him get the sponsors he needed to settle here.[29] He was a fortunate man even in bad times: he stayed with the Nazi regime's German Ambassador—an old friend of his father's—in Lisbon, where a darkroom in the embassy cellar was built,[30] and his good luck followed him to Australia.

Sievers was already a skilled professional photographer when he stepped off the boat in Fremantle to be greeted by one of his sponsors, the university academic Dr John Reynolds. His first impression of Australia—the corrugated iron roofs of Fremantle—horrified him. 'I would have gone back to Germany immediately', he said, 'if the Gestapo wouldn't have been waiting for me at the other end.'[31] But when he settled in Melbourne, because he couldn't stand Sydney's humidity, a friend drove him into the country. 'We went through huge forests that had been ringbarked', he said. 'I saw the bush for the first time … It was wonderful.'[32]

Wonderful too was his introduction to Melbourne. He spent his first evening dining at the Florentino with an American friend, and the friend's mother's friend—who happened to be Mrs Whiteman, the owner of Le Louvre, one of the most exclusive shops in Melbourne. And soon he met Mrs Casey, the wife of the conservative MP Richard Casey. This is Sievers' description of what happened:

> I was introduced to Mrs Casey on my first night in Melbourne … I had an American friend who knew Mrs Whiteman from Le Louvre, and she took me to dinner at the Florentino … [She] took me to Mrs Casey, and I became one of her young men … I was a friend of Mrs Casey, the very clever woman of an idiotic husband, and [later] I lived with them in East Melbourne …[33]

He also became friends with Richard's Casey's brother Dermot, who was an amateur archaeologist. It was Dermot who saved his cameras when the war broke out and enemy aliens—people with 'enemy' nationality—were forbidden to have them.[34]

When the war began, Sievers tried but failed to join the military. With wry amusement, he remembered his experience:

> When war broke out I went to the Town Hall on the first of September and the military asked me where I came from. 'German, you said? Get out, you bastard!' Then, a couple of months later, I was accepted into the air force, the RAAF, to be a teacher at Point Cook. But as soon as that became known in Canberra they protested, and I was called up to army headquarters here [Melbourne]. I said, 'Why can't I do it?' He said, 'Well, because an enemy alien cannot be an officer.' I said, 'I don't care a damn whether I'm an officer or not, just a private [will do].' He said, 'No, this job carries the rank of an officer.' Bureaucracy forever.[35]

He kept himself busy for a time taking photographs of servicemen, many sent to him by his friend Dermot Casey.[36] He also began to take pictures of his new environment, and his training and background in the Bauhaus tradition drew him to the symmetry and power of man-made objects—a subject that in post-war years would make him one of Australia's most significant photographers. Always, he said, 'my Bauhaus training was … to photograph craftsmanship, the divinity of man and industry.'[37]

This cultured man, who chose to live in a suburb far from Bergner's Carlton and Fitzroy, and who became friends with establishment figures as well as artists, architects and fashion photographers, was never captive to the world of glamour or power. He had a sharp, critical eye. He spoke scornfully of the Melbourne rich, who had Cézannes on their walls but 'where the men would stand at one end [of the room] and talk dirty jokes and the women would stand far away at the other end and talk about babies … It was an unbelievable thing to see this ancient business …'[38]

When he joined the 4th Employment Company in March 1942, he readily accepted his fellow soldiers—the Italians and Greeks and Hungarians and Jews from Poland, as well as the many aliens in this Company who came from Germany and Austria—but his attitude to some of the officers was more critical (a not uncommon view):

> In Albury, our captain was Captain Walker, VD, which we immediately translated into venereal disease … I think he was half-drunk most of the time, and he addressed us in a slurred voice: 'Well, I notice a lot of you chaps are Germans and Austrians. I just want to tell you the only Germans and Austrians I like are dead ones!' That was our introduction to the Australian Army.[39]

While he enjoyed the polyglot company, and the cultural activities, including a choir—'we sang Russian songs in Russian'[40]—Sievers chaffed at the waste of the men's skill and knowledge as they loaded and unloaded trains in Albury. The Americans showed more sense, he believed: 'they [were] clever enough to use people like us to put into the army and have right in front, because of their local knowledge. Whereas here, we were in stupid work and not allowed to go overseas and fight.'[41] He did not have a high opinion of the military hierarchy—another not uncommon response among the Employment Company soldiers.

Even when he saw Australian behaviour that, at one level, appalled him, he recognised something appealing: a casual, egalitarian spirit and a reluctance to condemn. On one occasion, he was working as a checker at the Albury railway station when he saw 'a German U-boat captain in his full uniform' hiding in a carriage under a tarpaulin. There had been a break-out from the Cowra prisoner-of-war camp. Sievers says:

> I called some of the civilian labourers who were also at the platform. I said, 'Look, I've got this chap here. Please watch him while I quickly go and get the military police.'... They said, 'Ah, let the poor bugger go.' It was unbelievable. I said, 'This is a German U-boat captain.' They said, 'Ah, let him go.'... I went and rang up, and ten minutes later the [military police] came with submachine guns. There were the three ... labourers sitting playing cards with the German submarine officer. If that wasn't Australian![42]

Later, he was to say: 'I am fiercely Australian, but I am also fiercely European.'[43]

Sievers and Bergner are just two of the aliens who spent the bulk of the war as labourers: soldiers who never fired a shot. Their work was essential, and entirely unglamorous. They have largely vanished from public memory, and the war historians have generally overlooked them. Many of these men stayed on in Australia after the war. They never lost the invisible luggage of memory and hope they brought here. A few, like Bergner and Sievers, became eminent. Almost all contributed immensely to the post-war flowering of the Australian economy and its culture.[44]

# Notes

## Introduction

1 Catherine Merridale, 'War, Death and Remembrance in Soviet Russia', in J Winter and E Sivan (eds), *War and Remembrance in the Twentieth Century*, Cambridge University Press, 1999, p. 61.

2 Yosl Bergner, letter to 6th Employment Company reunion, Melbourne, 16 February, 1994. Copy held by June Factor.

## 1 Coming to Australia: home is no longer home

1 Kurt Lippmann, interviewed by Yvonne Fein, 2003, Beth Weizmann Centre, Melbourne.

2 Robert Exiner, 6th Employment Company, 'From the Spree to the Yarra: Memories of an Emigration', *Journal of the Australian Jewish Historical Society*, vol. 12, 1993–95, pp. 546, 547.

3 It has proven difficult to establish the exact number of men who served in the alien Employment Companies. The total figure of approximately four thousand has been calculated from the available evidence, especially the Companies' official War Diaries. Of this number, probably fewer than a thousand came from Asia.

4 Earlier immigrants from Europe had the time and opportunity to become naturalised Australian citizens, and naturalised men could join the AIF—the fighting forces. Restrictions on naturalisation for non-Europeans made this much less common among immigrants from Asia.

5 Keith Steinhardt, 4th Employment Company, interviewed by June Factor, 13 January 2003.

6 S Lovas, 'Politics of Hungarian Migrants in Australia', MA thesis, University of Sydney, 1969, p. 99. Of the Jewish women Michele Langfield interviewed who arrived in Australia in the late 1930s, she writes: 'All those interviewed tried to emigrate to other countries other than Australia which was not their first choice of destination. This was because of its distance from Europe, their lack of knowledge about it and the expense involved.' Michele Langfield, 'Guilt That They Survived: Memories Of Jewish Women Who Arrived In Australia In The Late 1930s', *Australian Jewish Historical Society Journal*, vol. xv, no. 3, 2000, p. 396.

7 Emil Witton (Witkowski), 3rd Employment Company, response to questionnaire from June Factor, September 2005. In 1937 Chaim Weizmann, a leader of the Zionist movement in Britain, told the Peel Commission that 'the world is divided into places where [the Jews]

cannot live and places where they may not enter.' Cited in M Marrus, *The Unwanted: European Refugees in the Twentieth Century*, OUP, NY, 1985, p. 185.

8 Orpheus Kandiliotis, interviewed by June Factor, 26 July 2004.

9 NAA: MP 529/3: transcript of the Aliens Tribunal No. 2 hearing of Zammarchi's appeal against internment, 7 May 1941.

10 Louis Waller, interviewed by June Factor, 8 July 2002.

11 Walter Schnock, response to questionnaire from June Factor, 25 May 1995.

12 NLA ORAL TRC 4549: Wolfgang Sievers, interviewed by Barry York, 20 March 2000, p. 30. In this interview, p. 41, he tells of being invited by Robert Menzies, then a minister in the Australian Government, to a cocktail party on the ship coming to Australia. Menzies insisted on marvelling at the 'wonderful job the Nazis did in Germany'. That led to 'a rather violent argument'.

13 Wolfgang Sievers, interviewed by June Factor, 16 June 2003.

14 Ken Inglis, Seumas Spark and Jay Winter with Carol Bunyan, *Dunera Lives: A Visual History,* Monash University Publishing, 2018, pp. 66–8; Pamela Bone, 'Haven-Sent Happiness', *The Age,* 6 October 1990.

15 Remembered by KG Loewald and quoted in his article 'A *Dunera* Internee at Hay, 1940-41', *Historical Studies*, vol. 17, nos. 66–69, 1976–77, p. 513.

16 The number of men and boys on the *Dunera* was 2542, according to the Research Guide 'Safe Haven: Records of the Jewish Experience in Australia', written by Malcolm Turnbull and produced by the National Archives of Australia, 1999. This number included 251 German pro-Nazis and 200 Italian fascists. See also Konrad Kwiet, '"Be patient and reasonable!" The internment of German-Jewish refugees in Australia', in *Australian Journal of Politics and History*, vol. 31, no. 1, 1985, p. 70. The most recent study, *Dunera Lives: A Visual History* (2018), by Ken Inglis et al, offers 'around 2500 men and boys' p. xvii.

17 Cited in Virginia Tate's article 'Franz Philipp', *Art and Australia*, vol. 30, no. 4, Winter 1993.

18 *Dunera Lives,* by Ken Inglis et al, pp. 304–5 and Appendix 1.

19 Sol Encel, 'How the *Dunera* Helped Australia', *The Age,* 15 September 1972, p. 9.

20 The 8th Employment Company into which men from the *Dunera* were enlisted included men deported from Singapore on the *Queen Mary*.

21 KG Loewald, 'A *Dunera* Internee at Hay, 1940-41', *Historical Studies*, vol. 17, nos. 66–69, 1976–77, p. 513.

22 The Nuremberg Laws: The Reich Citizenship Law: First Regulation (14 November 1935), Article 4. https://www.jewishvirtuallibrary.org/the-reich-citizenship-law-first-regulation

23 Cited in D Dwork and RJ Van Pelt, *Flight from the Reich: Refugee Jews, 1933-1946*, W.W. Norton, NY, 2009, p. 95.

24 Richard Evans, *The Third Reich in Power 1933-1939*, Penguin, London, 2006, pp. 555–9.
25 Information about Emil Witkowski's (Witton's) experiences comes from my interviews with him between 2005 and 2008, his unpublished November 2006 memoir, 'My Memories' (copy in possession of author), and a letter he wrote to the German publication *Aktuell* in 2005 (translated by him into English) (copy in possession of author).
26 Emil Witkowski became an Australian citizen in February 1945, and changed his surname to Witton in November 1945.
27 Written by M Gibbs, Shenton Park, Western Australia; cited by Alan Gill, 'When friends were enemies', the *Sydney Morning Herald* 'Good Weekend', 1 September 1990, p. 21.
28 *The Go-Between* by LP Hartley, Hamish Hamilton, London, 1953.
29 David Potts, *The Myth of the Great Depression*, Scribe Publications, Melbourne, 2006.
30 United States Holocaust Memorial Museum, *Holocaust Encyclopedia.* http://www.ushmm.org/wlc/en/article.php?ModuleId=10005470
31 Aryan Christians were Christians who had been Jewish but had converted.
32 NLA: MS 4965: Brian Fitzpatrick papers, Extract of ACCL Minutes, 6 March 1939.
33 For an analysis of the ACCL's policies and activities regarding refugees, see Don Watson, *Brian Fitzpatrick: A Radical Life*, 1979, and James Waghorne and Stuart Macintyre, *Liberty: A History of Civil Liberties in Australia*, 2011.
34 Cited in AW Martin, *Robert Menzies – A Life*, vol. 1, 1894–1943, MUP, 1993, p. 235.
35 Eg NAA: A1608 F19/1/1: File from Prime Minister's Department: Assistance to Poland - Migration of Refugees. This document also reveals the struggle within the government on the subject of refugees from Europe. A request from the Polish Government in January 1941 (supported by the British Government) for Australia to accept sixty-six Polish refugees (90 per cent of them Jews) who had managed to reach Japan was reluctantly agreed to by Cabinet. However, the Australian Minister at Tokyo was informed that 'while the Government is agreeable to the admission of these refugees as a gesture to Poland, we are not desirous of giving effect to the decision if it can be avoided.' The response of the Australian Minister at Tokyo, in a note to the Minister for External Affairs, was unambiguous: 'It may have been thought that such a refusal in the case of a non-influential country such as Poland would have been of no particular importance or significance. I take this opportunity of expressing a directly contrary view. The refusal of Australia to receive this small number of Europeans would inevitably have become known to the representatives of other countries – whether allied, neutral or enemy. It is

reasonably certain that many would have reported the matter to their Governments. Such reports would make no friends for Australia. As long as the British Empire ruled the world, it did not matter much whether or not Australia had any foreign friends. If, however, during or after the present war, the immigration policy of Australia should come up for international discussion, it would, to use mild language, be unfortunate if we had unnecessarily antagonised peoples of European stock as well as the people of Australia. The willingness of Australia to receive English children did our country a great deal of good. Now that we cannot obtain British immigrants, whom we would prefer to any others, if we are difficult and grudging in admitting other European immigrants of certified health, character and loyalty, the final results may be very serious.'

36 NAA: A433 1943/2/46: Department of the Interior 8/3/1938.

37 Cited in Paul R Bartrop, 'The Australian Government's "Liberalisation" of Refugee Immigration Policy in 1938: Fact or Myth?' *Menorah: Australian Journal of Jewish Studies*, vol. 2, no. 1, June 1988, p. 69, sourced at NAA: A433 43/2/46: 'Refugees (Jewish and Others) - General Policy File'.

38 Australian House of Representatives, *Debates*, 2 December 1938, p. 2628. Lieutenant Colonel Thomas W White, DFC, VD, MP, Minister for Trade and Customs. https://historichansard.net/hofreps/1938/19381202_reps_15_158/#debate-1

39 The dictation test remained in force until 1958. By giving would-be immigrants, especially Asians, a dictation test in a language they were unlikely to know, the government was able to restrict 'unwanted' immigrants while asserting that Australia engaged in no racial discrimination. The original legislation passed in 1901 (the Immigration Restriction Act), declared that naturalisation was permissible for any 'aboriginal native of Asia, Africa, or the Islands of the Pacific, excepting New Zealand.' For a detailed account of the White Australia policy, see James Jupp, *From White Australia to Woomera: Story of Australian Immigration*, Cambridge University Press, 2007.

40 Cited in M Cathcart and K Darian-Smith (eds), *Stirring Australian Speeches*, MUP, Melbourne, 2004, p. 192.

41 M Langfield and P MacLean, 'Jewish Women Remember 1938-9', in AJ Hammerton and E Richards (eds), *Speaking to Immigrants: Oral Testimony and the History of Australian Immigration, Visible Immigrants: Six*, Australian National University, Canberra, 2002, p. 84.

42 Australian House of Representatives, *Debates*, 2 December 1938, p. 2628. Lieutenant Colonel Thomas W White, DFC, VD, MP, Minister for Trade and Customs. https://historichansard.net/hofreps/1938/19381202_reps_15_158/#debate-1

43 R Feiglin, 'Jewish Refugees from Hitler', *Australian Historical Bibliography Bulletin*, no. 9, April 1984, pp. 25–6.

44 Australian House of Representatives, *Debates*, 2 December 1938, p. 2628. Lieutenant Colonel Thomas W White, DFC, VD, MP, Minister for Trade and Customs. https://historichansard.net/hofreps/1938/19381202_reps_15_158/#debate-1
45 ibid.
46 CA Price, 'Immigration: 1949-1970', in G Greenwood and N Harper (eds), *Australia in World Affairs 1966-1970*, Cheshire, Melbourne, 1974, pp. 171–205. The precise number of Jews who came to Australia in this period is uncertain. See Hilary L Rubinstein, *The Jews in Australia: A Thematic History, vol.1: 1788 – 1945*, William Heinemann Australia, 1991, pp. 177–80.
47 According to a speech in parliament in February 1949, 'A total of 15,000 persons were evacuated to Australia *from nearby countries*, and were given sanctuary during the war ... 5473 were non-Europeans' (my emphasis). Australian House of Representatives, *Debates*, 9 February 1949, Arthur Calwell, Minister for Immigration, p. 60. https://historichansard.net/hofreps/1949/19490209_reps_18_201/#debate-13
48 NLA ORAL TRC 4549: Wolfgang Sievers, interviewed by Barry York, 20 March 2000, transcript p. 44.

## 2 Life before the army

1 Yosl Bergner, *What I Meant to Say: Stories and travels as told to Ruth Bondy*, Hed Arzi Book Publishing, Israel, 1997, pp.88–9.
2 ibid., p. 77.
3 ibid., p. 90.
4 ibid., p. 101.
5 ibid., p. 103.
6 Cited by Frank Klepner, *Yosl Bergner: Art as a Meeting of Cultures*, Macmillan, Melbourne, 2004, pp. 67, 70.
7 Talk by Saul Factor in Melbourne to the Campaign for International Co-Operation and Disarmament on 16 April 1986, at a function to mark his eightieth birthday and election as Honorary Life Member of CICD. Tape in the possession of June Factor. An abbreviated version of the talk was published in the newsletter *CICD Anti-War News & Views*, June 1986, registered by Australia Post Publication No. VBH 5166.
8 Interview with Kurt Langfelder by June Factor, 17 September 2004.
9 Robert Exiner, interviewed by June Factor, 31 January 1994.
10 George Strauss, *Margaret Holmes: a life of ecumenical service 1886-1981*, privately printed, Melbourne 2003, p. 57.
11 William D Rubinstein, 'Concluding Remarks' to 'The Future of Australian Jewish Historiography: A Panel Discussion', *Menorah: Australian Journal of Jewish Studies*, vol. 3, no. 1, issue 4, July 1989, p. 38. The responses of the Australian Jewish community to the arrival of Jewish immigrants in the

1930s has been a subject of considerable debate among historians. See, for example, Suzanne D Rutland, *Edge of the Diaspora: Two Centuries of Jewish Settlement in Australia*, Collins Australia, Sydney, 1988, and Hilary L Rubinstein, *The Jews in Australia: A Thematic History*, vol. 1, 1788-1945, William Heinemann Australia, Port Melbourne, 1991.

12 Stephen Lovas, 'Politics of Hungarian Migrants in Australia', MA thesis, University of Sydney, 1969, pp. 2–3.

13 NAA: A373 788: Department of Army Memorandum to Secretary, Department of Defence Co-ordination, n.d., probably January 1942.

14 ibid.

15 NAA: A373 788: Enemy Languages in Public Places – Publication of newspapers in foreign languages.

16 *The Westralian Judean*, Editorial: 'False Security', vol. 12, no. 138, 1 February 1941, p. 1.

17 *The Hebrew Standard of Australasia*, 'The New Australian: Mass Meeting at Maccabean Hall, Letter from Minister of Defence, Important Resolution Unanimously Adopted', vol. 44, no. 48, Sydney, 20 April 1939, p. 2.

18 ibid., Mr Israel Green, p. 2. The subject of the local Jewish community's responses to the arrival of Eastern and Middle European Jews in the 1930s has been widely discussed in books and journals. Two influential writers on this subject, with somewhat different perspectives, are Suzanne D Rutland (see, for example, her article 'Australian responses to Jewish refugee migration before and after World War II', *The Australian Journal of Politics and History*, vol. 31, no. 1, 1985), and Paul R Bartrop and Gabrielle Eisen (eds), *The Dunera Affair: A Documentary Resource Book,* Melbourne: Jewish Museum of Australia/Schwartz and Wilkinson, 1990. A refugee and vigorous writer from the period, George M Berger, produced three articles on Australia and the refugees (*The Australian Quarterly*, vol. xiii, no. 3, September 1941, vol. xiii, no. 4, December 1941, and vol. xiv, no. 2, June 1942) in which he writes most critically of the role of the Australian Jewish Welfare Society.

19 Wolfgang Sievers, interviewed by June Factor, 16 June 2003.

20 Jack Waller, 'A Fragment of Memory', unpublished memoir translated and edited by his son, Louis Waller, Melbourne 1997, p. 25.

21 Ilma Martinuzzi O'Brien, 'Internments and Arthur Calwell: the view from Carlton', *Italian Historical Society Journal*, vol. 1, no. 2, December 1993, p. 11.

22 Kurt Langfelder, son of Richard Langfelder, interviewed by June Factor, 17 September 2004.

23 Louis Waller, son of Jack Waller, interviewed by June Factor, 8 July 2002.

24 From an unpublished memoir by Albert Ceen, summarised and translated by his son Guido Ceen, private correspondence to June Factor.

25 ibid.

26 Robert Exiner, 'From the Spree to the Yarra: Memories of an Emigration', *Journal of the Australian Jewish Historical Society*, Vol. 12, 1993–95, pp. 553–4.

27 NAA: MP529/3: Tribunal 2/Zammarchi. Zammarchi gives a brief account of his early working years in Australia in Wendy Lowenstein, *Weevils in the Flour: An oral record of the 1930s depression in Australia*, Hyland House, Melbourne, 1978, pp. 158–61.

28 Speros Polites, interviewed by June Factor, 1 November 2002.

29 ibid.

30 Robert Exiner, 'From the Spree to the Yarra: Memories of an Emigration', *Journal of the Australian Jewish Historical Society*, Vol. 12, 1993–95, p. 536. Judah Waten, a Jewish writer who wrote in English, was also a well-known communist and an active member of the Jewish Council to Combat Fascism and Anti-Semitism, an organisation Exiner and many other Jewish immigrants supported.

31 Bart Srhoy, *Journey Beyond Origin*, Hesperian Press, Western Australia, 1998, p. iv.

32 NAA: A437 1946/6/250: 'A Record of the Civil Aliens Corps'.

33 NLA: MS4738 Box 38: Aliens Control Instructions No. 11.

34 On 31 December 1942 the government census counted 51 317 registered aliens, of whom 22 314 were categorised as enemy aliens. See Noel W Lamidey, *Aliens Control in Australia 1939-46*, Sydney, 1974, pp. 5–6.

35 NAA: SP1048/7 556/1/1220: Aliens Control (Prohibited Possessions) Order.

36 Robert Exiner, 'From the Spree to the Yarra: Memories of an Emigration', *Journal of the Australian Jewish Historical Society*, Vol. 12, 1993–95, p. 553.

37 There is disagreement among historians as to the exact number of people interned during World War II. The figure of (more than) 15 000 comes from Klaus Neumann, *In the Interest of National Security: Civilian Internment in Australia during World War II*, National Archives of Australia, Canberra, 2006, p. 2. According to an official document, the highest number of internees, 12 256, was recorded in June 1942 (NAA: MP742/1 255/15/1286: Prisoners of War & Internees in Australia [Statistics]). Kay Saunders says that fifty-seven nationalities were interned (Kay Saunders and Roger Daniels (eds), *Alien Justice: Wartime Internment in Australia and North America*, University of Queensland Press, St Lucia, Queensland, 2000). Internees included prisoners of war.

38 NAA: A1608 N19/1/1 Part 1: letter from FG Shedden, Secretary of the Department of Defence Co-Ordination, to the Secretary of the Prime Minister's Department, 7 September 1939. This government and the Labor government that followed were also conscious that mass internment 'would create an unnecessary disturbance in the economic life of the community'—see NAA: A571 1942/538: Supplement 2 to War Cabinet Agendum No. 242/1941, Compulsory Service for Enemy

Aliens. See also NAA: A638 116: Aliens Control – Treatment of Civilian Enemy Aliens.

39 This figure declined after the government developed the category 'refugee alien' to cover Jewish and some anti-fascist 'enemy' aliens, and after Italy withdrew from the war in September 1943. By October 1945 there were only 4541 civilians still in internment. See Noel W Lamidey, *Aliens Control in Australia 1939–46*, Sydney 1974, p. 8 and Appendix; NAA: MP742/1 255/15/1286: Prisoners of War & Internees in Australia [Statistics]. For an example of the process in one state, see Michael Bosworth, 'Internment', in *On the Homefront: Western Australia and World War II*, ed. Jenny Gregory, University of Western Australia Press, Nedlands, 1996, pp. 200–11.

40 This was the official category of non-alien Australians—the vast majority of the population at the time.

41 Figures provided by James C Docherty, *Historical Dictionary of Australia*, Oceanian Historical Dictionaries No. 1, The Scarecrow Press, Metuchen, New Jersey, 1992, p. 84. The numbers interned could vary from state to state, most particularly for the Italians: more than 2216 were interned in Queensland, but only 170 in Victoria. See Ilma O'Brien, 'Internment of Italian Born and Unnaturalised British Subjects of Italian Origin', *War Internment and Mass Migration: The Italo-Australian Experience 1940 – 1990*, eds R Bosworth and R Ugolini, Gruppo Editoriale Internazionale, 1992, p. 92.

42 Families of Templers, a German Lutheran sect, were deported from Palestine to Australia during World War II and interned for the duration of the war. A recollection of a period in detention as a Templer child at Tatura internment camp has been written by Bruno Werner Weinmann: 'A Schoolboy's Memories, Life in Camp 3, Tatura', available from the Tatura Museum, Hogan Street, Tatura, Victoria 3616. For a general summary of internment, see Klaus Neumann, *'A Doubtful Character': Wolf Klaphake.* https://web.archive.org/web/20070828220417/http://uncommonlives.naa.gov.au/life.asp?lID=1 updated 7 May 2004.

43 Julius Guest interviewed by June Factor, 17 April 2003.

44 Alan Gill, 'Memorial for the brave Dunera boys', the *Sun Herald*, 13 November 1994, p. 14. Ken Inglis, Seumas Spark and Jay Winter with Carol Bunyan, *Dunera Lives: A Visual History*, Monash University Publishing, 2018.

45 This episode in what may be called late British colonial history was briefly described in an earlier chapter and is now well documented by Australian historians. See, especially, *Dunera Lives*, by K Inglis, Seumus Spark and Jay Winter with Carol Bunyan.

46 Felix Werder, interviewed by June Factor, 5 June 2003.

47 The ill-treatment of the men by the soldiers guarding the detainees became the subject of debate in the House of Commons, and ultimately of

an apology from the British Government and some minor compensation. See, for example, Cyril Pearl, *The Dunera Scandal*, Angus & Robertson, Sydney, 1983, p. v.

48 Julius Guest interviewed by June Factor, 17 April 2003.

49 While the detainees were, in the end, not informed of where they were to be sent, there had been an earlier call for volunteers who wished to go to Canada.

50 Kurt Lewinski, 'The Dunera Diaries', extracts published in the *Sunday Age*, 5 August 1990. There are some 'Dunera boys' who challenge such bleak accounts—as in June Factor's interview with Bern Brent.

51 'Robert', interview in Wendy Lowenstein and Morag Loh (eds), *The Immigrants*, Hyland House, Melbourne 1977, p. 65.

52 Eric Eckstein, 'The Dunera Experience', letter in *The Age*, 29 August 2005.

53 Books include: Cyril Pearl, *The Dunera Scandal;* Benzion Patkin, *The Dunera Internees*, Cassell Australia, Stanmore, New South Wales, 1979; Paul R Bartrop and Gabrielle Eisen (eds), *The Dunera Affair: A Documentary Resource Book*, Jewish Museum of Australia, and Schwartz and Wilkinson, Melbourne, 1990; and Ken Inglis et al, *Dunera Lives: A Visual History,* Monash University Publishing, Melbourne, 2018; *The Dunera Boys*, Network 10 television series, 1985; National Library of Australia *Dunera Boys* exhibition, 2010.

54 Pamela Bone, 'Haven-sent happiness', *The Age*, 6 October 1990; Ken Inglis et al, *Dunera Lives: Profiles,* Monash University Publishing, Victoria, 2020, p. xvi.

55 Konrad Kweit, '"Be patient and reasonable!" The internment of German-Jewish refugees in Australia', *Australian Journal of Politics and History*, vol. 31, no. 1, 1985, pp. 70–1.

56 See Chapter 10 for a discussion of some of these groups.

57 Erwin Fabian, *Max und Erwin Fabian: Berlin, London, Melbourne*, Stiftung Stadtmuseum, Berlin, 2000, pp. 130–1.

58 Julius Guest, interviewed by June Factor, 17 April 2003.

59 ibid. Through the efforts of a number of individuals and organisations, including the Australian Student Christian Movement, Melbourne University accepted interned students under its External Studies scheme. See Paul R Bartrop and Gabrielle Eisen (eds), *The Dunera Affair: A Documentary Resource Book*, Jewish Museum of Australia and Schwartz & Wilkinson, Melbourne 1990, pp. 322–3; and George Strauss, *Margaret Holmes: a life of ecumenical service 1886-1981*, p. 67.

60 NAA: MP385/4 1940/271: Petition to the Governor-General, Lord Gowrie, 2 March 1941. While there is no evidence Lord Gowrie influenced the final release of these internees, he was certainly sympathetic to aliens detained without proper cause. His views are expressed in a letter to King George VI, written on 4 November 1940 (NLA MS2852:

Papers of Alexander Gore Gowrie), and his support for the work of Margaret Holmes from the Student Christian Movement (see George H Strauss, 'Margaret Holmes: a life of ecumenical service', privately printed by the author, Melbourne, March 2003, p. 53).

61 NAA: MP742/1 255/12/12: Letter from C Venn Pilcher to FM Forde re separation of refugee internees from Nazi internees, 1942.

62 C Willyan, *Memoirs*, 1948 unpublished ms, Fryer Library, University of Queensland, cited in Kay Saunders, '"Discovering" the subversive and the saboteur: the disjuncture between official records of internment policy and practice and the remembered experiences of internees in Australia in the Second World War', *Oral History of Australia Journal*, no. 13, 1991, p. 6.

63 ibid.

64 NAA: SP459/1 489/1/2187: Letter from Southern Command to Eastern Command, 15 July 1941.

65 Count von Luckner, cited in Kay Saunders, '"Discovering" the subversive and the saboteur: the disjuncture between official records of internment policy and practice and the remembered experiences of internees in Australia in the Second World War', *Oral History of Australia Journal*, no. 13, 1991, p. 6.

66 NAA: A376 T107: *Commonwealth of Australia Gazette*, no. 242, Canberra, 30 November 1940. The decision to establish such a tribunal probably followed the pattern established by the government in Britain.

67 NAA: A376 T107: Commonwealth of Australia National Security (Aliens Control) Regulations, Observations for the Guidance of Aliens Tribunals, Department of the Army, p. 2.

68 NAA: A376 T107: National Security (Aliens Control) Regulations: Regulation 20, Aliens Tribunal (Victoria) No. 2, 13 March 1941.

69 NAA: MP508/1 255/702/366: Letter re Guiseppe Zammarchy [sic] - Italian Internee - P.W./WA14523, 20 September 1941.

70 NAA: MP508/1 255/743/130: Guiseppe Zammarchi, 1940-41.

71 NAA: MP529/3: Aliens Tribunal No.2/ Zammarchi.

72 ibid., evidence of Zammarchi to the Aliens Tribunal, Wednesday, 7 May 1941.

73 ibid.

74 ibid., statement to Aliens Tribunal by chairman Mr C Book KC.

75 NAA: MP508/1 255/743/3: Letter from Charles Wm. Cullip, St Arnaud, 7 April 1941.

76 NAA: MP508/1 255/702/366: Letter re Guiseppe Zammarchy [sic] - Italian Internee - P.W./WA14523, 20 September 1941.

77 NAA: MP529/3: Tribunal 2/ Zammarchi, extract from report of Major Prentice of Eastern Command, 10 March 1941.

78 NAA: MP508/1 255/743/130: Report to G.O.C., Southern Command, on objections submitted by Giuseppe Zammarchi.

79 See Chapter 10 for an account of some of those who worked for the release of detainees.

80 Konrad Kwiet, 'Be Patient and reasonable'... *Australian Journal of Politics and History*, vol. 31, no. 1. 1985; NAA: A373 5752: Release of UK Internees in Australia; NLA: MS4738, Box 38: Calwell Papers, October 1942.

81 NAA: A6388 414 War Cabinet Agendum, Supplement No. 1 to Agendum No. 242/1941, Military Service for Aliens, p. 2.

82 ibid.

83 NAA: A6388 95 Voluntary Enlistment of Aliens in A.I.F. and A.M.F. and Supplementary Regulations relating to National Security (Supplementary) Regulations to Statutory Rules 1942, No. 40, Amendment of the National Security (Supplementary) Regulations, notified in the Commonwealth Gazette, 4 February 1942, Explanatory Memorandum for Executive Council.

84 Helmut Newton, *Autobiography*, Nan A. Talese/Doubleday, NY, 2002, pp. 106–7.

85 *The Australian Women's Weekly*, March 2004, p. 30.

86 *The Shepparton News*, 'Refugee Fruitpickers Finish Work in Shepparton: Some of Their Impressions', Monday, 13 April 1942, p. 3.

87 ibid.

88 Helmut Newton, *Autobiography*, Nan A. Talese Doubleday, NY, 2002, p. 112. Such a threat was not recalled by other interviewees.

89 Felix Werder, interviewed by June Factor, 5 June 2003.

90 Cyril Pearl, *The Dunera Scandal*, Angus & Robertson, Sydney, 1985 [1983], p. 201; Ken Inglis, Bill Gammage, Seumas Spark and Jay Winter with Carol Bunyan, *Dunera Lives: Profiles*, Monash University Publishing, Melbourne, 2020, p. xxvii.

91 '8 Aust Employment Coy. March', words and music written by Sergeant Lohde, cited in Paul R Bartrop and Gabrielle Eisen (eds), *The Dunera Affair: A Documentary Resource Book*, Jewish Museum of Australia and Schwartz & Wilkinson, Melbourne 1990, pp. 381–2.

92 The *Sydney Morning Herald*, 'A Plea for Refugees', 8 July 1940, p. 3; NAA: A1608 F19/1/1 Department of the Interior, Memorandum: Admission of Polish Refugees from Japan. For a detailed discussion of the changing rules regarding sponsorship, permits, etc, see Hilary Rubinstein, *The Jews in Australia: A Thematic History*, William Heinemann, Port Melbourne, 1991.

93 The National Archives of Australia Research Guide 'More People Imperative: Immigration to Australia 1901-39' by Michele Langfield lists a number of these organisations in Chapter 9, 'Refugees'. https://www.naa.gov.au/help-your-research/research-guides/more-people-imperative-immigration-australia-1901-39

94 Michele Langfield, 'The fortunate few: Jewish refugee policy and women's experiences in the 1930s', Margaret P Hamilton (ed.), *Oral History Association of Australia Journal*, No. 22, 2000, p. 44.
95 Robert Salter, 'Love thy Neighbour', a speech given by Salter on the occasion of his grandson David's bar mitzvah, November 1995, copy given to June Factor.
96 Bob James, 'The Knights of Labor and Their Context', pamphlet for the 6th Biennial Conference of the Australian Society for the Study of Labour History, held 1–4 October 1999 in Wollongong. http://www.takver.com/history/secsoc02.htm
97 Robert Salter, 'Love thy Neighbour', a speech given by Salter on the occasion of his grandson David's bar mitzvah, November 1995, copy given to June Factor.
98 Saul Factor, talk given to the Campaign for International Co-operation and Disarmament at a celebration of his eightieth birthday held in Melbourne on 6 April 1986. Extracts from the talk were published in *CICD Anti-War News & Views*, June 1986. The manuscript of the full talk, plus later elaboration by Saul Factor, is held by June Factor.
99 ibid.

## 3 Joining up

1 Saul Factor, 'Saul Remembers …', *CICD Anti-War News & Views,* Melbourne, June 1986.
2 The *Sydney Morning Herald*, 'Dictatorship: Attitude of Mr. Menzies, Possible Degeneration of Democracy', Tuesday, 15 November 1938, p. 13, and the *Sydney Morning Herald*, 'Viewpoint of Germany: Mr. Menzies' Plea for Understanding, Rearmament Defended', Monday, 12 December 1938, p. 11.
3 The Federal Treasurer, Mr Spender, reported in the *Sydney Morning Herald*, 'Progress of Loan. Treasurer Dissatisfied', 6 June, 1940, p. 9.
4 The social philosopher PH Partridge observed in 1951 that 'it was the Labour Party, which had regarded both military conscription and economic and social compulsion with great suspicion, which established the most far-reaching control to which Australians had ever had to submit', and that 'it has been shown on more than one occasion in Australian political history that a Labour government can bring pressure to bear on workers which it would be politically difficult for a non-Labour government to attempt.' PH Partridge, 'Depression and War, 1925 – 50', in Gordon Greenwood (ed.), *Australia: A Social and Political History*, Angus & Robertson, Sydney 1972, pp. 378–9. This is also the view of the historian and civil libertarian leader Brian Fitzpatrick, as expressed in a book published during the war: *A Short History of the Australian Labor Movement*, Rawson's Bookshop, Melbourne, 1944, p. 212.

5 SJ Butlin, *War Economy 1939-1942*, Australian War Memorial, Canberra, 1955.

6 PM John Curtin appealed to the American President FD Roosevelt on 26 December 1941, outlining the parlous circumstances in which Australia found itself, and asking for American assistance: 'It is in your power to meet the situation. Should the Government of the United States desire, we would gladly accept an American commander in the Pacific area.' Cited in Irene Dowsing, *Curtin of Australia*, Acacia Press, Blackburn, n.d. (preface by JF Cairns dated 1968), p. 108.

7 ibid., p. 106.

8 ibid., p. 117.

9 Paul Hasluck, *Australia in the War of 1939-1945: Volume II – The Government and the People 1942-1945*, Australian War Memorial, Canberra, 1970, p. 130.

10 Irene Dowsing, *Curtin of Australia*, Acacia Press, Blackburn, n.d. (preface by JF Cairns dated 1968) p. 118.

11 Until the passage of the Nationality and Citizenship Act 1948, which came into force on 26 January 1949, Australians were classified as British subjects. The use of the term 'race' as a synonym for nationality was common in this period, and can still be heard today, although less often.

12 In February 1942 military documents list fifty-nine 'alien' nationalities 'known to be resident in Australia': Department of the Army Military Board, 13 February 1942, NAA: SP459/1, 489/2/191: 'Definition of Aliens in Categories'. The government respected a longstanding convention against the conscription of citizens of neutral countries, such as Switzerland.

13 Irene Dowsing, *Curtin of Australia*, Acacia Press, Blackburn, n.d. (preface by JF Cairns dated 1968) p. 134.

14 A detailed account is provided in SJ Butlin and CB Schedvin, *War Economy 1942-1945*, Australian War Memorial, Canberra, 1977, pp. 3–33.

15 Aliens who did not enlist in the army could be conscripted into the Civil Aliens Corps. See Australian War Memorial, 1946/6/250. The population in 1914 was about 5 million; by 1939 it was 7 million.

16 Percentages are calculated from figures provided by Paul Hasluck, *The Government and the People 1939-1941*, Australian War Memorial, Canberra, 1965, pp. 399–40 and p. 613.

17 NAA: MP508/1 275/750/768: Enlistment of Aliens, 5 September 1939. The document incorrectly gives his name as ES Coppel.

18 ibid.

19 ibid., 21 November 1939.

20 NAA: A6338 95: Supplement to the Defence Committee Agenda for meeting of 15 February 1940.

21 ibid.

22 ibid.
23 NAA: A6338 95 582/401/103: Cable from Secretary of State for Dominion Affairs, London, to Prime Minister's Department, 27 September 1939.
24 NAA: A6338 95 54/301/19: Memorandum from FG Shedden, 'Enlistment of Aliens in the Australian Defence Forces'; for comment on the motive for the change to the requirement to swear an oath to the King, see NAA: A6338 95 3/2/274: Letter from War Book Officer, 13.1.1941 to Colonel Vail under heading Co-Ordination: Enlistment of Aliens.
25 NAA: 54/301/19: Memorandum on Enlistment of Aliens in the Australian Defence Forces from FG Shedden, Secretary of the Department of Defence Co-Ordination.
26 The *Herald*, 'Some Aliens May Join R.A.A.F.', 25 June 1940.
27 NAA: MP308/1 275/750/818, Naturalisation of Andrew Zanelli.
28 ibid., letter signed by PC Spender, 21 February 1941.
29 ibid., letter from J McEwen to the Hon PC Spender, Minister for the Army, 28 February 1941.
30 ibid., Department of the Army Minute Paper, 5 March 1941.
31 ibid., letter from Southern Command headed 'Enlistment of Aliens', 19 March 1941.
32 The *Argus*, 'First Aliens Enlisted', 5 April 1941, p. 5.
33 NAA: A6338 95: Department of Defence Minute Paper, Enlistment of Aliens in Australia, 26/1/1940.
34 NAA: SP459/1 489/2/337: Citation from the Director of Personal Services in letter from Major-General H.Q., New South Wales Line of Communication Area, May 1942.
35 NAA: SP459/1 430/14/322: Letter from Lieutenant-Colonel Clark, Army Headquarters, Victoria Barracks, Melbourne, to all Command Districts, 8 April 1941.
36 In the Routine Orders for the 19th Australian Labour Company, 13 October 1942, there is a section headed 'Nomonclature [sic] of the Forces', which sets out the definitions of the various army groupings that have been promulgated 'to ensure standardised usage and interpretation'. The previous occasional usage of AMF (Australian Military Forces) to denote army forces other than the AIF was to cease. See Australian War Memorial: 52 22/1/26: 19 Works Company, June 1942 – February 1943. As with other, similar, edicts, the confusing practice continued intermittently.
37 NAA: A6388 414: War Cabinet Agendum, Military Service for Aliens, from FM Forde, Minister for the Army, 10 January 1942.
38 NAA: 6388 414: War Cabinet Agendum No. 242/1941, Aliens – Service Under the Defence Act.
39 For a summary of regulations regarding enemy and refugee aliens from 1939 to February 1942, see NAA: A472 W6534: Attorney-General's Department. Minute Paper. Jewish Refugees - Statelessness.

40 Statutory Rules 1942, No. 39: Regulations Under the National Security Act 1939-1940, notified in the *Commonwealth Gazette* on 3 February 1942. Under another amendment of the National Security (Aliens Service) Regulations, August 1942, male enemy aliens (other than refugee aliens) could also be compelled to undertake 'such service in Australia as is directed by the Minister of State for the Interior, not being service in the Armed Forces' (NAA: A6388 414).
41 NAA: SP459/1 489/2/191: National Service (Aliens Service) Regulations – Registration and Enrolment, 1942.
42 NAA: MP742/1 275/2/38: War Cabinet Agendum No. 242/1941, Compulsory National Service for Neutral Aliens.
43 ibid., War Cabinet Minute, 24 November 1943.
44 NAA: A571 1942/538: Department of Works, Allied Works Council, War Cabinet Agendum.
45 *The Age* letter – 'Land Buying Aliens' by 'Soldier's Mother', Shepparton, 9 September 1940, p. 8.
46 *The Age* letter – 'Land Buying Aliens', by H Pollak, Hawthorn, 10 September 1940, p. 8.
47 NAA: A571 1942/538: War Cabinet Agendum No. 490/1942, National Service for Refugee and Enemy Aliens, 27/11/1942, stamped SECRET.
48 George M Berger, 'Australia and the Refugees', *The Australian Quarterly*, vol. xix, no. 2, June 1942, p. 74.
49 Helmut Graf, response to June Factor's questionnaire, 23 May 1995.
50 ibid.
51 Wolfgang Sievers, interviewed by June Factor, 16 June 2003.
52 Bart Srhoy, *Journey Beyond Origin*, Hesperian Press, Carlisle, Western Australia, 1998, p. 56.
53 ibid.
54 Emil Witton, letter to June Factor, 23 August 2005, and response later that year to questionnaire from June Factor. In 1941 the enemy alien nationalities were German, Austrian, Italian, Finnish, Rumanian, Hungarian and Bulgarian.
55 NAA: SP459/1 489/2/235: Letter from Secretary of the Military Board to all Command Bases, 14 March 1942.
56 NB different spellings of names, both while in the army, before and later.
57 June Factor's phone conversation with John Callinicos, 7 July 2004; also interview with Callinicos by George Paxinos.
58 NAA: MP508/1 275/701/199: 2nd Australian Imperial Force – Conditions of Enlistment, Extracts from Standing Orders for the 2nd AIF Chapter IV.
59 NAA: SP459/1 489/2/176: 3 February 1942, provides a telegram summary of the rules regarding enlistment of aliens.
60 An example of the range of occupations in one Company, the 8th, can be found in Cyril Pearl's *The Dunera Scandal*, Angus & Robertson, Sydney,

1983, p. 197. There is evidence from interviews with some of the men that they gained in physical fitness as a result of the work undertaken in the Employment Companies.

61 AWM: 52 22/1/36: War Diary, 28 Australian Employment Company, 16 July 1942.

62 AWM: 52 22/1/26: Medical Classification, 19th Employment Company.

63 AWM: 52 22/1/18: 9 Works Company, January – December 1944.

64 Erwin Fabian, taped account transcribed and edited by Brigid McCoppin, Melbourne, May – June 2000, in the catalogue for the exhibition *Max und Erwin Fabian: Berlin – London – Melbourne*, by Dominik Bartmann, Stadtmuseum Berlin, Ephraim-Palais, 2000.

65 Keith Steinhardt, interviewed by June Factor, 2003.

66 AWM: 54 883/5/4: [Security – National Security (Emergency Control) Regulations] National Security (Aliens Service) Regulation, December 1942.

67 Bart Srhoy, *Journey Beyond Origin*, Hesperian Press, Carlisle, Western Australia, 1998, pp. 67 and 68.

68 ibid., p. 70.

69 Robert Exiner, 'From the Spree to the Yarra: Memories of an Emigration', *Journal of the Australian Jewish Historical Society*, vol. 12, 1993–95, p. 555.

70 Frank Klepner, interviewed by June Factor, 16 April 2002.

71 Helmut Newton, *Autobiography*, Nan A. Talese/Doubleday, NY, 2003, p. 113.

## 4 We're in the army now

1 NAA: MP742/1 275/2/9: Enlistment of Aliens, 6 February 1942.

2 ibid.

3 ibid.

4 NAA: MP508/1 61/702/690: Enlistment of Aliens, 18 March 1942.

5 ibid., letter to the Hon FM Forde, Minister for the Army, 15 September 1942.

6 ibid., letter dated 14 April 1942.

7 The Regulations establishing the Army Labour Corps were signed by the Governor-General and the Minister for the Army on 4 February 1942—see NAA: MP927/1 A4/1/65: Regulations signed by the Minister for the Army, FM Forde, February 1942.

8 NAA: MP508/1 61/702/690: Minute Paper 8 April 1942 [6237]. A telegram marked SECRET from the Army Base in Melbourne, sent on 4 February 1942, outlined an elaborate classification of refugee aliens into those 'whose loyalty is undoubted', 'those against whom no suspicion exists', and 'those considered disloyal or about whom any suspicion exists'. The first category could be 'allotted to Labour Units without hindrance'; the second also, but with the qualification that the Commanding Officers were to 'confidentially observe [their] activities'; the last category was to

be drafted into 'civilian auxiliary service'—see NAA: MP7421/1 275/2/9: Allegations re Alien Labour Coys, Memo submitted by Sergeant Jackson.

9 ibid., Minute Paper Uniform – Labour Units, 2 May 1942.

10 ibid., Minute Paper – Labour Units C.M.F. – Uniforms, 30 April 1942.

11 The information provided by Keith Glyde in his publication *Distinguishing Colour Patches of the Australian Military Forces 1915-1951*, Claremont, Tasmania, 1999, is not entirely accurate in its description of the nature of the Employment Companies (p. 188).

12 The general rule of equality in pay is set out in the Explanatory Statement to the Defence (Labour Corps) Regulations, NAA: MP927/1 A4/1/65.

13 AWM: 52 22/1/27: 20 Works Company, January – December 1943.

14 AWM: 52 22/1/41: 33 Employment Company, January – June 1944.

15 NAA: MP742/1 275/2/32: Statement by Private Honigsberg K V377762, 2 March 1943.

16 AWM: 54 721/22/1: Account of formation, service and activities of 22nd Works Company.

17 In October 1942 the Quartermaster-General listed thirty-two Employment Companies 'with a total strength of 10,000 all ranks' and the expectation that the extra Companies to be established would result in over 14 000 men—see NAA: MP508/1 61/702/690: Colour Patches for Employment Companies, 27 October 1942.

18 An outline of each Company can be found in Graham McKenzie-Smith, *The Unit Guide – the Australian Army 1938-45*, Blue Sky Publications, 2018. For establishment details of Employment Companies, see AWM: 54 422/7/8: Provisional War Equipment Table for an Employment Company, July 1943.

19 ibid.

20 NAA: SP1048/7 S9/1/200: Employment of Labour Companies.

21 NAA: MP927/1 A4/1/65: Draft defence (Labour Corps) Regulations Explanatory Statement.

22 The distinction between the armed and non-armed Employment Companies was important for many in the non-armed Companies. Thus an entry in the War Diary of the 28th Employment Company based in the Northern Territory: 'As the members of the Coy are assentually [sic] soldiers and manual workers afterwards, it is necessary to keep up trg [training].' AWM: 52 22/1/30: War Diary 28th Employment Company, Alice Springs, 19 December 1943.

23 Henry Lippmann, interviewed by Rosemary Block, New South Wales State Library Oral History Program, 1994, Tape 7, p. 103.

24 Charles D'Aprano, 'The Heroes of Tocumwal', in his short story collection *Old Wine in New Bottles*, Winseray, Carlton, 1986, pp. 38–9.

25 NAA: MP508/1 275/705/48: Labour Coys (Aliens) Arming of Non-Alien Personnel.

26 ibid.
27 NAA: MP508/1 211/701/138: Medical Classification of Personnel.
28 NAA: MP927/1 A4/1/65 Statutory Rules 1942 No.44 Regulations Under the Defence Act 1903–1941.
29 NAA: A2421 61506 Medical Standard of Fitness on Enlistment and Classification of Personnel: Labour Units – Standards of Physical Fitness.
30 ibid.
31 Werner Lowenstein, interviewed by June Factor, April 2003.
32 Mitchell Library, MLMSS 6735: Ceen family papers, 1923–98, letter, Monday, 4 May 1942.
33 ibid., letter, 24 August 1942.
34 Letter to June Factor from Lieutenant Colonel JA Stirling, an historian of the British Pioneer Corps, 23 October 2002. The same information can be found on the website http://www.royalpioneercorps.co.uk/rpc/history.htm
35 NLA ORAL TRC 4549: Wolfgang Sievers interviewed by Barry York, 20 March 2000, p. 66. The official title in the Regulations signed by the Minister for the Army, FM Forde, in February 1942 refers to the establishment of 'an Army Labour Corps' (NAA: MP 927/1 A4/1/65: Draft Defence (Labour Corps) Regulations. Explanatory Statement). Earlier discussion in the Menzies government about the possible involvement of aliens in the military used the term 'Pioneer Corps' (NAA: A6388 95: War Cabinet Agendum, Aliens - Service Under the Defence Act, 12 July 1941). Information about the establishment, and other dates, of the various Companies comes from a variety of official sources, which do not always agree with each other. See Army Records Office, Victoria Barracks, Melbourne, list of Corps/Units (provided to June Factor on 11 November 2003) for what seems to be the most reliable source. See also NAA: MP742/1 240/8/31: Aust Labour and Aust Emp Coys – Redesignation Of.
36 See NAA: MP742/1 240/8/31: Redesignation of Employment Companies - Aust Labour Coys and Aust Employment Coys – Redesignation Of.
37 The 10th Employment Company was not designated as 'alien', although, according to official documents, its members were predominantly Greek and Aboriginal. See NAA: MP742/1, Department of Army Minute Paper, 110 [sic] Employment Coy, 16 September 1943. The 11th Labour Company was established in June 1942, renamed the 12th Labour Company in July 1942 and renamed the 12th Employment Company in October 1942. See Army Records Office, Melbourne, MP149 8 S16 4: Regimental Orders Part 2 RO717.
38 Ivan Rostkier, response to questionnaire from June Factor, 2 June 1995.
39 Nicholas Raftopoulos, response to questionnaire from June Factor, n.d. In his case, as in a number of others, the military record as listed on

the National Archives of Australia's nominal roll for World War II is not correct in every detail. In this case, his surname is misspelled (as Raftopulus), and his Company is listed as the 8th instead of the 6th.

40 Robert Salter, interviewed by June Factor, 6 November 2002.

41 John Cohen, interviewed by June Factor, 21 June 2002. The Department of Army's Director of Labour acknowledged, in a Minute Paper dated 18 December 1944, that 'It is apparent that in the majority of cases these men … are most desirous of being permitted the privilege of becoming members of the AIF and with very few exceptions they regard Australia as their adopted country, and a large percentage have indicated their desire to apply for Naturalization as soon as they are eligible.' He goes on to suggest that 'Whilst it may NOT be practicable for Aliens to be drafted, on a large scale, to other Units within the AIF it is felt that much would be gained of an AIF Emp Cpy to serve in an Operational zone (subject to security …) It is considered, therefore, that in view of their 2 ½ years good service the privilege of free naturalisation be extended to those who become eligible conditional on volunteering for the AIF.' NAA: MP742/1 115/1/173.

42 ibid.

43 Frank Klepner, interviewed by June Factor, 16 April 2002.

44 NAA: A373 8503: List of Aliens by Nationality at present serving in the Labour Corps of the Australian Military Forces.

45 Victor Chapkoun, from the 6th Employment Company, estimates there were about seventy Macedonians in his Company, and about a hundred and five in the 4th Employment Company—phone conversation with June Factor, 16 August 2004.

46 NAA: A 6122 Part 3: Statistical Returns of Resident Aliens.

47 NAA: SP459/1 489/2/191: Registration of Aliens.

48 NAA: A373 8503: List of Aliens by Nationality.

49 NAA: SP459/1 489/2/203: Registration of Volunteer Refugee Aliens.

50 NAA: MP742/1 92/1/193: Allocation and Posting of Personnel to Employment Coys, 25 January 1944.

51 The neutral aliens would all have been volunteers, as they were exempt from conscription.

52 Charles D'Aprano, interviewed by June Factor, 17 May 1999.

53 NAA: SP459/1 489/2/235: Military Board - National Security (Aliens Service) Regulations – Compulsory Action, 12 March 1942.

54 Speros Polites, interviewed by June Factor, 1 November 2002.

55 Orpheus Kandiliotis, interviewed by June Factor, 26 July 2004. In the court case, his name was spelled as Kandiliotes.

56 The *Launceston Examiner*, 'Call-up of Greek Melbourne', 23 December 1944, p. 9.

57 NAA: A472 W26336: High Court of Australia 1944, No. 22.

58 Commonwealth Law Report No. 70, pp. 60–83, 1945: High Court of Australia, Polites – Plaintiff, The Commonwealth and Another – Defendants. Kandiliotes – Plaintiff, The Commonwealth and Another – Defendants. Melbourne, 8, 9 March; 10 April 1945.
59 ibid., p. 73.

## 5 Officers and NCOs

1 'Captain Richardson, a former bank manager so he claimed, but in reality probably an ex-teller', Robert Exiner, 'From the Spree to the Yarra: Memories of an Emigration', *Journal of the Australian Jewish Historical Society*, vol. 12, 1993–95, p. 555.
2 Jack Friedman interviewed by June Factor, 4 November 2002.
3 Robert Exiner interviewed by June Factor, 6 November 2002.
4 Cary Roth, 'The Shire Ball', incomplete copy provided by Wolfgang Sievers.
5 Wolfgang Sievers, interviewed by June Factor, 16 June 2003.
6 ibid.
7 VD was an award for Volunteer Officers or Colonial Auxiliary Forces Officers.
8 Letter from Guido Ceen to June Factor, 9 December 2004.
9 Paul Fussell, *Wartime: Understanding and Behaviour in the Second World War*, OUP, 1989, p. 68.
10 Felix Werder, interviewed by June Factor, 5 June 2003.
11 John Cohen, interviewed by June Factor, 21 June 2002.
12 Wolfgang Sievers, interviewed by June Factor, 16 June 2003.
13 AWM: 52 22/1/3: 4th Employment Company War Diary, Albury 9 March 1943.
14 ibid.
15 *A Day in Camp*, created by Cary Roth, and written and illustrated by Tim Walton. According to a letter from Kurt Lippmann, a fellow soldier in the 4th Employment Company, after the war Roth became a watchmaker and Walton 'made a name for himself as a stage decorator.' (Letter to June Factor, 19 April 1994.)
16 ibid., p. 1. June Factor's copy a gift from Wolfgang Sievers.
17 ibid., p. 9.
18 The *Border Morning Mail*, 'Last Night's Reception. A Day of Interest', 16 October 1942, p. 4.
19 Wolfgang Sievers, interviewed by June Factor, 16 June 2003.
20 An example of standing orders against gambling is set out in the Routine Orders of the 6th Employment Company, 22 September 1942, AWM: 52 22/1/15.
21 John Cohen, interviewed by June Factor, 21 June 2002.
22 Andy Factor, interviewed by June Factor, 25 July 2002.
23 Gerard Herbst, 'United Under the Southern Cross (Exposé)', Australian War Memorial ms 1577.

24 Bern Brent, interviewed by June Factor, 16 November 1994.
25 ibid.
26 Andy Factor, interviewed by June Factor, 25 July 2002.
27 Speros Polites, interviewed by June Factor, 1 November 2002.
28 Orpheus Kandiliotis, phone conversation with June Factor, 4 August 2004.
29 Emil Witton, a written account of his life before, during and after the war, sent to June Factor in response to her questionnaire.
30 The Comforts Fund was a voluntary organisation providing those in the military with goods not available from the army—socks, cigarettes, razor blades, etc. See Museums Victoria: https://collections.museumvictoria.com.au/articles/10608
31 Emil Witton, 'A short description of my life before and after military service', sent to June Factor, 23 August 2005.
32 AWM MSS 1577: Gerard Herbst, 'United Under the Southern Cross (Exposé)', unpublished short memoir of life in the army.
33 ibid.
34 AWM: 62 76: Offensive Behaviour – Tocumwal, 8 January 1943.
35 ibid., two letters from Major LG Campbell, 10 January 1943 and 11 January 1943.
36 AWM: 54 883/5/4: Gerhard Steuerwald wrote an article he hoped to publish (from which the quotation is taken), but Army Intelligence forbade it.
37 Frank Klepner, cited in an article by Larry Schwartz, the *Sunday Age*, 23 June 2002.
38 Frank Klepner, interviewed by June Factor, 16 April 2002.
39 Andy Factor, interviewed by June Factor, 25 July 2002.
40 ibid.
41 ibid.
42 The *Sydney Morning Herald*, letter—'Botany Road Rang with German Song', FF Wheener, 2 May 1992, p. 24.
43 Wolfgang Sievers, interviewed by June Factor, 16 June 2003.
44 Robert Salter, interviewed by June Factor, 6 November 2002.
45 Mentioned in interviews with Andy Factor and Charles D'Aprano.
46 Charles D'Aprano, 'Flashback: Life in the Australian Army', in *Tears, Laughter and the Revolution*, p. 190, Insegna Publishers, Brunswick West, 1998.
47 Charles D'Aprano, interviewed by June Factor, 17 May 1999.
48 Werder joined, he said, because that seemed the only way he could get medical help for his sick father—something not possible, according to an officer, while he was in the Tatura Detention Centre. 'You think I volunteered for the army? You must be joking.' Interview with June Factor, 5 June 2003.
49 Felix Werder, interviewed by June Factor, 5 June 2003.
50 Fred Lester, response to questionnaire from June Factor, 2002.

51 Charles D'Aprano, interviewed by June Factor, 17 May 1999.
52 ibid.
53 Robert Exiner, 'From the Spree to the Yarra: Memories of an Emigration', *Journal of the Australian Jewish Historical Society*, vol. 12, 1993–95, p. 555.
54 AWM: 113 17/3/1: Alien Labour December 1942.
55 ibid., Alien Labour – 6 Employment Coy 5 December 1943.
56 ibid.
57 ibid., Alien Labour – 6 Employment Coy 5 December 1943.
58 None of the men from the 6th Company with whom I have communicated had any recollection of this inquiry, and knew of none of their fellow soldiers being consulted by the visiting officer.
59 Yosl Bergner, interviewed by Ranald Macdonald, ABC Melbourne, October 1990.
60 Frank Klepner, interviewed by June Factor, 16 April 2002.
61 AWM: 52 22/1/11: Routine Orders 6.7.43.
62 ibid., 18.7.43.
63 NAA: SP1008/1 451/1/605: Allegations Conveyed to Mr D Mulcahy, M.H.R. Regarding Alien Labour Companies [139]. While all the official documents refer to 5 NCOs, the Court and the final report list six men: two Sergeants and four Corporals.
64 ibid. Information given by Sergeant JW Jackson, V.C., D.C.M., 2nd Labour Corps, Ascot Military Camp, Sydney, to Mr D Mulcahy, MP, during the course of a discussion on Sunday, 13/9/42.
65 ibid.
66 ibid.
67 ibid., p. 379.
68 ibid., Report of Court, 5.10.42, p. 7.
69 ibid.
70 ibid., Court of Inquiry p. 56.
71 ibid., evidence given to the Inquiry by LF O'Brien, 18.9.1942, p. 34.
72 ibid., p. 35.
73 ibid., p. 31.
74 ibid., pp. 111–12.
75 ibid., Report of Court, p. 7. For Corporal West, who had heart trouble, the Court recommended that his request to be medically discharged be complied with.
76 ibid., Report of Court, p. 4.
77 ibid., p. 4.
78 ibid., letter to Minister for the Army from Major General AC Fewtrell, 14 November 1942.
79 ibid.
80 ibid.
81 NAA: MP742/1 275/2/9: Letter from FM Forde, Minister for the Army to D. Mulcahy, MHR, 4 March 1943.

82 AWM: 52 22/1/3: 4 Labour Company.
83 NAA: SP1008/1 451/1/605: Report of Court.
84 NAA: MP742/1 115/1/274: Australian Military Forces Minute Paper, Aliens in Employment Companies, 28 June 1945.
85 NAA: SP1008/1 451/1/605: Report of Court, Appendix (1), Statement of Nationalities of NCOs 2 Australian Labour Company as at 21 September 1942.
86 Charles D'Aprano, 'The Heroes of Tocumwal', in *Old Wine in New Bottles*, Winseray, Carlton, 1986, p. 37.
87 NAA: MP742/1 115/1/274: Australian Military Forces Minute Paper, Aliens in Employment Companies, 28 June 1945.
88 Letter from Albert Ceen to his wife, 21 December 1942, Ceen family correspondence, Mitchell Library, Sydney, MLMSS 6735.
89 Henry Lippmann, interviewed by Rosemary Block, New South Wales State Library, Oral History Program, 7 November 2003, Tape 6, p. 101 of transcript.
90 Orpheus Kandiliotis, interviewed by June Factor, 4 August 2004; Speros Polites interviewed by June Factor, 1 November 2002.
91 Gerhard Steurwald, unpublished article, AWM: 54 883/5/4.
92 Anon 1, interviewed by June Factor, July 2002.
93 Felix Werder, interviewed by June Factor, 5 June 2003.
94 Eric Eckstein, *A Thousand Bonds: An Autobiography*, unpublished ms, copy lent to June Factor by June and Julius Guest.
95 Letter from Alfred Ruskin to June Factor, 15 June 1995.
96 ibid.
97 ibid.
98 ibid.
99 Jack Friedman, interviewed by June Factor, 4 November 2002.

## 6 Hard yakka

1 Routine Orders were regular notices providing soldiers with military regulations, orders, instructions and other relevant information.
2 AWM: 54 255/4/3: Military History Section, Notes on Compilation of War Diaries.
3 ibid.
4 AWM: 52 22/1/13: 4 Labour Company War Diary.
5 AWM: 52 22/1/9: 5 Labour Group War Diary June – November 1945.
6 AWM: 52 22/1/19: 10th Employment Company War Diary, July to December 1942 [2063]. The importance of firewood emerges from a number of official documents. See, for example, a letter from the Prime Minister to the Attorney-General in March 1943, NAA: A373 3644, and a letter from the Minister for the Army to the Director-General of Allied Works in June 1942, NAA: A437 1946/6/250.

7 AWM: 52 22/1/10: 1st Australian Works Company War Diary, 1 – 6 July 1945.
8 AWM: 52 22/1/15: 6th Employment Company War Diary, 31 March 1942.
9 John Callinicos, telephone conversation with June Factor, 7 July 2004.
10 There is a reference in the War Diary of the 26th Employment Company in January 1945, when the Company was based in Perth: it supplied labour 'to replace civil labour at Fremantle Wharf' because of a strike. AWM: 52 22/1/32. There is also an entry in the War Diary of the 25th Labour Company, based in Osborne, a suburb of Adelaide, where, for a short period, the men refused to continue working at a Finsbury factory because the civilian workers called them scabs. The War Diary records that 'when explained to men that their actions could be construed as mutiny they immediately went back to work when called upon. Factory agreeing to remove all civilians from their vicinity.' AWM: 22/1/31 July 1942. In his interview with me, Bern Brent, of the 8th Employment Company, mentioned working on the wharves in Melbourne during a strike.
11 Robert Salter, interviewed by June Factor, 6 November 2002; Bern Brent, interviewed by June Factor, 16 November 1994.
12 Albert Ceen, extract from a letter sent to his wife, translated for June Factor by his son Guido Ceen.
13 Helmut Newton, *Autobiography*, Nan A. Talese/Doubleday, NY, 2003, p. 126.
14 Paul Seefeld, interviewed by June Factor, 10 February 2003.
15 Julius Guest, interviewed by June Factor, 17 April 2003.
16 AWM: 52 22/1/13: 4th Labour Company War Diary, 9 March 1942.
17 Mitchell Library: MLMSS 6735: Ceen family undated letter, probably 21 April 1942, translated from the Italian by Guido Ceen.
18 Paul Seefeld, interviewed by June Factor, 10 February 2003.
19 AWM: 52 22/1/13: 4th Labour Company War Diary, 16 June 1942.
20 Bern Brent, interviewed by June Factor, 16 November 1994.
21 Bart Srhoy, *Journey Beyond Origin*, Hesperian Press, p. 69.
22 ibid.
23 Robert Exiner, 'From the Spree to the Yarra: Memories of an Emigration', *Journal of the Australian Jewish Historical Society*, vol. 12, 1993–95, p. 555; Louis Waller, son of Jack Waller, interview by June Factor, 8 July 2002.
24 Email from John Pollak to June Factor, 15 July 2008.
25 Emil Witton, 'A short description of my life before and after military service', detailed response to questionnaire from June Factor.
26 John Cohen interviewed by June Factor, 21 June 2002.
27 ibid.
28 Mark Twain, *Following the Equator* (1897), cited in 'A Track to the Future', the *Sydney Morning Herald*, 10 January 2004.
29 See, for example, report in the *Argus*, 1 March 1941, p. 7, about rail transport given priority because of shortage of shipping.

30 Paul Hasluck provides a detailed description of the logistic difficulties posed by trying to ensure that both Sydney and the political capital, Canberra, were not neglected by government instrumentalities. See *Australia in the War of 1939-1945: The Government and the People 1939-1941*, Australian War Memorial, Canberra, 1965, pp. 475–8. General Douglas MacArthur, as the Supreme Commander for the South West Pacific, initially also based himself in Melbourne, before moving his headquarters to Brisbane.
31 Figures cited in Kate Darian-Smith, 'War and Australian Society', in Joan Beaumont (ed.), *Australia's War 1939-45*, Allen & Unwin, Sydney, 2000, p. 56.
32 Gerard Herbst, 'United under the Southern Cross (Expose´)', Mitchell Library MSS 1577.
33 Staff Sergeant J Feldmann, 'They're Asking About Australia', *Salt*, vol. 3, no. 9, 1 June 1942, p. 4. It was not until 2004 that all mainland capital cities were connected by standard-gauge rail.
34 AWM: 52 22/1/13: War Diary, 4th Labour Company, 13 March 1942.
35 Charles D'Aprano, 'The Heroes of Tocumwal', in *Old Wine in New Bottles*, short stories by Charles D'Aprano, Winseray, Melbourne, 1986, p. 35.
36 Erwin Fabian in *Max und Erwin Fabian: Berlin, London, Melbourne*, Stiftung Stadtmuseum, Berlin, 2000, p. 133.
37 AWM: 52 22/1/13: War Diary, 4th Labour Company, 16.3.42 – 31.3.42.
38 ibid.
39 Charles D'Aprano, 'The Heroes of Tocumwal' in *Old Wine in New Bottles*, short stories by Charles D'Aprano, Winseray, Melbourne, 1986, pp. 35–7.
40 Frank Klepner, interviewed by June Factor, 16 April 2002.
41 Jack Friedman, interviewed by June Factor, 4 November 2012.
42 Frank Klepner, interviewed by June Factor, 16 April 2002. Some of the men interviewed referred to tents sleeping five; others, to eight. This may result from the existence of different-sized tents and/or from faulty memory.
43 Andy Factor, interviewed by June Factor, 25 July 2002.
44 Orpheus Kandiliotis, interviewed by June Factor, 26 July 2004 and 4 August 2004.
45 Mitchell Library: MLMSS 6735: Ceen family papers, 1923–98, letter from Albert Ceen to his wife Flavia, undated but written sometime between 4 and 31 May 1942, translated from Italian by their son Guy (Guido) Ceen and sent to June Factor.
46 Summary and translation from Italian of material in letter from Albert Ceen to his wife, written between April and July 1942, by Ceen's son, Guido Ceen, and sent to June Factor.
47 Translation from Italian of letter dated 12 June; source as above.
48 NAA: MP742/1 115/1/39: Tocumwal: 6 Employment Coy, 11.1.43.
49 Guido Ceen, email to June Factor, 18 December 2004. This suggestion of fights between the Employment Company members and the American soldiers is not confirmed by any of my informants.

50 Albert Ceen, letter written April 1942, in the possession of Guido Ceen.
51 AWM: MSS 1577: Gerard Herbst, 'United under the Southern Cross (Expose')', 1993.
52 Letter from Yosl Bergner in Israel to Frank Klepner, dated 16 February 1994, to be read at a reunion of the 6th Employment Company. Copy held by June Factor.
53 Jack Friedman, interviewed by June Factor, 4 November 2002.
54 Charles D'Aprano, interviewed by June Factor, 17 May 1999.
55 This was one of my father's favourite stories of his time in the army.
56 Spiros Polites, interviewed by June Factor, 1 November 2002.
57 ibid.
58 Fred Cohn, 4th Employment Company, tape of his army experiences provided by his son, John Cohn.
59 Morry Nirens, interviewed by June Factor, 29 January 1995; Alan Gregory, *The Ever Open Door: A History of the Royal Melbourne Hospital 1848–1998*, Hyland House, South Melbourne, 1998, pp. 258–63. http://www.med-dept.com/unit_histories/4_gen_hosp. php
60 AWM: 52 22/1/13: 4 Labour Coy War Diary, 2 July 1942.
61 See, for example, AWM: 52 22/1/13: Army Diary, 4th Labour Company.
62 Alan Gill, 'How a Maori officer became a father figure to the "misfits"', the *Sydney Morning Herald*, 25 April 1992, p. 21.
63 Fred Lester, interviewed by June Factor, 17 December 2002.
64 Bruce Pennay, 'The Friendly Aliens at Albury Railway Station During the Second World War', an unpublished report from July 2000 into 'the historical context of the transhipment platform at Albury Railway Station', for the New South Wales State Rail Authority, n.d.
65 Paul Baxter, interviewed by June Factor, 26 August 2013.
66 Louis Waller, interviewed by June Factor, 8 July 2002.
67 NLA ORAL TRC 4549: Wolfgang Sievers, interviewed by Barry York, 20 March 2000, cassette 4, side A.
68 Army Records Office, Melbourne: MP 149 8 S16 4: Routine Orders Part 2, RO717, File No. 37, 5 May 1943.
69 ibid.
70 The small war graves section of the Tocumwal cemetery includes the graves of two members of the 8th Employment Company: Ulrich Siegmund Laufer, born in Berlin in May 1923, and Max Schwarz, born in Vienna in September 1917. Both men's date of death is given as 30 December 1943; they drowned while swimming in the Murray River.
71 Keith Steinhardt, interviewed by June Factor, 13 January 2003. A notice in the files of the 21 Works Company directs Employment Companies 'loading and unloading Chemical Warfare ammunition' to 'immediately requisition for sufficient anti-gas equipment to be issued for personnel of such Units'. (AWM:52 22/1/28 21 Works Company April-June

1944.) It appears this protection was not extended to those cleaning such ammunition.

72 Charles D'Aprano, interviewed by June Factor, 17 May 1999.
73 ibid.
74 Fred Cohn, audio tape provided by his son and daughter-in-law.
75 ibid.
76 ibid.
77 See, for example, AWM: 52 22/1/13 War Diary 1 April – 30 April 1942.
78 Jack Friedman, interviewed by June Factor, 4 November 2002.
79 Nicholas Raftopoulos, response to questionnaire sent by June Factor.
80 Nicholas Raftopoulos, interviewed by George Paxinos, 15 May 1985.
81 Extract from an unpublished memoir, written in Italian by Albert Ceen, translated and summarised by his son Guido Ceen.
82 Robert Exiner, interviewed by June Factor, 31 January 1994.
83 Kurt Langfelder, interviewed by June Factor, 17 September 2004.
84 See, for example, AWM: 52 22/1/29 22: Employment Company, Port Moresby, October – December 1943, Routine Orders, 14 November 1943.
85 Emil Witton, response to questionnaire from June Factor, September 2005.
86 ibid.
87 John Callinicos, interviewed by George Paxinos, 19 May 1985.
88 ibid.
89 Fred Lester, interviewed by June Factor, 17 December 2002.
90 AWM: 54 443/2/2: Department of the Army Minute Paper, Employment Coys, 12 November 1943.
91 ibid., 25 November 1943.
92 AWM: 54 443/2/2: Correspondence about Employment Companies.
93 ibid.
94 NAA: MP742/1 240/8/31: Department of the Army Minute Paper, 31 January 1944.
95 See, for example, AWM: 52 22/1/27: 20 Employment Company, 1 – 31 March 1944.
96 AWM: 52 22/1/41 33: Employment Company, January – June 1944.
97 See, for example, AWM: 52 22/1/7: War Diary 3rd Australian Labour Group, Brisbane, 14 September 1945.
98 NAA: MP742/1 115/1/274: letter from John Dedman, for Acting Prime Minister, to Senator John Fraser, Acting Minister for the Army, 23 May 1945.
99 NAA: MP742/1 115/1/274: July 1945, military list of 1692 alien personnel in five Employment Companies, of whom 237 are naturalised, 230 have applied for naturalisation, and 196 desire to apply for (free) naturalisation.
100 The prevention and treatment of venereal diseases was a serious concern for the military. There were regular genital ('short arm') inspections, lectures and films provided to servicemen, as well as the provision of condoms and

material for treatment. See, for example, NAA: A6388 498: National Security (Venereal Diseases and Contraceptives) Regulations; Michael Sturma, 'Public Health and Sexual Morality: Venereal Disease in World War II in Australia', *Signs*, vol. 13, no. 4, 1988 pp. 725–40; 'V.D. Spreads', *Salt*, vol. 6, no. 7, 7 June 1943, pp. 1–6.

101 Robert Exiner, interviewed by June Factor, 31 January 1994, and Robert Exiner, 'From the Spree to the Yarra: Memories of an Emigration', *Journal of the Australian Jewish Historical Society*, vol. 12, 1993–95, pp. 556–7.

102 Fred Lester, response to questionnaire from June Factor, and interview with June Factor, 17 December 2002.

103 Paul Baxter, interviewed by June Factor, 26 August 2013.

104 AWM: 52 22/1/2: Deputy Assistant Director Labour H.Q. Qld. L of C Area, January to May 1945, Appendix 2, 25 January 1945.

105 ibid., Appendix 3, 28 February 1945.

## 7 The enjoyment companies

1 C Moran and M Massam, 'A "Trace of History": Cartoons from the Australian War Memorial Christmas Books of the Second World War', *Journal of the Australian War Memorial*, (n.d.) https://www.awm.gov.au/journal/j39/cartoons/ Vane Lindesay, *Some Fragments Recalled*, Trojan Press for Vane Lindesay, Ripponlea, Melbourne, 2005.

2 David Walker, 'The Writers' War', in Joan Beaumont (ed.), *Australia's War 1939-45*, p. 159.

3 Robert Exiner, 'From the Spree to the Yarra ...' *Journal of the Australian Jewish Historical Society*, vol. 12, 1993–95, p. 555.

4 Information from David Nachintsky, a soldier in the 6th Employment Company, during a discussion with the author at the reunion of men from the 4th and 6th Employment Companies in Melbourne on 9 March 1994.

5 Eric Liffman, *Songs the People Love*, Vivid Publishing, Fremantle, Western Australia, 2015, p. 94.

6 Morry Nirens, interviewed by June Factor, 29 January 1995, and 'Maurice' in Morag Loh and Judith Winternitz, *Dinky-Di: The contributions of Chinese immigrants and Australians of Chinese descent to Australia's defence forces and war efforts 1899-1988*, p. 84.

7 A phrase now widely attributed to Australian men during the war, but whose authenticity is sometimes challenged.

8 *Instructions for American Servicemen in Australia 1942*, original edition prepared by Special Service Division, Services of Supply, United States Army, and first issued by War and Navy Departments Washington DC, 1942; reprinted by Penguin Australia, 2007, p. 17.

9 Andy Factor, interviewed by June Factor, 25 July 2002.

10 Yosl Bergner, letter to 6th Employment Company reunion, 1994; Charles D'Aprano, *Tears, Laughter and the Revolution*, pp. 218–19 and interview with June Factor, 17 May 1999.

11 Yosl Bergner, *What I Meant to Say*, pp. 108–9. The origin of this term is obscure, but its use in this context and, more broadly, in the Australian Jewish community is largely captured in the Wikipedia definition: 'It is used mainly in reference to the German Jews' legendary attention to detail and punctuality.' Those were not, however, characteristics of Yosl Bergner, who grew up in Warsaw.

12 Letter from George E Kaufmann to M/s Phyllida Fitzgerald, c/o Angus and Robertson Publishers, 15 March 1983.

13 Morag Loh and Judith Winternitz, *Dinky-Di: The contributions of Chinese immigrants and Australians of Chinese descent to Australia's defence forces and war efforts 1899-1988*, Fung Ho, p. 117.

14 AWM: 54 443/2/2: Department of the Army Minute Paper, 12 November 1943.

15 Remembered by the scientist Huntley Higgins in a conversation with June Factor, 3 February 2002.

16 AWM: 52 22/1/12: 3rd Employment Company War Diary, October-December 1944; AWM: 52 22/1/15: 6th Employment Company War Diary; Fred Lester, interviewed by June Factor, 17 December 2002.

17 Keith Steinhardt, interviewed by June Factor, 13 January 2003.

18 Cary Roth and Tim Walton, 'A Day in Camp', written and illustrated for the 4th Employment Company's 1st anniversary, 9 March 1943; the author's copies from Kurt Lippmann, 19 April 1994, and from Wolfgang Sievers in 2004.

19 Robert Salter, response to questionnaire from June Factor, and interview with June Factor, 6 November 2002.

20 AWM: 52 22/1/13: War Diary 25/7/42 and 22/1/43.

21 Fred Lester, interviewed by June Factor, 17 December 2002.

22 Robert Exiner, interviewed by June Factor, 31 January 1994.

23 Bern Brent, interviewed by June Factor, 16 November 1994.

24 Felix Werder, interviewed by June Factor, 5 June 2003.

25 Yossel Birstein, 'Weger', in *Facing the Holocaust: Selected Israeli Fiction*, edited by G Ramras-Rauch and J Michman-Melkman, Jewish Publication Society, Philadelphia, 1985, pp. 175 and 176. An earlier version of the story was published in *Ariel: A Quarterly Review of Arts and Letters in Israel*, no. 37, 1974.

26 AWM: 52 22/1/15: 6 Australian Employment Company, Routine Orders, 27 November 1942.

27 AWM: 52 22/1/11: 2 Employment Company War Diary, February and March 1943, Routine Orders, 17 February 1943.

28 Examples of the repetition in just one Company in one year include AWM: 52 22/1/13: 4 Labour Company, Routine Orders, 2 August 1942, 16 September 1942, 1 November 1942—though in this last there is the concession that 'Card games for small stakes are not included in this order.'
29 AWM: 52 22/1/11: 2nd Employment Company War Diary, January – June 1944, Routine Orders, 13 February 1944.
30 John Cohen, interviewed by June Factor, 21 June 2002.
31 Felix Werder, interviewed by June Factor, 5 June 2003.
32 AWM: 52 22/1/13: 4 Labour Company, 1 November 1942.
33 Emil Witton, response to questionnaire from June Factor, private correspondence.
34 Letter from Albert Ceen to his wife Flavia, translated by their son Guido Ceen, private correspondence.
35 Jack Friedman, interviewed by June Factor, 4 November 2002.
36 ibid.
37 Cary Roth and Tim Walton, 'A Day in Camp', illustrated poem created for the 4th Employment Company's 1st anniversary, 9 March 1943.
38 AWM: 52 22/1/13: Routine Orders, 6 May 1942.
39 AWM: 52 21/1/13: War Diary, 25/5/43.
40 AWM: 52 22/1/11: Routine Orders, 19 March 1945.
41 AWM: 52 22/1/17: 8th Employment Company Routine Orders, 12 March 1943.
42 ibid.
43 The ironic and affectionate term used by Felix Werder to describe the rich cultural life that developed both on the *Dunera* and at the Tatura internment camp: Felix Werder, interviewed by June Factor, 5 June 2003.
44 Mitchell Library: MLMSS 6735: Ceen family papers, 1923–98; this letter not dated but certainly from 1942.
45 Yossel Birstein, 'Weger', in *Facing the Holocaust: Selected Israeli Fiction,* edited by G Ramras-Rauch and J Michman-Melkman, Jewish Publication Society, Philadelphia, 1985, p. 183.
46 Bart Srhoy, *Journey Beyond Origin,* Hesperian Press, Carlisle, Western Australia, 1998, p. 71.
47 Many Jewish families in Germany, Austria and Hungary had converted to Christianity decades before the rise of Nazism. The Nazis generally chose not to recognise such conversions, leading to the departure of many such as Rado.
48 Wolfgang Sievers, interviewed by June Factor, 16 June 2003.
49 Klaus Loewald, 'The Eighth Employment Company', *Australian Journal of Politics and History*, vol. 31, 1985, p. 84.
50 Eric Liffman, Patricia and Kurt Liffman, *Songs the People Love*, Vivid Publishing, Fremantle, Western Australia, 2015, p. 114.
51 Ken Inglis, Seumas Spark and Jay Winter with Carol Bunyan, *Dunera Lives: A Visual History*, Monash University Publishing, 2018, p. 349.

52 See Warren A Bebbington and John Carmody, *Prerauer, Kurt (Curt) (1901-1967)*, *Australian Dictionary of Biography*, vol. 16, MUP, 2002.
53 NAA: SP1008/1 451/1/605: Proceedings of a Court of Inquiry, Victoria Barracks, Paddington, 16 September 1942, and letter to the Minister for the Army from Major General AC Fewtrell, October 1942.
54 Larry Schwartz, 'Fighting for WWII refugees' compassionate captain', *The Age*, 20 May 2005.
55 Andy Factor, interviewed by June Factor, 25 July 2002.
56 Yosl Bergner, *What I Meant to Say: Stories and Travels As Told to Ruth Bondy*, Hed Arzi Book Publishing, Israel, 1997, p. 109.
57 ibid.
58 AWM: 52 22/1/13: Routine Orders, January – June 1942.
59 AWM: 52 22/1/13: War Diary, 31 August 1942.
60 Andy Factor, interviewed by June Factor, 25 July 2002.
61 Bob Exiner, interviewed by June Factor, 31 January 1994.
62 Mitchell Library: MLMSS 6735: Ceen family papers, 1923–98; Alfred Ceen, letter to his wife, 2 October 1942.
63 Alfred Ruskin, response to questionnaire from June Factor, 15 June 1995.
64 Mitchell Library: MLMSS 6735: Ceen family papers, 1923–98; letter to Mr Orbuck, 2 February 1943.
65 ibid., letter to his wife, 27 April 1943.
66 Robert Exiner, response to questionnaire from June Factor, 25 May 1995, personal correspondence.
67 For a detailed account of this production, see Ken Inglis et al, *Dunera Lives: A Visual History*, Monash University Publishing, Clayton, Australia, 2018, pp. 342–46.
68 Mitchell Library: MLMSS 6735: Ceen family papers, 1923–98; Alfred Ceen, letter to his wife, 27 April 1943.
69 Cyril Pearl, *The Dunera Scandal*, Angus & Robertson, Sydney 1983, p. 201.
70 ibid.
71 Orpheus Kandiliotis, interviewed by June Factor, 26 July 2004, and further phone conversations.
72 Fred Lester, interviewed by June Factor, 17 December 2002.
73 ibid.
74 Mitchell Library: MLMSS 6735: Ceen family papers, 1923–98; Albert Ceen, letter to his son Guy as part of a letter to his wife and other son, Allan, Tocumwal, 20 June 1943.
75 AWM: 52 22/1/13: 4th Labour Company War Diary, Albury, 17 May 1942.
76 AWM: 52 22/1/12: April – June 1945. *Golden Hind* was a British ship moored for a time in Sydney Harbour.
77 AWM: 52 22/1/13: 4th Employment Company, April – June 1943, item dated 12/6/43.
78 ibid, July – September 1943, Routine Orders, 30 August 1943.

79 AWM: 52 22/1/19: War Diary, 10th Employment Company, July – December 1942.
80 AWM: 52 22/1/15: War Diary, 6th Employment Company, 22 May 1942.
81 AWM: 52 22/1/17: 8 Australian Employment Company War Diary, 2 January 1944—Private Max Schwarz drowned in December 1943. Abraham Kurz from the 4th Employment Company drowned, *Border Morning Mail*, 31 January 1944, p. 2, cited by Bruce Pennay. See also the two men from the 8th who drowned—noted in Chapter 6.
82 Mitchell Library: MLMSS 6735: Ceen family papers, 1923–98; Albert Ceen, letter to his wife, 29 December 1942.
83 ibid., letter to his wife from Tocumwal, 8 February 1943.
84 ibid., letter to his wife, 8 June 1943.
85 Orpheus Kandiliotis, interviewed by June Factor, 26 July 2004.
86 ibid., and Nicholas Raftopoulos, response to questionnaire from June Factor.
87 Orpheus Kandiliotis, interviewed by June Factor, 26 July 2004.
88 Bruce Pennay, Heritage Report, State Railway Authority, Sydney, 2000.
89 AWM: 52 22/1/13 4 Employment Company Routine Orders, 1 July 1942.
90 Robert Exiner, response to questionnaire from June Factor, 25 May 1995.
91 Robert Exiner, interviewed by June Factor, 31 January 1994.
92 See, for example, Srhoy, *Journey Beyond Origin*: 'greasy odd smelling mutton chop'.
93 Orpheus Kandiliotis, interview and further discussion with June Factor, 26 July 2004 and 4 August 2004.
94 ibid.
95 John Cohen, interviewed by June Factor, 21 June 2002.
96 AWM: 52 22/1/15: War Diary, 6th Employment Company, 17 November 1943.
97 See, for example, AWM: 52 22/1/22: Routine Orders, 22 Employment Company, 27 February 1943.
98 'The "50/50" dance came into being with a program evenly divided between the modern and the old dances so that both young and old could be catered for' in the 1930s: Peter Ellis, 'Old Time Dancing and Music, Part 2'. http://www.australian-heritage-dance.com/oldtime2.html
99 Charles D'Aprano interviewed by June Factor, 17 May 1999.
100 Charles D'Aprano, *Tears, Laughter and the Revolution*, Insegna Publishers, Brunswick West, 1998, p. 218.
101 Jack Friedman, interviewed by June Factor, 4 November 2002.
102 Cyril Pearl, *The Dunera Scandal*, Angus & Robertson, Sydney, 1985, p. 205.
103 ibid.
104 Henry Lippmann, interviewed by Rosemary Block, New South Wales State Library, Tape 7: 103.
105 ibid., Tape 7: 115.
106 ibid., Tape 7: 116.

107 AWM: 54 883/5/4: Security - National Security (Emergency Control) Regulations; National Security - (Aliens Service) Regulation - Copy of an article submitted by N321052, Private Steuerwald Gerhard of 3 Employment Coy, through his CO for permission to arrange publication through the Press.

108 Letter from Alfred Ruskin, Walter Schnock and Robert Exiner to Kurt Lippmann, 31 October 1942, provided to the writer by Walter Schnock on 25 May 1995. Despite the humour, the letter was mainly concerned with a serious matter—the establishment of the Association of Jewish Refugees (Vic). As Schnock wrote in his accompanying letter, the army's reference to these men as Friendly Enemy Aliens was not acceptable: 'We insisted at the time that we should be referred to as Friendly Refugee Aliens or some such description.'

109 Peter Coleman, 'Deep Impact', the *Weekend Australian*, 31 August – 1 September 2002, p. 8. See also Daniel Snowman, *The Hitler Émigrés: The Cultural Impact on Britain of Refugees from Nazism*, Chatto & Windus, and Tom Ambrose, *What Britain and America Gained from Europe's Cultural Exiles*, Peter Owen, 2001.

110 NLA ORAL TRC 4549: Wolfgang Sievers, interviewed by Barry York, 20 March 2000, p. 68.

111 Interview with Yosl Bergner in *Painting the Town: A Film about Yosl Bergner*, written by Charles Merewether and Sharon Connelly, directed by Trevor Graham, narrated by Max Gillies, Yarra Bank Films, 1987.

112 Yosl Bergner, *What I Meant to Say*, Hed Arzi Book Publishing, Israel, 1997, p. 112

113 Klaus Friedeberger, Biographical Notes.

114 Mitchell Library: MLMSS 6735: Ceen family papers, 1923–98.

115 From the summary and translation of Albert Ceen's letters and memoir by his son, Guido Ceen—material held by June Factor.

116 ibid.

117 Charles D'Aprano, interviewed by June Factor, 17 May 1999.

118 Joan Davis, '*Salt*: The journal of the Australian Army Education Service in the second world war', *Journal of the Australian War Memorial*, No. 17, October 1990, pp. 20–28.

119 AWM: 52 22/1/17: Company Routine Orders No. 332, 20/3/43.

120 AWM: 52 22/1/13: War Diary, 4th Employment Company, 15 May 1942.

121 Robert Exiner, interviewed by June Factor, 31 January 1994.

122 Bern Brent, interviewed by June Factor, 16 November 1994.

123 GH Strauss, *Margaret Holmes: a life of ecumenical service*, privately printed, 2003, p. 69.

124 John Cohen, interviewed by June Factor, 21 June 2002.

125 *Max und Erwin Fabian: Berlin – London – Melbourne*, Stiftung Stadtmuseum, Berlin, 2000, p. 132.

126 The historian Sean Scalmer details the many thousands of servicemen who attended the array of educational and cultural activities conducted by the AES, and asserts that 'The Australian "cultural renaissance" of the forties was shaped by the war': 'The Puzzle of *Meanjin* and the Historical Emergence of the Australian Intelligentsia', *Country and Calling: Journal of Australian Studies*, no. 62, 1999, p. 202.
127 Andrew Reeves, 'Laidler, Thomas Percival', in *Australian Dictionary of Biography*, MUP, vol. 9, 1983.
128 AWM: 52 22/1/17 Company Routine Orders No.175, 8th Employment Company War Diary, Camp Pell, Parkville, 14/10/42.
129 AWM: 52 22/1/13 4th Employment Company War Diary, Routine Orders, Albury, 21/3/43.
130 Ian Turner, 'My Long March', *Overland*, no. 59, Spring 1974, p. 29.
131 ibid., pp. 29–30. A letter from a knowledgeable writer details the vital role of music in the AES's work. He states that by the end of the war, 'more than 30,000 music recitals had been given to an attendance of almost two million.' Roger Jones, 'Lectures on opera (with whistled extracts)', The *Age*, 1 January 2000.
132 Vane Lindesay, letter to June Factor, 24 July 2002. For an account of the history of *Salt,* see Joan Davis, '*Salt*: The journal of the Australian Army Education Service in the second world war', *Journal of the Australian War Memorial*, no. 17, October 1990, pp. 20–9.

## 8 Most satisfactory service: the Chinese Employment Company

1 One admirable, and quite recent, exception is the two books by Ken Inglis, Bill Gammage, Seumas Spark and Jay Winter, with Carol Bunyan: *Dunera Lives: Profiles* (2020) and *Dunera Lives: A Visual History* (2018).
2 Brisbane *Worker*, 30 March 1901, p. 12, cited in CMH Clark, *A History of Australia*, vol. v, MUP, 1981, p. 190.
3 NAA: A373 7925/37, letter from the Secretary of the Department of the Interior to the Director-General of Security, 6 June 1945.
4 Australian House of Representatives, *Debates*, House of Representatives, 9 February 1949, vol. 201, pp. 60–4. https://historichansard.net/hofreps/1949/19490209_reps_18_201/#debate-13
5 Andrew Markus, 'Chinese Immigration under the "White Australia Policy"', in Paul Macgregor (ed.), *Histories of the Chinese in Australasia and the Pacific*, Museum of Chinese Australian History, Melbourne, 1995, p. 356; Barry York, 'The Chinese in Australia: exclusions and admissions 1901-1957', in Paul Macgregor (ed.), ibid., provides figures for numbers admitted in each year, and on what conditions, p. 376; Morag Loh and Judith Winternitz estimate 1600 workers from Nauru, between 1000–2000 refugees from New Guinea, and about 2000 seamen [pp. 33–4]. Wendy

Rankine suggests about 3000 in all, in 'The Chinese in Australia 1930-45: Beyond a History of Racism', MA thesis, Department of History, University of Melbourne, 1995, p. 141. According to the Director-General of Security, writing in June 1945, there were 7638 registered alien Chinese in Australia up to 31 March 1945 (NAA: A373 7925/37).

6 Barry York, 'The Chinese in Australia: exclusions and admissions', in Paul Macgregor (ed.), *Histories of Chinese in Australasia and the Pacific*, Museum of Australian Chinese History, Melbourne, 1995, pp. 366, 362.

7 ibid., p. 376.

8 Cited in Morag Loh and Judith Winternitz, *Dinky-Di: The contributions of Chinese immigrants and Australians of Chinese descent to Australia's defence forces and war effort 1899-1988*, Australian Government Publishing Service Press, Canberra, 1989, p. 107.

9 For a discussion of the militancy of the Chinese Seamen's Union, and the success of its efforts, and that of the Australian Seamen's Union, to gain legal confirmation of equal pay for the Chinese seamen, see Wendy Rankine's thesis 'The Chinese in Australia 1930-45: Beyond a History of Racism', MA thesis, Department of History, University of Melbourne, 1995, p. 68.

10 An example is Security concern in February 1945 about the activities of Jong Ngok Bew, who was Superintendent of the Chinese Section of the US Small Ships Camp at Bulimba, and who was 'assisting Chinese to obtain their discharge from the Small Ships Section and arranging for their transportation to Murwillumbah, whence they travel by train to Sydney.' The Security letter notes that Bew 'is an ex Secretary of the Chinese Seamen's Union.' NAA: 373 7925/37, letter from the Deputy Director of Security, New South Wales, to his counterpart in Queensland and copied to the Director-General of Security in Canberra, 26 February 1945.

11 Like the other alien Employment Companies, and a number of the non-alien Employment Companies, the 7th was first called a Labour Company. Within seven months, the name had changed to Employment Company.

12 NLA: MS 4738 Box 38: Aliens Control Instructions No.11, p. 4. NB 'The word "alien" is not defined either in the Constitution or in legislation. Under a former definition in the Citizenship Act, it used to mean anyone who was "not a British subject, an Irish citizen or a protected person". But this definition became out of date for an independent Australian nation and was removed in 1987 without being replaced.' Peter Prince, Australian Parliamentary Library Research Paper no. 3 200304, 24 November 2003.

13 NAA: MP508/1 115/702/20: letter from Secretary of the Military Board to Secretary of the Department of the Army, 28 May 1940.

14 ibid. By mid-1941, according to one historian, anti-Chinese regulations were 'increasingly ignored' in all the military services. Diana Guise, *Courage and Service: Chinese Australians and World War II*, Courage and Service Project, Marrickville, Sydney, 1999, p. 2.

15 NAA: MP1049 1877/12/105: Rankine, Wendy, 'Australia's Chinese Army Corps' in Jan Ryan (ed.), *Chinese in Australia and New Zealand: a Multidisciplinary Approach*, New Age International, New Delhi, 1995.

16 According to the historian Diana Giese, well before war's end there were Australian Chinese serving in all the services. See Diana Giese, *Courage and Service: Chinese Australian and World War II*, Courage and Service Project, Marrickville, Sydney, 1999.

17 NAA: MP508/1 240/701/158: Chinese Units in Australian Military Forces - Proposed formation of.

18 NAA: MP508/1 299/701/284: Chinese crews in 5 Military District - formed into 7 Labour Company (Chinese).

19 Wendy Rankine, 'Australia's Chinese Army Corps' in Jan Ryan (ed.), *Chinese in Australia and New Zealand: a Multidisciplinary Approach*, New Age International, New Delhi, 1995, p. 80.

20 ibid, p. 141.

21 NAA: A373 7925/37: letter to Deputy Director of Security, Brisbane, 23 November 1944.

22 NAA: A373 7925/37: letter from Queensland District Security Officer to Deputy Director of Security, Brisbane, 22 July1944.

23 An example is a comment in the 7th Employment Company War Diary on 9 March,1943, AWM: 52 22/1/16: 'There are many letters now being received from enemy-occupied China ... Letters from Hong Kong indicate that the Japanese have changed street and road names in that town.'

24 NAA: MP508/1 299/701/284: Chinese crews in 5 Military District - formed into 7 Labour Company (Chinese).

25 See, for example, the names of a number of 7th Employment Company Chinese non-commissioned officers in Wendy Rankine, 'Australia's Chinese Army Corps', in Jan Ryan (ed.), *Chinese in Australia and New Zealand: A Multidisciplinary Approach*, New Age International, New Delhi, 1995, p. 69.

26 ibid., p. 68.

27 Wendy Rankine, 'The Chinese in Australia 1930-45: Beyond a History of Racism', MA thesis, Department of History, University of Melbourne, 1995, p. 81.

28 Wendy Rankine, 'Australia's Chinese Army Corps', in Jan Ryan (ed.), *Chinese in Australia and New Zealand: A Multidisciplinary Approach*, New Age International, New Delhi, 1995, p. 70.

29 AWM: 52 22/1/16: 7 Employment Company War Diary, November and December 1942, entry 25.11.42.

30 ibid., entry 7 December 1942.

31 Wendy Rankine, 'Australia's Chinese Army Corps', in Jan Ryan (ed.), *Chinese in Australia and New Zealand: A Multidisciplinary Approach*, New Age International, New Delhi, 1995, p. 70.

32 NAA: A2700 419: Report to Cabinet on Enemy Alien Labour Corps, Western Australia by WJ Scully, Minister for Commerce and Agriculture, 9 January 1943. The positive aspects of this report were duly published in the *Canberra Times*, 18 January 1943, p. 4. NB there must have been considerable disquiet in trade union circles about the use of Labour Companies in a way that could displace civilian workers. This explains the letter from the Assistant Secretary of the Department of Defence Co-Ordination to the Secretary of the Department of the Army, April 1942, stating that Labour Companies would not displace civilian workers or skilled tradesmen. But of course they did, as many of these civilians were already in the military. See NAA: MP508/1 275/705/61: letter from the Assistant Secretary, Department of Army, Melbourne, to the Secretary of the Department in Melbourne, 30 April 1942.

33 Wendy Rankine, 'The Chinese in Australia 1930-45: Beyond a History of Racism', MA thesis, Department of History, University of Melbourne, 1995, p. 86.

34 ibid., pp. 88–9.

35 NAA: MP508/1 275/705/61: letter from the Assistant Secretary, Department of Army, Melbourne, to the Secretary of the Department in Melbourne, 30 April 1942.

36 Wendy Rankine, 'The Chinese in Australia 1930-45: Beyond a History of Racism', MA thesis, Department of History, University of Melbourne, 1995, p. 70.

37 AWM: 52 22/1/16: 7th Employment Company War Diary, entry 15 December 1942.

38 Wendy Rankine, 'The Chinese in Australia 1930-45: Beyond a History of Racism', MA thesis, Department of History, University of Melbourne, 1995, p. 71.

39 ibid, pp. 71–2.

40 AWM: 52 22/1/16: 7th Employment Company War Diary, entry 24 November 1942.

41 Noel Adams, 'Chinese Sailors Help Army', the *Canberra Times*, 6 September 1943, p. 3.

42 ibid.

43 AWM: 52 22/1/36: War Diary, 28 Employment Company July 1942 – March 1943.

44 ibid.

45 Graham McKenzie-Smith, 'Unit Guide: The Australian Army 1939-1945' (section sent to me in draft form, 2010), p. 2.5A-1.

46 AWM: 52 22/1/16: 7th Employment Company War Diary, entry 24.11.42.

47 NAA: A373 7925/37: Chinese Labour Corps, Bulimba (U.S. Small Ships Section), 6.6.45. According to one historian, about 1 in 10 Australians

served in the armed forces—a greater proportion than in the United States. Bruce T Swain, *A Chronology of Australian Armed Forces at War 1939-45*, Allen & Unwin, Crows Nest, New South Wales, 2001, p. 310.

48 GC Bolton, '1939-51', in FK Crowley (ed.), *A New History of Australia*, William Heinemann, Melbourne, 1974, p. 467.

49 NAA: A989 1943/40/39 Proposed importation of Chinese labour to work under US Army control and responsibility in New Guinea and Queensland.

50 ibid. Letter from Secretary of Department of Defence to Secretary of External Affairs, 3 December 1943, stamped SECRET.

51 NAA: A373 7925/37 Letter to Deputy Director of Security from FA Kearns, outlining the American proposal.

52 ibid.

53 The Chinese in the Native Labour Company had worked for the British Phosphate Company in Nauru and Ocean Island, and were brought to Australia by the Company as refugees. (Peter Dunn, 'The Native Labour Company in Australia during WW2: Native Labor Co (Chinese)', *Australia @ War*. https://www.ozatwar.com/ozatwar/nlc.htm) The Chinese seamen were employed by the New South Wales Metropolitan Water Sewerage and Drainage Board on the Warragamba pipeline project. NAA: A373 7925/37: letter from FA Keane to the Deputy Director of Security, 31 May 1943.

54 ibid.

55 Interview with Louis Wong in Morag Loh and Judith Winternitz, *Dinky-Di: The contributions of Chinese immigrants and Australians of Chinese descent to Australia's defence forces 1899–1988*, Australian Government Publishing Service, Canberra, 1989, p. 111.

56 Dennis Burchill, Wartime Memories of Bulimba. https://www.ozatwar.com/locations/wartimememoriesbulimba.htm

57 Drew Cottle and Angela Keys, 'Building the bridge of solidarity: The politics of the Chinese Youth League in Australia, 1939-73', *Journal of Chinese Australia*, Issue 2, October 2006, p. 3. See also letter from the Deputy Director of Security for New South Wales to the Deputy Director of Security for Queensland, 26 February 1945, (NAA: A373, File No. 7925/37).

58 NAA: A373 7925/37: Summary, Chinese Native Labour Co., Armstrong Paddock, Townsville, 5.6.44.

59 NAA: A373 7925/37: Letter from District Security Officer to Deputy Director of Security, Brisbane, 6 June 1944.

60 ibid. Letter from Townsville District Security Officer to Deputy Director of Security in Brisbane, 12 August 1944.

61 AWM: 60 13/1277/43: Telegram from Norforce to Landforces RPTD Milbase Brisbane, 19 August 1943, stamped SECRET.

62 Morag Loh and Judith Winternitz, *Dinky-Di: The contributions of Chinese immigrants and Australians of Chinese descent to Australia's defence forces and war effort 1899-1988*, Australian Government Publishing Service Press, Canberra, 1989, pp. 114–16.
63 NAA: A373 7925/37: Chinese Labour Corps 1943–44.
64 Morag Loh Judith Winternitz, *Dinky-Di: The contributions of Chinese immigrants and Australians of Chinese descent to Australia's defence forces and war effort 1899-1988*, Australian Government Publishing Service Press, Canberra, 1989, p. 117. Fung Hoi's reference to wearing US uniform does not accord with information from other Chinese, who refer to their continuing civilian status.
65 NAA: A373 9342: Chinese Employed by USA – Policy File.
66 See, for example, NAA: A373 7925/37: Bulimba (U.S. Small Ships Section).
67 NAA: A373 7925/37: 'Unrest Among Chinese Employed by U.S. Army', letter from District Security Officer to Deputy Director of Security, Brisbane, 19 July 1944.
68 ibid., Chinese Native Labour Company, Armstrong Paddock, Townsville.
69 ibid., U.S. Native Labour Company (Chinese).
70 ibid., Chinese aliens employed by U.S. Army – departure from Cairns.
71 ibid.
72 ibid., Chinese Native Labour Company, Armstrong Paddock, Townsville.
73 ibid.
74 ibid., Chinese aliens employed by U.S. Army – departure from Cairns.
75 ibid., Bulimba (U.S. Small Ships Section).
76 Dennis Burchill, Wartime Memories of Bulimba. https://www.ozatwar.com/locations/wartimememoriesbulimba.htm. See also 'Chinese Draw Knives in Brawl at Bulimba', the *Canberra Times*, 12 December 1944, p. 3 and the *Sydney Morning Herald*, 'Mob Clash in Brisbane', 12 December 1944, p. 3.
77 NAA: A373 7925/37: Bulimba (U.S. Small Ships Section).
78 ibid.
79 ibid.
80 NAA: A373 9342: Chinese Employed by U.S.A. Policy File.
81 AWM: 60 13/1277/43: 7th Australian Employment Company (Chinese).
82 NAA: A373 7925/37: Relations With Local Chinese – letter from Deputy Director of Security for Queensland to Director-General of Security, Canberra.
83 NAA: A373 7925/37: Letter from Deputy Director of Security for New South Wales to Deputy Director of Security for Queensland.
84 NAA: A373 7925/37: ibid.
85 Bill Lunney and Frank Finch, *The Forgotten Fleet: a history of the part played by Australian men and ships in the U.S. Army Small Ships Section in New Guinea, 1942-1945*, Forfleet Publishing, New South Wales, 1995.

86 David D Bruhn, *Maritime Books of Interest* – extract from Bill Lunney and Frank Finch, *The Forgotten Fleet: a history of the part played by Australian men and ships in the U.S. Army Small Ships Section in New Guinea, 1942-1945*, Forfleet Publishing, New South Wales, 1995. http://www.davidbruhn.com/maritimeworks
87 NAA: MP742/1 247/1/1219: Department of the Army Central Registry File: Miscellaneous claim for Subsistence & Leave, 7 Australian Employment Company.
88 NAA: A373 7925/37: Letter from Director General of Security re Alien Chinese Ex U.S. Forces.
89 The *Herald,* 'Germans and Austrians Want to Stay in Australia', 15 March 1944.
90 M Loh and J Winternitz, *Dinki-Di: The contributions of Chinese immigrants and Australians of Chinese descent to Australia's defence forces and war efforts 1899-1988*, Australian Government Publishing Service Press, Canberra, 1989, p. 37. NB Wendy Rankine's MA thesis, 'The Chinese in Australia 1930-45: Beyond a History of Racism', Department of History, University of Melbourne, 1995, p. 103, gives the figure as 1266—cites NAA: Queensland: C10/7 vol. 2. For more about the Chinese who left, see Rankine, p. 144. Barry York, 'The Chinese in Australia: Exclusions and Admissions 1901-1957' in Paul Macgregor (ed.), *Histories of the Chinese in Australasia and the Pacific*, Museum of Chinese Australian History, Melbourne, 1995, provides a table of Chinese departures from Australia; in 1945, there were 2029; in 1946, 1495, p. 370.
91 The *Sydney Morning Herald*, '"Stop-Go" Order to Chinese', 8 November 1945, p. 3.
92 Wendy Rankine, 'The Chinese in Australia 1930-45: Beyond a History of Racism', MA thesis, Department of History, University of Melbourne, 1995, p. 144.
93 ibid., pp. 145–6.
94 See, for example, Morag Loh and J Winternitz, *Dinki-Di: The contributions of Chinese immigrants and Australians of Chinese descent to Australia's defence forces and war efforts 1899-1988*, Australian Government Publishing Service Press, Canberra, 1989, p. 109, and Glenn Nicholls, 'Gone with hardly a trace: deportees in immigration policy', in *Does history matter?; making and debating citizenship, immigration and refugee policy in Australia and New Zealand*, eds Klaus Neumann and Gwenda Tavan, ANU E Press, Canberra, 2009.
95 Glenn Nicholls, 'Gone with hardly a trace: deportees in immigration policy', in *Does history matter?; making and debating citizenship, immigration and refugee policy in Australia and New Zealand*, eds Klaus Neumann and Gwenda Tavan, ANU E Press, Canberra, 2009, p. 13.

## 9 Refugees and rebels: Indonesians and Timorese in Employment Companies

1 Jan Lingard, *Refugees and Rebels: Indonesian Exiles in Wartime Australia*, Australian Scholarly Publishing, North Melbourne, 2008, p. 10. See also Margaret George, *Australia and the Indonesian Revolution*, MUP, 1980; Frank C Bennett Jr, *The Return of the Exiles: Australia's Repatriation of Indonesians 1945-47*, Monash University Publishing, Victoria, 2003; and Rupert Lockwood, *The Indonesian Exiles in Australia 1942 – 47*, Cornell University Press, 1976.

2 Jan Lingard, *Refugees and Rebels: Indonesian Exiles in Wartime Australia*, Australian Scholarly Publishing, North Melbourne, 2008, p. 10.

3 See Rupert Lockwood, *Black Armada: Australia and the struggle for Indonesian independence 1942-49*, Hale & Iremonger, New South Wales, 1982, and Lingard, ibid., Chapters 5 and 12.

4 Rupert Lockwood, *Black Armada: Australia and the struggle for Indonesian independence 1942-49*, Hale & Iremonger, New South Wales, 1982, p. 3. Lockwood, a communist, was the editor of the Communist Party of Australia's weekly newspaper, *Tribune*, which was the first publication to support Indonesian independence in Australia. See also Lockwood's long article, 'The Indonesian Exiles in Australia 1942 – 47', in *Indonesia* no. 10, Cornell University Southeast Asia Program, October 1970, pp. 37–56. See Frank C Bennett Jr, *The Return of the Exiles: Australia's repatriation of Indonesians 1945-47*, p. 65.

5 The exact number of men who were first enlisted in the 36th Employment Company is unclear. Lingard refers to 692 men drafted into the Company (p. 35), and there is an army document that refers to 695 Indonesian men interned at Cowra, New South Wales, who were to be released to become 'militarised civil labour' in Queensland (NAA: MP742/1 92/1/256, 36 Aust Employment Coy – Raising Of). But a note from Military Intelligence refers to the same situation as including '500 Javanese seamen' (ibid. 28 May 1942), and the Establishment figures for the Company refer to six platoons, which would total not much more than 360 men (Army Records Office, Melbourne, MP1498 S-1613 RO726). A Department of the Army Security document from the Director of Prisoners of War provides the figure of a total of 467 Javanese seamen interned at the Loveday Camp in South Australia and Cowra in New South Wales (NAA: MP742/1 92/1/256 Javanese Seamen, 13.6.1942). According to a document signed by the Quartermaster-General in January 1944, there were 618 men in the 36th Employment Company (NAA: MP742/1 240/8/31: Redesignation and New Colour Patch – Australian Employment Companies (Alien)). In summary, the Indonesians who served in the 36th Employment Company were largely seamen who had crewed the Dutch ships, and the political activists whom the Dutch had brought from their internment in Papua.

6 Connie Levett, 'Revealed: Australia's secret labour camps', the *Sun-Herald*, 21 December 2008.

7 Ron Witton, in his review of Lingard's book in the *Review of Indonesian and Malaysian Affairs*, vol. 42, no. 2, 2008, pp. 187–92, calls it 'the swamps of west Papua'.

8 Kay Saunders writes that 'over 600 political prisoners [were] sent from the Dutch East Indies [to] Australia after the Japanese invasion in 1942', in '"Discovering" the Subversive and the Saboteur: The Disjuncture between official records of internment policy and practice and the remembered experiences of internees in Australia during the Second World War', *Oral History Association of Australia Journal*, no. 13, 1991, p. 2.

9 An example from the archival record is a document from the Director of Prisoners of War, who, in June 1942, listed 403 Javanese seamen in Cowra and sixty-four in Loveday, with another forty to fifty expected. NAA: MP742/1 92/1/256: 36 Australian Employment Company Indonesian [2754]. Not all political prisoners were freed. There is a reference to Indonesian communist internees held at Liverpool Prisoner of War Camp in New South Wales as late as April 1944 (see NAA: A373 3550: Internment Camp Intelligence Reports), and the New South Wales Deputy Director of Security reported on a visit from Mrs Laura Gapp, of the Civil Rights Defence League in Sydney, to the Indonesian internee Noeroet, whose appeal for release in July 1944 was rejected (see NAA: A6122 1585 Australian Civil Rights Defence League Vol. 1, Interest taken by Mrs Laura Gapp, Civil Rights Defence League in Indonesian Internees and ex-Internees). Rupert Lockwood, in 'The Indonesian Exiles in Australia' p. 38, estimated close to ten thousand Indonesians came to Australia between 1942 and 1945. Lockwood, p. 42, also describes a note dropped from a train taking the Indonesians to the Liverpool prison camp that was picked up by a railway worker and passed on to Mrs Laura Gapp, and from her to Dr Evatt, a leading member of the Australian Government.

10 Lockwood, *Black Armada: Australia and the struggle for Indonesian independence 1942–49*, Hale & Iremonger, New South Wales, 1982, p. 3. Lingard, *Refugees and Rebels: Indonesian Exiles in Wartime Australia*, Australian Scholarly Publishing, North Melbourne, 2008, p. 26.

11 NAA: MP742/1 92/1/256: 36 Australian Employment Company Indonesian, Statutory Rules 1942, No. 360, Amendment of the National Security (Aliens Control) Regulations.

12 Lockwood, *Black Armada: Australia and the struggle for Indonesian independence 1942–49*, Hale & Iremonger, New South Wales, 1982, pp. 61–4, 92; Lingard *Refugees and Rebels: Indonesian Exiles in Wartime Australia*, Australian Scholarly Publishing, North Melbourne, 2008, p. 26. See also Ross Fitzgerald, 'The Tanah Merah exiles in Australia'. https://rossfitzgerald.com/2009/11/07/the-tanah-merah-exiles-in-australia/

13 NAA: MP742/1 92/1/256: Department of the Army Minute Paper, Javanese Seamen, 15 June 1942.
14 ibid.
15 NAA: A6122 150: Australian Council for Civil Liberties Security Files, Seventh Annual Report 1943, p. 3.
16 Cited in Jan Lingard, *Refugees and Rebels: Indonesian Exiles in Wartime Australia*, Australian Scholarly Publishing, North Melbourne, 2008, p. 92.
17 NAA: A6122 150: Australian Council for Civil Liberties Security Files, Seventh Annual Report 1943, p. 3.
18 NAA: MP 742/1 92/1/256: 36 Australian Employment Company Indonesian, Department of the Army Minute Paper, Javanese Seamen.
19 NAA: MP 742/1 92/1/256: 36 Australian Employment Company Indonesian, Department of the Army Minute Paper, Javanese Seamen: Employment by Allied Works Council.
20 NAA: MP 742/1 92/1/256; Allied Land Forces in South West Pacific Area – 36 Employment Company 'Indonesians', LHQ Melbourne, 12 January 1943.
21 ibid.
22 ibid.
23 Jan Lingard, *Refugees and Rebels: Indonesian Exiles in Wartime Australia*, Australian Scholarly Publishing, North Melbourne, 2008, p. 93, refers to uniforms, but the official description of Clothing and Necessities for the Indonesians does not describe military uniform. See NAA: MP 742/1 92/1/256: 36 Australian Employment Company Indonesian.
24 Peter Dunn, '3 Advanced Ordnance Depot (3AOD). Wallangarra Logistics Support Area, Qld', *Australia @ War*. https://www.ozatwar.com/ausarmy/3aod&1aad.htm
25 For a brief outline of the work of the men in the 36th Employment Company, see Lingard, *Refugees and Rebels: Indonesian Exiles in Wartime Australia*, Australian Scholarly Publishing, North Melbourne, 2008, p. 35.
26 Tutt, Ian, 'A History of Queensland's Explosive Reserves', *Queensland Government Mining Journal* (QGMJ) no. 1236, Spring 2009, pp. 22–4. https://geoscience.data.qld.gov.au/dataset/cr060132/resource/geo-doc1201750-cr060132
27 The Commonwealth Investigative Service notes this name for Molly Bondan in December 1948, when she is reported in *News Weekly* as joining 'the staff of foreign broadcasters on the Voice of Free Indonesia short wave station at Jogjakarta'. NAA: 6119 5505316: Bondan, Mary Allethea; *News Weekly*, 'Broadcaster', 24 November 1945.
28 M Bondan, *Spanning a Revolution: The Story of Mohamad Bondan and the Indonesian national movement*, Pustaka Sinar Harapan, Jakarta, 1992, cited in Frank C Bennett Jr, *The Return of the Exiles: Australia's Repatriation of Indonesians 1945-47*, Monash University Publishing, Clayton, 2003, p. 45.

See also Joan Hardjono and Charles Warner, *In Love with a Nation: Molly Bondan and Indonesia, her own story in her own words*, C. Warner, Picton, New South Wales, 1995.

29 Lingard, *Refugees and Rebels: Indonesian Exiles in Wartime Australia*, Australian Scholarly Publishing, North Melbourne, 2008, p. 44.

30 NAA: MP 742/1 92/1/256: 36 Australian Employment Company Indonesian, letter from Captain, Liaison Officer, 36 Aust. Emp. Coy to Major General VPH Stanke, O.B.E., G.O.C., Qld. L. of C. Area, Wallangarra, 3 May 1943.

31 ibid.

32 Lingard, *Refugees and Rebels: Indonesian Exiles in Wartime Australia*, Australian Scholarly Publishing, North Melbourne, 2008, p. 44.

33 AWM: 60 86/1/263: Explosion at 36 Employment Company Wallangarra.

34 ibid.

35 Lingard, *Refugees and Rebels: Indonesian Exiles in Wartime Australia*, Australian Scholarly Publishing, North Melbourne, 2008, p. 36.

36 NAA: MP 742/1 92/1/256 36 Australian Employment Company Indonesian, Minute Paper, Department of the Navy, Employment 700 Indonesian Sailors, 3 February 1943.

37 ibid.

38 K.P.M. (Koninklijke Paketvaart-Maatschappij) was the major Dutch shipping company in the region.

39 NAA: MP 742/1 92/1/256 36 Australian Employment Company Indonesian, Minute Paper, Department of the Navy, Employment 700 Indonesian Sailors, 3 February 1943.

40 ibid.

41 ibid., letter from the Captain of the 36th Employment Company in Wallangarra to the D.A.D. Labour in Brisbane, 23 February 1943.

42 ibid., letter from Boestami, sent to the Minister for the Army, Mr Forde, 19 February 1943.

43 ibid., letter headed Netherlands Indies Commission and dated 16 March 1944.

44 Lingard, *Refugees and Rebels: Indonesian Exiles in Wartime Australia*, Australian Scholarly Publishing, North Melbourne, 2008, p. 93.

45 ibid., cited in letter from the Minister for the Army to Dr van der Plas, dated 28 March 1944.

46 ibid., letter addressed to the Assistant Secretary, defence Division, Department of the Treasury, dated 27 March 1944.

47 ibid., letter dated 5 April 1944.

48 ibid., Department of Army Minute Paper headed 36 Aust Emp Coy – Indonesian, dated 27 April 1944.

49 Documents outlining the negotiations between the Australian and the NEI Governments about the men's outstanding pay can be found in NAA: MP742/1 247/1/829: Pay [of] Indonesian Personnel - 36th (Australian

Employment Company). The NEI Government generally did not reimburse the men the money they were owed.

50 ibid. Confidential document from the Adjutant-General to the Headquarters of the army in Queensland's Line of Communication and to the Rear Headquarters of the First Australian Army, dated 18 May 1944.

51 Army Records Office, Victoria Barracks, Melbourne. MP1498 S-16 ROs Pt2 RO726, 36 Aust Wks Coy (36 Aust Employment Coy crossed out).

52 Rupert Lockwood, 'Personal Interview with Mrs Gapp, May, 1964', cited in R Lockwood, 'The Indonesian Exiles in Australia', *Indonesia,* p. 44.

53 Lingard, *Refugees and Rebels: Indonesian Exiles in Wartime Australia*, Australian Scholarly Publishing, North Melbourne, 2008, p. 121. See also the documentary film *Indonesia Calling*, made for the Waterside Workers Federation in 1946 by Joris Ivens. https://www.youtube.com/watch?v=iAzfM9cQvZQ

54 Frank C Bennett Jr, *The Return of the Exiles: Australia's Repatriation of Indonesians 1945–47*, p. 65.

55 NLA: ORAL TRC 2381; Molly Bondan, interviewed by Campbell McKnight in 1989. http://nla.gov.au/nla.obj-216667029

56 ibid. See also Joan Hardjono and Charles Warner, *In Love with a Nation: Molly Bondan and Indonesia*, Charles Warner, Picton, New South Wales, 1995, and Stephen Gapps, 'Personal and Political – Australian Women and Indonesian Independence', Australian National Maritime Museum. https://www.sea.museum/2015/08/17/black-armada/personal-and-political--australian-women-and-indonesian-independence

57 Molly Bondan, interviewed by Campbell McKnight, session 2, 00.33.18, NLA: ORAL TRC 2381.

58 Cited in Margaret George, *Australia and the Indonesian Revolution*, MUP, 1980, p. 37.

59 Frank C Bennett Jr, *The Return of the Exiles: Australia's Repatriation of Indonesians 1945–47*, p. 205. LF Crisp, the biographer of Chifley, records a remark the Prime Minister made in January 1949: 'I thought the [Dutch] Government had made a colossal blunder, and that they were only assisting the upsurge of nationalism in the East.' *Ben Chifley: A Political Biography*, Angus & Robertson, London, 1977, p. 293.

60 ibid., p. 146.

61 ibid., p. 146.

62 An example of a particularly public battle over the repatriation of Indonesians was the Annie O'Keefe case. Annie, an Indonesian refugee, a widow with eight children, had remarried an Australian, but the government refused to accept the marriage, and wanted to deport her and her children. Her case went to the High Court in 1949 and she won. An account of this case was provided by a journalist, Paul Power, 'How One Refugee Signalled the End of the White Australia Policy', in the *Guardian*,

18 March 2014. http://www.theguardian.com/commentisfree/2014/mar/18/annie-white-australia-policy

63 Rupert Lockwood, *Black Armada: Australia and the struggle for Indonesian independence 1942-49*, Hale & Iremonger, New South Wales, 1982, p. 147.

64 The 36th Employment Company was disbanded on 2 May 1945, by which time most of the men had been withdrawn by the Dutch. NAA: MP 742/1 92/1/256: 36 Australian Company, Indonesian, document from the Adjutant-General, 18 May 1944.

65 This name, used for Timorese in a number of official documents, came from the name of the main city in West Timor: Koepang or Kupang. According to the geographer and historian DN Jeans, in the 1930s Timorese, known as Koepangers, were part of the multi-ethnic community in Broome, Western Australia—see his chapter, 'The Country', in *Australians 1938*, edited by Bill Gammage and Peter Spearitt, Fairfax, Syme & Weldon Associates, Sydney, 1987, pp. 258–9. The Australian World War II Nominal Roll includes other spellings: Kopang, Kopangele and Kopangse; and Timorese and Malays are often not clearly distinguished from each other (DVA's Nominal Rolls: World War II. https://nominal-rolls.dva.gov.au/ww2)

66 EP Chamberlain's monograph, *Forgotten Men: Timorese in Special Operations during World War II* [http://www.scribd.com/doc/29688334/Forgotten-Men-in-Special-Operations-during-World-War-II]; personal correspondence with the writer; Steven Farram, PhD thesis, 'From "Timor Koepang" to "Timor NTT": a political history of West Timor, 1901-1967', Charles Darwin University, 2004 [https://espace.cdu.edu.au/eserv/cdu:6450/Thesis_CDU_6450_Farram_S.pdf]; Dick Horton, *Ring of Fire: Australian Guerrilla Operations Against the Japanese in World War II*, Macmillan, Melbourne, 1983.

67 Ministry of the Interior - to the Prime Minister, Canberra, 19 January 1943 (NAA: A1608, J41/1/9 Part 2, p. 27), cited in EP Chamberlain, *Forgotten Men: Timorese in Special Operations during World War II.* http://www.scribd.com/doc/29688334/Forgotten-Men-Timorese-in-Special-Operations-during-World-War-II

68 One of many acknowledgements of the critical support of the Timorese: DVA (Department of Veterans' Affairs) (2020), *Japanese Advance (December 1941-March 1942)*, DVA Anzac Portal. https://anzacportal.dva.gov.au/wars-and-missions/world-war-ii-1939-1945/events/japanese-advance-december-1941-march-1942

69 AWM: 52 22/1/36: 28 Employment Company, August-November 1943 [2532]. On 23 February 2002 a talk given at the Australian War Memorial by Brad Manera, a military historian at the AWM, titled 'Remembering 1942: The battles on Timor, 20-23 February 1942', also made no mention of the support given to the Australians by the Timorese. The talk can be

found on the War Memorial website: https://www.awm.gov.au/articles/blog/1942-timor

70 EP Chamberlain, *Forgotten Men: Timorese in Special Operations during World War II*. http://www.scribd.com/doc/29688334/Forgotten-Men-in-Special-Operations-during-World-War-II, pp. 2, 19, 20, 36, 43.

71 ibid., p. 2.

72 AWM: 52 1/1/9 Headquarter Units, Allied Land Forces in S.W. Pacific Area, 30 May 1942.

73 Men came from other parts of Malaya and from Singapore. (See, for example, NAA: MP1498 S-16 8 ROs Pt 2 RO 721, 23 Employment Company (Koepangese).)

74 NAA: B883 WX36791: Attestation form from pearl worker Samsudin Bin Katib's service file. https://www.naa.gov.au/learn/learning-resources/learning-resource-themes/war/world-war-ii/attestation-form-pearl-worker-samsudin-bin-katibs-service-file

75 NAA: MP1498 S-16 8: Routine Orders Part 2, Routine Order 721, 23 Employment Company (Koepangese); MP1498 S-16 8: Routine Orders Part 2, Routine Order 717, 23 Employment Company (Koepangese).

76 ibid.

77 The work of 'Z' Special Unit (aka Z Force) is quite well documented. See, for example, DC Horton, *Ring of Fire: Australian Guerrilla Operations Against the Japanese in World War II*, Macmillan, Melbourne, 1983.

78 LS Black, Past President, 'Z' Special Unit Association, Victoria, 'The Story of "Z" Special Unit', *Double Diamond*, September 1992, p. 5.

79 DVA's Nominal Rolls: World War II. https://nominal-rolls.dva.gov.au/ww2

80 Rupert Lockwood, *Black Armada*, p. 147.

81 See, for example, the World War II Nominal Roll entry for Amat Bin Sujar (W65779) and Saleh Bin Amat (W65781).

82 Rupert Lockwood, *Black Armada*, p. 147.

83 EP Chamberlain, *Forgotten Men: Timorese in Special Operations during World War II*, p. 46.

## 10 Antagonists, allies and advocates

1 The *Shepparton News*, 'Enemy Aliens. Immediate Internment Urged', 30 March 1942, p. 4.

2 Letter – LATE No. 6215, 7th Btn. (South Yarra), 'Aliens in Australia', *The Age*, 27 May 1940, p. 8.

3 GC Bolton, '1939-51', in FK Crowley, *A New History of Australia*, William Heinemann, Melbourne, 1974, p. 361. For a discussion of the RSSIALA's history as a political pressure group, see GL Kristianson, *The Politics of Patriotism: The Pressure Group Activities of the Returned Servicemen's League*, ANU Press, Canberra, 1966. The organisation changed its name to the Returned Services League of Australia (RSL) in 1965.

4 A call by the Queensland RSL, reported in the *Border Morning Mail,* 'More Aliens Rounded Up', 6 March 1942, p. 6; 'Enemy Aliens. Soldiers Favour Internment', in the *Sydney Morning Herald*, 2 August 1940, p. 8.
5 E Hardy Johnston, letter to the editor, 'Refugees and the War', the *Sydney Morning Herald,* 3 August 1940, p. 7.
6 The *Shepparton News*, 'Enemy Aliens. R.S.L. Resolutions', 2 July 1942, p. 3.
7 NAA: A1608 N19/1/1: Part 2, Prime Minister's Department.
8 The *Sydney Morning Herald*, 'Enemy Aliens Cannot Join Air Force', 6 February 1942, p. 6; Letter from 'Two Australians' (Edgecliff) and 'Restrictions on Aliens', the *Sydney Morning Herald*, 6 February 1942, p. 3.
9 NAA: MP508/1 61/702/690: Letter from Mr SJ Barry (Leichhardt) to Prime Minister John Curtin, 14 April 1942.
10 Letter from V377, 392, Private GHN 8th Labor, 'Alien Labor Corps', *The Age,* 11 May 1942, p. 2.
11 George Hans Nadel, born in Vienna in 1923, the post-war author of a number of books, including *Australia's colonial culture: ideas, men and institutions in mid-nineteenth century eastern Australia,* Melbourne: FW Cheshire, 1957.
12 Ezra Norton, *Truth*, 16 October 1938, p. 23, cited in Suzanne D Rutland, 'Australian responses to Jewish refugee migration before and after World War II', *Australian Journal of Politics and History*, vol. 31. no. 1, 1985, p. 40.
13 The *Argus*, 'Industrial Danger. Alien Workers' and 'Rich Refugees Arrive in Three Ships', 9 May 1939, p. 9.
14 NAA: A6122 1883, Security files about the Jewish Council to Combat Fascism and Anti-Semitism.
15 ibid., Victoria Police Report, 'Possible Anti-Semitism in Prahran', 31 July 1943.
16 ibid., Commonwealth Security Service (Victoria), Anti-Semitism, 30 October 1943.
17 ibid.
18 *Smith's Weekly*, 'Over-generous payments to refugees', 25 April 1942, p. 3.
19 The *Bondi Daily*, Editorial, 4 July 1940.
20 The *Sydney Morning Herald*, 19 May 1940, p. 5.
21 NAA: MP529/3: Tribunal 2/Zammarchi, p. 2.
22 NLA: MS4738 Box 38: Security Service Classification of Aliens & Allied Matters.
23 ibid. Papers of Arthur Calwell, Series II – Aliens Classification and Advisory Committee, 1942-46, October 1942.
24 NAA: A1608 N19/1/1/ Part 1: Position of Aliens and Refugees in Time of War.
25 ibid.
26 The *Daily Telegraph*, 'Where Can They Go', 8 July 1938, p. 6.
27 The *Sydney Morning Herald* , Editorial, 13 October 1940.
28 ibid., 'Injustice to Refugees', 20 October 1943, p. 6.

29 Bruce Pennay, Heritage Report (unpublished), NSW State Railway Authority, Sydney, 2000.

30 *1,000,000 Jews in the Armies of Freedom*, Jewish Council to Combat Fascism and Anti-Semitism, Melbourne, c.1944.

31 Philip Mendes, 'The Jewish Council to Combat Fascism and Anti-Semitism – A History', 17 October 2010.

32 NAA: A6122 1883: The Jewish Council to Combat Fascism and Anti-Semitism, Security file.

33 See, for example, ibid., letter to the Deputy Director, Security Service, 4 March 1943.

34 Michele Langfield, 'The fortunate few…', *Oral History of Australia Journal*, no. 22, 2000, p. 39; NAA: MP 508/1 255/744/265: Pen Club Melbourne Centre, letter to Minister for the Army, 31 May 1941; CV Pilcher et al, 'Treatment of Refugees. An Appeal for Justice. Cruel Propaganda', the *Sydney Morning Herald*, 1 August 1940, p. 6; the *Sydney Morning Herald*, 'Progress of Loan. Treasurer Dissatisfied', 6 June 1940, p. 9; the *Sydney Morning Herald*, 6 June 1940, p. 9; NAA: A472 W8422, Treatment of Refugee Aliens, letter from General Secretary of ALP New South Wales, 25 August 1942, and list of vice-presidents of the Australian Council for Civil Liberties, 14 May 1943; NAA: A373 890: Jewish Refugees in Australia, letter from T Playford, Premier of South Australia, to the Prime Minister, 23 June 1942.

35 NAA: A6122 1585: Australian Civil Rights Defence League Vol. 1.

36 ibid., letter from Security Service in Sydney, 19 July 1943, Subject: Civil Rights Defence League.

37 ibid., Australian Civil Rights Defence League.

38 NAA: A6122 1585: Australian Civil Rights Defence League Vol. 1, Extract from Camp Intelligence reports No. 22.

39 Laura Gapp, 'Aliens in Australia', the *Sydney Morning Herald*, 22 May 1943, p. 6.

40 UK Parliament, Hansard, Aliens (Treatment on Ships), Debate in the House of Commons, 25 February 1941, Mr Wedgwood MP.

41 The *Sydney Morning Herald*, PA Smith, 'The Persecution of Aliens', 25 July 1940, p. 3.

42 The *Advocate*, 'Horror of Nazi Persecution in Poland', Melbourne, 20 June 1940, p. 17; Kate Darian-Smith, 'War and Australian Society' in Joan Beaumont (ed.), *Australia's War 1939-45*, pp. 57–8.

43 Alan Gill, 'The enemy alien who loved us', the *Sydney Morning Herald*, 24 May 2003. (https://www.smh.com.au/national/the-enemy-alien-who-loved-us-20030524-gdgtae.html). Gill added that 'It is claimed the prelate made no such effort to assist the Jewish majority', but evidence suggests otherwise.

44 Letter provided to June Factor by Marjorie Coppel's son, Dr Charles Coppel.

45 Letter from the Victorian Refugee Immigration Appeals Committee, Melbourne, 23 May 1941; The *Advocate*, 'German Internees in Australia: A Plea for Justice', 29 May 1941, p. 6. There is also Mannix's early support for persecuted German Jews in the *Hebrew Standard of Australasia*, published 5 May 1933, p. 4, and his endorsement of a petition on behalf of Jewish refugees in that paper's issue of 1 July 1943, 'Jewish National Fund, Plea for Bulgarian Jews. Statement to the Press', p. 7.

46 GH Strauss, *Margaret Holmes: A life of Ecumenical Service*, privately printed, Melbourne, 2003, p. 52.

47 After Holmes published an article in the Australian Student Christian Movement journal, the *Intercollegian*, in October 1941, she and another woman activist, Miss Duncan, were for a time 'barred from further visits to the [internment] camps', because the article 'breached security by divulging the internees' whereabouts'. See GH Strauss, ibid., p. 56.

48 Klaus Loewald, 'The Eighth Australian Employment Company', *Australian Journal of Politics and History*, vol. 31, 1985, p. 84.

49 Dr Maurice Laserson, *Bishop Charles Venn Pilcher D. D. : A Biographical Study*, A. K Murray & Co., Sydney, June, 1949.

50 Pilcher had considerable involvement with Jewish organisations and causes before World War II. See Leon Gettler, *An Unpromised Land*, Fremantle Arts Centre Press, Perth, 1993.

51 Charles Venn Pilcher, 'Refugees Offer to Serve', the *Sydney Morning Herald*, 23 May 1940, p. 5.

52 C Venn Pilcher, S Roberts, PA Smith and C Williamson, 'Treatment of Refugees. An Appeal for Justice. Cruel Propaganda', the *Sydney Morning Herald*, 1 August 1940, p. 6. The signatories included the heads of a number of Protestant churches in New South Wales and a couple of professors.

53 See, for example, NAA: 742/1 115/1/48: letter dated 6 August 1942.

54 The new category was introduced by government regulation in February 1942 NAA: A472 W6534: (National Security [Aliens Service] Regulations, Statutory Rules 1942, No. 39, 3 February 1942). It took some time to penetrate military practice—for example, see NAA: SP459/1 489/2/553, letter from Captain DM Bradshaw, Army Headquarters, Victoria Barracks, to every State Army Line of Communication Area, 13 February 1943.

55 See, for example, NAA: MP742/1 275/705/129: letter from Venn Pilcher to Mr Forde, Minister for the Army.

56 NAA: MP508/1 4/703/1116: letters between Bishop Venn Pilcher and Mr Forde, Minister for the Army.

57 NAA: MP508/1 4/703/1217: letter from FM Forde, Minister for the Army, to Bishop Pilcher, 2 March 1942.

58 NLA: MS2852: letter from Earl of Gowrie, Governor-General of Australia, to King George VI, 4 November 1940.

59 Konrad Kwiet, '"Be patient and reasonable!": The internment of German-Jewish refugees in Australia', *Australian Journal of Politics and History*, vol. 31, no. 1, 1985, p. 65.
60 The *Courier Mail*, 'Ban on Jewish Immigrants. No Landing in Brisbane', 6 October 1938, p. 7.
61 Brian Fitzpatrick, *The Australian Commonwealth: A Picture of the Community 1901-1955*, FW Cheshire, Melbourne, 1956, p. 244.
62 NLA: MS 4965/1/3844: Brian Fitzpatrick papers. ACCL 9th Annual Report, 1945.
63 Don Watson, *Brian Fitzpatrick: A Radical Life,* Hale & Iremonger, Sydney, 1979, p. 89.
64 Letter on Victorian Refugee Immigration Appeals Committee letterhead, 23 May 1941, signed by Marjorie Coppel, Honorary Secretary. Letter provided to writer by Marjorie Coppel's son, Dr Charles Coppel.
65 Letter to Professor Wright, University of Melbourne, 6 June 1941. Letter provided to writer by Marjorie Coppel's son, Dr Charles Coppel.
66 ibid.
67 ibid.
68 ibid.
69 United Associations of Women, 11 June 1941, letter signed by Jessie Street. Letter provided to writer by Marjorie Coppel's son, Dr Charles Coppel.
70 NAA: A6122 Item 150: Australian Council for Civil Liberties Security Files, From Major Ronald S. Browne, Inspector, to G.S.O. (M.I.) Southern Command, 18 June 1941.
71 NLA: MS 4965/1/3890: Brian Fitzpatrick Papers, ACCL 9th Annual Report, 1945.
72 In July 1943 the ACCL had one of its five vice-presidents in the Labor government, and its president and two other vice-presidents as members of parliament. See NLA: MS 4965/1/3720: Brian Fitzpatrick papers, ACCL 7th Annual Report, 6 July 1943.
73 Australian House of Representatives, *Debates,* 27 March 1942, p. 462, Arthur Fadden, Leader of the Opposition, https://historichansard.net/hofreps/1942/19420327_reps_16_170/#subdebate-22-0
74 Australian House of Representatives, *Debates,* 27 March 1942, pp. 520–1, John Curtin, PM. https://historichansard.net/hofreps/1942/19420327_reps_16_170/#subdebate-22-0
75 Cited in SD Rutland, 'Australian responses to Jewish refugee migration before and after World War II', *Australian Journal of Politics and History*, vol. 31, no. 1, 1985, p. 44.
76 See Don Watson, *Brian Fitzpatrick: A Radical Life,* Hale & Iremonger, Sydney, 1979.
77 The JCCFAS was an affiliated society of the ACCL; NLA: MS4965 1/1/3749; Brian Fitzpatrick papers. Notes re report to Executive Committee re 'Affiliated Society', 6 March 1944.

78 Brian Fitzpatrick, *Refugees – Hitler's Loss Our Gain*, Jewish Council to Combat Fascism and Anti-Semitism, Melbourne 1944, University of Melbourne Library, McLaren Collection.

79 It appears the returned servicemen's organisation is by now better known as the RSL than the RSSAILA—that is the acronym used by Fitzpatrick throughout the pamphlet.

80 Brian Fitzpatrick, *It Can Happen Here! The case of an A.I.F. Soldier, A Naturalised British Subject*, Australian Council for Civil Liberties, Melbourne, n.d., c.1944; Mitchell Library: 328.63/A SLNSW.

81 NLA: MS 4965/13/6334 Brian Fitzpatrick papers, 'Civil Liberties in Australia', 3XY broadcast, 18 July 1943.

82 ibid.

83 ibid.

84 See Don Watson, *Brian Fitzpatrick: A Radical Life,* and E James Waghorne and Stuart Macintyre, *Liberty – a History of Civil Liberties in Australia*, UNSW Press, Randwick, 2011.

85 See, for example, NAA: A6335 12: Report by informant on 'Communist inner cell' in the ACCL.

86 NLA: MS4965/1/3890 Brian Fitzpatrick papers, Australian Council for Civil Liberties 9th Annual Report, 1945, section 11.

87 Paul Hasluck, *Australia in the War of 1939–45 Vol. 1: The Government and the People 1939–41*, Australian War Memorial, Canberra, 1965 [1952], p. 177.

88 ibid., p. 186.

89 ibid., p. 187.

## 11 Religion and politics

1 Joan Rydon, *A Federal Legislature: the Australian Commonwealth Parliament 1901–1980*, Melbourne, Oxford University Press, 1986, p. 39.

2 *The Religion Report*, ABC Radio National, 3 September 2003.

3 Norman Abjorensen, 'When did Catholics take over the Liberal Party?', 5 December 2007 https://www.crikey.com.au/2007/12/05/abjorensen-when-did-catholics-take-over-the-liberal-party/

4 NAA: A6122 1883: The Jewish Council to Combat Fascism and Anti-Semitism. At the same time, Security was investigating the Council. An inquiry into it in February 1943 resulted in a report setting out briefly the organisation's development and concluding that 'in my opinion there is no security risk attached to the above-named council'. See ibid. Commonwealth Security Service (Victoria), Appendix B, 22 February and 24 February 1943.

5 ibid.

6 FB Smith, 'Sunday Matters', in Bill Gammage and Peter Spearitt (eds), *Australians 1938*, Fairfax, Syme & Weldon, Sydney, 1987, p. 401.

7 ibid.

8 Paul R Bartrop, *Australia and the Holocaust*, Australian Scholarly Publishing, North Melbourne, 1994.
9 Henry Lippmann, interviewed by Rosemary Block, State Library of New South Wales, Oral History Program, 1994, Tape 7:103.
10 NAA A1608 F19/1/1: Question of Admitting Polish and Czech Refugees from Nazi Oppression, 23 January 1941, p. 2.
11 NAA: A1608 N19/1/1: Part 1, Memorandum from Department of Defence to Secretary, Prime Minister's Department, n.d.
12 NAA A1608 N19/1/1: Part 1, Position of Aliens and Refugees in Time of War.
13 ibid.
14 ibid. Memorandum for Secretary, Prime Minister's Department, 7 September 1939.
15 The *Sydney Morning Herald,* 'Refugee Aliens' Status. Regulations Changed', 19 October 1943, p. 6.
16 Jewish prayer book – *Service Prayer Book for The Solemn Days for Jewish Members of the Australian Forces,* 2nd edn., published in August 1943 by 'the Australian Army Chaplains' Department under the Supervision of the Australian Hebrew Chaplains' Conference, January 1943'.
17 Henry Lippmann, interviewed by Rosemary Block, New South Wales State Library, Oral History Program, Tape 11:171.
18 AWM: 52 22/1/17: 8 Employment Co., Routine Orders 21/09/1942.
19 AWM: 52 22/1/17: 8 Employment Co., Routine Orders 26/03/43.
20 AWM: 52 22/1/17: 8 Employment Co., Routine Orders 12/03/43.
21 Yosl Bergner, *What I Meant to Say*, Hed Arzi Book Publishing, Israel, 1997, pp. 109–10.
22 Fred Lester, interviewed by June Factor, 17 December 2002.
23 Such church services also occurred in military detention barracks. See, for example, the Church of England padre holding a service at the Bendigo Detention Barracks in February 1941: AWM: 52 18/3/15: January to June 1941, 8 February 1941, Bendigo Detention Barracks.
24 AWM: 52 22/1/15: 6 Employment Company March – August 1942, 30/08/42.
25 Ian Turner, 'My Long March', *Overland* no. 59, Spring 1974, p. 29. The term 'emu parade' was so widely known and used that it sometimes appears, without irony, in the army's War Diaries, as, for example, in that of the 10th Employment Company: AWM: 52 22/1/19: 10 Employment Company, 16 May 1943.
26 Bart Srhoy, *Journey Beyond Origin*, Hesperian Press, Carlisle, Western Australia, 1998, p. 81.
27 A Fabian, 'The Jewish Chaplaincy in Australia', in Gerald Pynt (ed.), *Australian Jewry's Book of Honour World War II*, Australian Federation of Jewish Ex-Servicemen & Women, 1973, p. 125.

28 Julius Guest, interviewed by June Factor, 17 April 2003.
29 Rabbi Dr A Fabian, 'The Jewish Chaplaincy in Australia', in Gerald Pynt (ed.), *Australian Jewry's Book of Honour World War II,* p. 127.
30 AWM: 52 22/1/13: 4th Employment Company War Diary, October to December, 1942, 7/12/42.
31 In an interview, Robert Exiner refers to an occasion when Rabbi Danglow visited the 6th Employment Company and made a 'big speech for king and country ... and how lucky we were that we had the privilege to serve in the Australian Army. He was booed, and he never came again.' Robert (Bob) Exiner, interview with June Factor, 31 January 1994.
32 Bruce Pennay, 'The Friendly Aliens At Albury Railway Station During The Second World War', unpublished report to the NSW Railways, p. 5; sourced from the *Border Morning Mail,* 'Greek Notables to Visit Albury', 13 October 1942.
33 NAA: 52 22/1/13: War Diary 4th Employment Company, Routine Orders, 28 March 1943.
34 AWM: 52 22/1/19: 10th Employment Company, January – October 1943, War Diary, 25 August 1943.
35 Charles D'Aprano, interviewed by June Factor, 17 May 1999.
36 Fred Lester, interviewed by June Factor, 17 December 2002.
37 AWM: 52 22/1/13 April – June 1943, 4th Employment Company War Diary, Albury 25/5/43.
38 ibid., 25 May 1942.
39 John Callinicos, telephone conversation with June Factor, 7 July 2004.
40 See Katharine Massam and John H Smith, 'Images of God: civil religion and Australia at war 1939 – 1945, *Australian Religious Studies Review,* vol. 11. no. 2, 1998, pp. 57–71.
41 Paul Hasluck, *Australia in the War of 1939 – 1945, vol.1: The Government and the People 1939 – 1941*, Australian War Memorial, Canberra, 1965 [1952], p. 236.
42 ibid., p. 237.
43 ibid, p. 238.
44 Oriel Gray, *Exit Left: Memoirs of a Scarlet Woman,* Penguin Books, Melbourne, 1985, pp. 60 and 97.
45 For a description of the pre-May 1940 newspapers, see Hasluck, *Australia in the War of 1939 – 1945, vol.1: The Government and the People 1939- 1941*, Australian War Memorial, Canberra, 1965 [1952] pp. 237–8.
46 NAA: SP3300/2 Portus 24: Professor GV Portus, 'What Does Patriotism Mean?' 5 March 1944.
47 NAA: SP300/2 Murdoch 24: Walter Murdoch, 'Understanding the Foreigner', 23 July 1944, pp. 1 and 6.
48 *Salt* was initially called the Australian Army and Air Force Education Journal, but by the last issue of the first year of publication, 1941, it was labelled Authorised Australian Army Education Journal. By volume 6

in 1943, the word 'Authorised' had been dropped. For a useful outline of the role and functions of *Salt*, see Joan Davis, '*Salt:* The journal of the Australian Army Education Service in the second world war', *Journal of the Australian War Memorial*, no. 17, October 1990, pp. 20–8.

49 Sean Scalmer, 'The Puzzle of *Meanjin* and the Historical Emergence of the Australian Intelligentsia', *Journal of Australian Studies*, no. 62, 1999, p. 202 [4790].

50 Darryl Dymock, *A Sweet Use of Adversity: the Australian Army Education Service in World War II and its Impact on Australian Adult Education*, University of New England Press, Armidale, 1995, p. 15.

51 The *Kalgoorlie Miner*, 'Our Education System. Army Revelations. One in Twenty-five Cannot Read', 24 June 1943.

52 'Finding Work in a World of Experts' by PC Greenland, vocational training expert, *Salt*, vol. 1, no. 13, 22 December 1941, p. 32.

53 AWM: 38 3DLR 6673/206: Australian Army Education Service – Its Objects and Activities.

54 G Lyle, 'The Legacy is Limited', *Australian Highway*, vol. 29, no. 2, April 1947, p. 25.

55 John Cohen, interviewed by June Factor, 21 June 2002.

56 Robert Salter, interviewed by June Factor, 6 November 2002.

57 Vane Lindesay, letter to June Factor, 8 July 12002 [not page numbered]; Joan Davis, '*Salt* – The Journal of the Australian Army Education Service in the second world war', *Journal of the Australian War Memorial*, no. 17, October 1990, pp. 20–9.

58 *Salt*, 'Free-beer and Free-dom' (Editorial), vol. 1, no. 10, 1 December 1941, p. 1.

59 AWM: 52 22/1/31: 25th Employment Company, November and December 1942, Routine Orders, Cheltenham, 22 November 1942.

60 AWM: 52 22/1/13: 4th Employment Company, January – March 1943, War Diary 21/3/43.

61 Tom Heenan, 'Milner, Ian Frank (1911-1991)', *Australian Dictionary of Biography*, vol. 19, 2021. https://adb.anu.edu.au/biography/milner-ian-frank-16424

62 Roger Jones, 'Lectures on Opera (with whistled extracts)', letter published in *The Age*, 1 January 2000.

63 NAA: A6122 221: Part 1, CPA Interest in the Australian Armed Forces, Extract from *Post and Telegraph Censorship Bulletin* No. 74, For Period 7 March to 20 March, 1944. Political. Communism.

64 NAA: 52 5/12/42, Appendix II, War Cabinet Agendum No. 260/1942.

65 CEW Bean, 'The Value of "Salt"', the *Sydney Morning Herald*, 30 May 1942, p. 6.

66 *The Morning Bulletin* (Rockhampton), '"Salt" Defended', 9 December 1942, p. 4.

67 *Salt*, vol. 8 no. 6, 22 May 1944, p. 22.

68 Rankin's question to the Acting Prime Minister, Ben Chifley, published in *Smith's Weekly* under the heading 'Politics Now Flavour: "Salt"', 9 June 1945.
69 Ian Turner, 'My Long March', *Overland*, no. 59, Spring 1974, p. 29.
70 *Smith's Weekly*, '"Salt" Demobbed', 27 April 1946, p. 19.
71 ibid.
72 *Salt*, vol. 6, no. 11, 2 August 1943, p. 1.
73 *Salt*, vol. 3, no. 3, 20 April 1942.
74 Vane Lindesay, *Some Fragments Recalled – A Life So Far*, p. 37.
75 NAA: A612 444: Subject: Jewish Communist Activities, 9 April 1943, letter to Director-General of Security.
76 Heather Radi, 'Street, Lady Jessie Mary', *Australian Dictionary of Biography*, vol. 16, 2006. http://adb.anu.edu.au/biography/street-lady-jessie-mary-11789; Fay Anderson, 'Max Crawford: Necessity and Freedom', PhD thesis, Department of History, University of Melbourne, 2002, p. 158.
77 The *Advertiser*, 'Sheepskins for Russia £10,000 Appeal', Friday, 9 July 1943, p. 2.
78 Curtin, John, *Diary of a Labour Man 1917-1945: 1945 Prime Minister.* (http://john.curtin.edu.au/diary/primeminister/1945.html). An early historian, Paul Hasluck, in vol. 2 of his history of Australia in World War II, *Australia in the War of 1939-1945: The Government and the People 1942-1945*, lists four groups as responsible for security and surveillance: 'the Investigative Branch of the Attorney-General's Department; officers of Military Intelligence; the policemen of the "Military Police Intelligence Section" working in close collaboration with the Military Intelligence officers; and military officers who formed State branches of a Security Service … set up under the Attorney-General but advisory to the Army.' p. 728. See a much later and more detailed account in John Fahey, *Australia's First Spies: The remarkable story of Australia's intelligence operations 1901 – 45*, Allen & Unwin, Sydney, 2018, for a discussion of the various intelligence organisations.
79 Stuart Macintyre, *The Reds: The Communist Party of Australia from origins to illegality*, Allen & Unwin, Sydney, 1998, p. 394.
80 The 4000 figure is from the 'Report of the Work of the Central Committee from the 13th to 14th National Congress, Central Committee, Australian Communist Party', Sydney, June 1945, cited in Beverley Symons, 'All-Out for the People's War: "Red Diggers" in the Armed Forces and the Communist Party of Australia's Policies in the Second World War', BA Honours thesis, University of Wollongong, 1993, p. 42.
81 Fay Anderson, 'Max Crawford: Necessity and Freedom', PhD thesis, November 2002, History Department, University of Melbourne.
82 AWM: 22/1/26 19: Works Company, January to June 1945, Routine Orders, 10 January 1945.
83 ibid.

84 Jack Friedman, interviewed by June Factor, 4 November 2002.
85 AWM: MSS 1577: Gerard Herbst, 'United under The Southern Cross (Expose)'.
86 Ivan Rostkier, response to questionnaire from June Factor, 2 June 1995.
87 Richard Haese, *Rebels and Precursors: The Revolutionary Years of Australian Art*, Allen Lane, Ringwood, Victoria, 1981 p. 88.
88 Frank Klepner, interviewed by June Factor, 16 April 2002.
89 Caroline Moore, 'Charles D'Aprano: Italo-Australian Left-Activist', *The Hummer*, vol. 2, no. 6, Winter 1996. https://www.labourhistory.org.au/hummer/vol-2-no-6/charles-daprano/
90 Charles D'Aprano, response to questionnaire from June Factor.
91 Charles D'Aprano, interviewed by June Factor, 17 May 1999.
92 ibid.
93 Fred Lester, interviewed by June Factor, 17 December 2002.
94 Charles D'Aprano, interviewed by June Factor, 17 May 1999.
95 ibid.
96 Cited by Bruce Pennay, 'The Friendly Aliens At Albury Railway Station During The Second World War' (unpublished report to NSW Railways), p. 6.
97 NAA: A6122 221: Part 1, CPA Interest in the Australian Armed Forces, vol. 2, SECRET, Extract from Security Report of Vic. L of C Area, 20 September 1943.
98 The National Archives of Australia summarises security agencies during World War II as largely military intelligence units. See NAA. http://www.naa.gov.au/collection/explore/security/index.aspx
99 NLA: MS4738, Box 38, Security Service: Classification of Aliens & Allied Matters, 12 October 1942.
100 NAA: A6122 444: 11 March 1943, Letter on Jewish Communist Activities to the Deputy Director of Security for Victoria.
101 NAA: A6122 444: Melbourne, 9 April 1943, Letter re Jewish Communist Activities.
102 ibid.
103 NAA: A6122 221: Part 2, CPA Interest in defence forces: Australian Armed Forces, vol. 2, part 2.
104 Kay Saunders, *War on the Homefront: State Intervention in Queensland 1938 – 1948*, University of Queensland Press, St Lucia, 1993, p. 65.
105 NAA: A6335 10: Part 1, Communism – Fighting Services, letter titled Communists and American Forces from Lieutenant-Colonel in Western Australia to HQ3 Australian Corps, 16 May 1942, and letter from the Director-General of Security to all Deputy Directors of Security, titled Communist Party – Negro Soldiers, 23 May 1942; A373 2837 Unrest among US Negro Soldiers.
106 AWM: 52 22/1/17, Company Routine Orders No. [not decipherable], Headquarters, 8th Labour Coy, Area 5 Camp Pell, Parkville, 19/6/42.

107 AWM: 52 22/1/13: 4th Employment Company War Diary, October-December 1942, 18.11.42.
108 NAA: A6122 221 Part 2 CPA Interest in Defence Forces: Australian Armed Forces, Vol. 2 Part 2, Contact With Party Apparatus.
109 Guido Ceen, correspondence to June Factor, 18 December 2004.
110 See, for example, AWM: 52 22/1/17 8th Company Routine Orders No. 154, 23/9/42.
111 See, for example, NAA: H373 File No. 7925/37 Bulimba (U.S. Small Ships Section), 9.10.44 .
112 AWM: 52 22/1/26: Box 3677, 19 Works Company, March to December 1943, 1/5/43.
113 NAA: A376 T57, Circular Memorandum No. 8794/35, 25 August 1944.
114 NAA: A6122 Part 1 CPA Interest in the Australian Armed Forces, vol. 2, Secret, May 1943, Communist Activities Within The Army.
115 Beverley Symons, 'All-Out For The People's War: "Red Diggers" in The Armed Forces And The Communist Party Of Australia's Policies In The Second World War', BA (Hons) thesis, University of Wollongong, 1993, pp. 70–1.

## 12 Now the bloody war is over

1 'Now the bloody war is over' was the opening line of a song popular at the time. See Warren Fahey, *Digger's Songs*, Australian Military History Publications, Loftus, New South Wales, 1996.
2 Australian War Memorial (AWM), 'Victory in Europe (VE Day)'. https://www.awm.gov.au/articles/encyclopedia/ve_day
3 AWM: 52 18/3/20: 12th Employment Company, March and April 1943, January – September 1945.
4 AWM: 52 22/1/8: 4th Labour Group, January to November 1945.
5 Steve Waldon, 'Finally. Peace broke out and the people partied', *The Age*, 13 August 2005, p. 8.
6 Morag Loh and Judith Winternitz, *Dinky-Di:The Contribution of Chinese Migrants and Australians of Chinese Descent to Australia's Defence Forces and War Efforts1899 – 1988*, AGPS Press, Canberra, 1989.
7 The Yiddish title translates as *Contributions to an Anthology*, and the editor is noted as a 'colleague'. Printed by York Press in Melbourne in 1944.
8 Louis Waller, 'Growing Up Under Rabbi Danglow: Memories 1940 – 1945', *Journal of the Australian Jewish Historical Society*, vol. x, part 4, 1988, p. 267.
9 See, for example, AWM 52 22/1/28: 21st Employment Company, January to April 1943, 'Unsuitable Personnel'.
10 *Salt*, vol. 7, no. 3, 11 October 1943, p. 23; Melbourne *Argus*, '172 "Reserved" Occupations. Provisional List Issued. Enlistment Restrictions', 28 September 1939, p. 2; AWM: 52 22/1/39, 31 Works Company, May – August 1945, Routine Order no. 98, 8 August 1945.

11 Frank Klepner, interviewed by June Factor, 16 April, 2002.
12 Julius Guest, interviewed by June Factor, 17 April 2003.
13 DVA, Service Record: World War Two Service, Liffmann, Erich. https://nominal-rolls.dva.gov.au/veteran?id=606830&c=WW2#R
14 Bob Exiner, interviewed by June Factor, 31 January, 1994.
15 Eric (Erich) Eckstein, 'A Thousand Bonds: An Autobiography', unpublished memoir.
16 Orpheus Kandiliotis, interviewed by June Factor, 4 August 2004.
17 ibid.
18 Frank Klepner, interviewed by June Factor, 16 April 2002.
19 *Salt*, vol. 10, no. 12, 1945, pp. 47–8.
20 *Salt*, vol. 10, no. 13, 27 August 1945, pp. 2–3.
21 *Salt*, vol. 11, no. 4, 22 October 1945, p. 28.
22 Robert Exiner, 'From the Spree to the Yarra: Memories of an Emigration', *Journal of the Australian Jewish Historical Society*, vol. 12, 1993–95, p. 558.
23 Australian Military Forces Demobilization Procedure Book No. 348920 belonging to Erich Liffmann.
24 See https://www.awm.gov.au/wartime/45/article
25 GL Kristianson, *The Politics of Patriotism: The Pressure Group Activities of the Returned Servicemen's League*, ANU Press, Canberra, 1966, p. 75.
26 ibid.
27 JP Pomeroy, 'Morale on the Homefront in Australia during the Second World War', PhD thesis, University of Sydney, 1995. For the perspective of a key public servant of the time, see Herbert C Coombs, 'An insider's perspective on social engineering', *Australia's War 1939-45: Study Guide and Reader*, Deakin University, Geelong, 1994, Reading 5.13, p. 325ff.
28 AWM: Digest of Decisions and Announcements and Important Speeches by the Prime Minister, 46 (12 November – 6 December 1942), p. 22.
29 Herbert C Coombs, 'An insider's perspective on social engineering', *Australia's War 1939-45: Study Guide and Reader*, 1981, Deakin University, *Reading* 5.13, p. 325ff.
30 Quoted by Mr Dedman in parliamentary debate, 29 March 1946.
31 NLA, Brian Fitzpatrick papers, MS 4965/1/3892 Australian Council for Civil Liberties, 10 Years of the Council.
32 NAA: MP742/1 84/1/928; University Courses for Aliens of Enemy Origins, p. 6044ff.
33 NAA: MP742/1, 84/1/928, Australian House of Representatives, *Debates*, 29 March 1946.
34 ibid., p. 15.
35 Bruce Pennay, 'Historical Outline and Context: The Battle of Albury', in his unpublished Heritage Report to the NSW State Railway Authority, 2000.
36 NAA: MP742/1 115/1/173 October 1944 Department of the Army Minute Paper Employment of Aliens in AMF, October 1944.

37 MP742/1 84/1/928 Australian House of Representatives, *Debates*, 29 March 1946, p. 19.
38 Australian House of Representatives, *Debates*, 1 May 1942, p. 845. https://historichansard.net/hofreps/1942/19420501_reps_16_170/#debate-3p
39 Arthur Calwell, 'Pop. 7,000,000 – Not Enough', *Salt*, vol. 10, no. 13, 27 August 1945, p. 45.
40 Michael McKernan, *All In! Australia during the Second World War*, Nelson, Melbourne, 1983, p. ix.
41 NAA: MP 742/1 115/1/315.
42 The *Herald*, 'Germans and Austrians Want to Stay in Australia', 15 March 1944.
43 Example from the Application for Naturalization form filled in by Pasquale (Charles) D'Aprano, 6th Employment Company in January 1946. (NAA: A435 1946/4/953).
44 NAA: MP 742/1 115/1/274; Aliens in Employment Companies, note to the Prime Minister from the Minister for the Army, 24 January, 1945.
45 Australian House of Representatives, *Debates*, 17 May 1945, p. 1866.
46 NAA: MP 742/1 115/1/274.
47 GL Kristianson, *The Politics of Patriotism: the Pressure Group Activites of the Returned Servicemen's League*, ANU Press, Canberra, 1966, p. 224.
48 NAA: A6119 242: Sol Factor, F/3/70 Vol. 1; Letter headed Commonwealth of Australia Department of Labour and National Service, Man Power Rehabilitation Section, date obscured, from the Supervisor of the Man Power Rehabilitation Section to Mr MW Tomlinson, Department of Security, Cavendish House, 159 Flinders Lane, Melbourne C.1.
49 Bob Exiner, interviewed by June Factor, 31 January 1994.
50 Civilian clothing was not always readily available, so ex-servicemen were permitted to wear their military uniform for up to six months. AWM 52 22/1/5: Headquarters 1 Labour Group Routine Orders, item 59.
51 Klaus Friedeberger, Biographical Notes; Ken Inglis, Seumas Spark and Jay Winter with Carol Bunyan, *Dunera Lives: A Visual History*, Monash University Publishing, 2018, p. 448.
52 Andy Factor, interviewed by June Factor, 25 July 2002, p. 1543.
53 GC Bolton, *1939 – 51*, in FK Crowley (ed.), *A New History of Australia*, William Heineman, Melbourne, 1974, p. 479.
54 GL Kristianson, *The Politics of Patriotism: The Pressure Group Activities of the Returned Servicemen's League*, ANU Press, Canberra, 1966, p. xxvii.
55 Charles D'Aprano, response to questionnaire from June Factor, 1995.
56 Orpheus Kandiliotis, interviewed by June Factor, 26 June 2004.
57 Keith Steinhardt, interviewed by June Factor, 13 January 2003.
58 The *Argus*, 'Solo Pianist Who Worked on Sydney Wharves', 29 July 1946, p. 4.

59 Felix Werder, interviewed by June Factor, 5 June 2003.
60 GL Kristianson, *The Politics of Patriotism: The Pressure Group Activities of the Returned Servicemen's League*, ANU Press, Canberra, 1966, p. 206.
61 NAA: A6122 222: Australian Legion of Ex-Servicemen and Women.
62 See, for example, the Australian Greek Ex-Servicemen's Organisation.
63 Henry Lippmann suggested in an interview that some men wouldn't march because 'They feel they have been discriminated against at the time'. Interview with Henry Lippmann conducted by Rosemary Block, New South Wales State Library, Australian Oral History Program, Tape 14: 210.
64 Alan Gill, the *Sydney Morning Herald*, 25 April 1992.
65 Henry Lippmann interviewed by Rosemary Block, New South Wales State Library, Australian Oral History Program, Tape 7: 117.
66 Fred Lester, interviewed by June Factor, 17 December 2002.
67 Jack Friedman, interviewed by June Factor, 4 November 2002.
68 Yossel Birstein's response to June Factor's questionnaire.
69 *The Age*, 15 September 1952, p. 9.
70 A recent overview of a number of the men in the 8th Employment Company: Ken Inglis, Bill Gammage, Seumas Spark and Jay Winter, with Carol Bunyan, *Dunera Lives: Profiles*, Monash University Publishing, Melbourne, 2020.
71 Orpheus Kandiliotis, conversation with June Factor, 12 October 2004.

## 13 Bergner and Sievers: two 'alien' artists in the Employment Companies

1 Yosl Bergner, *What I Meant to Say: Stories and travels as told to Ruth Bondy*, Hed Arzi Book Publishing, Israel, 1997, p. 43.
2 Bergner's father, Zacharia Chana Bergner, was a poet, essayist and leading Jewish cultural activist in Poland, who took the name Melech Ravitch. He came to Australia in 1933, in search of a possible 'Jewish homeland' in the Kimberleys, and lived here until 1937. For Yosl Bergner's matter-of-fact account of his father, see his memoir, *What I Meant to Say: Stories and travels as told to Ruth Bondy*, Hed Arzi Book Publishing, Israel, 1997.
3 ibid., p. 82.
4 ibid., p. 88.
5 Cited by Frank Klepner, *Yosl Bergner: Art as a Meeting of Cultures*, Macmillan, Melbourne, 2004, pp. 67, 70.
6 Bernard Smith, *Noel Counihan: Artist and Revolutionary*, OUP, Melbourne, 1993, p. 184.
7 Yosl Bergner, interviewed by Ranald Macdonald for the Australian Broadcasting Corporation, Melbourne, October 1990. See also Richard Haese, *Rebels and Precursors: The Revolutionary Years of Australian Art*, Allen Lane, Ringwood, 1981, p. 85.

8 Frank Klepner, *Yosl Bergner: Art as a meeting of cultures*, Macmillan, Melbourne, 2004, p. 74.
9 Albert Tucker, cited in Klepner, *Yosl Bergner: Art as a meeting of cultures*, Macmillan, Melbourne, 2004, p. 77.
10 Smith, *Noel Counihan: Artist and Revolutionary*, OUP, Melbourne, 1993, p. 167.
11 Bergner, *What I Meant to Say: Stories and travels as told to Ruth Bondy,* Hed Arzi Book Publishing, Israel, 1997, p. 113. Frank Klepner's Book *Yosl Bergner: Art as a meeting of cultures* includes three pencil sketches of Aboriginal Australians dated 1938; a painting titled *Aborigines in Fitzroy* dated 1941; and then a number of paintings of Indigenous people done between 1942 and 1944, part of the period Bergner spent in the 6th Employment Company. Klepner's book has an interesting chapter that discusses Bergner's interest in Aboriginal Australians as influencing other painters (pp. 91–107).
12 Klepner, *Yosl Bergner: Art as a Meeting of Cultures*, Macmillan, Melbourne, 2004, p. 9.
13 Bergner, interviewed by Ranald Macdonald for the Australian Broadcasting Corporation, Melbourne, October 1990.
14 P Heinrichs, 'Wandering Son Returns', *The Age,* 26 August 1978, p. 19, cited in Klepner, *Yosl Bergner: Art as a Meeting of Cultures*, Macmillan, Melbourne, 2004, p. 91.
15 Bergner, interviewed by Ranald Macdonald for the Australian Broadcasting Corporation, Melbourne, October 1990.
16 Bergner, in a documentary made by Yarra Bank Films in 1987, called *Painting the Town: A Film about Yosl Bergner*, written by Charles Merewether and Sharon Connelly, directed by Trevor Graham and narrated by Max Gillies.
17 Cited in Smith, *Noel Counihan: Artist and Revolutionary*, OUP, Melbourne, 1993, p. 182.
18 Frank Klepner, interviewed by June Factor, 16 April 2002.
19 The Australian War Memorial dates the painting 1944. Klepner calls it *End of a Day's Work, Tocumwal*, and dates it 1942–43 (*Yosl Bergner: Art as a Meeting of Cultures*, Macmillan, Melbourne, 2004, plate 40). Before him, the art historian Richard Haese uses the same title as Klepner but gives the date as 1941 (*Rebels and Precursors: The Revolutionary Years of Australian Art*, Allen Lane, Ringwood, 1981, p. 158). As Bergner is notorious for both not dating his pictures and changing their names ('Sometimes I date my paintings and sometimes not' (Klepner, p. 105), this confusion is understandable, although Haese's date is definitely wrong, as Bergner didn't join the 6th Employment Company until April 1942.
20 Frank Klepner, *Yosl Bergner: Art as a meeting of cultures*, Macmillan, Melbourne, 2004, p. 91.

21 ibid., pp. 51, 72.
22 ibid., p. 41.
23 Wolfgang Sievers, interviewed by Barry York, 20 March 2000, (NLA: ORAL TRC 4549, p. 36).
24 Wolfgang Sievers, interviewed by June Factor, 16 June 2003.
25 Wolfgang Sievers, *Images of Germany: Australian Insights*, small pamphlet-size publication, n.d., p. 13.
26 ibid.
27 Wolfgang Sievers, interviewed by Barry York, 20 March 2000, (NLA: ORAL TRC 4549, p. 30).
28 ibid.
29 Sievers, interviewed by June Factor, 16 June 2003.
30 Wolfgang Sievers, interviewed by Barry York, 20 March 2000, (NLA: ORAL TRC 4549, pp. 23-4).
31 ibid., p. 41.
32 ibid., p. 47.
33 Sievers, interviewed by June Factor, 15 June 2003. Maie Casey was the wife of Richard Casey, then a Cabinet minister in the conservative Australian Government. Mrs Casey was interested in the arts and enjoyed the company of artists.
34 ibid.
35 ibid.
36 Sievers, interviewed by Barry York, 20 March 2000, (NLA: ORAL TRC 4549, p. 65).
37 ibid., p. 97.
38 ibid., p. 61.
39 Sievers, interviewed by June Factor, 16 June 2003.
40 ibid.
41 ibid., p. 55.
42 ibid. p. 70.
43 ibid. p. 116,
44 In his book *The Hitler Refugees* (Chatto & Windus, London, 2002), the British historian Daniel Snowman has explored the remarkable cultural contribution made to Britain by refugees from Nazism.

# Bibliography

## Interviews


Block, Rosemary, Interview with Henry Lippmann [interview transcript], 1994–5, New South Wales State Library, Oral History Program.

—Interview with Henry Lippmann [interview transcript], 7 November 2003, New South Wales State Library, Oral History Program.

Factor, June, Interview with Robert Exiner [interview transcript], 31 January 1994.

—Interview with Bern Brent [interview transcript], 16 November 1994.

—Interview with Morry Nirens [interview transcript], 29 January 1995.

—Interview with Charles D'Aprano [interview transcript], 17 May 1999.

—Interview with Yosl Bergner [interview transcript], 16 April 2002.

—Interview with Frank Klepner [interview transcript], 16 April 2002.

—Interview with John Cohen [interview transcript], 21 June 2002.

—Interview with Anon 1 [interview transcript], July 2002.

—Interview with Louis Waller [interview transcript], 8 July 2002.

—Interview with Andy Factor [interview transcript], 25 July 2002.

—Interview with Speros Polites [interview transcript], 1 November 2002.

—Interview with Jack Friedman [interview transcript], 4 November 2002.

—Interview with Robert Exiner [interview transcript], 6 November 2002.

—Interview with Robert Salter [interview transcript], 6 November 2002.

—Interview with Fred Lester [interview transcript], 17 December 2002.

—Interview with Keith Steinhardt [interview transcript], 13 January 2003.

—Interview with Paul Seefeld [interview transcript], 10 February 2003.

—Interview with Julius Guest [interview transcript], 17 April 2003.

—Interview with Werner Lowenstein [interview transcript], 25 April 2003.

—Interview with Felix Werder [interview transcript], 5 June 2003.

—Interview with Wolfgang Sievers [interview transcript], 16 June 2003.

—Interview with Orpheus Kandiliotis [interview transcript], 26 July 2004.

—Interview with Orpheus Kandiliotis [interview transcript], 4 August 2004.

—Interview with Kurt Langfelder [interview transcript], 17 September 2004.

—Interviews with Emil Witton [interview transcript], between 2005–8

—Interview with Paul Baxter [interview transcript], 26 August 2013.

Fein, Yvonne, Interview with Kurt Lippmann [interview transcript, Beth Weizmann Jewish Community Centre, Melbourne], c. 2003.

Paxinos, George, Interview with Nicholas Raftopoulos [interview transcript], 15 May 1985.

—Interview with John Callinicos [interview transcript], 19 May 1985.

## Memoirs

Ceen, Albert, unpublished memoir, summarised and translated by his son Guido Ceen.

Cohn, Fred, audiotape of his army experiences provided by his son John Cohn.

Eckstein, Eric, 'A Thousand Bonds: An Autobiography', unpublished memoir, n.d.

Waller, Jack, 'A Fragment of Memory', unpublished memoir translated and edited by his son, Louis Waller, Melbourne, 1997.

Weinmann, Bruno Werner, 'A Schoolboy's Memories, Life in Camp 3, Tatura', available from the Tatura Museum, Hogan Street, Tatura, Victoria, 3616.

Witton (Witkowski), Emil, 'My Memories', unpublished memoir, November 2006.

## Responses to questionnaires

Birstein, Yossel, response to questionnaire from June Factor, n.d.

D'Aprano, Charles, response to questionnaire from June Factor, 1995.

Exiner, Robert, response to questionnaire from June Factor, 25 May 1995.

Graf, Helmut, response to questionnaire from June Factor, 23 May 1995.

Lester, Fred, response to questionnaire from June Factor, 17 December 2002.

Raftopoulos, Nicholas, response to questionnaire from June Factor, n.d.

Rostkier, Ivan, response to questionnaire from June Factor, 2 June 1995.

Ruskin, Alfred, response to questionnaire from June Factor, 15 June 1995.

Salter, Robert, response to questionnaire from June Factor, 6 November 2002.

Schnock, Walter, response to questionnaire from June Factor, 25 May 1995.

Witton (Witkowski), Emil, response to questionnaire from June Factor, 16 November 2005.

## Letters and personal communication

Australian Military Forces Demobilization Procedure Book No. 348920, belonging to Erich Liffmann.

Bergner, Yosl, letter to 6th Employment Company reunion, 16 February 1994. Copy held by June Factor.

Callinicos, John, phone conversation with June Factor, 7 July 2004.

Ceen, Albert, letter to his wife Flavia, translated by their son Guido Ceen, private correspondence.

Ceen, Albert, letter written April 1942, in the possession of Guido Ceen.

Ceen, Guido, letter to June Factor, 9 December 2004.

Ceen, Guido, correspondence to June Factor, 18 December 2004.

Chapkoun, Victor, phone conversation with June Factor, 16 August 2004.

Coppel, Marjorie, letter from Victorian Refugee Immigration Appeals Committee to JB Chifley, Treasurer in the Curtin Labor government, 23 May 1941.

Coppel, Marjorie, letter to Professor Wright, University of Melbourne, 6 June 1941.
Higgins, Huntley, conversation with June Factor, 3 February 2002.
Kandiliotis, Orpheus, phone conversation with June Factor, 4 August 2004.
Kandiliotis, Orpheus, conversation with June Factor, 12 October 2004.
Kaufmann, George E, letter to M/s Phyllida Fitzgerald, c/o Angus and Robertson Publishers, 15 March 1983 [source no longer known].
Lindesay, Vane, letter to June Factor, 18 July 2002.
—letter to June Factor, 2 July 2002.
Lippmann, Kurt, letter to June Factor, 19 April 1994.
Nachintsky, David, discussion with June Factor, 9 March 1994.
Pollack, John, email to June Factor, 15 July 2008.
Ruskin, Alfred, Walter Schnock and Robert Exiner, letter written to Kurt Lippmann, 31 October 1942, provided to June Factor by Walter Schnock on 25 May 1995.
Stirling, Lieutenant Colonel JA, letter to June Factor, 23 October 2002.
United Associations of Women, letter to the Victorian Refugee Immigration Appeals Committee, signed by Jessie Street, 11 June 1941.
Victorian Refugee Immigration Appeals Committee, letter signed by Marjorie Coppel, 23 May 1941.
Witton (Witkowski), Emil, 'A short description of my life before and after military service', letter to June Factor, 23 August 2005.
—letter to the German publication *Aktuel,* 2005 (translated by him into English).

## Government, parliamentary and High Court records

Australian House of Representatives, *Debates,* 2 December 1938, p. 2628. Lieutenant-Colonel Thomas W White, DFC, VD, MP, Minister for Trade and Customs. https://historichansard.net/hofreps/1938/19381202_reps_15_158/#debate-1
—*Debates,* 27 March 1942, pp. 520–1, John Curtin, PM. https://historichansard.net/hofreps/1942/19420327_reps_16_170/#subdebate-22-0
—*Debates,* 27 March 1942, p. 462, Arthur Fadden, Leader of the Opposition. https://historichansard.net/hofreps/1942/19420327_reps_16_170/#subdebate-22-0
—*Debates,* 1 May 1942, p. 845, Arthur Calwell, Minister for Immigration. https://historichansard.net/hofreps/1942/19420501_reps_16_170/#debate-3
—*Debates,* 17 May 1945, p. 1866, John Curtin, PM. https://historichansard.net/hofreps/1945/19450517_reps_17_182/#debate-0
—*Debates,* 29 March 1946, George Bowden, Hon. Member for Gippsland. (NAA: MP742/1 84/1/928)
—*Debates,* 29 March 1946, Mr Dedman, Minister for Post-War Reconstruction. (NAA: MP742/1 84/1/928)

—*Debates*, 29 March 1946, Charles Morgan, Hon. Member for Reid. (NAA: MP742/1 84/1/928)
—*Debates*, 9 February 1949, pp. 60–4. Arthur Calwell, Minister for Immigration. https://historichansard.net/hofreps/1949/19490209_reps_18_201/#debate-13
Commonwealth Law Report No. 70, pp. 60–83, 1945: High Court of Australia, Polites – Plaintiff, The Commonwealth and Another – Defendants. Kandiliotes – Plaintiff, The Commonwealth and Another – Defendants. Melbourne, 8, 9 March; 10 April 1945. https://www.ato.gov.au/law/view/document?Mode=type&TOC=%2205%3ACases%3AHigh%20Court%3A1945%3APolites%20v.%20Commonwealth%20-%20(10%20April%201945)%3A%230107%23Judgment%20by%20Williams%20J%3B%22&DOCID=%22JUD%2F70CLR60%2F00007%22
Department of Veterans' Affairs (DVA), Nominal Rolls: World War II. https://nominal-rolls.dva.gov.au/ww2
Department of Veterans' Affairs (DVA), 'Japanese advance (December 1941 – March 1942)', *Anzac Portal.* https://anzacportal.dva.gov.au/history/conflicts/australia-and-second-world-war/events/japanese-advance-december-1941march-1942-4
Department of Veterans' Affairs (DVA), Service Record: World War Two Service, Liffmann, Erich. https://nominal-rolls.dva.gov.au/veteran?id=606830&c=WW2#R
Digest of Decisions and Announcements and Important Speeches by the Prime Minister. No. 46, 12 November – 6 December 1942, p. 22. John Curtin Prime Ministerial Library: JCPML00110/51. https://jcpml-link.library.curtin.edu.au/dtlimg.pl?a=JCPML00110%2F51&p=1
UK Parliament, Hansard, House of Commons, Aliens (Treatment on Ships), vol. 369, Tuesday 25 February 1941, Mr Wedgwood, MP. https://hansard.parliament.uk/Commons/1941-02-25/debates/c898c99c-3d89-4a96-9068-61e7a6209883/Aliens(TreatmentOnShips)?highlight=%27wedgwood%27#contribution-e3448451-1eb7-4c73-9183-99e68147b487

## Archives and libraries

**Army Records Office, Victoria Barracks, Melbourne:** List of Corps/Units provided on 11 November 2003.
—MP1498 S-16 4; ROs Part 2, RO717, File No. 37, 5 May 1943.
—MP1498 S-16 13; ROs Part 2, RO726, Note from Military Intelligence.
—MP1498 S-16 13; ROs Part 2, RO726, 36 Aust. Works Coy (36 Aust. Employment Coy crossed out).

**Australian War Memorial (AWM):** 38 3DLR 6673/206; Australian Army Education Service – Its Objects and Activities.
—52 1/1/9; Headquarter Units, Allied Land Forces in SW Pacific Area, 30 May 1942.

—52 1/17/8; Australian Employment Company War Diary, 2 January 1944.
—52 22/1/2; Deputy Assistant Director Labour HQ Qld. L of C Area, January – May 1945.
—52 22/1/3; 4 Labour Company.
—52 22/1/3; 4 Employment Company War Diary, Albury, 9 March 1943.
—52 22/1/5; Headquarters 1 Labour Group, Routine Orders, Item 59.
—52 22/1/7; 3 Australian Labour Group War Diary, Brisbane, 14 September 1945.
—52 22/1/8; 4 Labour Group, January to November 1945.
—52 22/1/9; 5 Labour Group War Diary, June – November 1945.
—52 22/1/10; 1 Australian Works Company War Diary, 1 – 6 July 1945.
—52 22/1/11; 2 Employment Company War Diary, February and March 1943, Routine Orders 17 February 1943.
—52 22/1/11; Routine Orders 6 July 1943.
—52 22/1/11; Routine Orders 18 July 1943.
—52 22/1/11; 2 Employment Company War Diary, January – June 1944, Routine Orders 13 February 1944.
—52 22/1/11; Routine Orders 19 March 1945.
—52 22/1/12; 3 Employment Company War Diary, October – December 1944.
—52 22/1/12; 3 Employment Company, April – June 1945.
—52 22/1/13; 4 Labour Company War Diary.
—52 22/1/13; Routine Orders January – June 1942.
—52 22/1/13; 4 Labour Company War Diary, 9 March 1942.
—52 22/1/13; 4 Labour Company War Diary, 16 – 31 March 1942.
—52 22/1/13; War Diary, 1 April – 30 April 1942.
—52 22/1/13; Routine Orders, 6 May 1942.
—52 22/1/13; 4 Employment Company War Diary, 15 May 1942.
—52 22/1/13; 4 Labour Company War Diary, Albury, 17 May 1942.
—52 22/1/13; 4 Employment Company, April – June 1943, War Diary, Albury, 25 May 1942.
—52 22/1/13; 4 Labour Company War Diary, 16 June 1942.
—52 22/1/13; 4 Employment Company, Routine Orders, 1 July 1942.
—52 22/1/13; 4 Labour Company War Diary, 2 July 1942.
—52 22/1/13; War Diary, 31 August 1942.
—52 22/1/13; 4 Labour Company, Routine Orders August – November 1942.
—52 22/1/13; 4 Labour Company, 1 November 1942.
—52 22/1/13; 4 Employment Company War Diary, October – December 1942, 18 November 1942.
—52 22/1/13; 4 Employment Company War Diary, October – December, 1942, 7 December 1942.
—52 22/1/13; War Diary, 25 July 1942 and 22 January 1943.
—52 22/1/13; 4 Employment Company War Diary, Routine Orders, Albury, 21 March 1943.
—52 22/1/13; 4 Employment Company, January – March 1943, War Diary, 21 March 1943.

—52 22/1/13; 4 Employment Company War Diary, Albury, 22 March 1943.
—52 22/1/13; 4 Employment Company, April – June 1943, War Diary, Albury, 25 May 1943.
—52 22/1/13; 4 Employment Company, April – June 1943, item dated 12 June 1943.
—52 22/1/13; 4 Employment Company, July – September 1943, Routine Orders, 30 August 1943.
—52 22/1/15; 6 Employment Company War Diary.
—52 18/3/15; January – June, 1941, Bendigo Detention Barracks, 8 February 1941.
—52 22/1/15; 6 Employment Company War Diary, 31 March 1942.
—52 22/1/15; 6 Employment Company War Diary, 22 May 1942.
—52 22/1/15; 6 Employment Company March – August 1942, 30 August 1942.
—52 22/1/15; 6 Employment Company Routine Orders , 22 September 1942.
—52 22/1/15; 6 Australian Employment Company, Routine Orders, 27 November 1942.
—52 22/1/15; 6 Employment Company War Diary, 17 November 1943.
—52 22/1/16; 7 Employment Company War Diary, entry 24 November 1942.
—52 22/1/16; 7 Employment Company War Diary, November and December 1942, entry 25 November 1942.
—52 22/1/16; 7 Employment Company War Diary, entry 15 December 1942.
—52 22/1/16; 7 Employment Company War Diary, 9 March 1943.
—52 22/1/17; Company Routine Orders No. [not decipherable], Headquarters, 8 Labour Company, Area 5 Camp Pell, Parkville, 19 June 1942.
—52 22/1/17; 8 Employment Company, Routine Orders, 21 September 1942.
—52 22/1/17; 8 Company Routine Orders No. 154, 23 September 1942.
—52 22/1/17; 8 Employment Company War Diary, Company Routine Orders No.175, Camp Pell, Parkville, 14 October 1942.
—52 22/1/17, 8 Employment Company, Routine Orders, 12 March 1943.
—52 22/1/17; Company Routine Orders No. 332, 20 March 1943.
—52 22/1/17; 8 Employment Company, Routine Orders 26 March 1943.
—52 22/1/18; 9 Works Company, January – December 1944.
—52 22/1/19; 10 Employment Company War Diary, July – December 1942.
—52 22/1/19; 10 Employment Company, 16 May 1943.
—52 22/1/19; 10 Employment Company, January – October 1943, War Diary, 25 August 1943.
—52 18/3/20; 12 Employment Company, March and April 1943, January – September 1945.
—52 22/1/22; 22 Employment Company Routine Orders, 27 February 1943.
—52 22/1/26; Medical Classification, 19 Employment Company.
—52 22/1/26; 19 Australian Labour Company Routine Orders, 13 October 1942, 19 Works Company, June 1942 – February 1943.
—52 22/1/26; Box 3677; 19 Works Company, March – December 1943, 1 May 1943.

—52 22/1/26; 19 Works Company, January to June, 1945, Routine Orders 10 January 1945.
—52 22/1/27; 20 Works Company, January – December 1943.
—52 22/1/27; 20 Employment Company, 1 – 31 March 1944.
—52 22/1/28; 21 Employment Company, January to April 1943, 'Unsuitable Personnel'.
—52 22/1/28; 21 Works Company April – June 1944.
—52 22/1/29; 22 Employment Company, Port Moresby, October – December 1943, Routine Orders 14 November 1943.
—52 22/1/30; 28 Employment Company War Diary, Alice Springs, 19 December 1943.
—52 22/1/31; 25 Labour Company, War Diary, July 1942.
—52 22/1/31; 25 Employment Company, November and December, 1942, Routine Orders, Cheltenham, 22 November 1942.
—52 22/1/32; 26 Employment Company War Diary, January 1945.
—52 22/1/36; 28 Australian Employment Company War Diary, July 1942 – March 1943; 16 July 1942.
—52 22/1/36; 28 Employment Company War Diary, July, 1942 – March 1943.
—52 22/1/36; 28 Employment Company, August – November 1943.
—52 22/1/39; 31 Works Company, May – August, 1945, Routine Order no. 98, 8 August 1945.
—52 22/1/41; 33 Employment Company, January – June 1944.
—54 255/4/3; Military History Section, Notes on Compilation of War Diaries.
—54 422/7/8; Provisional War Equipment Table for an Employment Company, July 1943.
—54 443/2/2; Department of the Army Minute Papers, Employment Companies, November 1943.
—54 443/2/2; Department of the Army Minute Paper, 12 November 1943.
—54 721/22/1; Account of Formation, Service and Activities of 22 Works Company.
—54 883/5/4; [Security – National Security (Emergency Control) Regulations] National Security (Aliens Service) Regulation, December 1942.
—54 883/5/4; National Security – (Aliens Service) Regulation – Copy of an article submitted by N321052, Private Steuerwald, Gerhard of 3 Employment Coy, through his CO for permission to arrange publication through the Press, December 1942.
—55 443/2/2; Correspondence about Employment Companies.
—60 13/1277/43; 7 Australian Employment Company (Chinese).
—60 13/1277/43; Telegram from Norforce to Landforces RPTD Milbase Brisbane, 19 August 1943, stamped SECRET.
—60 86/1/263; Explosion at 36 Employment Company Wallangarra.
—62 76; Offensive Behaviour – Tocumwal, 8 January 1943.
—62 76: Two letters from Major LG Campbell, 10 January 1943 and 11 January 1943.

—113 17/3/1; Alien Labour, December 1942.
—113 17/3/1; Alien Labour – 6 Employment Company, 5 December 1943.
—MSS 1577; Gerard Herbst, 'United Under the Southern Cross (Exposé)', 1993, unpublished short memoir of life in the army.
—R 940.541294 L963f + V: Lunney, Bill and Frank Finch, *The Forgotten Fleet: a History of the Part Played by Australian Men and Ships in the U.S. Army Small Ships Section in New Guinea, 1942-1945*, Forfleet Publishing, New South Wales, 1995.

**Mitchell Library (ML), State Library of New South Wales:** 328.63/A SLNSW: Fitzpatrick, Brian, *It Can Happen Here! The Case of an A.I.F. Soldier, A Naturalised British Subject*, Australian Council for Civil Liberties, Melbourne, n.d, c.1944.
—MLMSS 6735: Ceen family papers, 1923–98, Albert Ceen.
—MLMSS 6735: Ceen family papers, 1923–98, Albert Ceen, undated letter to his wife.
—MLMSS 6735: Ceen family papers, 1923–98, Albert Ceen, letter to his wife from Tocumwal, 8 February 1942.
—MLMSS 6735: Ceen family papers, 1923–98, Albert Ceen, letter to his wife, 29 December 1942.
—MLMSS 6735: Ceen family papers, 1923–98, Albert Ceen, letter to Mr Orbuck, 2 February 1943.
—MLMSS 6735: Ceen family papers, 1923–98, Albert Ceen, letter to his wife, 27 April 1943.
—MLMSS 6735: Ceen family papers, 1923–98, Albert Ceen, letter to his wife, 8 June 1943.
—MLMSS 6735: Ceen family papers, 1923–98, Albert Ceen, letters written 20 June 1943, Tocumwal.
—MLMSS 6735: Ceen family papers, 1923–98, Albert Ceen, letter to son Guy as part of letter to his wife and other son, Allan, Tocumwal, 20 June 1943.

**The National Archives of Australia (NAA):** Research Guide, 'Immigration to Australia 1901-39'. http://www.naa.gov.au/publications/research_guides/guides/immig/chapt09/
—A52 5/12/42, Appendix II, War Cabinet Agendum No. 260/1942.
—A52 22/1/13: War Diary 4 Employment Company, Routine Orders, 28 March 1943.
—A373 788: Department of Army Memorandum to Secretary, Department of Defence Co-ordination, n.d., probably January 1942.
—A373 788: Enemy Languages in Public Places – Publication of newspapers in foreign languages.
—A373 890; Jewish Refugees in Australia, letter from T Playford, Premier of South Australia to the Prime Minister, 23 June 1942.
—A373 2837; Unrest among US Negro Soldiers.

—A373 3550; Internment Camp Intelligence Reports, 1944.
—A373 3644; Letter from the Prime Minister to the Attorney-General, March 1943.
—A373 5752; Release of UK Internees in Australia.
—A373 7925/37; Letter from FA Keane to the Deputy Director of Security, 31 May 1943.
—A373 7925/37; Summary, Chinese Native Labour Co., Armstrong Paddock, Townsville, 5 June 1944.
—A373 7925/37; Letter from District Security Officer to Deputy Director of Security, Brisbane, 6 June 1944.
—A373 7925/37; Letter from Queensland District Security Officer to Deputy Director of Security, Brisbane, 22 July 1944.
—A373 7925/37; Letter from Townsville District Security Officer to Deputy Director of Security in Brisbane, 12 August 1944.
—A373 7925/37; Letter to Deputy Director of Security, Brisbane, 23 November 1944.
—A373 7925/37; Letter from the Secretary of the Department of the Interior to the Director General of Security, 6 June 1945.
—A373 7925/37; Letter written by the Director General of Security, June 1945.
—A373 7925/37; Chinese Labour Corps, Bulimba (U.S. Small Ships Section), 6 June 1945.
—A373 7925/37; Letter to Deputy Director of Security from F.A. Kearns, outlining the American proposal.
—A373 7925/37; Chinese Labour Corps 1943–44.
—A373 7925/37; Chinese Native Labour Company, Armstrong Paddock, Townsville.
—A373 7925/37; U.S. Native Labour Company (Chinese).
—A373 7925/37; 'Unrest Among Chinese Employed by U.S. Army', letter from District Security Officer to Deputy Director of Security, Brisbane, 19 July 1944.
—A373 7925/37; Bulimba (U.S. Small Ships Section).
—A373 7925/37; Chinese aliens employed by US Army – departure from Cairns.
—A373 7925/37; Relations With Local Chinese – letter from Deputy Director of Security for Queensland to Director-General of Security, Canberra.
—A373 7925/37; Letter from the Deputy Director of Security, New South Wales, to Deputy Director of Security for Queensland and copied to the Director-General of Security in Canberra, 26 February 1945.
—A373 7925/37; Letter from Director General of Security re Alien Chinese Ex U.S. Forces, June 1945.
—A373 8503; List of Aliens by Nationality.
—A373 8503; List of Aliens by Nationality at present serving in the Labour Corps of the Australian Military Forces.
—A373 9342; Chinese Employed by USA – Policy File.
—A376 T57; Circular Memorandum No. 8794/35, 25 August 1944.

—A376 T107; *Commonwealth of Australia Gazette*, no. 242, Canberra, 30 November 1940.
—A376 T107; Commonwealth of Australia National Security (Aliens Control) Regulations, Observations for the Guidance of Aliens Tribunals, Department of the Army.
—A376 T107; National Security (Aliens Control) Regulations: Regulation 20, Aliens Tribunal (Victoria) No. 2, 13 March 1941.
—A433 43/2/46: Refugees (Jewish and Others) – General Policy File.
—A433 1943/2/46; Department of the Interior, Refugees (Jewish and Others) – General Policy File, 8/3/1938.
—A435 1946/4/953; Application for Naturalization form, Pasquale (Charles) D'Aprano, 6 Employment Company, January 1946.
—A437 1946/6/250; A Record of the Civil Aliens Corps.
—A437 1946/6/250; Letter from the Minister for the Army to the Director-General of Allied Works, June 1942.
—A472 W6534: *Commonwealth of Australia Gazette*, Statutory Rules 1942, No. 39: Regulations Under the National Security Act 1939-1940, 3 February 1942.
—A472 W6534; Attorney-General's Department. Minute Paper. Australian Jewish Welfare Society. Question of nationality of Jewish refugees – Statelessness.
—A472 W6534; National Security [Aliens Service] Regulations, Statutory Rules 1942, No. 39, 3 February 1942.
—A472 W8422; Treatment of Refugee Aliens, letter from General Secretary of ALP NSW, 25 August 1942.
—A472 W26336; High Court of Australia 1944 No. 22.
—A571 1942/538; Supplement 2 to War Cabinet Agendum No. 242/1941, Compulsory Service for Enemy Aliens.
—A571 1942/538; Department of Works, Allied Works Council, War Cabinet Agendum.
—A571 1942/538; War Cabinet Agendum No. 490/1942, National Service for Refugee and Enemy Aliens, 27/11/1942, stamped SECRET.
—A638 116; Aliens Control - Treatment of Civilian Enemy Aliens.
—A989 1943/40/39; Proposed importation of Chinese labour to work under U.S. Army control and responsibility in New Guinea and Queensland.
—A989 1943/40/39; Letter from Secretary of Department of Defence to Secretary of External Affairs, 3 December 1943, stamped SECRET.
—A1608 F19/1/1; Question of Admitting Polish and Czech Refugees from Nazi Oppression, 23 January 1941.
—A1608 F19/1/1; File from Prime Minister's Department: Assistance to Poland – Migration of Refugees.
—A1608 F19/1/1; Department of the Interior, Memorandum: Admission of Polish Refugees from Japan.
—A1608 J41/1/9; Part 2, Ministry of the Interior – to the Prime Minister, Canberra, 19 January 1943.

—A1608 N19/1/1; Part 1, Position of Aliens and Refugees in Time of War.
—A1608 N19/1/1; Part 1, Letter from FG Shedden, Secretary of the Department of Defence Co-Ordination, to the Secretary of the Prime Minister's Department, 7 September 1939.
—A1608 N19/1/1; Part 1, Memorandum from Department of Defence to Secretary, Prime Minister's Department, n.d.
—A1608 N19/1/1; Part 2, Prime Minister's Department, letter to Right Hon. WM Hughes from the Hon. Secretary, Mossman Sub-branch R.S.S.A.I.L.A.
—A1608 N19/1/1; Memorandum for Secretary, Prime Minister's Department, 7 September 1939.
—A2421 61506; Medical Standard of Fitness on Enlistment and Classification of Personnel: Labour Units – Standards of Physical Fitness.
—A2700 419; Report to Cabinet on Enemy Alien Labour Corps, Western Australia by WJ Scully, Minister for Commerce and Agriculture, 9 January 1943.
—A6119 242: Sol Factor, F/3/70 Vol. 1; Commonwealth of Australia, Department of Labour and National Service, Man Power Rehabilitation Section, letter from the Supervisor of the Man Power Rehabilitation Section to Mr MW Tomlinson, Department of Security, Cavendish House,159 Flinders Lane, Melbourne C.1., date obscured.
—A6119 5505316; Bondan, Mary Allethea.
—A6122 Part 3; Statistical Returns of Resident Aliens.
—A6122 150; Australian Council for Civil Liberties Security Files, Seventh Annual Report, 1943.
—A6122 221; Part 1, CPA Interest in the Australian Armed Forces, vol. 2, SECRET, Extract from Security Report of VIC L OF C AREA, 20 September 1943.
—A6122 221; Part 1, CPA Interest in the Australian Armed Forces, Extract from Post and Telegraph Censorship Bulletin No. 74, For Period 7 March to 20 March, 1944. Political. Communism.
—A6122 221; Part 1, CPA Interest in the Australian Armed Forces, vol. 2, SECRET, May 1943, Communist Activities Within The Army.
—A6122 221; Part 2, CPA Interest in Defence Forces: Australian Armed Forces, vol. 2, part 2.
—A6122 221; Part 2 CPA Interest in Defence Forces: Australian Armed Forces, vol. 2 part 2, Contact With Party Apparatus.
—A6122 222; Australian Legion of Ex-Servicemen and Women.
—A6122 444; Subject: Jewish Communist Activities 9 April 1943, Letter to Director-General of Security.
—A6122 444; 11 March 1943, Letter on Jewish Communist Activities to the Deputy Director of Security for Victoria.
—A6122 444; Melbourne, 9 April 1943, Letter re Jewish Communist Activities.

—A6122 Item 150; Australian Council for Civil Liberties Security Files, From Major Ronald S Browne, Inspector, to G.S.O. (M.I.) Southern Command, 18 June 1941.
—A6122 1585; Australian Civil Rights Defence League, Vol. 1.
—A6122 1585; Letter from Security Service in Sydney, 19 July 1943. Subject: Civil Rights Defence League.
—A6122 1585; Australian Civil Rights Defence League.
—A6122 1585; Australian Civil Rights Defence League Vol. 1, Extract from Camp Intelligence reports No. 22.
—A6122 1585; Australian Civil Rights Defence League – Indonesian Refugees, Vol. 1, Interest taken by Mrs. Laura Gapp, Civil Rights Defence League in Indonesian Internees and ex-Internees.
—A6122 1883; The Jewish Council to Combat Fascism and Anti-Semitism.
—A6122 1883; Security files about the Jewish Council to Combat Fascism and Anti-Semitism.
—A6122 1883; Commonwealth Security Service (Victoria), Appendix B, 22 and 24 February and February 1943.
—A6122 1883; Letter to the Deputy Director, Security Service, 4 March 1943.
—A6122 1883: Victoria Police Special Branch, 'Possible Anti-Semitism in Prahran', letter from Office of Chief Commissioner of Police to Prahran C.I.B, 31 July 1943.
—A6122 1883: Commonwealth Security Service (Victoria), 30 October 1943.
—A6335 10; Part 1, Communism – Fighting Services, Letter titled Communists and American Forces from Lieutenant-Colonel in Western Australia to HQ3 Australian Corps, 16 May 1942.
—A6335 10; Part 1, Communism – Fighting Services, Letter from the Director-General of Security to all Deputy Directors of Security, titled Communist Party – Negro Soldiers, 23 May 1942.
—A6335 12; Report by informant on 'Communist inner cell' in the Council.
—A6338 95; Department of Defence Minute paper, Enlistment of Aliens in Australia, 26 January 1940.
—A6388 95; Voluntary Enlistment of Aliens in A.I.F. and A.M.F. and Supplementary Regulations relating there to National Security (Supplementary) Regulations to Statutory Rules 1942, No. 40, Amendment of the National Security (Supplementary) Regulations, notified in the Commonwealth Gazette, 4 February 1942, Explanatory Memorandum for Executive Council.
—A6388 95; War Cabinet Agendum, Aliens – Service Under the Defence Act, 12 July 1941.
—A6338 95; Supplement to the Defence Committee Agenda for meeting of 15 February 1940.
—A6338 95 3/2/274; Letter from War Book Officer, 13 January 1941 to Colonel Vail under heading Co-Ordination: Enlistment of Aliens.

—A6338 95 54/301/19; Memorandum on Enlistment of Aliens in the Australian Defence Forces from FG Shedden, Secretary of the Department of Defence Co-Ordination.
—A6338 95 582/401/103; Cable from Secretary of State for Dominion Affairs, London, to Prime Minister's Department, 27 September 1939.
—A6388 414; Commonwealth of Australia National Security (Aliens Service) Regulations, August 1942.
—A6388 414; War Cabinet Agendum, Supplement No. 1 to Agendum No. 242/1941, Military Service for Aliens, p. 2.
—A6388 414; War Cabinet Agendum, Military Service for Aliens, from FM Forde, Minister for the Army, 10 January 1942.
—A6388 414; War Cabinet Agendum No. 242/1941, Aliens – Service Under the Defence Act.
—A6388 498; National Security (Venereal Diseases and Contraceptives) Regulations.
—B883 WX36791; Attestation form from pearl worker Samsudin Bin Katib's service file. https://www.naa.gov.au/learn/learning-resources/learning-resource-themes/war/world-war-ii/attestation-form-pearl-worker-samsudin-bin-katibs-service-file
—H373 File No. 7925/37; Bulimba (U.S. Small Ships Section), 9 October 1944.
—MP308/1 275/750/818; Naturalisation of Andrew Zanelli.
—MP308/1 275/750/818; Letter signed by PC Spender, 21 February 1941.
—MP308/1 275/750/818; Letter from J McEwen to the Hon. PC Spender, Minister for the Army, 28 February 1941.
—MP308/1 275/750/818; Department of the Army Minute Paper, 5 March 1941.
—MP308/1 275/750/818; Letter from Southern Command headed Enlistment of Aliens, 19 March 1941.
—MP385/4 1940/271; Appeal to His Excellency the Governor-General Lord Gowrie, 2 March 1941.
—MP508/1 4/703/1116; Letters between Bishop Venn Pilcher and Mr Forde, Minister for the Army.
—MP508/1 4/703/1217; Letter from FM Forde, Minister for the Army to Bishop Pilcher, 2 March 1942.
—MP508/1 61/702/690; Enlistment of Aliens, 18 March 1942.
—MP508/1 61/702/690; Uniform and Colour Patches for E. Cos.
—MP508/1 61/702/690; Minute Paper Uniform – Labour Units, 2 May 1942.
—MP508/1 61/702/690; Minute Paper – Labour Unit C.M.F. – Uniforms, 8 April 1942.
—MP508/1 61/702/690; Letter to Mr. J. Curtain [*sic*], Prime Minister, from SJ Barry, dated 14 April 1942.
—MP508/1 61/702/690; Minute Paper – Labour Units C.M.F. – Uniforms, 30 April 1942.

—MP508/1 61/702/690; Letter to Hon. FM Forde, Minister for the Army, 15 September 1942.
—MP508/1 61/702/690; Colour Patches for Employment Companies, 27 October 1942.
—MP508/1 115/702/20; Letter from Secretary of the Military Board to Secretary, Department of the Army, 28 May 1940.
—MP508/1 211/701/138; Medical Classification of Personnel.
—MP508/1 240/701/158; Chinese Units in Australian Military Forces – Proposed formation of.
—MP508/1 255/702/366; Letter re Guiseppe Zammarchy [*sic*] – Italian Internee – P.W./WA14523, 20 September 1941.
—MP508/1 255/743/3; Letter from Charles Wm. Cullip , St Arnaud, 7 April 1941.
—MP508/1 255/743/130; Guiseppe Zammarchi, 1940–41.
—MP508/1 255/743/130; Transcript of the Aliens Tribunal No. 2, Hearing of Zammarchi's appeal against internment, 7 May 1941; Report to G.O.C., Southern Command, on objections submitted by Giuseppe Zammarchi.
—MP508/1 255/744/265; Pen Club Melbourne Centre, Letter to Minister for the Army, 31 May 1941.
—MP508/1 275/701/199; 2 Australian Imperial Force – Conditions of Enlistment, Extracts from Standing Orders for the 2 A.I.F. Chapter IV.
—MP508/1 275/705/48; Labour Coys (Aliens) Arming of Non-Alien Personnel.
—MP508/1 275/705/61; Letter from the Assistant Secretary, Department of Army, Melbourne, to the Secretary of the Department in Melbourne, 30 April 1942.
—MP508/1 275/750/768; Enlistment of Aliens, 5 September 1939.
—MP508/1 275/750/768; Enlistment of Aliëns, 21 November 1939.
—MP508/1 299/701/284; Chinese crews in 5 Military District – formed into 7 Labour Company (Chinese).
—MP529/3; Transcript of the Aliens Tribunal No. 2, Hearing of Zammarchi's appeal against internment, 7 May 1941.
—MP529/3 Tribunal 2/Zammarchi; extract from report of Major Prentice of Eastern Command, 10 March 1941.
—MP 529/3; Transcript of the Aliens Tribunal No. 2, Hearing of Zammarchi's appeal against internment, 7 May 1941; Extract from report of Major Prentice of Eastern Command, 10 March 1941.
—MP529/3; Transcript of the Aliens Tribunal No. 2, Hearing of Zammarchi's appeal against internment, 7 May 1941; Evidence of Zammarchi to the Aliens Tribunal, Wednesday 7 May 1941.
—MP529/3; Transcript of the Aliens Tribunal No. 2, Hearing of Zammarchi's appeal against internment, 7 May 1941; Statement to Aliens Tribunal by chairman Mr. C. Book K.C.

—MP742/1 84/1/928; University Courses for Aliens of Enemy Origins.
—MP742/1 84/1/928; Commonwealth of Australia, Parliamentary Debates, House of Representatives, 29 March 1946, Mr Dedman, Minister for Post-War Reconstruction.
—MP742/1 84/1/928; Commonwealth of Australia, Parliamentary Debates, House of Representatives, 29 March 1946, George Bowden, Hon. Member for Gippsland.
—MP742/1 84/1/928; Commonwealth of Australia, Parliamentary Debates, House of Representatives, 29 March 1946, Charles Morgan, Hon. Member for Reid.
—MP742/1 92/1/193; Allocation and Posting of Personnel to Employment Coys, 25 January 1944.
—MP742/1 92/1/256; 36 Aust Employment Coy – Raising Of.
—MP742/1 92/1/256; Javanese Seamen, 13 June 1942.
—MP742/1 92/1/256; 36 Australian Employment Company Indonesian.
—MP742/1 92/1/256; 36 Australian Employment Company Indonesian, Department of the Army Minute Paper, Javanese Seamen.
—MP742/1 92/1/256; 36 Australian Employment Company Indonesian, Department of the Army Minute Paper, Javanese Seamen, Employment by Allied Works Council.
—MP742/1 92/1/256; 36 Australian Employment Company Indonesian, Statutory Rules 1942, No. 360, Amendment of the National Security (Aliens Control) Regulations.
—MP742/1 92/1/256; 36 Australian Employment Company Indonesian, June 1942.
—MP742/1 92/1/256; Department of the Army Minute Paper, Javanese Seamen, 15 June 1942
—MP742/1 92/1/256; 36 Australian Employment Company Indonesian, Minute Paper, Department of the Navy, Employment 700 Indonesian Sailors, 3 February 1943.
—MP742/1 92/1/256; Allied Land Forces in South West Pacific Area – 36 Employment Company 'Indonesians', LHQ Melbourne, 12 January 1943.
—MP742/1 92/1/256; Letter from Boestami, sent to Minister for the Army, Mr Forde, 19 February 1943.
—MP742/1 92/1/256; Letter from the Captain of the 36 Employment Company in Wallangarra to the D.A.D. Labour in Brisbane, 23 February 1943.
—MP742/1 92/1/256; Letter headed Netherlands Indies Commission and dated 16 March 1944.
—MP742/1 92/1/256; Letter addressed to the Assistant Secretary, Defence Division, Department of the Treasury, dated 27 March 1944.
—MP742/1 92/1/256; Letter from Minister for the Army to Dr van der Plas, dated 28 March 1944.

—MP742/1 92/1/256; Letter dated 5 April 1944.
—MP742/1 92/1/256; Department of Army Minute Paper headed 36 Aust Emp Coy – Indonesian, dated 27 April 1944.
—MP742/1 92/1/256; 36 Australian Employment Company Indonesian, letter from Captain, Liaison Officer, 36 Aust. Emp. Coy to Major-General VPH Stanke, O.B.E., G.O.C., Qld. L. of C. Area, Wallangarra, 3 May 1943.
—MP742/1 92/1/256; 36 Australian Company, Indonesian, document from Adjutant-General, 18 May 1944.
—MP742/1 92/1/302; Department of Army Minute Paper, 110 [*sic*] Employment Coy, 16 September 1943.
—MP742/1 115/1/39; Tocumwal: 6 Employment Coy, 11 January 1943.
—MP742/1 115/1/48; Letter written by C Venn Pilcher, 6 August 1942.
—MP742/1 115/1/173; Department of the Army Minute Paper, Employment of Aliens in AMF, October 1944.
—MP742/1 115/1/173; Department of Army Minute Paper, 18 December 1944.
—MP742/1 115/1/274; Australian Military Forces Minute Paper, Aliens in Employment Companies, 28 June 1945.
—MP742/1 115/1/274; Aliens in Employment Companies, Note to the PM from Frank Forde, Minister for the Army, 24 January 1945.
—MP742/1 115/1/274; Military list of 1692 alien personnel in five Employment Companies.
—MP742/1 115/1/274; Letter from John Dedman, for Acting Prime Minister, to Senator John Fraser, Acting Minister for the Army, 23 May 1945.
—MP742/1 115/1/274; Australian Military Forces Minute Paper, Aliens in Employment Companies, 28 June 1945.
—MP742/1 115/1/315; Letter from Arthur Calwell to Frank Forde, Minister for the Army, 20 November 1945.
—MP742/1 240/8/31; Department of the Army Minute Paper, 31 January 1944.
—MP742/1 240/8/31; Redesignation of Employment Companies – Aust Labour Coys and Aust Employment Coys – Redesignation Of.
—MP742/1 240/8/31; Redesignation and New Colour Patch – Australian Employment Companies (Alien).
—MP742/1 247/1/829; Pay [of] Indonesian Personnel - 36 Australian Employment Company.
—MP742/1 247/1/829; Confidential document from the Adjutant-General to the Headquarters of the Army in Queensland's Line of Communication and to the Rear Headquarters of the First Australian Army, 18 May 1944.
—MP742/1 247/1/1219; Department of the Army Central Registry File: Miscellaneous claim for Subsistence & Leave, 7 Australian Employment Company.
—MP742/1 255/12/12; Letter from C Venn Pilcher to FM Forde re separation of Refugee Internees from Nazi Internees, 1942.

—MP742/1 255/15/1286; Prisoners of War & Internees in Australia [Statistics].
—MP742/1 275/2/9; Enlistment of Aliens, 6 February 1942.
—MP742/1 275/2/9; Allegations re Alien Labour Coys, Memo submitted by Sgt Jackson, 28 September 1942.
—MP742/1 275/2/9; Letter from FM Forde, Minister for the Army to D Mulcahy, MHR, 4 March 1943.
—MP742/1 275/2/32; Statement by Pte Honigsberg K V377762, 2 March 1943.
—MP742/1 275/2/38; War Cabinet Agendum No. 242/1941, Compulsory National Service for Neutral Aliens.
—MP742/1 275/2/38; War Cabinet Agendum No. 242/1941, Compulsory National Service for Neutral Aliens, War Cabinet Minute, 24 November 1943.
—MP742/1 275/705/129; Letter from Bishop Venn Pilcher to Mr Forde, Minister for the Army.
—MP927/1 A4/1/65; Draft Defence (Labour Corps) Regulations. Explanatory Statement.
—MP927/1 A4/1/65; Statutory Rules 1942 No. 44 Regulations Under the Defence Act 1903–1941.
—MP927/1 A4/1/65; Draft Defence (Labour Corps) Regulations. Explanatory Statement.
—MP927/1 A4/1/65; Regulations signed by the Minister for the Army, FM Forde, February 1942.
—MP927/1 A4/1/65; Explanatory Statement to the Defence (Labour Corps) Regulations.
—MP1049 1877/12/105: Wendy Rankine, 'Australia's Chinese Army Corps' in Jan Ryan (ed.), *Chinese in Australia and New Zealand: a Multidisciplinary Approach*, New Age International, New Delhi, 1995.
—MP1498 S-16 8; Routine Orders Part 2, Routine Order 721, 23 Employment Company, (Koepangese).
—MP1498 S-16 8; Routine Orders Part 2, Routine Order 717, 23 Employment Company, (Koepangese).
—SP300/2; Murdoch 24, Walter Murdoch, 'Understanding the Foreigner', 23 July 1944, pp. 1, 6.
—SP459/1 430/14/322; Letter from Lt-Colonel Clark, Army Headquarters, Victoria Barracks, Melbourne to all Command districts, 8 April 1941.
—SP459/1 489/1/2187; Letter from Southern Command to Eastern Command, 15 July 1941.
—SP459/1 489/2/176; Telegram Summary of the Rules Regarding Enlistment of Aliens, 3 February 1942.
—SP459/1 489/2/191; Registration of Aliens.
—SP459/1 489/2/191; National Service (Aliens Service) Regulations – Registration and Enrolment, 1942.

—SP459/1 489/2/191; Department of the Army Military Board, 'Definition of Aliens in Categories', 13 February 1942.
—SP459/1 489/2/203; Registration of Volunteer Refugee Aliens.
—SP459/1 489/2/235; Military Board – National Security (Aliens Service) Regulations – Compulsory Action, 12 March 1942.
—SP459/1 489/2/235; Letter from Secretary of the Military Board to all Command Bases, 14 March 1942.
—SP459/1 489/2/337; Citation from the Director of Personal Services in letter from Major-General H.Q., New South Wales Line of Communication Area, May 1942.
—SP459/1 489/2/553; Letter from Captain DM Bradshaw, Army Headquarters, Victoria Barracks, to every State Army Line of Communication Area, 13 February 1943.
—SP1008/1 451/1/605; Court of Inquiry, 1942, p. 56.
—SP1008/1 451/1/605; Allegations Conveyed to Mr. D. Mulcahy, MHR Regarding Alien Labour Companies.
—SP1008/1 451/1/605; Proceedings of a Court of Inquiry, Victoria Barracks, Paddington, 16 September 1942, and letter to the Minister for the Army from Major-General A.C. Fewtrell, October 1942.
—SP1008/1 451/1/605; Evidence given to the Inquiry by L. F. O'Brien, 18 September, 1942, p. 34.
—SP1008/1 451/1/605; Information given by Sergeant JW Jackson, V.C., D.C.M., 2 Labour Corps, Ascot Military Camp, Sydney, to Mr D Mulcahy, MP, during the course of a discussion on Sunday, 13 September 1942.
—SP1008/1 451/1/605; Report of Court, Appendix (1), Statement of Nationalities of NCOs 2 Australian Labour Company as at 21 September 1942.
—SP1008/1 451/1/605; Report of Court, 5 October, 1942, p. 7.
—SP1008/1 451/1/605; Letter to Minister for the Army from Major-General AC Fewtrell, 14 November 1942.
—SP1048/7 S9/1/200; Employment of Labour Companies.
—SP1048/7 556/1/1220; Aliens Control (Prohibited Possessions) Order.
—SP3300/2; Portus/24, Professor GV Portus, 'What Does Patriotism Mean?', 5 March 1944.

**National Library of Australia (NLA):** MS 4738 Box 38; Papers of Arthur Calwell. Aliens Control Instructions No. 11, October 1942.
—MS 4965/1; Brian Fitzpatrick papers. Extract of ACCL Minutes, 6 March 1939.
—MS 4965/1/3844; Brian Fitzpatrick papers. ACCL 9th Annual Report, 1945.
—MS 4965/1/3720; Brian Fitzpatrick papers. ACCL 7th Annual Report, 6 July 1943.
—MS 4965/1/3749; Brian Fitzpatrick papers. Notes re report to Executive Committee re 'Affiliated Society', 6 March 1944.

—MS 4965/13/6334 Subseries (13n) No. 1; Brian Fitzpatrick papers. 'Civil Liberties in Australia', radio broadcast, 3XY Melbourne, 18 July 1943.
—MS 4965/1/3890; Brian Fitzpatrick papers, Australian Council for Civil Liberties 9th Annual Report, 1945, section 11.
—MS 4965/1/3892; Brian Fitzpatrick papers, Australian Council for Civil Liberties, 10 Years of the Council.
—MS 2852; Papers of Alexander Gore Gowrie, Extract from letter from Earl of Gowrie to King George VI re internees, 4 November 1940.
—MS 4738, Box 38; Papers of Arthur Calwell, Series II – Aliens Classification and Advisory Committee 1942 – 46, October 1942.
—MS 4738, Box 38; Aliens Control Instructions No. 11.
—ORAL TRC 2381; Molly Bondan interviewed by Campbell McKnight, 12 – 13 January 1989 [audio file]. http://nla.gov.au/nla.obj-216667029
—MS 4738, Box 38; Security Service Classification of Aliens & Allied Matters, 12 October 1942.
—MS 4738, Box 38; Papers of Arthur Calwell: Security Service: Classification of Aliens & Allied Matters, 12 October 1942.
—ORAL TRC 4549; York, Barry, Interview with Wolfgang Sievers [interview transcript], 20 March 2000.

**University of Melbourne Library,** McLaren Collection; Fitzpatrick, Brian, *Refugees – Hitler's Loss Our Gain*, Jewish Council to Combat Fascism and Anti-Semitism, Melbourne, 1944.

## Books

*1,000,000 Jews in the Armies of Freedom*, Jewish Council to Combat Fascism and Anti-Semitism, Melbourne, c.1944.
Ambrose, Tom, *What Britain and America Gained from Europe's Cultural Exiles*, Peter Owen, London, 2001.
Bartrop, Paul R, and Gabrielle Eisen (eds), *The Dunera Affair: A Documentary Resource Book,* Jewish Museum of Australia, and Schwartz and Wilkinson, Melbourne, 1990.
Bartrop, Paul R *Australia and the Holocaust*, Australian Scholarly Publishing, North Melbourne, 1994.
Bennett Jr, Frank C, *The Return of the Exiles: Australia's Repatriation of Indonesians 1945–47*, Monash University Publishing, Clayton, 2003.
Bergner, Yosl, *What I Meant to Say: Stories and Travels As Told to Ruth Bondy*, Hed Arzi Book Publishing, Israel, 1997.
Birstein, Yossel, 'Weger', in G Ramras-Rauch and J Michman-Melkman (eds), *Facing the Holocaust: Selected Israeli Fiction,* Jewish Publication Society, Philadelphia, 1985. Also in *Ariel: A Quarterly Review of Arts and Letters in Israel*, no. 37, 1974.

Bolton, G, '1939–51', in FK Crowley (ed.), *A New History of Australia*, William Heinemann, Melbourne, 1974.

Bosworth, Michael, 'Internment', in Jenny Gregory (ed.), *On the Homefront: Western Australia and World War II*, University of Western Australia Press, Nedlands, WA, 1996.

Butlin, SJ, *War Economy 1939–1942*, Australian War Memorial, Canberra, 1955.

Butlin, SJ and CB Schedvin, *War Economy 1942-1945*, Australian War Memorial, Canberra, 1977.

Cathcart, M and K Darian-Smith (eds), *Stirring Australian Speeches*, Melbourne University Publishing, Carlton, 2004.

Clark, CMH, *A History of Australia*, vol. v, Melbourne University Press, Carlton, 1981.

*Contributions to an Anthology*, York Press, Melbourne, 1944.

Coombs, Herbert C, 'An Insider's Perspective on Social Engineering', in *Australia's War 1939–45: Study Guide and Reader*, Deakin University, Geelong, Victoria, 1994. Reading 5.13, p. 325ff.

Crisp, LF, *Ben Chifley: A Political Biography*, Angus & Robertson, London, 1977 [1961].

D'Aprano, Charles, 'The Heroes of Tocumwal', in *Old Wine in New Bottles*, Winseray, Carlton, 1986.

D'Aprano, Charles, 'Flashback: Life in the Australian Army', in *Tears, Laughter and the Revolution*, Insegna Publishers, Brunswick West, 1998.

Darian-Smith, Kate, 'War and Australian Society', in Joan Beaumont (ed.), *Australia's War 1939–45*, Allen & Unwin, Sydney, 2000.

Docherty, James C, *Historical Dictionary of Australia*, Oceanian Historical Dictionaries No. 1, The Scarecrow Press, Metuchen, New Jersey, 1992.

Dowsing, Irene, *Curtin of Australia*, Acacia Press, Blackburn, n.d. (preface by JF Cairns dated 1968).

Dwork, D and RJ Van Pelt, *Flight from the Reich: Refugee Jews, 1933–1946*, WW Norton, New York, 2009.

Dymock, Darryl, *A Sweet Use of Adversity: the Australian Army Education Service in World War II and its Impact on Australian Adult Education*, University of New England Press, Armidale, 1995.

Evans, Richard, *The Third Reich in Power 1933-1939*, Penguin, London, 2006.

Fabian, A, 'The Jewish Chaplaincy in Australia', in Gerald Pynt (ed.), *Australian Jewry's Book of Honour World War II, Australian Federation of Jewish Ex-Servicemen & Women*, Griffin Press, Adelaide, 1973, p. 125.

Fabian, Erwin, *Max und Erwin Fabian: Berlin, London, Melbourne*, exhibition catalogue, Stiftung Stadtmuseum, Berlin, 2000.

Fabian, Erwin, taped account transcribed and edited by Brigid McCoppin, Melbourne, May – June 2000, in *Max und Erwin Fabian: Berlin, London, Melbourne*, by Dominik Bartmann, exhibition catalogue, Stiftung Stadtmuseum, Berlin, 2000.

Fahey, John, *Australia's First Spies: The Remarkable Story of Australia's Intelligence Operations 1901–45*, Allen & Unwin, Sydney, 2018.
Fahey, Warren, *Digger's Songs: Songs of the Australians in Eleven Wars*, Australian Military History Publications, Loftus, New South Wales, 1996.
Fitzpatrick, Brian, *A Short History of the Australian Labor Movement*, Rawson's Bookshop, Melbourne, 1944.
Fitzpatrick, Brian, *The Australian Commonwealth: A Picture of the Community 1901–1955*, FW Cheshire, Melbourne, 1956.
Fussell, Paul, *Wartime: Understanding and Behaviour in the Second World War*, Oxford University Press, 1989.
George, Margaret, *Australia and the Indonesian Revolution*, Melbourne University Press, Carlton, 1980.
Gettler, Leon, *An Unpromised Land,* Fremantle Arts Centre Press, Perth, 1993.
Glyde, Keith, *Distinguishing Colour Patches of the Australian Military Forces 1915–1951*, Keith Glyde, Claremont, Tasmania, 1999.
Gray, Oriel, *Exit Left: Memoirs of a Scarlet Woman,* Penguin Books, Melbourne, 1985.
Guise, Diana, *Courage and Service: Chinese Australians and World War II*, Courage and Service Project, Marrickville, Sydney, 1999.
Haese, Richard, *Rebels and Precursors: The Revolutionary Years of Australian Art*, Allen Lane, Ringwood, Victoria, 1981.
Hardjono, Joan and Charles Warner, *In Love with a Nation: Molly Bondan and Indonesia, Her Own Story in Her Own Words*, C Warner, Picton, New South Wales, 1995.
Hartley, LP, *The Go-Between*, Hamish Hamilton, London, 1953.
Hasluck, Paul, *Australia in the War of 1939-1945: Volume I – The Government and the People 1939–1941*, Australian War Memorial, Canberra, 1965 [1952].
—*Australia in the War of 1939–1945: Volume II – The Government and the People 1942–1945*, Australian War Memorial, Canberra, 1970.
Horton, DC, *Ring of Fire: Australian Guerrilla Operations Against the Japanese in World War II*, Macmillan, Melbourne, 1983.
Inglis, Ken, et al, *Dunera Lives: A Visual History,* Monash University Publishing, Melbourne, 2018.
—*Dunera Lives: Profiles,* Monash University Publishing, Melbourne, 2020.
Jeans, DN, 'The Country', in Bill Gammage and Peter Spearitt (eds), *Australians 1938*, Fairfax, Syme & Weldon Associates, Sydney, 1987.
Jupp, James, *From White Australia to Woomera: Story of Australian Immigration*, Cambridge University Press, 2007.
Klepner, Frank, *Yosl Bergner: Art as a Meeting of Cultures*, Macmillan, Melbourne, 2004.
Kristianson, GL, *The Politics of Patriotism: The Pressure Group Activities of the Returned Servicemen's League*, ANU Press, Canberra, 1966.
Lamidey, Noel W, *Aliens Control in Australia 1939–46*, N Lamidey, Sydney, 1974.

Langfield, M and P MacLean, 'Jewish Women Remember 1938–9', in AJ Hammerton and E Richards (eds), *Speaking to Immigrants: Oral Testimony and the History of Australian Immigration*, *Visible Immigrants: Six*, Australian National University, Canberra, 2002.

Laserson, Dr Maurice, *Bishop Charles Venn Pilcher D.D.: A Biographical Study,* AK Murray & Co., Sydney, June 1949.

Liffman, Eric, Patricia and Kurt Liffman, *Songs the People Love*, Vivid Publishing, Fremantle, Western Australia, 2015.

Lindesay, Vane, *Some Fragments Recalled*, Trojan Press for Vane Lindesay, Ripponlea, Melbourne, 2005.

Lingard, Jan, *Refugees and Rebels: Indonesian Exiles in Wartime Australia*, Australian Scholarly Publishing, North Melbourne, 2008.

Lockwood, Rupert, *Black Armada: Australia and the Struggle for Indonesian Independence 1942–49*, Hale & Iremonger, Sydney, New South Wales, 1982.

Loh, Morag and Judith Winternitz, 'Maurice' in *Dinky-Di: The Contributions of Chinese Immigrants and Australians of Chinese Descent to Australia's Defence Forces and War Efforts 1899–1988*, Australian Government Publishing Service, Canberra, 1989.

Lowenstein, Wendy and Morag Loh (eds), 'Robert' in *The Immigrants*, Hyland House, Melbourne, 1977.

Lowenstein, Wendy, *Weevils in the Flour: An Oral Record of the 1930s Depression in Australia*, Hyland House, Melbourne, 1978.

McKenzie-Smith, Graham, *The Unit Guide – the Australian Army 1939–45*, Blue Sky Publications, Newport, New South Wales, 2018.

McKernan, Michael, *All In! Australia during the Second World War*, Nelson, Melbourne, 1983.

Macintyre, Stuart, *The Reds: The Communist Party of Australia from Origins to Illegality*, Allen & Unwin, Sydney, 1998.

Markus, Andrew, 'Chinese Immigration under the "White Australia Policy"', in Paul Macgregor (ed.), *Histories of the Chinese in Australasia and the Pacific*, Museum of Chinese Australian History, Melbourne, 1995.

Marrus, M, *The Unwanted: European Refugees in the Twentieth Century*, Oxford University Press, New York, 1985.

Martin, AW, *Robert Menzies – A Life*, vol. 1, 1894–1943, Melbourne University Press, Carlton, 1993.

Merridale, Catherine, 'War, Death and Remembrance in Soviet Russia', in J Winter and E Sivan (eds), *War and Remembrance in the Twentieth Century*, Cambridge University Press, Cambridge, 1999.

Murray-Smith, Stephen, 'Memories of Melbourne University', in Hume Dow (ed.), *Memories of Melbourne University: Undergraduate Life in the Years since 1917*, Hutchinson of Australia, Melbourne, 1983.

Nadel, George Hans, *Australia's Colonial Culture: Ideas, Men and Institutions in mid-nineteenth century Eastern Australia,* FW Cheshire, Melbourne, 1957.

Neumann, Klaus, *In the Interest of National Security: Civilian Internment in Australia during World War II*, National Archives of Australia, Canberra, 2006.

Newton, Helmut, *Autobiography*, Nan A. Talese/Doubleday, New York, 2003.

O'Brien, Ilma Martinuzzi, 'Internment of Italian Born and Unnaturalised British Subjects of Italian Origin', in R Bosworth and R Ugolini (eds), *War Internment and Mass Migration: The Italo-Australian Experience 1940–1990*, Gruppo Editoriale Internazionale, 1992.

Partridge, PH, 'Depression and War, 1925–50', in Gordon Greenwood (ed.), *Australia: A Social and Political History*, Angus & Robertson, Sydney, 1972 [1951].

Patkin, Benzion, *The Dunera Internees*, Cassell Australia, Stanmore, New South Wales, 1979.

Pearl, Cyril, *The Dunera Scandal*, Angus & Robertson, Sydney, 1985 [1983].

Potts, David, *The Myth of the Great Depression*, Scribe Publications, Melbourne, 2006.

Price, CA, 'Immigration: 1949–1970', in G Greenwood and N Harper (eds), *Australia in World Affairs 1966–1970*, Cheshire, Melbourne, 1974.

Rankine, Wendy, 'Australia's Chinese Army Corps', in Jan Ryan (ed.), *Chinese in Australia and New Zealand: A Multidisciplinary Approach*, New Age International, New Delhi, 1995.

Rubinstein, Hilary L, *The Jews in Australia: A Thematic History, vol. 1: 1788–1945*, William Heinemann Australia, Port Melbourne, 1991.

Rydon, Joan, *A Federal Legislature: the Australian Commonwealth Parliament 1901–1980*, Oxford University Press, Melbourne, 1986.

Rutland, Suzanne D, *Edge of the Diaspora: Two Centuries of Jewish Settlement in Australia*, Collins Australia, Sydney, 1988.

Saunders, Kay and Roger Daniels (eds), *Alien Justice: Wartime Internment in Australia and North America*, University of Queensland Press, St Lucia, Qld, 2000.

Saunders, Kay, *War on the Homefront: State Intervention in Queensland 1938–1948*, University of Queensland Press, St Lucia, Qld, 1993.

Sievers, Wolfgang, *Images of Germany: Australian Insights*, small pamphlet-size publication, n.d.

*Service Prayer Book for The Solemn Days for Jewish Members of the Australian Forces,* 2nd edn, published August 1943 by the Australian Army Chaplains' Department Under the Supervision of the Australian Hebrew Chaplains' Conference, January 1943.

Smith, Bernard, *Noel Counihan: Artist and Revolutionary*, Oxford University Press, Melbourne, 1993.

Smith, FB, 'Sunday Matters', in Bill Gammage and Peter Spearitt (eds), *Australians 1938*, Fairfax, Syme & Weldon, Sydney, 1987.

Snowman, Daniel, *The Hitler Émigrés: The Cultural Impact on Britain of Refugees from Nazism*, Chatto & Windus, London, 2002.

Srhoy, Bart, *Journey Beyond Origin*, Hesperian Press, Carlisle, Western Australia, 1998.

Strauss, George, *Margaret Holmes: A Life of Ecumenical Service 1886–1981*, privately printed, Melbourne, March 2003.

Swain, Bruce T, *A Chronology of Australian Armed Forces at War 1939–45*, Allen & Unwin, Crows Nest, New South Wales, 2001.

Turnbull, Malcolm, '*Safe Haven: Records of The Jewish Experience in Australia*', National Archives of Australia, Canberra, 1999.

United States Army Service Forces, Special Service Division, *Instructions for American Servicemen in Australia 1942*, War and Navy Departments, Washington, DC, 1942; reprinted by Penguin Australia, 2007.

Waghorne, James and Stuart Macintyre, *Liberty: A History of Civil Liberties in Australia*, UNSW Press, Randwick, New South Wales, 2011.

Walker, David, 'The Writers' War', in Joan Beaumont (ed.), *Australia's War 1939–45*, Allen & Unwin, St Leonards, New South Wales, 2000.

Watson, Don, *Brian Fitzpatrick: A Radical Life*, Hale and Iremonger, Sydney, 1979.

York, Barry, 'The Chinese in Australia: Exclusions and Admissions 1901–1957', in Paul Macgregor (ed.), *Histories of the Chinese in Australasia and the Pacific, Proceedings of an International Public Conference held at the Museum of Chinese Australian History, Melbourne, 8–10 October 1993*, Museum of Chinese Australian History, Melbourne, 1995, pp. 361–77.

## Journal articles

Bartrop, Paul R, 'The Australian Government's "Liberalisation" of Refugee Immigration Policy in 1938: Fact or Myth?', *Menorah: Australian Journal of Jewish Studies*, vol. 2, no. 1, June 1988, p. 69.

Berger, George M, 'Australia and the Refugees', Part 1, *The Australian Quarterly*, Australian Institute of Policy and Science, St. Leonards, New South Wales, vol. xiii, no. 3, September 1941.

—'Australia and the Refugees', Part 2, *The Australian Quarterly*, Australian Institute of Policy and Science, St. Leonards, New South Wales, vol. xiii, no. 4, December 1941.

—'Australia and the Refugees', Part 3, *The Australian Quarterly*, Australian Institute of Policy and Science, St. Leonards, New South Wales, vol. xix, no. 2, June 1942.

Black, LS, 'The Story of "Z" Special Unit', *Double Diamond*, September 1992, pp. 5–6.

Cottle, Drew and Angela Keys, 'Building the Bridge of Solidarity: The Politics of the Chinese Youth League in Australia, 1939–73', *Journal of Chinese Australia*, Issue 2, October 2006.

Davis, Joan, '*Salt*: The Journal of the Australian Army Education Service in the Second World War', *Journal of the Australian War Memorial*, no. 17, October 1990.

Exiner, Robert ,'From the Spree to the Yarra: Memories of an Emigration', *Journal of the Australian Jewish Historical Society*, vol. 12, 1993–95.
Feiglin, R, 'Jewish Refugees from Hitler', *Australian Historical Bibliography Bulletin*, no. 9, April 1984.
Feldmann, S/Sgt J, 'They're Asking About Australia', *Salt*, vol. 3, no. 9, 1 June 1942.
Greenland, PC, 'Finding Work in a World of Experts', *Salt*, vol. 1, no. 13, 22 December 1941.
Holmes, Margaret, 'Student Internees in Australia', *Intercollegian*, Australian Student Christian Movement, October 1941.
Kwiet, Konrad, '"Be Patient and Reasonable!" The Internment of German-Jewish Refugees in Australia', *Australian Journal of Politics and History*, vol. 31, no. 1, 1985.
Langfield, Michele, 'Guilt That They Survived: Memories Of Jewish Women Who Arrived In Australia In The Late 1930s', *Australian Jewish Historical Society Journal*, vol. xv, no. 3, 2000.
Langfield, M, 'The Fortunate Few: Jewish Refugee Policy and Women's Experiences in the 1930s', in Margaret P Hamilton (ed.), *Oral History Association of Australia Journal*, no. 22, 2000.
Lockwood, Rupert, 'The Indonesian Exiles in Australia 1942–47', in *Indonesia*, no. 10, Cornell University Southeast Asia Program, October, 1970.
Loewald, Klaus, 'A *Dunera* Internee at Hay, 1940-41', in *Historical Studies*, vol. 17, nos. 66–69, 1976–77.
Loewald, Klaus, 'The Eighth Employment Company', *Australian Journal of Politics and History*, vol. 31, 1985.
Lyle, G, 'The Legacy is Limited', *Australian Highway*, vol. 29, no. 2, April 1947.
Massam, Katharine and John H Smith, 'Images of God: Civil Religion and Australia at War 1939–1945', *Australian Religious Studies Review*, vol. 11. no. 2, Australian Association for the Study of Religions, Adelaide, 1998.
O'Brien, Ilma Martinuzzi, 'Internments and Arthur Calwell: the View from Carlton', *Italian Historical Society Journal*, vol. 1, no. 2, December 1993.
Rubinstein, William D, '"Concluding Remarks" to "The Future of Australian Jewish Historiography: A Panel Discussion"', *Menorah: Australian Journal of Jewish Studies*, vol. 3, no. 1, issue 4, July 1989.
Rutland, Suzanne D, 'Australian Responses to Jewish Refugee Migration Before and After World War II', *The Australian Journal of Politics and History*, vol. 31, no. 1, 1985.
Saunders, Kay, '"Discovering" the Subversive and the Saboteur: the Disjuncture Between Official Records of Internment Policy and Practice and the Remembered Experiences of Internees in Australia in the Second World War', *Oral History of Australia Journal*, no. 13, 1991.
*Salt*, 'Free-beer and Free-dom' (Editorial), vol. 1, no. 10, 1 December 1941.
—'They Don't Forget', vol. 3, no. 3, 20 April 1942.
—'V.D. Spreads', vol. 6, no. 7, 7 June 1943, pp. 1–6.

—'Axis Soldiers Don't Vote', vol. 6, no. 11, 2 August 1943, p. 1.
—vol. 7, no. 3, 11 October 1943, p. 23.
—vol. 8, no. 6, 22 May 1944, p. 22.
—vol. 10, no. 12, 1945, pp. 47–8.
—vol. 10, no. 13, 27 August 1945, pp. 2–3.
—'Pop. 7,000,000 – Not Enough', Arthur Calwell, vol. 10, no. 13, 27 August 1945, p. 45.
—'This Way Out', vol. 11, no. 4, 22 October 1945, p. 28.
Scalmer, Sean, 'The Puzzle of *Meanjin* and the Historical Emergence of the Australian Intelligentsia', *Country and Calling: Journal of Australian Studies*. no. 62, 1999.
Sturma, Michael, 'Public Health and Sexual Morality: Venereal Disease in World War II in Australia', *Signs*, vol. 13, no. 4, 1988.
Tate, Virginia, 'Franz Philipp', *Art and Australia*, vol. 30, no. 4, Winter, 1993.
Turner, Ian, 'My Long March', *Overland*, no. 59, Spring, 1974.
Waller, Louis, 'Growing Up Under Rabbi Danglow: Memories 1940–1945', *Journal of the Australian Jewish Historical Society*, vol. x, part 4, 1988.
Witton, Ron, review of Jan Lingard's book *Refugees and Rebels: Indonesian Exiles in Wartime Australia*, in *Review of Indonesian and Malaysian Affairs*, vol. 42, no. 2, 2008.

## Newspapers and periodicals

Adams, Noel, 'Chinese Sailors Help Army', *Canberra Times*, 6 September 1943, p. 3.
*Advertiser* (Adelaide), 'Sheepskins for Russia £10,000 Appeal', 9 July 1943, p. 2.
*Advocate* (Melbourne), 'Horror of Nazi Persecution in Poland', 20 June 1940, p. 17.
—Letter – 'German Internees in Australia: A Plea for Justice', 29 May 1941, p. 6.
*Age*, Letter – 'Aliens in Australia', LATE No. 6215, 7th Btn. (South Yarra), 27 May 1940, p. 8.
—Letter – 'Land Buying Aliens', 'Soldier's Mother' (Shepparton), 9 September 1940, p. 8.
—Letter – 'Land Buying Aliens', H Pollak (Hawthorn), 10 September 1940, p. 8.
—Letter – 'Alien Labor Corps', V377392. Pte. G.H.N. 8th Labor, 11 May 1942, p. 2.
—Letter – 'Lectures on Opera (with whistled extracts)', Roger Jones (Mount Macedon), 1 January 2000.
—Letter – 'The *Dunera* Experience', Eric Eckstein (Dandenong), 29 August 2005.
*Argus*, 'Industrial Danger. Alien Workers', and 'Rich Refugees Arrive in Three Ships', 9 May 1939, p. 9.
—'172 "Reserved" Occupations. Provisional List Issued. Enlistment Restrictions', 28 September, 1939, p. 2.

—'Railways Get More Traffic. Shipping Dislocation', 1 March 1941, p. 7.
—'First Aliens Enlisted. Ex-German Baron', 5 April 1941, p. 5.
—'Solo Pianist Who Worked on Sydney Wharves', 29 July 1946, p. 4.
*Australian Women's Weekly*, March 2004, p. 30.
*Bondi Daily*, Editorial, 4 July 1940.
Bone, Pamela, 'Haven-Sent Happiness', *Age* 'Extra', 6 October 1990.
*Border Morning Mail* (Albury, New South Wales), 'More Aliens Rounded Up', 6 March 1942, p. 6.
—'Greek Notables to Visit Albury', 13 October 1942, p. 2.
—'Last Night's Reception. A Day of Interest', 16 October 1942, p. 4.
—'Man Drowned at Noreuil Park', 31 January 1944, p. 2.
*Canberra Times*, 'Enemy Aliens' Labour Corps for W.A.', 18 January 1943, p. 4.
—'Chinese Draw Knives in Brawl at Bulimba', 12 December 1944, p. 3.
Coleman, Peter, 'Deep Impact', *Weekend Australian*, 31 August – 1 September 2002.
*Courier Mail*, 'Ban on Jewish Immigrants. No Landing in Brisbane', 6 October 1938, p. 7.
*Daily Telegraph*, 'Where Can They Go', 8 July 1938, p. 6.
Encel, Sol, 'How the *Dunera* Helped Australia', *Age*, 15 September 1972, p. 9.
Gapp, Laura, 'Aliens in Australia', *Sydney Morning Herald*, 22 May 1943, p. 6.
Gill, Alan, 'When Friends Were Enemies', *Sydney Morning Herald* 'Good Weekend', 1 September 1990.
—'How a Maori Officer became a Father Figure to the "Misfits"', *Sydney Morning Herald*, 25 April 1992, p. 21.
—'The enemy alien who loved us', *Sydney Morning Herald*, 24 May 2003. https://www.smh.com.au/national/the-enemy-alien-who-loved-us-20030524-gdgtae.html
—'Memorial for the brave *Dunera* boys', *Sun-Herald*, 13 November 1994, p. 14.
*Hebrew Standard of Australasia*, 'Persecution of German Jews. Melbourne Meeting. Sum of £7100 Subscribed', 5 May 1933, p. 4.
—'The New Australian: Mass Meeting at Maccabean Hall, Letter from Minister of Defence, Important Resolution Unanimously Adopted', vol. 44, no. 48, 20 April 1939, p. 2.
—'Jewish National Fund, Plea for Bulgarian Jews. Statement to the Press', 1 July 1943, p. 7.
*Herald*, 'Some Aliens May Join R.A.A.F.', 25 June 1940.
—'Germans and Austrians Want to Stay in Australia', 15 March 1944.
*Kalgoorlie Miner*, 'Our Education System. Army Revelations. One in Twenty-five Cannot Read', 24 June 1943, p. 4.
*Launceston Examiner*, 'Call Up of Greek Melbourne', 23 December 1944, p. 9.
Levett, Connie, 'Revealed: Australia's Secret Labour Camps', *Sun-Herald*, 21 December 2008.
Lewinski, Kurt, 'The Dunera Diaries', extracts published in *Sunday Age*, 5 August 1990.

*Morning Bulletin* (Rockhampton, Qld), '"Salt" Defended', 9 December 1942, p. 4.
*News Weekly*, 'Broadcaster', 24 November 1945.
Power, Paul, 'How One Refugee Signalled the End of the White Australia Policy', *Guardian*, 18 March 2014.
Rankin, George, 'Politics Now Flavour: "Salt"', *Smith's Weekly*, 9 June 1945, p. 3.
Schwartz, Larry, 'Companies Dismissed: the "Aliens" History Forgot', *Sunday Age*, 23 June 2002.
—'Fighting for WWII Refugees' Compassionate Captain', *Age*, 20 May 2005.
*Shepparton News*, 'Enemy Aliens. Immediate Internment Urged', 30 March 1942, p. 4.
—'Refugee Fruitpickers Finish Work in Shepparton: Some of Their Impressions', Monday, 13 April 1942.
—'Enemy Aliens. R.S.L. Resolutions', 2 July 1942, p. 3.
*Smith's Weekly*, 'Over-generous Payments to Refugees', 25 April 1942, p. 8 .
—'"Salt" Demobbed', 27 April 1946, p. 19.
*Sydney Morning Herald*, 'Dictatorship: Attitude of Mr. Menzies, Possible Degeneration of Democracy', Tuesday, 15 November 1938, p. 13.
—'Viewpoint of Germany: Mr. Menzies' Plea for Understanding, Rearmament Defended', Monday, 12 December 1938, p. 11.
—19 May 1940, p. 5.
—Letter – Charles Venn Pilcher, 'Refugees' Offer to Serve', 23 May 1940, p. 5.
—'Progress of Loan. Treasurer Dissatisfied', 6 June 1940, p. 9.
—Letter – 'Austrian', 'A Plea for Refugees', 8 July 1940, p. 3.
—Letter – PA Smith, 'The Persecution of Aliens', 25 July 1940, p. 3.
—Letter – The Right Rev. CV Pilcher, Prof. Stephen Roberts, The Right Rev. PA Smith and Charles Williamson, Esq., 'Treatment of Refugees. An Appeal for Justice. Cruel Propaganda', 1 August 1940, p. 6.
—'Enemy Aliens. Soldiers Favour Internment. "Total Precaution"', 2 August 1940, p. 8.
—Letter – E Hardy Johnston, 'Refugees and the War', 3 August 1940, p. 7.
—Editorial, 13 October 1940.
—Letter – 'Two Australians' (Edgecliff), 'Restrictions on Aliens', 6 February 1942, p. 3.
—'Enemy Aliens Cannot Join Air Force', 6 February 1942, p. 6.
—Letter – CEW Bean, 'The Value of "Salt"', 30 May 1942, p. 6.
—'Refugee Aliens' Status. Regulations Changed', 19 October 1943, p. 6.
—'Injustice to Refugees', 20 October 1943, p. 6.
—'Mob Clash in Brisbane. Mounted Men as Picket Lancers', 12 December 1944, p. 3.
—'"Stop-Go" Order to Chinese', 8 November 1945, p. 3.
—Letter – 'Botany Road Rang with German Song', FF Wheener, 2 May 1992, p. 24.
—'A Track to the Future', 10 January 2004. https://www.smh.com.au/national/a-track-to-the-future-20040110-gdi4qj.html

Symonds, Saul, *The Hebrew Standard of Australasia*, Sydney, 20 April 1939.
Waldon, Steve, 'Finally. Peace Broke Out and the People Partied', *Age*, 13 August 2005, p. 8.
*Westralian Judean*, Editorial, 'False Security', vol. 12, no. 138, 1 February 1941.

## Theses and unpublished reports

Anderson, Fay, Max Crawford: Necessity and Freedom, PhD, Department of History, University of Melbourne, 2002.
Lovas, S, Politics of Hungarian Migrants in Australia, MA thesis, University of Sydney, 1969.
Pennay, Bruce, 'The Friendly Aliens at Albury Railway Station During the Second World War', unpublished report, NSW State Railway Authority, July 2000.
Pennay, Bruce, 'Historical Outline and Context: The Battle of Albury', unpublished report, NSW State Railway Authority, July 2000.
Pomeroy, JP, Morale on the Homefront in Australia During the Second World War, PhD, University of Sydney, 1995.
Rankine, Wendy, The Chinese in Australia 1930–45: Beyond a History of Racism, MA thesis, Department of History, University of Melbourne, 1995.
Symons, Beverley, All-Out for the People's War: 'Red Diggers' in the Armed Forces and the Communist Party of Australia's Policies in the Second World War, BA (Hons), University of Wollongong, 1993.

## Internet publications

Abjorensen, Norman, 'When did Catholics Take Over the Liberal Party?', 5 December 2007. https://www.crikey.com.au/2007/12/05/abjorensen-when-did-catholics-take-over-the-liberal-party/
Australian War Memorial (AWM), 'Victory in Europe (VE) Day'. https://www.awm.gov.au/articles/encyclopedia/ve_day
Bebbington, Warren A and John Carmody, 'Prerauer, Kurt (Curt) (1901–1967)', *Australian Dictionary of Biography*, vol. 16, 2006 [2002]. https://adb.anu.edu.au/biography/prerauer-kurt-curt-11455
British Pioneer Corps, *The Pioneer*. http://www.royalpioneercorps.co.uk/rpc/history.htm
Bruhn, David D, *Maritime Books of Interest*, n.d. http://www.davidbruhn.com/maritimeworks
Burchill, Dennis, *Wartime Memories of Bulimba*. https://www.ozatwar.com/locations/wartimememoriesbulimba.htm
Chamberlain, Ernest Patrick, *Forgotten Men: Timorese in Special Operations during World War II*, SCRIBD, n.d. http://www.scribd.com/doc/29688334/Forgotten-Men-in-Special-Operations-during-World-War-II
Curtin, John, *Diary of a Labour Man 1917–1945: 1945 Prime Minister*. http://john.curtin.edu.au/diary/primeminister/1945.html

Dunn, Peter, '3 Advanced Ordnance Depot (3AOD). Wallangarra Logistics Support Area, Qld', *Australia @ War*. https://www.ozatwar.com/ausarmy/3aod&1aad.htm (updated 23 January, 2020)

Dunn, Peter, 'The Native Labour Company in Australia During WW2: Native Labor Co (Chinese)', *Australia @ War*. https://www.ozatwar.com/ozatwar/nlc.htm

Ellis, Peter, 'Old Time Dancing and Music, Part 2'. http://www.australian-heritage-dance.com/oldtime2.html

Farram, Steven, From 'Timor Koepang' to 'Timor NTT': a political history of West Timor, 1901–1967, PhD, Charles Darwin University, 2004. https://espace.cdu.edu.au/eserv/cdu:6450/Thesis_CDU_6450_Farram_S.pdf

Fitzgerald, Ross, 'The Tanah Merah Exiles in Australia', 7 November 2009. https://rossfitzgerald.com/2009/11/07/the-tanah-merah-exiles-in-australia/

Gapps, Stephen, 'Personal and Political – Australian Women and Indonesian Independence', Australian National Maritime Museum. https://www.sea.museum/2015/08/17/black-armada/personal-and-political--australian-women-and-indonesian-independence (posted 17 August 2015).

Gregory, Alan, *The Ever Open Door: A History of the Royal Melbourne Hospital 1848-1998*, Hyland House, South Melbourne, 1998. http://www.med-dept.com/unit_histories/4_gen_hosp.php

Heenan, Tom, 'Milner, Ian Frank (1911-1991)', *Australian Dictionary of Biography*, vol. 19, 2021 [2014]. https://adb.anu.edu.au/biography/milner-ian-frank-16424

James, Bob, 'The Knights of Labor and Their Context', pamphlet for the 6th Biennial Conference of the Australian Society for the Study of Labour History, Wollongong, 1 – 4 October, 1999. http://www.takver.com/history/secsoc02.htm

James, Karl, *Soldiers to Citizens*, Australian War Memorial. https://www.awm.gov.au/wartime/45/article

Langfield, Michele, Research Guide: 'More People Imperative: Immigration to Australia, 1901-39', National Archives of Australia, 1999. https://www.naa.gov.au/help-your-research/research-guides/more-people-imperative-immigration-australia-1901-39

Mendes, Philip, 'The Jewish Council to Combat Fascism and Anti-Semitism – A History', *Galusaustralis.com,* 17 October 2010. http://www.galusaustralis.com

Moore, Caroline, 'Charles D'Aprano: Italo-Australian Left-Activist', *The Hummer*, vol. 2, no. 6, Winter, 1996. https://www.labourhistory.org.au/hummer/vol-2-no-6/charles-daprano/

Moran, C and M Massam, 'A "Trace of History": Cartoons from the Australian War Memorial Christmas Books of the Second World War', *Journal of the Australian War Memorial* n.d. https://www.awm.gov.au/journal/j39/cartoons/

Museums Victoria, Collections: *Australian Comforts Fund, World War II, 1939-1946*. https://collections.museumvictoria.com.au/articles/10608

National Archives of Australia (NAA). http://www.naa.gov.au/collection/explore/security/index.aspx

Neumann, Klaus, '*A Doubtful Character*': *Wolf Klaphake*. https://web.archive.org/web/20070828220417/http://uncommonlives.naa.gov.au/life.asp?lID=1 updated 7 May, 2004.

Nicholls, Glenn, 'Gone with Hardly a Trace: Deportees in Immigration Policy', in Klaus Neumann and Gwenda Tavan (eds), *Does History Matter?; Making and Debating Citizenship, Immigration and Refugee Policy in Australia and New Zealand*, ANU E Press, Canberra, 2009. http://press-files.anu.edu.au/downloads/press/p109651/mobile/ch01.html

The Nuremberg Laws: The Reich Citizenship Law: First Regulation (14 November 1935), Article 4. https://www.jewishvirtuallibrary.org/the-reich-citizenship-law-first-regulation

Prince, Peter, 'We Are Australian – The Constitution and Deportation of Australian-born Children', Australian Parliamentary Library, Research Paper no. 3 200304, 24 November 2003. https://www.aph.gov.au/About_Parliament/Parliamentary_Departments/Parliamentary_Library/pubs/rp/rp0304/04RP03

Radi, Heather, 'Street, Lady Jessie Mary (1889-1970)', *Australian Dictionary of Biography*, vol. 16, 2006 [2002]. http://adb.anu.edu.au/biography/street-lady-jessie-mary-11789

Reeves, Andrew, 'Laidler, Thomas Percival (Percy) (1884-1958)', *Australian Dictionary of Biography*, vol. 9, 2006 [1983]. https://adb.anu.edu.au/biography/laidler-thomas-percival-percy-7010

Tutt, Ian, 'A History of Queensland's Explosive Reserves', *Queensland Government Mining Journal* (QGMJ) no. 1236, Spring, 2009, pp. 22–24. https://geoscience.data.qld.gov.au/dataset/cr060132/resource/geo-doc1201750-cr060132

United States Holocaust Memorial Museum, Holocaust Encyclopedia. http://www.ushmm.org/wlc/en/article.php?ModuleId=10005470

## Radio, television and film

*The Dunera Boys*, television program, directed by Ben Lewin, Network Ten, Australia, October 1985.

*Indonesia Calling*, film, directed by Joris Ivens, produced by the Waterside Workers Federation, 1946. https://www.youtube.com/watch?v=iAzfM9cQvZQ

Macdonald, Ranald (October 1990), radio program, interview with Yosl Bergner for the Australian Broadcasting Corporation (ABC), Melbourne [interview transcript].

*Painting the Town: A Film about Yosl Bergner*, film, written by Charles Merewether and Sharon Connelly, directed by Trevor Graham, narrated by Max Gillies, Yarra Bank Films, Melbourne, 1987.

*The Religion Report*, radio program, ABC Radio National, 3 September 2003.

## Talks, poems and exhibitions

*The Dunera Boys: Seventy Years On*, exhibition, National Library of Australia, Canberra, ACT, 2010. https://www.nla.gov.au/whats-on/exhibitions/dunera-boys

Factor, Saul, Talk to the Campaign for International Co-Operation and Disarmament, 16 April 1986. Tape in the possession of June Factor. See also 'Saul Remembers…' in the newsletter *CICD Anti-War News & Views*, June 1986.

Manera, Brad, Remembering 1942: The battles on Timor, 20-23 February 1942, talk presented at the Australian War Memorial, 23 February 2002. https://www.awm.gov.au/articles/blog/1942-timor

Roth, Cary, *The Shire Ball*, provided by Wolfgang Sievers.

Roth, Cary and Tim Walton, *A Day in Camp*, illustrated ballad created for the first anniversary of the 4th Employment Company, 9 March 1943.

Salter, Robert, 'Love Thy Neighbour', speech given on the occasion of his grandson David's bar-mitzvah, November 1995, copy given to June Factor.

# Index

# D

## W



## Y



## Z